The Art of Manipulating Fabric

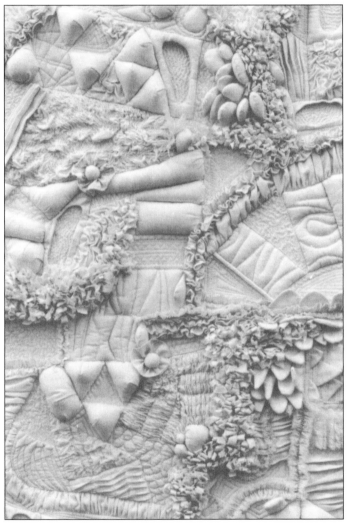

Colette Wolff

krause
publications

700 E. State Street • Iola, WI 54990-0001
Telephone: 715/445-2214

Published in Iola, Wisconsin, 54990 by Krause Publications

Editors: Robbie Fanning, Rosalie Cooke

Production: Rosalie Cooke

Book design: Rosalyn Carson

Cover design: Anthony Jacobson

Photography: Michael Kagan

Line art: Colette Wolff

Proofreader: Meredith Phillips

Manufactured in the United States of America

Library of Congress Cataloging in Publication Data

Wolff, Colette.
    The art of manipulating fabric / Colette Wolff.
        p.   cm.
    Includes bibliographical references and index.
    ISBN 0-8019-8496-3 (pbk.)
    1. Sewing. 2. Fancy work. I. Title.
TT705.W54 1996
646.2—dc20   96-32201
                                        CIP

    4 5 6 7 8 9 0   5 4 3 2 1 0 9 8

Other Books Available from Krause Publications

SEWING

A Step-by-Step Guide to Your New Home Sewing Machine, by Jan Saunders

Adventures with Polarfleece®, by Nancy Cornwell

Alphabet Stitchery by Hand & Machine, by Carolyn Vosburg Hall

Bridal Couture, by Susan Khalje

Claire Shaeffer's Fabric Sewing Guide, by Claire B. Shaeffer

Complete Book of Machine Embroidery, by Robbie and Tony Fanning

Contemporary Machine Embroidery, by Deborah Gonet

Embellishments: Adding Glamour to Garments, by Linda Fry Kenzle

Garments with Style, by Mary Mulari

Jan Saunders' Wardrobe Quick-Fixes, by Jan Saunders

Life Is Not A Dress Size, by Rita Farro

Made with Lace, by Ginny Barnston

More Sweatshirts with Style, by Mary Mulari

Pattern-Free Fashions, by Mary Lee Trees Cole

Sew & Go Baby, by Jasmine Hubble

Sew & Go, by Jasmine Hubble

Sew Any Patch Pocket, by Claire B. Shaeffer

Sew Any Set-In Pocket, by Claire B. Shaeffer

Sew Sensational Gifts, by Naomi Baker and Tammy Young

Shirley Adams' Belt Bazaar, by Shirley Adams

Snap It Up!, by Jeanine Twigg

Stretch & Sew® Guide to Sewing on Knits, by Ann Person

Sweatshirts with Style, by Mary Mulari

Teach Yourself Machine Embroidery, by Susan Rock

Texture with Textiles, by Linda McGehee

Your Sewing Machine, by Jan Saunders

SERGING

ABC's of Serging, by Tammy Young and Lori Bottom

Distinctive Serger Gifts & Crafts, by Naomi Baker and Tammy Young

Innovative Serging, by Gail Brown and Tammy Young

New Creative Serging Illustrated, by Pati Palmer, Gail Brown and Sue Green

A New Serge in Wearable Art, by Ann Boyce

Sew & Serge Pillows! Pillows! Pillows!, by Jackie Dodson and Jan Saunders

Serge a Simple Project, by Tammy Young and Naomi Baker

Serge it in an Hour or Less, by Cindy Cummins

Serge Something Super for Your Kids, by Cindy Cummins

Sew & Serge Terrific Textures, by Jackie Dodson and Jan Saunders

Serged Garments in Minutes, by Tammy Young and Naomi Baker

Ultimate Serger Answer Guide, by Naomi Baker, Gail Brown and Cindy Kacynski

RIBBON ART

Glorious Ribbons, by Christine Kingdom

More Ribbon Embroidery by Machine, by Marie Duncan and Betty Farrell

Quick and Easy Ways with Ribbon, by Ceci Johnson

Ribbon Embroidery by Machine, by Marie Duncan and Betty Farrell

Seasonal Creations, by Marie Duncan and Betty Farrell

Secrets of Fashioning Ribbon Flowers, by Helen Gibb

QUILTING

All Quilt Blocks are Not Square, by Debra Wagner

Best-Loved Designers' Collection Quick-Sew Quilts, by America's Top Designers

Cat Quilts and Crafts, by LaVera Langeman

Complete Book of Machine Quilting, by Robbie and Tony Fanning

Complete Miniature Quilt Book, by Dinah Travis

Contemporary Quilting Techniques, by Patricia Cairns

Creative Triangles for Quilters, by Janet B. Elwin

Dye It! Paint It! Quilt It!, by Joyce Mori and Cynthia Myerberg

Fast Patch® Kids Quilts, by Anita Hallock

Fast Patch®, by Anita Hallock

Heirloom Quilts, by the editors of Workbasket

Japanese Folded Patchwork, by Mary Clare Clark

Magic of Crazy Quilting, by Marcia Michler

New Work of Our Hands, by Mae Rockland Tupa

Precision Pieced Quilts using the Foundation Method, by Jane Hall and Dixie Haywood

Quilt As You Go, by Sandra Millett

Sashiko and Beyond, by Saikoh Takano

Scrap Quilts Using Fast Patch®, by Anita Hallock

Shirley Botsford's Daddy's Ties, by Shirley Botsford

Stars Galore and Even More, by Donna Poster

Stitch 'n' Quilt, by Kathleen Eaton

Super Simple Quilts, by Kathleen Eaton

Techniques of Japanese Embroidery, by Shuji Tamura

Three-Dimensional Pieced Quilts, by Jodie Davis

Traditional Quilts, Today's Techniques, by Debra Wagner

Ultimate Scrap Quilt, by Joyce Mori

ADDITIONAL TOPICS

Crafts – Crafting with Flowers & Nature – Ceramics – Doll Clothing – Floorcloths – Dollmaking with Papier Mache and Paperclay – Beadwork – Handmade Paper – Home Decorating – Jewelry – Kids Crafts – Needlecraft – Painted Wood – Pottery – Paper Crafts

Acknowledgments

Looking back, I remember with the deepest gratitude all those friends who listened. They let me talk about what was and still is an obsessive and rather passionate preoccupation with the subject of cloth, its manipulations, and all the ramifications thereof. They allowed me to "let off steam" so I could return to the solitary pursuit re-energized. With special acknowledgments to Ann Bradley, Dee Danley-Brown, Norma Ellman, Sylvia Fishman, Almuth Palinkas, Susan Prokop, and Dee Dee Triplett, who were in positions to extend help of a more tangible kind, thank you one and all. I would be seriously remiss if I didn't thank my husband, Ted Wolff, for all those caffé lattes during late night times of stress. My thanks to the creative team who worked to get this book into print: To Michael Kagan, whose eye for lighting and insistence on black-and-white perfection produced such outstanding photographs; to Rosalie Cooke, whose patient and conscientious editing challenged me to "go that extra distance"; to Rosalyn Carson, who assembled the material with computer magic into the handsome pages that follow; to my bi-coastal editors, Kathy Conover in Pennsylvania and Robbie Fanning in California, who coordinated everything—but particularly, first and last, to Robbie, who kept the faith, and then some, and more.

Contents

Foreword

Perhaps you're familiar with the volume of letters between Maxwell Perkins, the famous Scribner's editor, and such authors as F. Scott Fitzgerald and Ernest Hemingway. I'm thinking of publishing a similar one for the letters and phone calls between me and Colette Wolff on this book.

It started innocently enough in the early 1980s. Colette owned a mail-order catalog in New York City called Platypus, which published her toy and doll designs and sold supplies. I wrote a column for a magazine called *Needle and Thread*. My readers told me about her catalog; I wrote for a copy and was impressed; I mentioned the catalog in a column; and she wrote to thank me. We became long-distance friends.

Over the years, I was continually bowled over not only with the quality of her work, but its scope— quiltmaking, toymaking, dollmaking, costuming. Was there anything this woman could not do—and do well? Furthermore, she had the rare talent of being not only a consummate craftsperson, but a gifted graphic artist, an exceptionally clear writer, and an outstanding teacher.

In the middle 1980s I initiated a series of books for Chilton Book Company. Naturally, I approached Colette about doing a book. She had written a series of quilt articles on three-dimensional fabric forms and felt that we needed a book showing all the possibilities of manipulating fabric, organized by technique. In the early stages, we called the book *Fabric in Relief*, undoubtedly a foreshadowing of our feeling when the book would finally be finished. One of my early notes is dated June 22, 1987. "Colette says she can be done with the book by June 1988."

I advanced her $100 for materials, an entirely laughable amount, considering that 20 yards of material went into the pleating samples alone. Another note in my file says, "July 1989—CW received *another* 200 yards of unbleached muslin."

The defining characteristic of consummate, gifted, exceptional, outstanding talent is that they do not skim the surface. If they discover a side channel and it opens into another major river, they follow the current. And that's why this book turned into Niagara Falls. Colette would promise a delivery date, then write, "I keep promising myself that I won't add any more samples or techniques, and then something appears, and must be included, and so it goes."

Periodically, I would be in the same town as Colette and she would show me the samples. Always, I would be staggered at the workmanship and the possibilities. Who but Colette could have made darts into works of art? I began to drag other people into the meetings, merely for the pleasure of watching their faces as she pulled out some samples. At one point someone at Chilton asked her to ship her samples to Philadelphia for a meeting. Colette politely asked, "All 23 boxes?"

Like the boxes, the book grew and grew. The due dates were postponed, then again. As we approached the end, I had a sudden case of the willies. What if she got hit by a crazy New York taxi and her husband gave all her samples to Goodwill? I called him and made him promise to will me the samples if anything happened to her.

Then the payoff came: I had the extreme pleasure of editing a manuscript that was nearly perfect. A seminal book like this one comes along only once or twice in an editor's lifetime. And that was before seeing Michael Kagan's photos.

So here it is—finally! I wish I could watch your face and eavesdrop as you look through this book. Are you drawn to circular forms, as I am? Look at the yo-yos gone ku-ku on page 27 or the circular smocking over pleats on page 135. Perhaps you like an underlying grid. Look how she made pleats on a Perfect Pleater, backed them with iron-on interfacing, cut them into squares, and reassembled them into a block on page 123.

But I must return to my work as an editor. The first item on the agenda is to remind Colette that April 8, 1988, she wrote, "Relief techniques take the quilt in such new directions that I feel following *Fabric in Relief* with a second and smaller book particularly for quilters is a ripe idea. More on that at a later time."

Robbie Fanning
Series Editor

Preface

This is a book of ideas about sewing cloth. The ideas are techniques that change the look and feel of a piece of cloth with the assistance of a threaded needle. They texturize, embellish, inflate, and support. They create puckers, folds, waves, puffs, projections, and openings. With stitching by hand or machine, they resurface, reshape, restructure, and reconstruct a flat, supple piece of cloth into cloth with an entirely different disposition.

Most of these techniques materialized sometime during the long history of cloth. Along the way, persons who handled cloth modified, varied, and altered the elemental techniques into more techniques. The techniques acquired identifying names like *gathering, pleating, tucking, smocking, quilting*, words that are now part of our everyday vocabulary. The techniques have history and longevity; they are as valid now as they were back then. Today, anyone interested in the what, why, when, and how of these techniques can find information scattered all over the place in printed materials and actual sewn-cloth examples.

Some years ago, I needed to research tucks for a project, and confronted "all over the place" when I started looking. A bit from this book, a lot from that book, clues from seeing actual applications—eventually I collected a mass of information. A few of the tucks I discovered didn't seem like tucks. To understand distinctions, I investigated pleats; that led to curiosity

about smocking, shirring, gathering, and how they relate. Always the sources were a bit here, a lot there, with clues from pictures and presentations—and almost always the sources associated a technique with one particular usage.

I was frustrated because the information I needed wasn't put together in one place in a manner that allowed me to pick and choose and make my own decisions regarding application. Embroiderers and needlepointers have any number of manuals that show and describe the stitches of their craft, isolated from anything those stitches are used to produce. Similar directories exist for those who knit, crochet, knot, and weave. I wanted that kind of comprehensive, orderly reference for the sewing techniques identified with fabric manipulation.

So I set out on a journey to sew, write, and draw this book.

I had a working objective: To catalog fabric manipulation techniques, emphasizing what they are, what they do to a piece of cloth, and how it's done, detached from associations with product. For me, doing that meant generalized instructions with enough specifics to be a guide for you, the reader, to consult when adapting a technique to the project of your choice. It meant diagrams to clarify the directions and photographs showing examples of the techniques without revealing any particular environment. It also meant finding a surrogate for the overwhelming range of fabric possibilities, one generic fab-

ric that would adjust to the requirements of differing techniques and present those techniques on even terms.

I chose a medium-weight, even-weave, 100% cotton unbleached muslin. To increase the muslin's softness and manageability, it was washed with detergent, spin-dried, dampened, and ironed before use. When sewn into samples, its plain, smoothly woven surface doesn't distract from the main point, the manipulation. Its bland color proved exceptionally receptive to the light and shadow of black-and-white photography.

The subjects in the book directed their own organization. The Chapter titles which break down into techniques, the technique definitions that expand into Procedures which are then amplified with Notes and stretched with Variations, and the technical information pertinent to more than one technique collected under Basics at the beginning of the Chapters—the structure became obvious as work progressed. The pictures clustered after the how-to's explaining construction are grouped together in sequences that emphasize relationships. I wanted to make it visually convenient for you to observe a particular manipulation as it develops and changes, so that you can make discoveries of your own.

Getting the Most from this Book

Start with the pictures. Riffle through the pages until one or a cluster of the photographed manipulations catches your eye. Stop, consider, then look at the drawings relevant to your immediate interest.

Find out if there are similar manipulations elsewhere in the book. Compare. Search for connections and contrasts that spark each other. Build combinations. When you need to know, read the instructions for your chosen techniques. If you're so inclined, you can certainly start at the beginning with the illustrated text and refer to the pictures as you read, but take it in small doses.

This is a book of ideas about sewing cloth for you to interpret as you see fit. "Fit," meaning "proper, becoming, suitable; adjusted or altered to the substance, form, or size required." *Every technique in this book will be changed, more or less, by what you bring to it from outside.* You'll need to integrate the technique you've chosen with the situation you want to put it in, and the fabric you have in mind.

Qualifications that will affect the "fit" of a technique include:

Fabric.
A technique exposed to the weight and pliability of the unbleached muslin used in this book may be wrong for the fabric in your hand. Then again, your fabric could transform a technique into something special, or you could manage an unusual merger of fabric and technique for an unexpected and unique result.

Color/texture/pattern.
These beautiful distractions affect light and shadow and the noticeability of a manipulation in ways that can't always be foreseen. Some techniques will be overwhelmed by the color/texture/pattern in the fabric. Some will be intensified.

Design.
The visual, bas-relief elements of a manipulation need to be arranged into a pleasing composition. Depending on the technique, stitching, seamlines, folds, projections, depressions, edges, and openings are components of manipulated design.

Scale and proportion.
Think about juxtaposing big and small in adjacent techniques, or distorting the customary relationship of size between a technique and its setting. Visualize a technique expanded to fit within a gigantic format like a hanging for the atrium of a skyscraper, or believably miniaturized to doll house and doll figure standards.

Practical applicability.
Will the technique behave when it's moved? Will normal handling, strain, or pressure affect the technique adversely? Will it survive laundering or dry cleaning? Will the firmness, insulation, or weight added by the technique contribute to the purpose intended?

Skill.
Sewing craftsmanship affects the installation of a technique for better or worse. Mishaps inevitably occur, but when they do, don't give up. Booboos are innovations in disguise.

Between the techniques, underneath the descriptions, and around the procedures described in this book, there are deviations and mutations waiting to be discovered. Invent your own modifications. Imagine "what would happen if...." Test and experiment. Cloth and what we do with it is a restless study, as restless as the cloth itself. Approach with a spirit of adventure.

Controlled
Crushing

PART ONE

Gathering converts the edge of a piece of fabric into mini-folds bunched together on thread stitched close to the edge. Gathering shortens the fabric at the stitching line. Beyond the gathered stitching, the full extent of the fabric erupts into irregular, rolling folds.

A field of fabric gathered only at the top drops in spreading, fluctuating folds to a floating, lower edge. When fields or strips of fabric are gathered on opposite sides, variable folds flow unfastened between constricted edges. Fabric shapes gathered all around project loose folds that inflate into the center.

GATHERING

1 Gathering

Note: This chapter begins with BASICS, indicated by a gray band located underneath the relevant columns.

GATHERING BASICS

GATHERING METHODS

There are five ways to gather: by hand, by machine, automatically, with elastic, and through channels. Hand, machine, automatic, and one kind of elastic gathering are standard, stitched-thread methods. Other kinds of elastic gathering and channel gathering are specialty variations that use different means to gather.

Thread-based hand and machine gathering involves two procedures: (1) stitching across the designated edge of the fabric within the seam allowance; (2) pulling on the loose thread dangling unsecured from the end of the stitching with one hand while using the other hand to push the fabric into itself along the tautly held thread. The sparsity or density of the mini-folds created by the gathering, in combination with stitch length, determine fullness, which is the amount and depth of the folds liberated from the stitches. Long stitches tightly gathered release the most abundant fullness.

Hand gathering depends on running stitches. Because sewing thread is vulnerable to breaks under tension, use doubled or extra-strong thread in the needle. Anchor the first stitch with a good-sized knot at the end of the thread. For **plain hand gathering**, draw the fabric up onto the thread of a single row of even running stitches (Fig. 1-1).

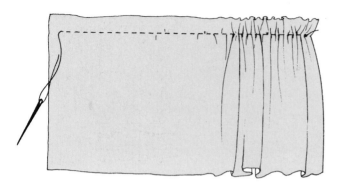

Fig. 1-1. Equally-spaced running stitches, partially gathered.

If the thread-gathered mini-folds are skimpy, the fullness produced in the rest of the fabric will be slight. Plentiful, close mini-folds produce generous fullness. However, fabric firmly crushed into copious mini-folds on a single row of running stitches tends to muddle at the gathered edge, especially if the stitches are enlarged. **Stroking** imposes order on such dense gathering. Sliding the tip of a blunt needle up and under a surface stitch, "stroke" and straighten the groove of fabric beneath the stitch from the top edge of the fabric down. One after the other, stroke the grooves behind adjacent stitches into shallow, leveled, tidy folds (Fig. 1-2).

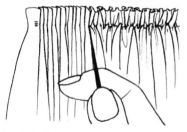

Fig. 1-2. Stroking running-stitched gathering into orderly folds.

Regular hand gathering accumulates on two or three rows of even running stitches. The resulting mini-folds, neat and more easily controlled than those formed on plain hand gathering, fill a band as wide as the combined rows of stitching, usually spaced ¼″ (6mm) or less apart (Fig. 1-3). **Gauging** is a variation of regular hand gathering used when extravagant fullness is the goal and a long length of fabric must be gathered to a very short measurement. Gauging stitches are uneven—short on the right side and long on the wrong side of the material. The stitch in

Fig. 1-3. Fabric gathered on two rows of hand or machine-stitching.

front sets the distance between mini-folds; the stitch in back sets the depth. Sew at least two, preferably three, parallel rows of identically spaced and vertically aligned stitches across the fabric's edge. Push the fabric on the threads into tightly packed, uniform folds that collapse to one side in flattened layers when the gauge-gathered edge is seamed to another piece of fabric (Fig. 1-4). (For an additional gauged gathering technique, refer to "Butted Cartridge Pleats" on page 107.)

Machine gathering is faster than hand gathering. Like hand gathering, stitch length affects fullness. Longer stitch lengths gather into deeper mini-folds which release more fullness in the fabric beyond the stitching. For **straight-stitched machine gathering**, gather the fabric onto the bobbin thread of one, two, or three rows of straight stitching sewn with the upper tension loosened. Use extra strong thread in the bobbin to improve break resistance.

Zigzag machine gathering tolerates the strain of lengthy or heavy-fabric gathering when even strong sewing thread in the bobbin snaps from the pulling and pushing. The fabric slides into gathers on sturdy string or cord loosely confined inside a tunnel of zigzag stitches (Fig. 1-5). To increase the efficiency of zigzag gathering: (1) Color-mark the string or cord with after-gathering target measurements, one mark indicating a point to be anchored to the fabric, a second mark indicating the target length for the gathering. (2) Start sewing by catching the anchoring mark on the string or cord with a couple of straight stitches; change to a zigzag that encloses the string or cord inside thread for the length of the stitching line. (3) Gather until the target mark

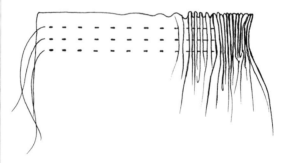

Fig. 1-4. The deep gathers produced on three rows of gauged hand stitching look like fine pleats.

Fig. 1-5. Two rows of zigzag stitching encase one gathering cord caught with stitches where each row starts.

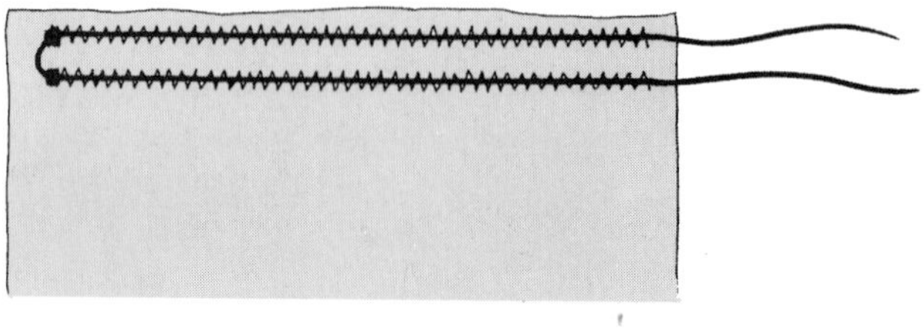

on the string or cord appears. Another zigzag-gathering method, less strong than the above, utilizes bobbin thread: (1) Stop after the first stitch and bring the bobbin thread to the surface; (2) pull the bobbin thread out to the length of the fabric to be gathered; (3) zigzag over the bobbin thread; (4) gather on the bobbin thread.

Whether gathering on hand or machine stitching, fabric can be pushed along from the unsecured end of the stitches to the beginning where the gathering thread is knotted, tied, or anchored—or the fabric can be worked into gathers by pushing it in toward the center from each end of the gathering thread, both unsecured. To gather a very long piece of fabric, divide the length into manageable segments and stitch and gather each segment separately.

When gathering stitches cross seams that join two pieces of fabric together, the extra layer of fabric at the seam allowances thickens the gathering. To detach the seam allowances from the stitching, notch the seam allowances to the point where machine-sewn gathering stitches cross, or suspend machine sewing on either side of the seam allowances (Fig. 1-6). If hand sewing, continue without catching the seam allowances in the stitches.

After gathering to the target measurement, secure the gathering (1) with tiny stitches overcast in place (handsewing); (2) by tying the bobbin thread to the needle thread (machine sewing), including any zigzagged string or cord in the tie; (3) by winding the thread figure-8 style around a pin inserted into the fabric at the last stitch (a temporary fastening). Gathers are usually distributed evenly along the length of the stitching, but may also change from light to heavy, if desired. Gathering remains adjustable with its thread base susceptible to breaks until it is permanently stabilized (refer to "Stabilizing Gathered Stitching" on page 6). Stabilizing is

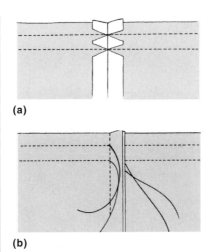

(a)

(b)

Fig. 1-6. When machine-stitching to be gathered crosses structural seam allowances: (a) Notch the seam allowances in advance. (b) Interrupt the stitching to free the seam allowances.

easier to manage when the seam that connects the gathered edge to another piece of fabric runs between two rows of gathering, one (or two) inside the seam allowance and one just outside the seam allowance. After seaming, remove the gathered stitching thread that shows in front.

For some purposes, automatic, elastic, and channel gathering may be more practical than the hand and machine gathering methods previously described. With *automatic gathering*, the quality and quantity of the bunched mini-folds is machine-set *while sewing* rather than arranged by maneuvering *after sewing*. Two attachments, the easy-to-use gathering foot (Fig. 1-7) and the more complicated, but versatile, ruffler (Fig. 1-8), convert flat fabric into gathered or finely pleated fabric.

Fig. 1-7. The gathering foot is as easy to use as a regular presser foot. The longest stitch length combined with tightened upper tension produces the fullest gathers.

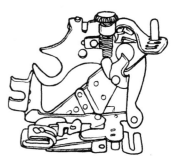

Fig. 1-8. The ruffler attachment traps puckers or pleats into stitches as it sews. It generates fullness ranging from slight to lavish with different stitch lengths combined with settings selected on the attachment.

Both lock a bit of extra fabric into the stitches as sewing proceeds. With the gathering foot or ruffler attached to the machine, sew until the automatically gathered fabric reaches target size. To estimate the fabric requirement, automatically gather a short sample of the fabric, measure before and after gathering, and use those measurements in this formula:

> [ungathered sample length
> ÷ gathered sample length]
> x target measurement
> = Estimated Fabric Length

Automatically gathered fabric may also be trimmed to size by securing the thread where it's cut with tiny dabs of fabric glue. Although automatic gathering traps extra fabric within the stitches, the gathering retains some adjustability until stabilized.

Elastic gathering with elastic thread, elastic cord, or elastic bands adds stretchability to automatic fullness. (1) Straight stitching with elastic thread in the bobbin gathers the fabric softly: Wind the elastic around the bobbin by hand, stretching it slightly; while stitching, hold the fabric taut before and behind the needle. (2) The fullness created by cord elastic caught inside a zigzagged seam increases to the degree the elastic is stretched during stitching, and the fabric is gathered on the elastic after stitching.

(3) A band of elastic, cut to or slightly less than target length, sewn directly to the fabric with zigzag stitching, gathers if the elastic is stretched to fabric length during the stitching (Fig. 1-9).

(4) Fabric may also be gathered on elastic inserted into a channel of fabric.

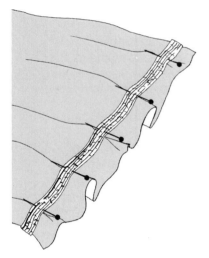

Fig. 1-9. Length of elastic, divided into quarters, pinned at the divisions to fabric, also divided into quarters. To sew, replace the pins with machine basting that crosses the elastic. Segment by segment, stretch the elastic to match the fabric while zigzag stitching.

One kind of *channel gathering* starts with a casing formed either by a hem at the edge or a tape applied across the fabric. Openings at the ends or internal slits allow access into the channel created between the two layers of fabric. The fabric slides into gathers over a gathering element—a length of string, cord, tape, ribbon, elastic, rope, chain, wire, dowel, or rod—moved through the hem or tape casing. To facilitate gathering, the casing channel should fit loosely around the element inside.

Another kind of channel gathering exposes the gathering element to view. A row of loops attached to the fabric's edge, or holes or slots that pierce the fabric, create channels with open spaces through which the gathering element moves in and out. Two features exclusive to all channel gathering: The gath-

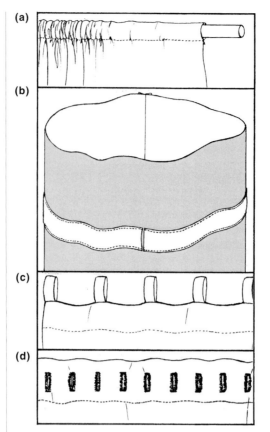

Fig. 1-10. (a) Gathering on a rod inserted through a hem. (b) Casing of tape sewn around a tube of fabric. A drawstring pulled through the casing with a bodkin or safety pin will gather the tube. (c) Loops caught in the seam joining fabric and facing will be slipped over a rod and pushed closer to gather the fabric. (d) Hemmed edge prepared for gathering on ribbon woven through buttonhole perforations.

ers may be adjusted and re-adjusted at any time, and the gathering element may be removed at any time, returning the fabric to its ungathered state. (Fig. 1-10)

STABILIZING GATHERED STITCHING

Stabilizing fixes hand and machine gathering. It ends the shifting of gathers on the thread, prevents the gathering thread from snapping, and conceals the gathering stitches.

Stabilizing may be *visible*—a binding, extension, foundation stay, or ruffled edge, or *invisible*—a stay or facing. Where they connect, the stabilizing fabric matches the gathered stitching in length and shape, and the stabilizing fabric adds one or more layers to a fabric already thickened by bunched gathers. During the stabilizing process, the gathering stitches disappear from sight.

A *binding* visibly stabilizes the gathering and encloses the stitching and seam allowances front and back inside a tunnel of smooth fabric. A bound edge is neat and firm, and adds three or four layers of binding fabric to the bulk of the gathering.

Binding a gathered edge with a long, narrow strip of fabric is a two-seam operation. To prepare the binding strip for methods #1 and #2, turn the seam allowance along one lengthy edge to the back and press. For method #1, sew the unturned edge of the binding to the gathered edge with right sides together. Bring the binding up and over the seam allowances, then handsew the turned edge of the binding to the joining seam/gathering in back (see (a) in Fig. 1-11). For method #2, sew the unturned edge of the binding, *wrong* side up, to the *wrong* side of the gathering. Bring the binding up and over the seam allowances to the front, covering all previous stitching, and edgestitch next to the turned edge of the binding (see (b) in Fig. 1-11). To prepare for method #3, which removes one layer of fabric from the binding, serge one long edge of the binding strip. With right sides together, sew the unserged edge of the binding to the gathered edge. Fold the serged edge to the back, pulling it down below the stitching. With right side up, stitch in the ditch, against the fold of the binding, catching the serged edge of the binding in the seam (see (c) in Fig. 1-11). Note that a finished binding wider than the seam allowances will feel empty above the enclosed seam allowances.

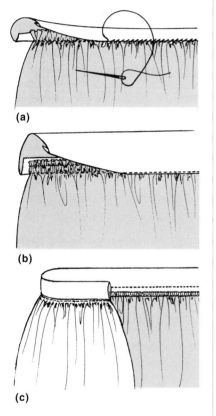

Fig. 1-11. Binding a gathered edge:
(a) With no stitching visible in front.
(b) With edgestitching visible in front.
(c) With "in the ditch" stitching hidden in front.

An *extension* of fabric covers the seam allowances and gathering stitches in front, but not in back. To add an extension, either (1) sew the extension to the gathered fabric with edges matching and right sides together, or (2) edgestitch next to the turned edge of an extension placed on top of the gathering stitches, or (3) combine (1) and (2)

(Fig. 1-12). Two or more rows of edgestitching reinforce the seam and add firmness while compressing the bunched gathers in the seam allowance underneath.

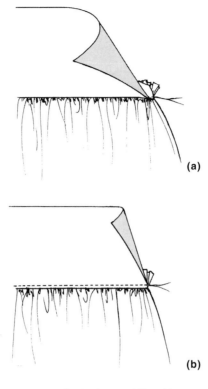

Fig. 1-12. Gathering stabilized by a fabric extension attached (a) with an invisible seam, (b) with visible edgestitching.

A *foundation stay* surrounds a contoured and gathered insertion with fabric. Method #1 fills a cutout in the foundation fabric with a gathered insertion. Sew the turned edge of the cutout over the gathered edge of the insertion with edgestitching by machine or blindstitching by hand (Fig. 1-13).

For Method #2, fabric shapes gathered on opposite sides or all around are appliquéd to matching outlines marked on the surface of a foundation stay. Edges gathered on straight machine stitching are the easiest to manage. Before gathering, turn the edge under on the stitching and heat press or finger crease.

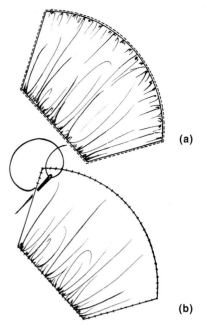

Fig. 1-13. Sewing a gathered insertion into a cutout in a foundation stay with (a) edgestitching and (b) blindstitching. Edgestitching emphasizes the outline of the cutout; for more emphasis, satin stitch over the edgestitching.

After gathering, blindstitch the edge to the outline: Catch the gathering thread and several threads of the fabric in the needle before pushing it through the foundation and out ⅛″ (3mm) ahead, just in front of the gathered edge, ready for the next stitch (see (a) in Fig. 1-14).

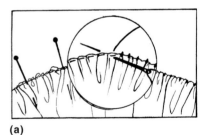

(a)

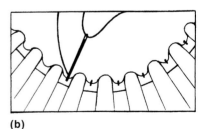

(b)

Fig. 1-14. Gathered appliqué options: (a) Blindstitch an edge gathered on machine stitching. (b) Flute an edge gathered on hand stitching.

Fluting is a hand-appliqué technique unique to hand-gathered edges. It arranges gathers into grooves between standing folds. Gather the already turned edge of the fabric on the thread of equally spaced running stitches (the larger the stitches, the higher the "flutes"). Distribute the gathers evenly. Start each tacking stitch by stroking the groove with a needle from the inside out to the edge; at the edge, catch several threads of the fabric in the needle before stabbing it through the outline on the foundation. Bring the needle up in front of the next groove and continue (see (b) in Fig. 1-14). Remove the gathering thread when all the grooves have been tacked.

An invisible *stay* is an underlining that controls gathering before it is stabilized in a finished manner. If the fabric is soft and slinky, a partial stay steadies the gathered edge before binding or adding an extension. A full edge-to-edge stay makes a gathered insertion easier to handle while sewing into a cutout inside a foundation stay (Fig. 1-15). When the layer of fabric added by a permanent stay is undesirable, use a temporary stay—paper or a commercial product developed for the purpose—which can be torn away when its usefulness is over.

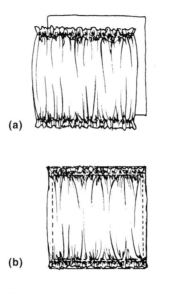

(a)

(b)

Fig. 1-15. (a) Target-sized stay for a gathered square (b) which is stayed when the two are basted together

An invisible *facing* is a lining that stabilizes as well as finishes a gathered edge. Sewn to the gathered fabric with edges matching and right sides together, a facing, when turned over to the back, also turns the gathered seam allowance to the inside. A facing for single-edge gathering has a loose edge in back; opposite-edge and all-sides gathering need full edge-to-edge facings (Fig. 1-16).

The *ruffled edge* is a decorative, frilly finish for the gathered edge. When the stitching to be gathered is sewn a distance away from the fabric's edge, the strip of fabric between the stitching and the edge breaks into a ruffle after gathering. To stabilize: (1) With the edge of an extension slipped beneath the gathering stitches, topstitch over the gathering stitches, then cover them with decorative stitching or an appliqué. Or topstitch next to the gathering stitches and remove the gathering thread after topstitching. (2) Sew a stay of tape to the back of the gathering stitches, flaunting the gathers for decorative effect in front. (3) Sew a decorative stay of ribbon, tape, or braid on top of the gathering stitches in front (Fig. 1-17). (Refer to "Edge Finishing for Ruffles" on page 43.)

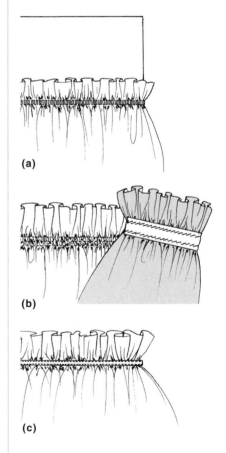

(a)

(b)

(c)

Fig. 1-17. Stabilizing a ruffled edge: (a) With an extension slipped underneath the satin-stitched gathering stitches. (b) With a tape handsewn to the back of the gathering stitches. (c) With a tape edgestitched over the gathering stitches.

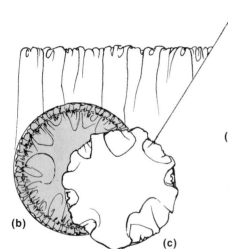

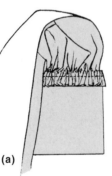

(a)

(b)

(c)

Fig. 1-16. (a) Partial facing stabilizing a gathered edge. (b) Gathered edge of a fabric circle stitched to a target-sized facing before (c) turning right side out through a slash in the facing. The gathered circle rolls at the edge and inflates.

"Stabilizing gathered stitching" doesn't apply to stretchable elastic gathering, but if the elastic is inside a channel, it needs *stops* to prevent retreat into the channel. Other channel-gathering elements of fiber, such as string, cord, tape, and ribbon, need stops as well. Depending on the element and the situation, the ends can be stopped by fastening to the fabric, or they can be enlarged beyond channel capacity with knots, beads, tassels, or baubles (Fig. 1-18). For encircling channels, the ends can be tied or tacked together, or connected with hooks, snaps, buttons, or Velcro. Non-fiber gathering elements such as chain, wire, dowel, or rods are stopped with suitable hardware devices.

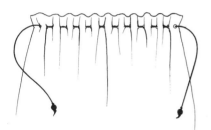

Fig. 1-18. Stops at the ends of a drawstring block accidental removal. A stop could be a large knot or, as shown, a bead held in place between knots.

FURROWING

With tiny tacking stitches **furrowing** creates a controlled relief of meandering, swirling grooves and crests from the fabric that balloons between all-sides-gathered edges appliquéd to a foundation stay. The tacks start widely spaced and get closer and closer, always reducing the inflated fabric left between previous tacks, adding more ridges to the developing maze.

Mark the surface of a foundation stay with the outline of the gathered shape to be furrowed. Cut the fabric to be gathered and furrowed two times larger than the outline on the foundation, even larger for dense furrowing with deep crevices. Dot the fabric in the center and at equally spaced points between the center and the edges. Mark the back of the foundation stay, behind the outline, with similarly spaced dots. Stretch the stay in a hoop. Gather the fabric and appliqué it to the outline marked on the stay.

Push a threaded needle straight up and out through the center dot marked on the stay in back and the center dot marked on the swelling fabric above. Take a stitch three or four threads-of-the-fabric wide and push the needle straight down through the stay and out the back. Pull on the thread to bring the fabric down to foundation level. Secure with a second stitch over the first. In back, move the needle to an adjacent dot position and make another double-tack, pulling the dot above and the dot below together. When all the dots have been anchored, refine the remaining bulges with more tacks to make new furrows. Use the needle's point to assist the grooving as tacking continues. (Fig. 1-19)

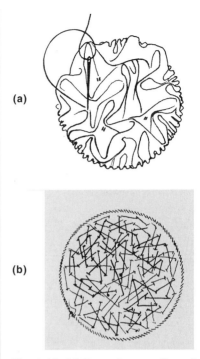

(a)

(b)

Fig. 1-19. (a) Furrowing a puffy, gathered appliqué with double-tacks. (b) When the furrowing is finished, thread crisscrosses the foundation in back.

The height of the crests between furrows diminishes as the number of tacks increases. With a densely furrowed surface, the crests have little room for collapse, but a layer of batting or loose fiberfill inserted between the gathered fabric and the foundation stay adds support.

SINGLE-EDGE GATHERING

—one side of a piece of fabric reduced to a smaller measurement when crushed onto pulled thread stitching, elastic, or over channelled elements. Below the gathered edge, the loose fabric drops and spreads in graceful, unstructured folds to a floating lower edge.

PROCEDURES

1. Decide how much fullness the fabric below the gathered edge should display—slight, moderate, generous, abundant. Set an after-gathering target measurement for the gathered edge. To estimate the length of ungathered fabric needed to produce the desired fullness in the gathered fabric, multiply the target measurement by the amount indicated in the following chart:

slight fullness	= [target] x	1 ½
moderate fullness	= [target] x	2
generous fullness	= [target] x	3
abundant fullness	= [target] x	4 (+ more)

   As the difference between the target measurement and the length of the fabric gathered to match that target increases, the fullness released by the gathering also increases.

2. Add width to the estimated length for the ungathered fabric, and cut the fabric. If necessary, piece the fabric to achieve the necessary length.

3. Divide the edge to be gathered into halves, quarters, or eighths, and mark the divisions between segments with pins, nips, notches, or chalk. Equate to similar but smaller divisions on a gauge—a ruler, a strip of paper or fabric—that represents the target measurement.

4. Gather the edge (refer to "Gathering Methods" on page 3), segment by segment, to fit the target measurement. Distribute the gathers as desired.

5. Stabilize the gathering (refer to "Stabilizing Gathered Stitching" on page 6).

NOTES & VARIATIONS

The standard for single-edge gathering is "cut, stitch, and gather on the straightgrain of woven fabric; stabilize horizontally and straight." Also, "stitching on the crossgrain is preferred over stitching on the lengthgrain because the folds released from crossgrain gathering hang more naturally than folds from lengthgrain gathering." However, deviations from these standards to suit specific circumstances are normal for gathered applications. For example:

Draped single-edge gathering extends to two adjacent edges of a squared piece of fabric. As a result, the released folds drape toward the center, and the floating edge, without the ripples and waves typical of straight-hanging folds, descends to a point (see (a) in Fig. 1-20). Stabilizing the gathered edge at an angle tighter or wider than the original angle alters the curve of the draping and the length of the point.

For *contoured single-edge gathering*, the gathered edge veers from the straight and horizontal while retaining a floating edge that ripples and waves. A straight, gathered edge may be stabilized to slant up or down, and, because of its flexibility, to curve or angle. When a straight, gathered edge is stabilized to arch or angle upward, the folds released from the contoured stabilizing deepen and swell, and the silhouette of the floating edge imitates in reverse the contour at the top (see (b) in Fig. 1-20). Straightening the floating edge by trimming places it off-grain.

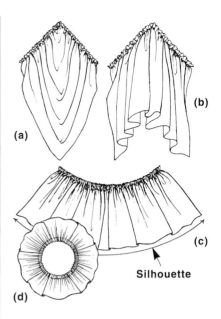

Fig. 1-20. Single-edge gathering variations: (a) Folds released from adjacent-edge gathering drape.
(b) Straight, gathered edge stabilized at an angle. (c) Straight, gathered edge stabilized to curve. (d) Straight, gathered edge stabilized in a flat circle becomes a ruffle.

Stabilizing a straight, gathered edge to dip in a curve stretches folds out of the floating edge, more so as the depth of the curve increases, unless (1) the fabric is lengthy and weighty enough to hang straight down from the gathering, or (2) the widening silhouette of the floating edge is considered in advance (see (c) in Fig. 1-20). Instead of the gathered-edge target measurement, use the silhouette of the floating edge as the target measurement to estimate the length of ungathered fabric needed to produce the desired fullness in a floating edge hanging from concave stabilizing.

When an application requires a straight, on-grain, floating edge with the desired fullness hanging perpendicular and even from a contoured gathering edge, the fabric needs to be cut from a pattern. (1) Make a full-size pattern, without a seam allowance, of the target shape the gathered fabric is to match. (2) Slash a copy of that pattern into strips, cutting in the direction the folds will hang. (3) Tape the strips to another piece of paper, spread apart to stretch out the pattern and add the desired fullness-after-gathering to the target edge. (4) Connecting the separated strips with lines, re-draw the outline—which becomes the pattern for the fabric to be gathered. **Variation:** Spread the strips more at the bottom than at the top to add flare to the folds released from the gathered edge (Fig. 1-21). Add a seam allowance to the final pattern.

For applications so large that working with a full-size target pattern is impractical, reduce the target dimensions and shape to a workable scale for pattern drafting purposes. Record actual-size measurements on the scaled-down gathering pattern and apply those measurements when cutting the fabric.

Stayed single-edge gathering doesn't have a floating edge. The dimensional folds released from the gathering stitches diminish and disappear at the opposite edge which is stretched smooth and stayed flat to prevent ripples and movement. To maintain a flat, straight, stayed edge, the opposite edge can be gathered only up to the point where the sides begin to drag the stayed edge out of alignment. Too much gathering will force the stayed edge to curve up. When one edge is stayed in a curve that encircles, like a tube of fabric sewn to a circular cutout in a foundation, the opposite edge, tightly gathered, closes the circular opening with folds that radiate from a central point—provided the width of the tube equals the radius of the circular cutout. Less than the radius—an opening surrounded by gathers: More than the radius—the gathering closes but puffs (Fig. 1-22).

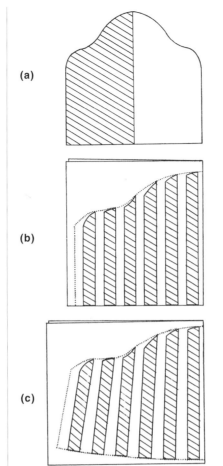

(a)

(b)

(c)

Fig. 1-21. Slash-and-spread pattern drafting for an inset gathered on a contoured edge: (a) One-half of the mirror-image target pattern (b) slashed into narrow strips which are spread out on folded paper. The re-drawn outline is the gathered inset pattern. (c) Adding optional flare to the floating edge by increasing the spread at the bottom.

Fullness multiplies with each addition to a buildup of *tiered single-edged gathering* because the ungathered edge of one tier stabilizes the gathered edge of the next tier. The gathered edge of fabric strip #2 is sewn to the ungathered edge of strip #1; gathered tier #3 is sewn to the ungathered edge of tier #2; and so on. Each tier increases the length of the gathered edge for the next tier (Fig. 1-23). If the tightness of the gathering is also increased for successive tiers, fullness will increase extravagantly.

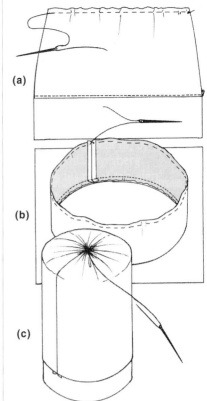

(a)

(b)

(c)

Fig. 1-22. (a) Gathering limited by the opposite edge which is stayed flat and straight. (b) Tube stitched into a circular cutout will flatten and almost close in the center when tightly gathered. (c) Tube stayed over a rigid form with the end of the tube closed by gathering.

Fig. 1-23. From lightly gathered stitching at the top, fullness increases gradually but dramatically when gathering is tiered.

Another variation of stayed single-edge gathering involves pattern drafting to enlarge the edge to be gathered, but not the opposite edge. The steps followed when drafting the pattern duplicate those described for Fig. 1-21 with a crucial difference—instead of slashing the target pattern into strips, the cuts stop ¹⁄₁₆″ (1.5mm) from the edge opposite the edge to be gathered. Sticking the slashed target pattern to another piece of paper, fan out the strips to enlarge the edge designated for gathering. Filling in the spaces, outline the gathering pattern (Fig. 1-24). Use the original target pattern as a stay for the gathered piece. Add seam allowances to final patterns.

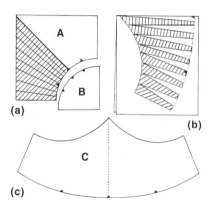

Fig. 1-24. Slash-and-spread pattern drafting for stayed single-edge gathering: (a) One-half of target pattern A (b) slashed but hinged at the opposite edge, fanned out on folded paper to enlarge the edge designated for gathering, and with the expanded edge re-drawn. (c) Pattern C cut out and marked with a notched edge that, when gathered, will match the notches on patterns A and B.

1-1—Lightly gathered on machined stitching, muslin enlarged 1¹⁄₂ times the target dimension ripples softly at the floating edge.

SINGLE-EDGE GATHERING

1-2—Muslin gathered moderately full on machine-sewn stitching loses 50% of its original length.

1-3—Close gathering on three rows of machine stitching reduces the muslin to one-third its original length and releases generous folds below the gathering.

1-4—Lavish fullness with deep folds descends from hand-stitched gauged gathering, which condensed the muslin used for this sample to 17% of its original length.

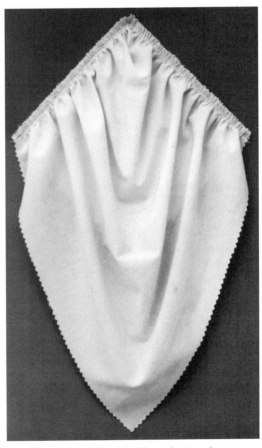

1-5—The draped folds caused by gathering adjacent edges of a muslin square to half their length.

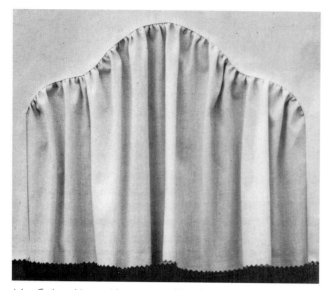

I-6—Gathered inset with a contoured heading set into a cutout in a foundation stay. (For the pattern, see Fig. I-21.)

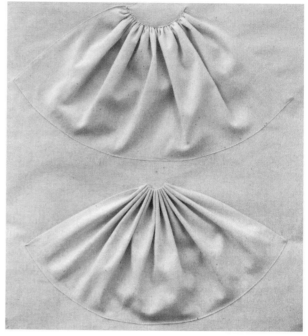

I-7—Gathered from identical rectangles of muslin, two fan-shaped applications with stayed edges shaped into curves controlled by the density of the gathering.

SINGLE-EDGE GATHERING

I-8—Cut from a pattern enlarged for gathering on one side and stayed horizontally, the loose, lower edge of the gathered sample falls into a curve.

I-9—Three tiers, each gathered fuller than the tier above, increase the circumference of the floating edge extravagantly without bulky gathers thickening the binding at the top.

SINGLE-EDGE GATHERING

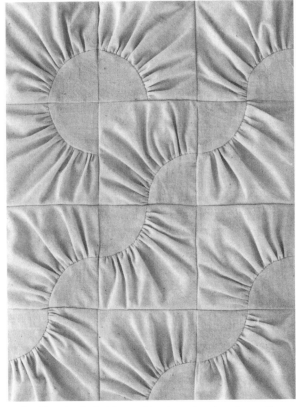

I-10—"Drunkard's Path," a traditional patchwork pattern, with patches dimensionalized by folds that radiate from a curved, gathered seam. The gathered patches were stayed before assembly. (For the pattern, see Fig. 1-24.)

I-11—Strips with one edge set into a circular cutout before tightly gathering the opposite edge. After gathering, (left) a strip less wide than the radius of the cutout leaves a center opening; (center) a strip as wide as the radius releases folds that radiate from a central pinpoint; (right) a strip wider than the radius inflates the muslin into a dome.

OPPOSITE-EDGE GATHERING

—opposite sides of a piece of fabric made smaller when crushed onto pulled thread stitching, elastic, or over channelled inserts. The freed fabric between the gathered edges collects into variable, directed folds.

PROCEDURES

To gather the opposite edges of a length of fabric, adapt the procedures described for "Single-edge Gathering" on page 10.

NOTES & VARIATIONS

Opposite-edge gathering requires opposite-edge stabilizing to anchor both gathered edges and maintain the released folds in a directional and taut or slack condition. The folds can move straight between the gathered edges, or they can drape, puff, radiate, or skew. The formation of the sculpted folds that are liberated between the gathered edges is the primary design focus of opposite-edge gathering.

When opposite-gathered edges are stitched to a stay that is smaller than the gathered fabric, the cramped folds in between either drape or puff. For *draped opposite-edge gathering*, the released folds must be horizontal and lengthy enough to droop of their own weight when the gathered edges are stabilized closer together (Fig. 1-25).

For *puffed opposite-edge gathering*, the folds released between the gathered edges must be relatively short, as they are between the gathered edges of a narrow strip of fabric. Instead of draping, the folds thrust upward when the gathering stitches are topstitched to an even narrower stay, breaking up into swirling ridges and peaks (Fig. 1-26). The draped or puffed effect grows more pronounced as the stay becomes smaller. Unlike draped opposite-edge gathering, puffed opposite-edge gathering can be rotated in any direction, and the elevations collapse under pressure.

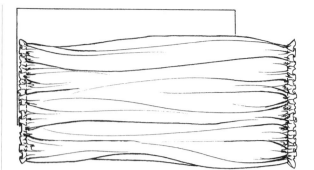

Fig. 1-25. Opposite-edge gathering before stabilizing to a shorter stay—which will cause the long, loose horizontal folds to drape.

Fig. 1-26. Strip of fabric gathered on opposite edges, stabilized to a stay that's smaller than the strip is wide, puffs up into craggy folds.

Skewed opposite-edge gathering fixes the folds into a diagonal relationship with the edges. After stabilizing the left edge by basting the gathering stitches to a stay, pull the right edge downward forcefully before basting that gathered edge to the stay. To prevent the pulled edge from wandering while topstitching, match the edge to a guideline marked on the stay (Fig. 1-27). Skewing decreases the original width of the gathered fabric.

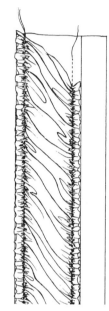

Fig. 1-27. Opposite-edge gathering skewed by tugging the right edge down to angle the folds before basting to the stay.

Curved opposite-edge gathering arcs and turns. Curvature is forced by gathering a segment on one side of the fabric strip tightly (the inner curve), the segment directly opposite lightly (the outside curve), and stabilizing the edges accordingly (Fig. 1-28).

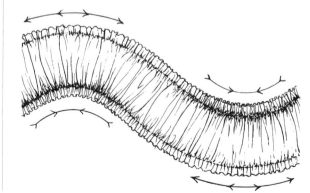

Fig. 1-28. Strip of opposite-edge gathering that curves when sections of one edge are gathered tighter than the sections immediately opposite.

OPPOSITE-EDGE GATHERING

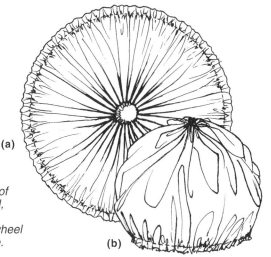

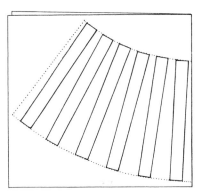

(a)

(b)

Fig. 1-29. Long strips of fabric with ends joined, gathered on opposite edges, (a) fashion a wheel and (b) create a dome.

Fig. 1-30. Using the slash-and-spread method to draft an opposite-edge-gathering pattern that will be gathered more on one edge than the other and stayed to a rectangle.

For *circular opposite-edge gathering*, the ends of a fabric strip are sewn together. One edge—the inside edge—needs very tight gathering on large stitches (the larger the stitches, the smaller the central opening). The opposite edge—the outside of the circle—is lightly gathered. The gathered strip can be manipulated into a flat, wheel-like shape or an elevated, domed form, as determined by the amount of gathering on the outside edge. Both have deep folds, collected around a central axis, that diminish as they radiate toward the outer edge (Fig. 1-29). To gather the outer edge, the strip must be longer than the circumference of the target circle to which the outer edge will eventually be stabilized. Use the target circle's circumference (circumference = diameter x 3.14) as the target measurement when estimating the length needed to gather the outer edge. A strip as wide as the radius of the intended circular outline will gather flat within that outline. A strip wider than the radius of the intended circular outline, when gathered on opposite edges, will elevate in the center within that outline.

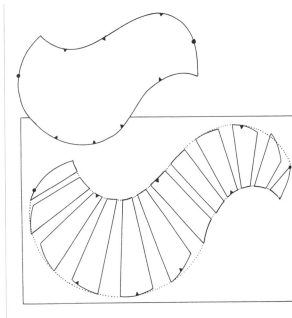

Fig. 1-31. Using the slash-and-spread method to draft an opposite-edge-gathering pattern, based on an unusually shaped target; to be gathered unequally along selected portions of the outline. Match points (▲) direct the adjustment of the gathers.

When none of these fit the situation, draft slash-and-spread patterns for the opposite-edge gathering. Insertions of a target shape covered with folds that cross from a densely gathered edge to a lightly gathered edge (Fig. 1-30), or a target shape with an unusual outline covered with folds that cross from edge to edge (Fig. 1-31), need patterns. Slash a copy of the target shape straight across from edge to edge in the direction of the folds; spread the pieces apart on another piece of paper to enlarge the edges for gathering and stick to the paper; draw a new outline that fills in the spaces. Add seam allowances after drafting patterns.

After stabilizing the gathered edges in a finished manner, arrange the unfastened folds agreeably, stretching and pinning the edges to a padded board if needed. Steam with an iron held above the gathering. Allow to cool and dry before moving.

I-12—Muslin gathered on and stretched between dowels inserted into hems.

I-13—Muslin gathered on and draped between dowels inserted into hems.

I-14—Trapezoid of muslin with its slanting edges gathered before stitching to a rectangular stay as wide as the top of the trapezoid. The released folds drape with increasing depth to a pendant lower edge.

OPPOSITE-EDGE GATHERING

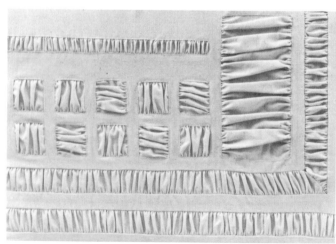

I-15—Muslin patterned with a design that contrasts smooth fabric with the dimensional, directional folds of automatically gathered inserts.

I-16—Construction that exploits the direction of gathered folds to distinguish between the parts of a pieced design. Border gathering around the central squares is skewed; stayed single-edge gathering fills the eight triangles outside the border. All pieces were stayed before assembly.

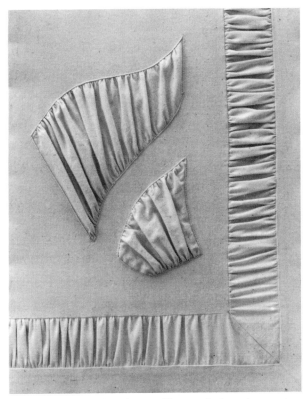

I-17—Generously gathered inserts fill unusually shaped cutouts in a muslin foundation. The gathers in the border start smooth at the corner and gradually increase in density.

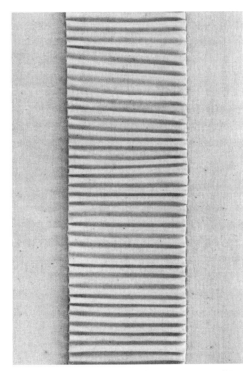

I-18— Corrugated gathering drawn up on matching rows of evenly spaced running stitches. The grooves were stroked and the edges fluted when appliquéd to the foundation.

OPPOSITE-EDGE GATHERING

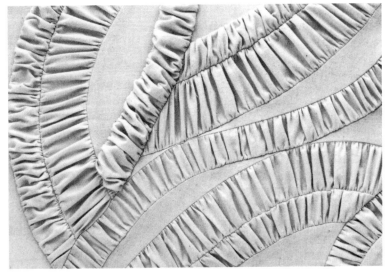

I-19—Serpentine construction of gathered strips curved by adjusting the gathers, accented with areas of smooth fabric. All elements were stitched to a paper stay outlined with the design. The three puffed strips have permanent stays of fabric.

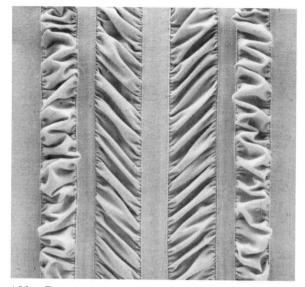

I-20 —The strips in the center are skewed, the strips on the sides puff to a height of 3/4" (2cm).

I-21—Medallion constructed from straight strips of muslin gathered to radiate and encircle. Stitched to a stiffened foundation, folds spread out from a central opening walled with deep gathers, to a circle of topstitching that releases a ruffled edge. The surrounding ring of curved gathering is puffed.

OPPOSITE-EDGE GATHERING

I-22—Straight strips gathered into two domed shapes, one an airy fabrication of billowing muslin, the other molded and steam-set over a rounded, solid form.

ALL-SIDES GATHERING

—a fabric shape condensed into a smaller version of itself when its entire edge is drawn up on pulled thread stitching, elastic, or over channelled inserts, inflating the fabric between the gathers.

PROCEDURES

1. Select target shapes with simple, uncomplicated outlines. To draft an all-sides-gathered pattern for a target, enlarge the target pattern by an equal amount all around to allow for puffing. As a broad rule-of-thumb, estimate a height for the inflated fullness and enlarge by that amount (see Fig. 1-32). Divide the curved edges of the gathering pattern into halves and quarters, marking the divisions with notches. Divide long straight edges in a similar manner. Mark the target pattern with comparably spaced notches.

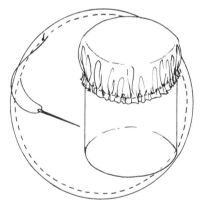

Fig. 1-32. To cover a round form with a circle of fabric gathered all around, measure the form across the diameter of the top and down the sides to the points where the covering will stop. The measurement includes enlargement for height.

2. Gather all around the edge of fabric cut from the gathering pattern, matching the gathered length between notches or sides to the length between related notches or sides on the target pattern, or on a stay cut or outlined from the target pattern. Distribute the gathers evenly. (Refer to "Gathering Methods" on page 3.)

3. Stabilize the gathered edges and shape, choosing a method that suits the requirements of the application (refer to "Stabilizing Gathered Stitching" on page 6).

NOTES & VARIATIONS

The standard for all-sides gathering is a square gathered to a smaller square, an oval gathered to a smaller oval, a circle gathered to a smaller circle, or variations thereof, with the edges stabilized appropriately. The air-supported fragility of the fabric that billows up between the edges is part of the appeal of all-sides gathering. An all-sides-gathered application needs an environment where such qualities are assets.

Furrowing is an unusual adjunct to all-sides gathering, utilizing needle and thread to collapse the puffy, unsteady folds deliberately. Furrowing converts the ballooning fabric between the stabilized edges into a maze-like relief of ridges and crevices with tiny tacking stitches (refer to "Furrowing" on page 9).

Puffs head a sublist of handsewing techniques that limit all-sides gathering to small circles. Gather a little circle of fabric very tightly around the edges, stand the bunched gathers on foundation fabric, and tack securely. With the needle's point, tease open and spread out the bundled fabric above the gathers to make a puff that looks something like a squatty toadstool (Fig. 1-33). A puff finishes slightly less than one-half its original circular diameter.

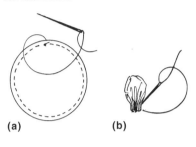

(a)   **(b)**

(c)

Fig. 1-33. To make a puff: (a) Stitch around the edge of a small fabric circle. (b) Gather tightly and tack the gathers to foundation fabric. (c) Cap the puff over its base.

The **ruffled puff** carries the puff concept a step further. Center the puff circle inside a larger circle of fabric. Stitch on the outline of the puff circle and gather, winding the thread around the gathering several times before securing. Attach the gathers between the ruffle and the puff to a foundation (Fig. 1-34).

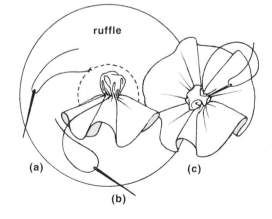

ruffle

(a)   **(c)**

(b)

Fig. 1-34. To make a ruffled puff: (a) Stitch around the inner circle, and (b) gather tightly. (c) Tack the gathers to a foundation.

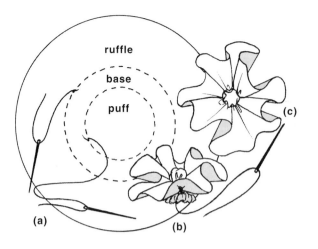

ruffle

base

puff

(a)

(b)

(c)

Fig. 1-35. For a ruffled puff on a base: (a) Stitch around both inner circles. (b) Gather tightly, pushing the gathered ring of base fabric down. (c) Tack the base to a foundation.

Massed ruffled puffs extend the coverage of frilly ruffles and nestled puffs to an area defined by the number of ruffled puffs attached to the foundation: The trick—attach so closely that adjacent ruffled edges are forced upward. The **ruffled puff on a base** snuggles the puff inside a fuller ruffle raised from a cushion of gathers. Outline two concentric circles spaced about ½″ (1.3cm) apart, centered inside a larger circle of fabric. With two threaded needles, stitch on the outlines. Gather both rows tightly while pushing the puff circle in the center up, and the gathered fabric between the rows down to form a base under the puff and ruffle. Sew the base to a foundation (Fig. 1-35). (Refer to "Edge Finishing for Ruffles" on page 43.)

With *puff gathering*, the puffs and the folds connecting the puffs reconstruct the fabric into a patterned relief. Puff gathering starts with a stencil of cut-out circles arranged on a grid (Fig. 1-36).

Using the stencil, trace the pattern onto the right side of the fabric. Stitch and gather each circular outline tightly. Push the puffs up and spread out the bunched puff fabric with the point of the needle. Gather the edges of the fabric to match the measurements of the puff-gathered interior of the fabric. A lightweight lining tacked to the gathering behind the puffs steadies the fabric overall and prevents puff-gathering threads from breaking under stress.

Star gathering describes the reverse side of puff gathering when it becomes the right side. Dimple-like points surrounded by radiating folds replace the puffs. Trace the circular outlines on the back of the fabric and proceed as described for puff gathering. For **pierced star gathering**, the dimples expand into round openings. Pierced-star-gathering stencils have circles at least twice as large in diameter as the target openings after gathering. Cut out on the circular outlines traced on the front of the fabric. With a scanty seam allowance clipped and turned under while sewing, gather each circle on overcast stitching pulled tight around a removable gauge like a pencil or dowel. Use strong thread and secure the gathered stitching well to deter future accidents.

For puff gathering and its variations, the connecting folds released by the gathering become longer as the distance between circles increases, and deeper as the circles increase in size.

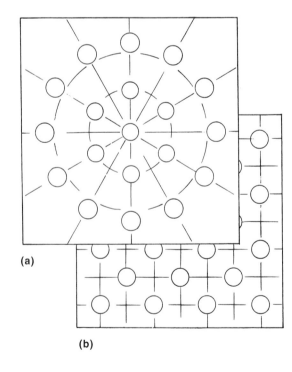

(a)

(b)

Fig. 1-36. Two puff or star gathering stencils (a) planned on a radiating grid bisected by concentric circles, (b) drawn on a squared grid. The circles are spaced more than their width apart to prevent the puffs from bumping into each other.

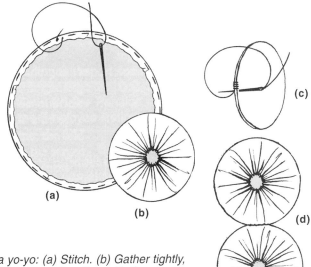

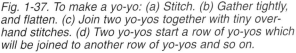

(a)

(b)

(c)

(d)

Fig. 1-37. To make a yo-yo: (a) Stitch. (b) Gather tightly, and flatten. (c) Join two yo-yos together with tiny overhand stitches. (d) Two yo-yos start a row of yo-yos which will be joined to another row of yo-yos and so on.

Yo-yos squash the inflated result of all-sides gathering and show a ring of gathers on the top. A yo-yo begins as a circle of fabric cut twice as large in diameter as the intended yo-yo. Turning the seam allowance inside, sew next to the fold with large, even running stitches: *Large running stitches = small center opening; small running stitches = large center opening.* Gather tightly and flatten the baggy fabric into a circle surrounding an inner circle of gathers. A multiplication of round yo-yos joined together where they touch creates a fabric or trim uniquely textured with gathers and openings (Fig. 1-37).

Appliquéd to a foundation fabric, yo-yos are elements for surface decoration. Outline a smaller circle, the perimeter of the finished yo-yo, inside the circle of fabric cut for the yo-yo. Because the fabric between the inner circle and the outer edge will be turned toward the center of the yo-yo by the gathering, the distance between the inner circle and the outer edge should be less than the radius of the inside circle. Turning the seam allowance inside, sew next to the fold with large, even running stitches, but don't gather until the yo-yo is attached to the foundation with stitching around the inner circle. Stabilize the gathered edge with fluting that spaces the grooves in the gathers (Fig. 1-38). When same-size circles are appliquéd, the finished size and appearance of the yo-yos may be changed by varying the size of the inner circle, which will also change the size of the opening framed by the gathers, and by placing the inner circle off-center.

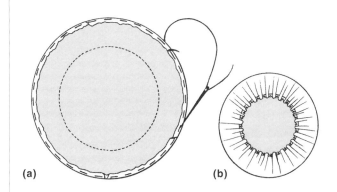

(a)

(b)

Fig. 1-38. To appliqué a yo-yo: (a) Stitch through the turned seam allowance, sew to the foundation fabric around the inner circle, and gather. (b) Flute the edge while stabilizing the gathers.

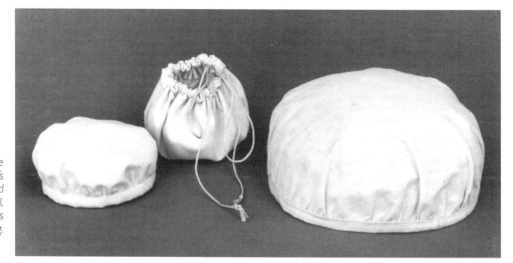

I-23—Three gathered-circle
structures, (left) one that puffs
naturally, (right) one molded
and steam-set over a bowl,
(center) one that pouches
from a channelled drawstring.

I-24—Border design with puffings
made from larger ovals gathered
and hand-stitched into smaller
oval cutouts, above an insertion
of opposite edge gathering.

ALL-SIDES GATHERING

I-25—Pieced design that contrasts puffed shapes and smooth areas.
Except for the cluster of puffs tacked to the surface, all gathered
pieces were stayed before assembly.

I-26—Scattered puffs accent a design of
gathered circular elements: (top) Six ruffled
puffs, three with centered puffs on top, three
attached with the puffs underneath. (bottom) Three strips with ends joined, tightly
gathered on one edge.

I-27—(lower right) Massed ruffled puffs, (left) four ruffled puffs, (center) puffs, (upper right) three ruffled puffs on bases.

I-28—Puff-gathering design. Faint lines on the fabric indicate the squared grid that regulates the pattern.

I-29—Star gathering (the puff-gathering design, reversed).

ALL-SIDES GATHERING

I-30—Radial design that combines star and puff gathering. If the bordering puffs were twice as large, or if there were 24 instead of 12, the circumference would shrink and the center would elevate into a dome.

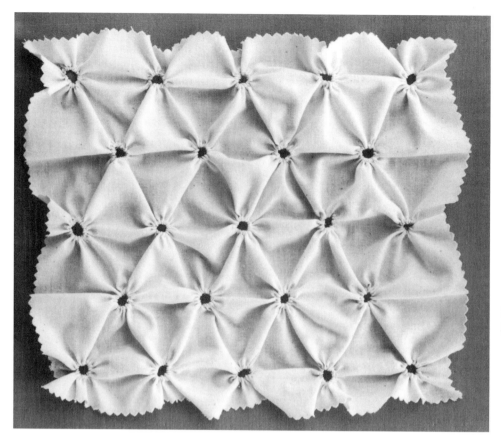

I-31—Pierced star gathering.

ALL-SIDES GATHERING

I-32—Assembly of yo-yos that could be continued to any size.

I-33—Row of yo-yos inserted as an openwork border.

I-34—Appliquéd yo-yos with
fluted stabilizing around the
larger openings.

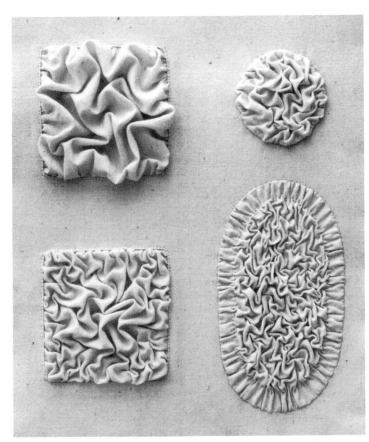

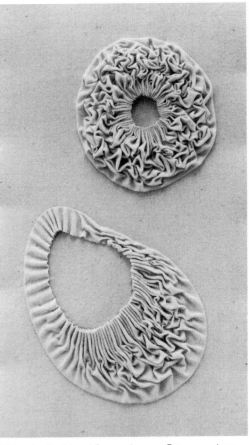

I-35—Furrowing examples started with muslin cut twice as large as the target
shape: (top left) Widely spaced tacks—the deepest furrows. (lower left) More
tacking reduces the height of the crests. (top right) Closely spaced tacks—crests
twice as high as the crests (lower right) in the densely tacked oval with a band
of gathering around the furrowing.

I-36—Appliquéd and furrowed yo-yos. Extreme enlargement outside the appliqué-stitching outlines provided the
swelling fabric for furrowing.

S hirring configures fabric with bands of soft, rolling folds released between rows of gathering. The pinched, puckery, stitching lines that bisect shirred fabric run parallel or diagonal to the fabric's edge, cross each other, or form multi-directional patterns. With its network of gathered stitching separated by zones of fabric crowded with variable folds, shirring shrinks the original fabric while adding substance to the decorative fabric it creates.

S H I R R I N G

2 Shirring

SHIRRING

—fabric contracted to a smaller size when gathered on multiple rows of stitching sewn straight across the designated area in parallel rows.

PROCEDURES

1. Set an after-shirring target measurement for the shirred fabric to match. Decide how much fullness the fabric released between the rows of gathering stitches should display—slight, moderate, generous. To estimate the length of unshirred fabric needed to produce the desired fullness in the shirred fabric, multiply the target measurement by the amount indicated in the chart below:

   slight fullness   = [target] x 1 ½
   moderate fullness = [target] x 2
   generous fullness = target] x 3 (+ more)

2. Adding a second measurement for the non-shirred length, cut the fabric. Note that shirred fabric shrinks slightly *across* the gathered stitching. (For example, a 12″ (30.5cm) square shirred to 6″ (15cm) may shrink ¼″ (6mm) from its non-shirred 12″ (30.5cm) length. As the number of gathered rows increases, shrinkage increases.)

3. Plan a shirring pattern with parallel stitching lines spaced out over the shirring area. Mark the stitching lines on the reverse side of the fabric with a fabric-safe marker or lightly pressed folds, or depend on a sewing machine attachment. Divide lengthy sewing lines into segments—halves, quarters—that will be matched to corresponding segments on a target gauge.

4. To prepare the fabric for gathering, cover the marked lines with ungauged, hand-sewn running stitches, machine-sewn straight stitching, or zigzag stitching over string or cords (refer to "Gathering Methods" on page 3). Leave at least 3″ (7.5 cm) of thread, string, or cord at one end (hand sewing) or both ends (machine sewing) of each seam.

5. Gather each row of stitching to a specific target measurement. Hand hold the fabric, or pin or tack one end or the center of each row to a flat surface marked with target measurements. Grasp the dangling threads, strings or cords at the ends of two or more adjacent rows of stitching in one hand; use the other hand to crush the fabric into itself on the tautly held threads. Gather inch by inch, working back and forth across the fabric, until all rows of stitching are gathered to size (Fig. 2-1).

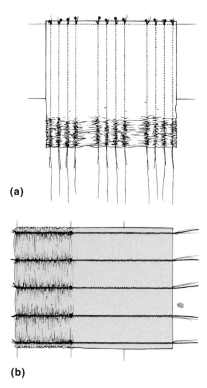

(a)

(b)

Fig. 2-1. Fabric prepared for shirring: (a) Pinned at the end of each machine-sewn row to one of two target lines marked on the surface underneath. (b) Tacked at the center of each zigzagged row to the midpoint between two target lines marked on the surface.

Secure hand-stitched gathering with tiny stitches, one over the other. Secure machine-stitched gathering by tying the bobbin and needle threads together and then machine stitching across the knots. If rows of shirring end inside the fabric rather than inside the seam allowance, capture the knotted threads with a tiny tuck (Fig. 2-2). Adjust the shirring evenly.

6. To set the shirring, pin to a flat surface, stretching gently, and steam with an iron held above the fabric. Allow to cool and dry before moving.

7. Stabilize thread-gathered shirring with an invisible stay stitched to the back (Fig. 2-3), and/or sew the shirring to the stay by topstitching over each gathered row (Fig. 2-4).

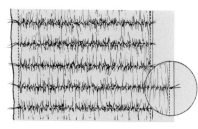

Fig. 2-2. On the left, gathered stitching that stops at the fabric's edge secured with bobbin-and-needle-thread knots and a vertical line of machine stitching that crosses each knot. On the right, gathered stitching that stops within the fabric secured with bobbin-and-needle-thread knots and a vertical pin tuck that catches each knot inside the tuck seam.

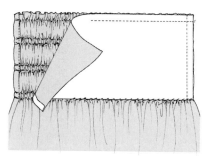

(a)

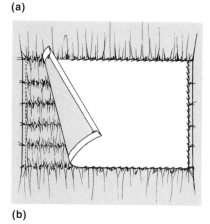

(b)

Fig. 2-3. Shirring stabilized with a stay hand-stitched to the last row of gathering stitches by catching the gathering thread and one or two threads of the fabric in each stitch: (a) Stay hand-stitched on one side and machine-basted to the seam allowances around the other three sides. (b) Stay hand-stitched to the gathering stitches and bordering pin tucks.

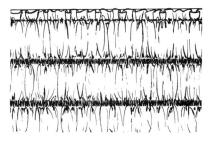

Fig. 2-4. Shirring, with a stay underneath, stabilized by satin stitching over the rows of gathering stitches.

If a layer of fabric underneath the shirring is undesirable, use a temporary stay and stabilize with narrow ribbon or tapes stitched over each gathered row (Fig. 2-5). For shirring gathered on sturdy string or cords, stabilizing is optional.

Fig. 2-5. Shirring stabilized with tape or ribbon machine-stitched over the rows of gathered stitching.

NOTES & VARIATIONS

Fully shirred fabric is gathered from one side to the other on stitching spaced out from top to bottom. Partially shirred fabric is confined to an area isolated in the middle of the fabric, a section that runs down the center of the fabric, or a section that crosses the top or bottom of the fabric. When the shirred section is a heading, the released fabric falls in spreading folds to a floating edge.

Always locate the last row of gathering stitches within the seam allowance for shirring that will be attached to an extension or inset behind a cutout within foundation fabric. If a gathered edge isn't meant to become the seam allowance for a future seam, the edge may be finished with a ruffle. (Refer to "Stabilizing Gathered Stitching" on page 8.)

Stabilizing prevents the gathering threads from breaking and also secures the distribution of the gathers. With a stay underneath, topstitching over each gathered row locks the arrangement in place; next best—hidden tacking stitches spaced out along each row. When rows of gathered stitching are topstitched to a permanent or temporary stay with decorative hand or machine stitching, shirring is sometimes called *mock smocking* (Fig. 2-4 and refer to "Mock Smocking" on page 133).

If all the stitched rows are gathered to the same target measurement, a rectangle of fabric shirrs into a smaller rectangle or a square. But if each row is gathered looser than the previous seam, the seams will curve, the sides of the shirred fabric at the ends of the stitching will fan outward, and the density of the connecting folds will gradually diminish. Rows of stitching spaced around a long strip of fabric with ends seamed together may be gathered with unequal density to convert the circle of fabric into a wheel with radiating folds controlled by concentric seamlines, or the circle of fabric can be gathered over a rigid form into a domed shape (refer to "circular opposite-edge gathering" on page 17). Shirred fabric acquires stiffness across the seams, a useful attribute for structured applications.

One-step automatic gathering, no stabilizing, and stretchable adaptability are three reasons for the popularity of *elastic shirring*. Machine-gathered with elastic thread in the bobbin or elastic cord inside zigzagged tunnels, elastic shirring clings and conforms when stretched over a solid, curvy substructure. (Refer to "Gathering Methods" on page 5.)

Automatically gathered shirring results when the rows are sewn with a gathering foot, a specialized machine attachment that crimps each stitch (refer to "Gathering Methods" on page 5). Tension and stitch settings regulate the density of

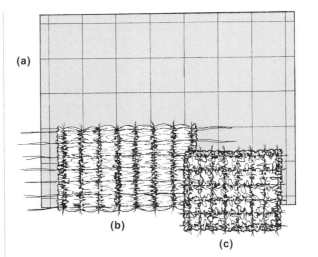

Fig. 2-6. For waffle or cross shirring: (a) Mark stitching lines on the back of the fabric. (b) After stitching, gather parallel rows in one direction. (c) Gather the crossing rows.

the gathering—a high tension combined with the longest stitch causes the fullest gathering; shorter stitches decrease fullness. Test before shirring with the gathering foot. The tightness of the gathers, the width of the foot, and the nature of the fabric affect the manageable distance between rows. Within its limitations, automatic gathering with the gathering foot speeds all kinds of shirring.

The pockets of puffy, crumpled fabric that spring up between crisscrossing rows of gathered stitching characterize *waffle or cross shirring*. Stitched by hand or machine over a grid of lines marked on the wrong side of the fabric, the fabric is gathered in one direction to the target measurement and then the cross-stitched lines are gathered to the target measurement (Fig. 2-6). When straight stitching by machine, skip the needle over previously stitched rows to avoid sewing through the thread, a catch that would impede the gathering process. Before steam setting the waffle shirring, push out and pull up the fabric released between the rows, stretch and pin the ends of the stitched rows to a padded board, steam, and allow to cool and dry before moving. To stabilize, hand tack a stay to the back of the shirring at the points where stitching lines cross.

For *puffed shirring*, the loose folds between rows of gathered stitching are elevated into a jumble of swirling ridges when adjacent rows are

pushed toward each other as they're topstitched to a stay. Mark the stay with lines that repeat the shirred stitching lines but space the lines closer together (the tighter the spacing compared to the shirred spacing, the higher the puff). Pin match the gathered rows to corresponding lines on the stay and topstitch over the gathering stitches (Fig. 2-7).

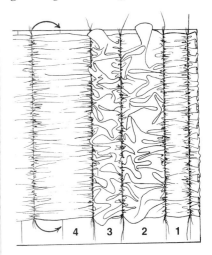

Fig. 2-7. To puff shirring while topstitching to a stay, shorten the space between adjacent gathered rows. In this diagram, topstitched section 1 has not been puffed, sections 2 and 3 are puffed, section 4 will be puffed when the gathered stitching is topstitched to the guideline marked on the stay.

An alternate method: Elevate the folds over a dowel or tube temporarily inserted between the shirring and stay, and topstitch over the gathered stitching with a zipper foot on the machine.

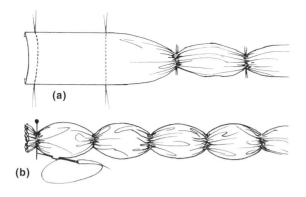

(a)

(b)

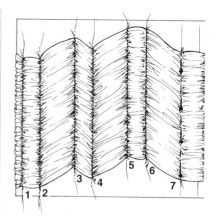

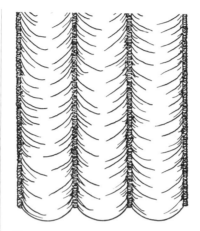

Fig. 2-8. Puffed trim: (a) Shirr a fabric strip on spaced out rows of machine stitching. (b) Push the gathered rows closer together and blindstitch the curving edges in between to a foundation.

Fig. 2-10. Skewed shirring pattern: After seam 1, seam 2 is not skewed; seams 3, 4, and 5 are skewed; seam 6 is not skewed; seam 7, pin-matched to a line on the stay, will be skewed when topstitched. When the skewed angle turns up, turn the shirring so that topstitching always moves down, following the descending slant of the skewed folds.

A variation of puffed shirring, **puffed trim** embellishes foundation fabric with chains of oval or circular fabric puffs connected by rows of gathered stitching. Puffed trim starts with a narrow strip of fabric: (1) Press the seam allowances on the long edges underneath. (2) At measured intervals spaced out along the length of the strip, stitch across the strip and gather tightly. (3) Reducing the distance between the gathered intersections to puff the intervening fabric, blindstitch the folded edges to a foundation, shaping scalloped outlines and securing the gathered stitching as sewing proceeds (Fig. 2-8). Shorten the distance between intersections to increase the outward curve of the edges attached to the foundation.

For shirring to puff, the distance between the gathered rows must be short enough for the folds to stay aloft when the rows are bunched. As the distance between gathered rows increases, the folds in between begin to droop instead of puff when adjacent rows are forced closer and, eventually, longer folds drape of their own weight. Although similar to puffed shirring in construction, the scale of *draped shirring* is comparatively large (Fig. 2-9). Draped shirring needs to hang from vertical gathering, whereas puffed shirring holds up whatever its position.

The relationship between folds and rows of gathered stitching changes from perpendicular to diagonal when shirring is skewed.

Fig. 2-9. Large, heavy application of draped shirring gathered on cords inside tapes (see Fig. 2-11). Rigid reinforcement from side to side at the top and bottom of the tapes keeps the sides straight.

Skewed shirring requires a stay about as wide as the shirred fabric measured across the gathered rows, but longer than the rows to allow space for angling. (If the stay fabric is limp, stiffen it with paper or a commercial product which can be torn away after the stitching, or starch it.) After topstitching the first row to the stay, pull the folds released from the gathered stitching up or down forcefully and hold in that slanted position while topstitching the next row of gathered stitching. Measure as topstitching proceeds to maintain a straight and even distance from previous rows (Fig. 2-10). Skewing shortens the across-row measurement of the shirred fabric.

Channel shirring is gathered on cords or rods concealed inside fabric conduits (refer to "Gathering Methods" on page 6). The folds are released between seams stitched in pairs, each pair spaced to enclose a

gathering element inserted between two fabric layers. A full or partial underlining or a tape behind every pair of seams makes up the second layer (Fig. 2-11). After shirring the fabric to size on channelled cords or rods, stops at the ends of the cords or rods prevent the gathering from coming undone but allow the gathering to be readjusted at any time.

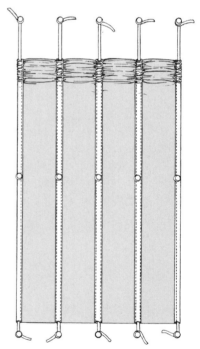

Fig. 2-11. Shirring in progress on cords confined inside hems on the outside, and in channels of tape on the inside of the fabric.

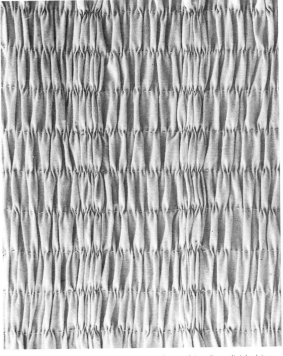

II-1—Handstitched shirring with each stitching line divided into five segments. Gathered segment by segment, two tightly gathered segments interrupt the looser gathering in the center and side segments.

SHIRRING

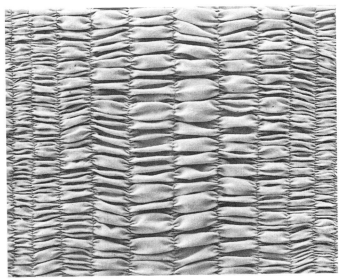

II-2—Machine-stitched shirring gathered on bobbin threads.

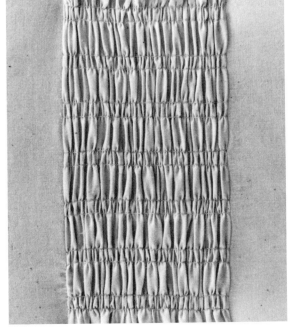

II-3—Vertical pintucks, which look like seams from the front, neatly finish the ends of the gathered rows of stitching, and separate the shirred section from the smooth fabric at the sides.

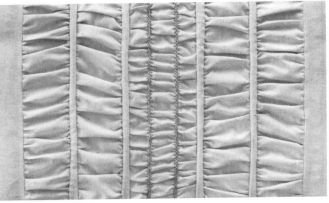

II-4—Shirring stabilized with tapes and braids that cover rows of stitching automatically gathered with a gathering foot. To apply thin braid and gather in the same operation, insert the braid into the needle hole in the gathering foot and bring it out behind the foot before starting to gather the fabric.

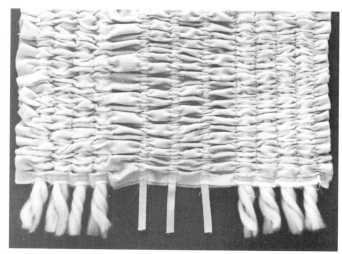

II-6—Channel shirring over soft yarn and twill tape. The seamlines separating the yarn channels on the left look muddled compared to the defined seamlines on the right—where the seams are bobbin-thread gathered to match the length of the yarn over which the fabric is channel-gathered.

II-5—(top) Shirring gathered on cords that are loosely confined inside zigzagged stitching. (bottom) Shirring produced on cords closely confined inside zigzag stitching is much more distinct and controlled.

SHIRRING

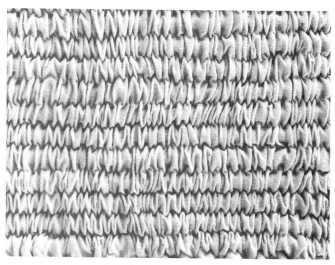

II-7—Stable, thick, firm textile created by gathering the stitching between rows of snugly channelled cable cord. To prepare for gathering, cords were seamed into doubled fabric with extra-strong thread in the bobbin. The fabric was pushed onto the cords as bobbin-thread gathering progressed.

II-8—Long rectangle of muslin shirred into a half-circle by graduating the gathering of successive seams from very tight in the center to light on the outside. After topstitching to a foundation stay, the original straight-stitched gathering threads were pulled out of the shirring.

SHIRRING

II-9—Circular insertions gathered on concentric seams into smaller circles. (left) Two circles automatically gathered with a gathering foot also rise unavoidably into cones. (right) With hand gathering to control density, a large circle shirrs into a flat medallion around a center of ballooning fabric, which was settled with furrowing.

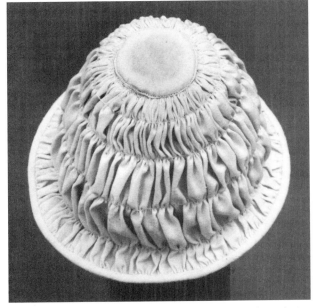

II-10—Sculpted form shaped by adjusting the gathering density of successive rows to conform to the domed shape of a mold. Loosening the gathers on the outside row created the flaring rim edged with binding.

II-11—With elastic thread in the bobbin and the muslin stretched taut in a hoop, free-motion machine stitching in a meandering pattern produces stretchy shirring with a crinkly texture.

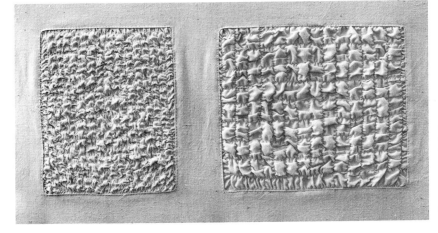

II-12—Two examples of waffle or cross shirring automatically gathered with a gathering foot. After gathering in one direction, the gathering foot had to pull the heavier weight of the shirred muslin, causing slightly looser gathering during cross stitching.

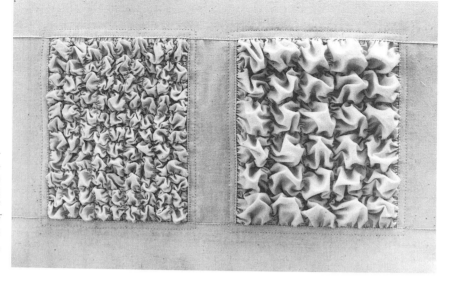

II-13—Waffle or cross shirring bobbin-thread gathered to one-half the original size of the fabric. The example on the right, based on a grid of 2" (5cm) squares gathered to a target of 1" (2.5cm) squares, releases swellings of muslin that peak 1" (2.5cm) above gathered-stitching level.

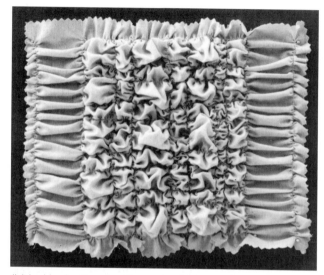

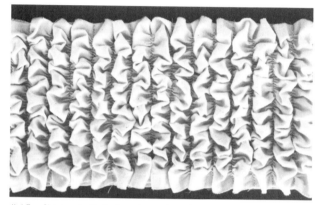

II-15—Shirring puffed when the gathered rows were topstitched to a stay with folds elevated over a dowel and a zipper foot attached to the machine.

II-14—Hand-gathered waffle or cross shirring, machine-stitched on an irregular grid, centered between bands of plain shirring.

SHIRRING

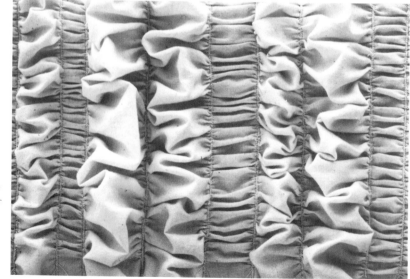

II-16—High-relief puffed shirring separated by bands of low-relief plain shirring.

II-17—Puffed trim applied to foundation fabric.

SHIRRING

II-18—A band of horizontal shirring at the top releases fullness into the fabric below. Widely spaced rows of vertical shirring, gathered on ribbons inside channels of zigzagged thread, create horizontal folds and draping at the lower edge. To secure the hemline shirring, the channelled ribbon was bowtied to another length of ribbon tacked to the top of each channel.

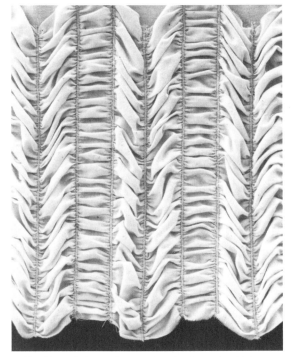

II-19—Skewed shirring between bands of straight shirring.

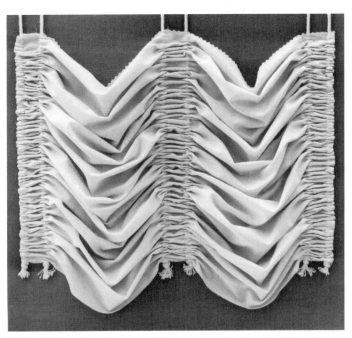

II-20—Shirring drapes between widely spaced, vertical bands of channel gathering.

PATTERN SHIRRING

—fabric automatically shirred with the gathering foot following a design of lines that twist and turn back and forth as they cross the fabric.

PROCEDURES

1. Plan a repeating pattern of continuous lines that move in curves and/or angles from one side of the fabric to the other (Fig. 2-12).

2. Trace the design onto the wrong side of the fabric with a fabric-safe marker.

3. With the gathering foot attached to the machine (refer to "Gathering Methods" on page 5), stitch-and-gather each line of the design. Sew slowly, stopping to lift the presser foot and pivot the fabric on the needle when seamline direction requires readjustment. In general, light to moderate gathering suits shirring to a pattern.

4. Stretching gently, pin the edges of the pattern-shirred fabric to a padded surface and steam with an iron held above the shirring. Allow to cool and dry before moving.

NOTES & VARIATIONS

Test several repeats of the design on a sample of the designated fabric to determine the appropriate stitch length and tension setting for automatic gathering and to assess overall design effectiveness. The pattern may be difficult to follow if the gathering is too full or the scale of the design is too small. To estimate the amount of fabric required for a specific application, measure a sample of the fabric before and after a test shirring of the pattern and equate with the target measurements.

Meander shirring is improvised. Instead of following a pattern, the design wanders freely forward and backward, sideways, across, and around, developing configurations of puckers, folds, and puffs as stitching-and-gathering proceed. Variations in the spacing and irregularities in the stitching path produce diversity in the relief of meander shirring. Stitch length and tension adjustments that modify the tightness/lightness of the gathering add more dimension. The foot's gathering action can be manually reduced by inhibiting the fabric from moving easily toward the needle. To increase fullness, jam the fabric by holding it down with a finger as it emerges behind the gathering foot; after an inch or so of fabric builds up in back of the foot, release it and repeat.

Because of the density and complexity of the gathered stitching, pattern- and meander-shirred fabrics are relatively strong and may not need protection from stress and strain, but if the shirring, because of the pattern, acquires some elasticity, stabilizing may be required. Baste a stay to the shirred fabric around the outside and tack it at intervals to the gathered stitching.

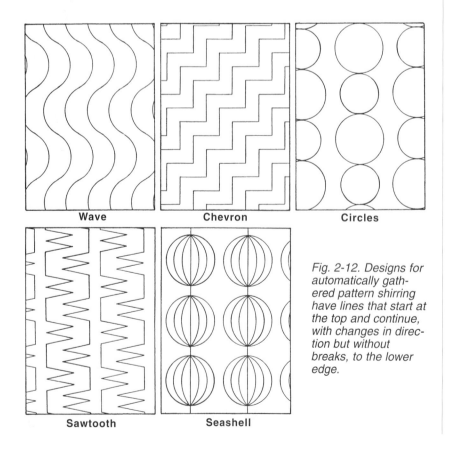

Wave   **Chevron**   **Circles**

Sawtooth   **Seashell**

Fig. 2-12. Designs for automatically gathered pattern shirring have lines that start at the top and continue, with changes in direction but without breaks, to the lower edge.

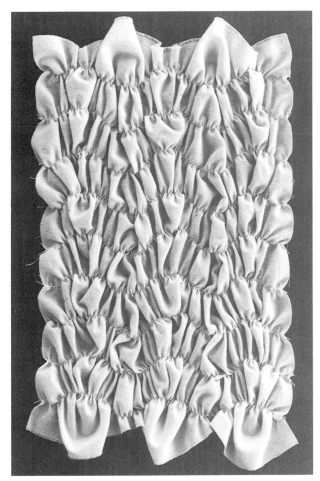

II-21—The curves of the wave pattern require slow automatic gathering (for the pattern, see Fig. 2-12).

II-22—The angled lines of the chevron pattern need stop-and-pivot automatic gathering (for the pattern, see Fig. 2-12).

PATTERN SHIRRING

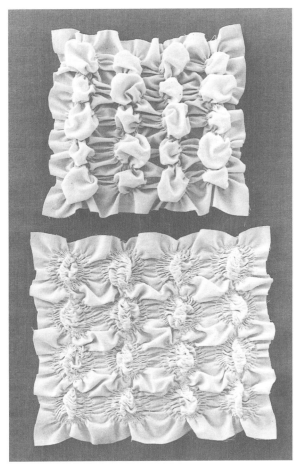

II-23—(top) Rows of puffy circles develop when deeply curving lines that cross each other are automatically gathered. (bottom) With the seashell pattern, additional lines of gathering reduce the puffing inside the circles (for the patterns, see Fig. 2-12).

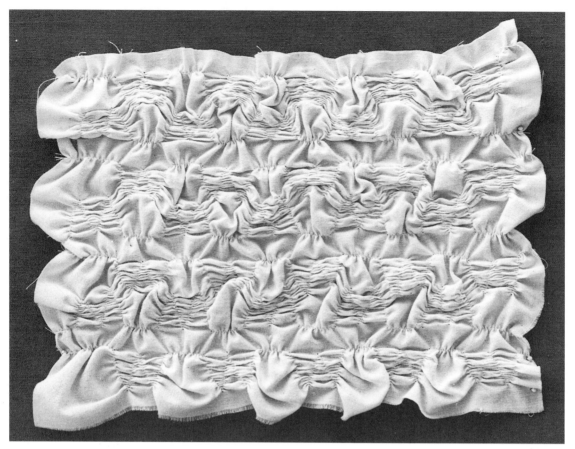

II-24—The sawtooth pattern (for the pattern, see Fig. 2-12).

PATTERN SHIRRING

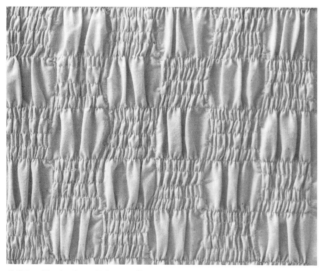

II-25—Checkerboard shirring fills alternate squares of a grid marked on the fabric. The squares, which have an uneven number of automatically gathered lines, are completed in diagonal sequence.

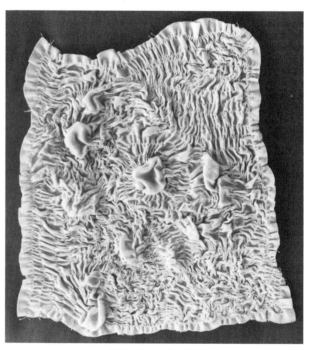

II-26—Meander shirring is improvised as automatic gathering proceeds.

*Supplementary
Fullness*

PART TWO

A *ruffle* is a strip of fabric reduced in length by gathering or pleating which releases folds that configure its floating edge. Attached to another piece of fabric, ruffles add the dimensionality of multiple folds and fluttering edges to the surface they adorn.

A ruffle is always smaller than the whole assembly of which it is a part. Within its setting, it can be narrow or wide and have one or two floating edges that hang down, stand up, or extend sideways. Ruffles are flexible, adjusting to straight, curving, and angled lines of application, and they inspire simple or elaborate arrangements, alone or in combination, separated or crowded, localized or allover.

RUFFLES

3 Making Ruffles

RUFFLE BASICS

EDGE FINISHING FOR RUFFLES

Choose an edge finish before making the ruffle. Anything imposed on the ruffle strip to finish the edge, whether it's a layer of stitched thread or another layer of fabric, not only protects the edge of the ruffle but also affects the swirling expansiveness and endurance of the ruffle's float after it's gathered or pleated. A soft, unlayered edge finish has the least effect on the float; a firm, layered edge finish changes the sweep of the float (Fig. 3-1).

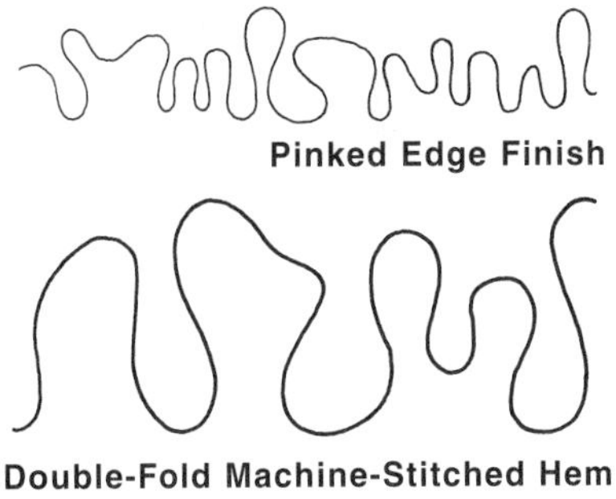

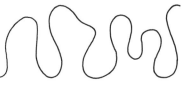

Pinked Edge Finish

Double-Fold Machine-Stitched Hem

Fig. 3-1. Demonstrating the difference an edge finish can make, the edge profiles of two muslin ruffles (same 1¼″ (3cm) width, identically gathered).

Note: This chapter begins with BASICS, indicated by a gray band located underneath the relevant columns.

Select an edge finish for its appearance as well as its impact on the float. The finish can be minimized (a selvedge or doubled fabric), it can blur the edge (a fringed or doubled-and-puffed ruffle), or flaunt it (a satin-stitched or contoured-and-faced ruffle). A few edge finishes have no right- or wrong-side association. There are no-sew, folded-and-seamed, and thread-bound edge finishes. With some, lines of stitched thread are obvious on both sides of the ruffle; with others, the stitching is inconspicuous.

Coordinate the edge finish with the nature of the fabric, the width of the ruffle, the density of the gathering or pleating, and the practical requirements of the application. Test one or more edge finishes on a scrap of the ruffle fabric before making a final decision. Before gathering or pleating the ruffle, always finish the edge or edges of the ruffle strip.

A *plain cut* edge, appropriate for non-woven materials, has no effect on the float and adds nothing to the definition of the ruffle's edge. Cut from woven fabric, an edge straight-cut on the grain without additional finishing quickly starts to unravel. If straight-cut on the bias, the edge will eventually fuzz.

The *pinked* edge of a woven fabric ruffle eventually fuzzes out but resists ravelling. Pinking doesn't alter the float of the ruffle but contributes a distinctive sawtooth outline to the edge.

When the *selvedge* of the fabric is used as the edge of a ruffle, the edge is self-finished. The combination of a selvedge, which is firmer than the weave between selvedges, and fabric cut on the lengthgrain, which is firmer than the crossgrain of the fabric, perks up the float of a ruffle.

The soft, indefinite quality of a ruffle with a *fringed* edge increases with the depth of the fringing. When the fringing stops just short of the gathering line, a ruffle with a fringed edge looks more like thick fringe than a ruffle. For a **ravelled-fringe edge**, threads parallel to the edge are removed, one by one, from the weave of the fabric. As the fringing deepens, avoid snags and breaks by dividing lengthy edges into manageable sections with perpendicular cuts. Stitch with a narrow zigzag across the base of the fringe to prevent coarse weaves from unravelling further. With cuts perpendicular to the edge, a **snip-fringed ruffle** is slashed into tiny, uniform strips along its entire length (Fig. 3-2). After gathering, deeply fringed ruffles tend to twist and need patient unwinding as application proceeds.

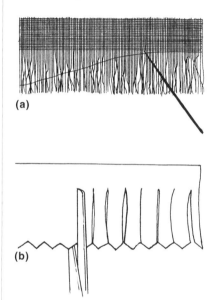

Fig. 3-2. (a) Sturdy needle extracting threads from the fabric's weave for a ravelled-fringe edge finish.
(b) Snipped-fringe finish slashed at the inside angles of a pinked edge.

Fusing allows the edge of a ruffle to be turned without sewing. Insert a strip of paper-backed, fusible transfer web inside a single-fold hem and, following the manufacturer's directions, bond the layers together with a hot iron (Fig. 3-3). With heat, the webbing dissolves into an adhesive that also prevents the cut edge of the fabric from ravelling and stiffens the floating edge of the ruffle.

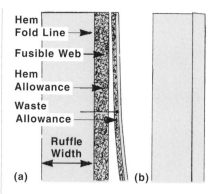

Fig. 3-3. Fusing a single-fold edge finish: (a) Prepare the ruffle strip as shown. (b) Fold at the inner edge of the fusible web and heat bond the hem.

A fold finishes the floating edge or edges of a ruffle made from *doubled fabric*. Doubling adds body to the whole ruffle and bulk to the bunched gathers or pleat folds at the stitching line. Cut a single-edged ruffle strip twice as wide as the ruffle plus two seam allowances; match the long edges to double the ruffle strip. Cut the strip for a ruffle with two sides (a double-edged ruffle) twice as wide as both ruffles plus two seam allowances; turn one seam allowance to the back and press; lap the seam allowances over the centered stitching line to double the ruffle strip (Fig. 3-4). Edge folds can be sharply creased or, if the ruffle strip is cut on the bias, unpressed and softly rolled. After application, a doubled-and-gathered ruffle with unpressed edge-folds may be puffed by pulling the layers apart.

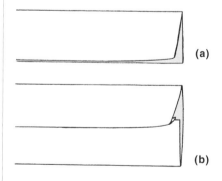

Fig. 3-4. Doubled-fabric ruffle strips with pressed folds finishing the floating edges: (a) Single-edged ruffle strip. (b) Double-edged ruffle strip with four layers of fabric at the centered stitching/gathering/pleating line.

Folds on a seam finish the edge of a ruffle when it's lined with a duplicate of itself. A ruffle with a *lining* has four layers of fabric plus a seam at the floating edge or edges, and the rest of the ruffle, including the stitching line, is two layers thick. For a lined ruffle, cut the ruffle strip with a seam allowance added to ruffle width at the floating edge or edges, and cut a lining to match. Sew the lining to the ruffle with right sides together, turn right side out with the seam or seams on folds, and press (Fig. 3-5). Options: Contour the seam joining the lining to the ruffle; edgestitch next to the turned edge.

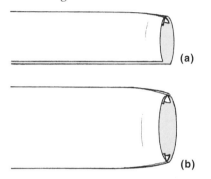

Fig. 3-5. When a ruffle strip is lined, each side of (a) a single-edged ruffle, or (b) a double-edged ruffle, is the right side, and each side may be cut from a different fabric.

Folds on a seam edge a ruffle strip finished with a *facing*, but, unlike linings, facings are never as wide as ruffle strips and never cover stitching lines. For a faced ruffle, cut the ruffle strip with a seam allowance added to ruffle width at the floating edge; cut the facing shorter than ruffle width plus two seam allowances. Application is a two-seam process: (1) Sew the facing to the floating edge of the ruffle and turn the facing right side out, folding it on the seam. (2) With its seam allowance turned under, sew the other edge of the facing to the ruffle strip, enclosing all seam allowances in the process. An **invisible facing** is sewn to the ruffle strip with right sides together and then turned to the back of the ruffle.

A **decorative facing** is sewn right side down to the back of the ruffle strip and turned to the front of the ruffle. Options: Contour the floating edge. Contour the inside edge of a decorative facing. Edge-stitch after turning to steady the folding and firm the edge. (Fig. 3-6)

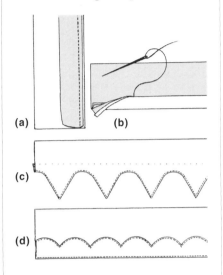

Fig. 3-6. (a) Invisible facing sewn to a ruffle strip, (b) turned to the back and slipstitched. (c) Invisible facing with a contoured and edgestitched floating edge, slipstitched in back. (d) Decorative facing with both edges edgestitched.

A *binding* wraps the floating edge of a ruffle in a separate strip of fabric which makes the edge five fabric layers thick. The traditional binding is a bias strip cut twice as wide as the *visible* width of the binding in front, plus two seam allowances. Press the seam allowance along one edge of the binding to the inside. Application involves two seams: (1) Sew the unfolded edge of the binding to the ruffle strip. (2) After turning the binding over to the other side of the ruffle, sew the folded edge of the binding to the ruffle (Fig. 3-7).

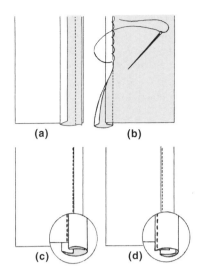

Fig. 3-7. Three ways to bind the edge of a ruffle strip: (a) Machine-stitch the binding to the strip with right sides together. Either (b) hand stitch the folded edge to the joining seam in back, or (c) pull the binding's folded edge beyond the joining seam in back; from the front, machine-stitch "in the ditch." (d) Sew the binding right side down to the back of the strip, turn the binding to the front, and edgestitch.

With a binder foot attached to the machine, one seam does the job. The binder's slots align the folded edge of the binding on top of the ruffle to the hidden, also folded, edge of the binding underneath so that one seam neatly catches both folds (Fig. 3-8). **Variation:** A no-sew binding, cut without seam allowances, backed with fusible web, folded and bonded over the edge of the ruffle.

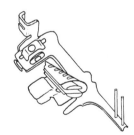

Fig. 3-8. The binder attachment applies folded binding to the edge of a ruffle strip in one operation.

The aristocrat of double-fold edge finishes, a tiny *hand-rolled hem* turns the edge softly with fine hand stitching that's invisible except for miniscule pricks bordering the front. Purists accomplish the rolling with only a hand-held needle and thread, but a line of staystitching next to the trimmed edge contributes a measure of control to the cut edge of delicate fabrics. When cutting the ruffle, add ¼″ (6mm) to ruffle width for the hem allowance and add a waste allowance to be trimmed away after staystitching. The stitching process rolls the hem (Fig. 3-9).

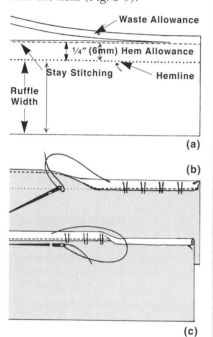

Fig. 3-9. Hand-rolled hem:
(a) Prepare the ruffle strip.
(b) To slipstitch: Turn the hem allowance down ⅛" (3mm). Take a ¼" (6mm) stitch in the hem allowance just below the turn. Moving straight down, pick up one or two threads of the fabric just below the hemline. Moving straight up, take another ¼" (6mm) stitch in the hem allowance below the turn. Continue for 1" (2.5cm). Stopping after a stitch below the turn, (c) pull the thread taut to roll the hem, and resume stitching.

A *shell hem* finishes the edge of a ruffle with a dainty scallop. Preparation for a **hand-stitched shell hem** involves adding a ¼″ (6mm) hem allowance to ruffle width when cutting the fabric strip. Turn the hem allowance down ⅛″ (3mm) and press; turn it over itself another ⅛″ (3mm) and press. Thread, brought over the top of the hem while stitching and pulled taut, bites into the fold to create a twisty edging (Fig. 3-10).

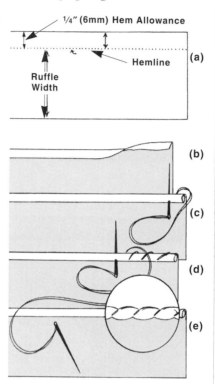

Fig. 3-10. (a) Ruffle strip for a shell hem. (b) Double fold hem allowance and press. (c) The stitching: Bury the thread knot inside the outer hem fold. Bring the needle down and ahead by 1/4" (6mm); push it through the inner hem fold and out in back. (d) Carry the needle up and over the top and repeat, making several stitches and flips over the hem. (e) Pull the thread taut and continue.

A **machine-sewn shell hem** requires a tightened stitch that swings over the edge, leaving a trail of stitches in front. Before cutting the strip and pressing a double-fold hem into the edge, test on scrap fabric to correlate hem width to the bite of the machine stitch (Fig. 3-11).

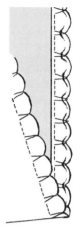

Fig. 3-11. Machine-stitched shell hem shaped by an overedge stitch with needle-thread tension increased.

The straight-stitched *double-fold hem* is a neat and sturdy edge finish for a ruffle. Add a small hem allowance when cutting the ruffle strip. Turn the hem allowance twice and press. Edgestitch next to the inside fold of the narrow hem (Fig. 3-12).

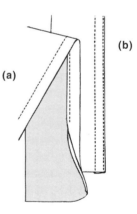

Fig. 3-12. (a) Straight-stitching a double-fold hem. (b) Optional edgestitching of the outer fold firms and accents the floating edge.

Vary the appearance of the stitching by machine sewing with a decorative stitch or, if a no-seam look is desirable in front, hand sew the hem. The hemmer foot, a timesaver when yards of ruffles need a finish, combines the double folding and straight stitching of little hems into one smooth and consistent operation (Fig. 3-13).

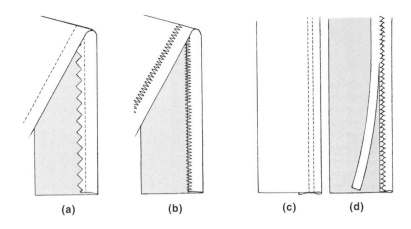

Fig. 3-13. Hemmer foot.

Fig. 3-14. One-seam flat hems: (a) Straight-stitched when cut with a pinked edge. (b) Zigzag-stitched when the edge is straight-cut. (c) Stitched from the front with a twin-needle, and (d) trimmed in back next to the stitches.

A machine-stitched *flat hem* edges ruffles with one seam visible in front, one fold, and one additional layer of fabric. In back, the single-fold hem stops at a cut edge which needs appropriate attention to discourage fraying—unless the fabric is firmly non-woven. Cut ruffle strips with a hem allowance added to ruffle width, and a waste allowance, if needed. For a **one-seam flat hem**, turn the hem allowance to the back, press, and secure with a straight, zigzagged, or twin-needle seam (Fig. 3-14). For a **two-seam flat hem**, staystitch, oversew with thread, or attach tape to the straight-cut edge before turning, pressing, and stitching to secure the hem (Fig. 3-15).

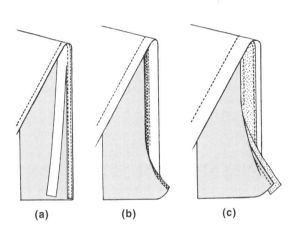

Fig. 3-15. Two-seam flat hems: (a) For sheer, flimsy fabrics, or knits, staystitch next to the hemline; straight stitch a scant 1/4" (6mm) from the staystitching; trim the excess hem fabric. (b) For firm, stable fabrics, zigzag or overlock the edge before turning and stitching. (c) For heavier fabrics, sew one edge of a tape over the cut edge and the other edge to the ruffle.

A solid covering of thread wraps the straight edge of a ruffle strip finished with *satin-stitched edging*. The tidy, smooth appearance of perfect satin stitching depends on coordinating the method of application with sewing thread and ruffle fabric. Using scrap fabric, test first. Select a medium-to-wide zigzag, reduce stitch length to 0 or almost, and guide the ruffle strip under the presser foot so that the needle just misses the edge when it swings to the right. As the chosen method requires, cut ruffle strips without any allowances added to ruffle width at the floating edge, with a waste allowance only, or with a hem allowance and a waste allowance.

(1) The one-seam/one-layer method lays satin stitching directly over the straight-cut edge of stable fabric with a close weave. To contour the edge with this method, choose a decorative stitch appropriate for satin stitching, such as the scallop, and trim on the outer needle holes of the stitching. (2) The two-seam/one-layer method primes the edge with zigzagging. Satin stitching covers the zigzag stitches. (3) For fabric that tends to ravel, the one-seam/two-layer method replaces the cut edge with a fold and bolsters the edge with a second thickness for the satin stitching to envelop. (4) The two-seam/two-layer methods control

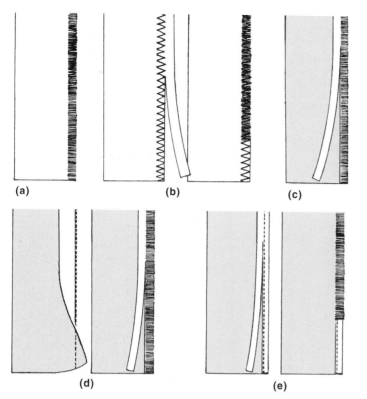

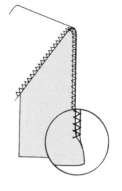

Fig. 3-18. Ruffle strip finished with hairline edging loses a tiny fraction of its original width.

(a)   **(b)**   **(c)**

(d)   **(e)**

Fig. 3-16. Satin-stitched edgings: (a) Sewn directly over the cut edge. (b) Sewn over an edge trimmed after zigzag-stitched preparation. (c) Sewn over a folded edge with the waste allowance trimmed after satin stitching. (d) Sewn over an edge turned on a staystitched fold with the waste allowance trimmed after satin stitching. (e) Sewn over a tiny, straight-stitched single-fold hem that disappears under the satin-stitched covering.

soft, shifty fabric with straight stitching that stabilizes the folded edge before satin stitching covers all. (Fig. 3-16) To prevent the cupping that occurs when satin stitching, sew with an overedge foot attached to the machine (Fig. 3-17).

Fig. 3-17. Medium-to-wide satin-stitched edgings lie flat when sewn with an overedge foot.

The finest of the thread-bound edgings, the *hairline edging*, is tiny, firm, and secure. Select a medium-to-wide zigzag stitch and raise the upper- thread tension to 7, 8, or 9. With the ruffle strip wrong side up, sew with the needle just missing the edge when it swings to the right. As the needle swings back to the left, the tightened tension brings bobbin thread up and around to the top and the fabric's edge with it, trapping a fold inside the stitching. A hairline edging emerges half the width of the medium-to-wide zigzag setting on the machine (Fig. 3-18).

Before zigzagging a hairline edge into fluid, sheer fabric, add stability by staystitching next to the edge. As zigzag-stitch length moves closer to 0, the firmness of the edging increases. A **single-fold hairline edging**, zigzagged or satin-stitched over a tiny one-fold hem previously pressed into the edge, is extra firm and neat.

A *wired edge* is stiff and holds its own. Thin, plastic-coated wire buried inside the fold of a hairline edging enables the floating edge of the ruffle to be curved, twisted, and angled into eccentric configurations. While sewing, guide the wire under the presser foot, laying it next to the edge where it will be enclosed inside the fold caused by the action of the tension-tightened zigzag or satin stitching (Fig. 3-19). Options: For an extra-firm edge without stiffness, substitute thin cord, extra-strong thread, or monofilament fishing line for the wire. Enclose the firming or stiffening element inside a tiny single-fold hem before zigzagging over the edge.

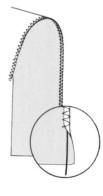

Fig. 3-19. Thin wire enclosed inside a hairline edging.

A *lettuce edge* finishes a ruffle strip cut from a knit with a frilly, fluttery edging. A *wavy edge* finishes a ruffle strip cut on the bias of woven fabric with a rolling, twisty edging. Both require stretchiness to achieve the effect. Select sewing machine settings for a hairline edging as previously described. While sewing, stretch out the edge progressing under the needle, holding the fabric in front and back of the presser foot. Stop to stretch out the section coming up when it becomes necessary. The zigzag-stitched edge will retain the stretch while the body of the ruffle strip returns to its unstretched condition (Fig. 3-20).

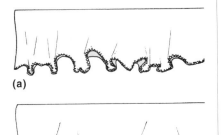

(a)

(b)

Fig. 3-20. (a) Lettuce edging on a jersey knit. (b) Wavy edging on bias-cut muslin.

An *overlocked edge* requires a serger. Overlocked stitching encloses the cut edge of a ruffle strip inside a laddered chain of loopy threads (Fig. 3-21). With stitch length shortened for dense thread coverage, the satin-stitched edgings described and illustrated previously can be duplicated by overlocking with a serger. The serger knife eliminates trimming the waste allowance with scissors.

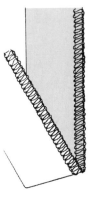

Fig. 3-21. Overlocked stitching finishes the edge of a ruffle strip.

A *rolled overlocked edging* is the serger version of hairline edging, the zigzag finish described previously—with a procedural difference. A rolled overlocked edge is stitched with the right side of the fabric up. On a serger with a 3-thread stitch, tightened lower looper tension forces the upper looper thread to roll around to the back of the fabric, turning the edge to the back with the thread.

GATHERED SINGLE-EDGED RUFFLE

—a strip of fabric with one long edge gathered to a shorter target measurement and attached to flat fabric. The opposite edge floats in irregular, serpentine folds.

PROCEDURES

1. Choose an appropriate and effective edge finish for the ruffle (refer to "Edge Finishing for Ruffles" on page 43). To set a width for the ruffle strip, add a seam allowance to the finished width selected for the ruffle and include allowances for the selected edge finish (Fig. 3-22).

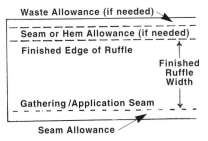

Fig. 3-22. Fabric strips cut for gathered single-edged ruffles must include measurements for finished ruffle width and a seam allowance beside the gathering seam, with measurements added to the floating edge if and as required for the chosen edge finish.

2. Decide how much fullness the gathered ruffle should display—slight, moderate, generous, abundant. Set an after-the-gathering target measurement for the ruffle. To estimate the length of the strip needed to produce the desired fullness in the ruffle, multiply the target measurement by the amount indicated in the following chart:

slight fullness   = [target] x 1½
moderate fullness = [target] x 2
generous fullness = [target] x 3
abundant fullness = [target] x 4 (+ more)

To evaluate fullness, gather matching lengths of the ruffle fabric, identical in width and finish, using different ratios from the chart.

3. Cut the ruffle strips to size:

   ◆ Align the edges of strips cut on the straightgrain of the fabric with threads in the weave. To extend the length of a ruffle strip, sew the short edges of two strips together with right sides facing and edges matching; press the seam allowances open (Fig. 3-23). (For a continuous ruffle strip cut on the straightgrain, refer to Fig. 10-1 on page 207.)

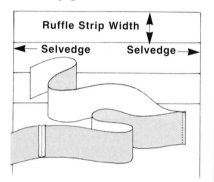

Fig. 3-23. Crossgrain ruffle strips. To have a selvedge edge finish, a longer ruffle strip, and extra fabric firmness—cut lengthgrain ruffle strips.

   ◆ For bias-cut strips, mark the fabric with lines that cross the weave at a 45-degree angle. To extend the length of a ruffle strip, sew the angled edges of two strips together with right sides facing and seamlines matching at the ends; press the seam allowances open (Fig. 3-24). (For a continuous ruffle strip cut on the bias, refer to Fig. 9-18 on page 200.)

4. Apply the selected finish to one long edge of the ruffle strip.

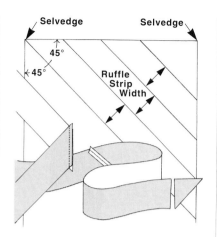

Fig. 3-24. Bias ruffle strips. Accurate measurements between cutting lines are taken at right angles to both lines.

5. Gather the unfinished edge to the target measurement (refer to "Gathering Methods" on page 3), sewing beside the designated seamline inside the seam allowance. To deal with a lengthy ruffle strip gathered on pulled-thread stitching, divide the edge to be gathered into halves, quarters, or eighths; mark the divisions between segments with pins, nips, notches, or chalk. Equate to similar but smaller divisions on a target gauge. Gather segment by segment to the target measurement. Distribute the gathers evenly.

6. Pin the gathered edge of the ruffle strip to the fabric where it is to be applied; baste directly over the gathering stitches. Machine sew the final seam immediately beside the basting/gathering stitches, hiding all construction stitching and the gathered seam allowance in the process of application:

   ◆ Within a seam connecting two pieces of fabric (Fig. 3-25).

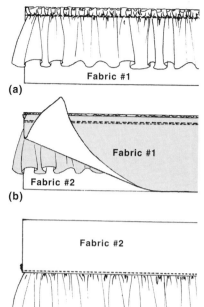
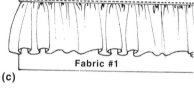

Fig. 3-25. To insert a ruffle into a seam: (a) Baste the ruffle to fabric #1. (b) Pin fabric #2 over the ruffle, turn the assembly over, and stitch beside the basting. (c) Optional edgestitching.

   ◆ As a hem ruffle that lies on top of the fabric to which it is attached, or extends out from the fabric to which it is attached. For top ruffles, cover the seam allowances with binding (refer to Fig. 1-11 on page 7). For ruffle extensions, options for treating seam allowances include: (1) Zigzag stitching or serging over the edges (Fig. 3-26); (2) covering with a lining or invisible facing (refer to Fig. 4-9 on page 70); (3) covering with a decorative facing (sew the ruffle right side up to the wrong side of the fabric and turn the facing to the front); (4) edgestitching after application.

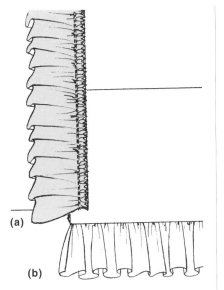

(a)

(b)

Fig. 3-26. Ruffled extension to a hem: (a) Sew the ruffle to the fabric's edge. Zigzag or overlock the seam-allowance edges. (b) Ruffled hem.

- To a foundation in a tiered arrangement (Fig. 3-27). The floating edge of the ruffle above overlaps and covers the application details of the ruffle below. The seam allowance of the ruffle at the top may be covered with binding, appliquéd tape, or an extension of fabric. The ruffle at the bottom may be treated as an extended hem ruffle.

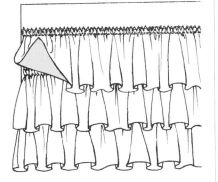

Fig. 3-27. Tiered ruffles applied to a foundation with straight stitching over the gathered stitching, and zigzag stitching over the edge of the ruffle's seam allowance.

- At the edge of an element that will be appliquéd to a foundation (Fig. 3-28).

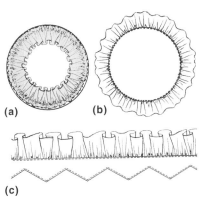

(a)　　　　(b)

(c)

Fig. 3-28. (a) Ruffle basted to the edge of a circle before (b) edgestitching the circle to a foundation. (c) Ruffle attached to a band edgestitched to a foundation.

NOTES & VARIATIONS

A ruffle of soft, thin fabric can be gathered much more tightly than a ruffle of stiff, heavy fabric. Because a ruffle cut on the bias tends to absorb gathers at the stitching line, a bias-cut ruffle may be gathered much more tightly than a ruffle cut on the straightgrain of the same fabric. To produce attractive fullness at the floating edge, a wide ruffle needs tighter gathering than a narrow ruffle.

Ruffle strips may be gathered on thread stitched by hand or straight- or zigzag-stitched by machine. One row may be enough for narrow strips gathered with light to moderate density, but tighter gathering is more easily controlled with two rows of stitching. When yards of ruffle strips need gathering, automatic gathering using the gathering foot or ruffler attachment is a fast and efficient alternative. (Refer to "Gathering Methods" on page 5.)

As gathering density increases, seam allowances accrue more bulk. To flatten the bunched gathers, (1) press a ruffle's seam allowance (only the seam allowance), leaning hard on the iron; (2) crush the seam allowance accumulation under straight, zigzagged, or overlocked stitching; (3) edgestitch through all layers after applying the ruffle; (4) or any combination of the above. Bulky seam allowances contribute an underlying firmness to applications with rows of gathered single-edged ruffles floating on the surface.

The gathered edge of a single-edged ruffle is flexible, permitting curved and even angled applications. A ruffle sewn around a curve, circle, or angle will stretch out and curl at the floating edge unless it is gathered extra tightly at the source. Add length to the ruffle strip to allow for the dense gathering curved and angled applications require. Conversely, a ruffle sewn inside a curve, circle, or angle will bulge with squeezed folds at the floating edge unless the gathering is lightened. For a ruffle applied around a curve or circle—more gathering; for a ruffle applied inside a curve or circle—less gathering (Fig. 3-29).

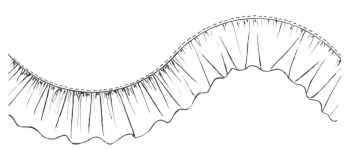

Fig. 3-29. To prepare a ruffle for application in a wavy line, divide the ruffle strip into longer segments gathered closely for outside curves and shorter segments gathered loosely for inside curves.

The ends of ruffles that encircle are stitched together, but other ruffle applications start and finish with loose ends. The ends of ruffles that stop at the edge of the foundation fabric will be caught in the seam that eventually completes the edge. The ends of ruffles that stop within the foundation fabric should taper or fan into the application seam (Fig. 3-30).

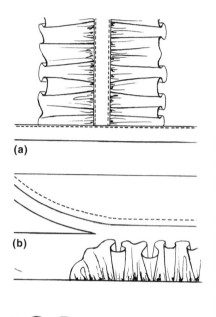

(a)

(b)

(c)

Fig. 3-30. (a) Ruffles with straight-cut ends anchored in a binding. (b) To taper out: Curve the gathering stitches into the edge; trim, gather, and attach the ruffle from start to tapered end. (c) To fan out: Pull the straight-cut, ungathered end down to the seamline and catch in the stitching.

When a ruffle is lined or faced (refer to "Edge Finishing for Ruffles" on page 45), contouring the floating edge, an option, shifts the edge silhouette from straight to a shaped outline that angles and curves. If a lining or facing isn't appropriate but a simply contoured floating edge is the desired profile, contour the gathering edge. With the gathering edge contoured, the floating edge of the ruffle strip remains straight for easy application of the desired edge finish (Fig. 3-31).

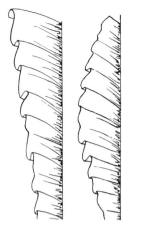

Fig. 3-31. Two ruffles with widths that change from broad to narrow because the gathering edge of the strip was contoured.

A *single-shell ruffle* has a gathering edge shaped in a scallop pattern. Gathering straightens out the curves, making the gathered stitching/application line straight—and making the floating edge scalloped to reflect the silhouette originally cut into the gathering edge (Fig. 3-32). If a single-shell ruffle is cut from doubled fabric (refer to "Edge Finishing for Ruffles" on page 44), the shells can be puffed after application.

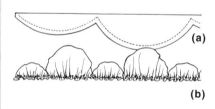

(a)

(b)

Fig. 3-32. (a) Single-shell ruffle pattern with curved outlines that are elongated versions (b) of the after-gathering shell shapes.

An application of *layered single-edged ruffles* compounds the decorative effect of frilly edges. Two or more ruffles, gathered separately to avoid nestled folds at the gathered stitching, are stacked one on top of the other with gathered edges matching, and sewn to the foundation as one. Whether the ruffles are equal or unequal in width, the floating edge of the upper ruffle sits on top of the folds of the ruffle below, increasing the total elevation of the float (Fig. 3-33).

Fig. 3-33. Two ruffles, the upper ruffle shorter than the ruffle underneath, applied as one to the fabric's edge.

The floating edge of a *puffed single-edged ruffle* disappears in a cloud of billowy fabric. The puffed ruffle starts with a doubled-fabric ruffle strip (refer to "Edge Finishing for Ruffles" on page 44). If the edges of the ruffle strip are cut on the straightgrain, skew the alignment at the starting corner when stitching the edges together for gathering. If the ruffle strip is cut on the bias, skewing is unnecessary. Don't press the fold at the floating edge. After gathering and application, pull the two layers of the ruffle apart to pouf the body of the ruffle (Fig. 3-34). Ruffles less than 1″ (2.5cm) wide frustrate efforts at separating the layers. Doubled ruffles of crisp fabric 2″ (5cm) wide or more puff with the most buoyancy; doubled ruffles of soft, limp fabric hardly puff at all. To stabilize the puff, tack the spreading ruffle fabric at intervals to each side of the application seam. For puffings that stop where the foundation fabric ends, gather around the tubular opening, flatten, and baste to the seam allowance.

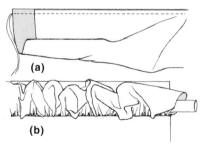

(a)

(b)

Fig. 3-34. (a) Doubled-fabric ruffle strip cut on the straightgrain and skewed at each end to prepare for puffing. (b) Separating the gathered layers with the help of a dowel.

III-2—Ruffles gathered from strips cut 200% longer than the target measurement. The bottom ruffle is twice the width of the ruffle on top and appears less full. The edge finish, a single-fold flat hem satin-stitched over the fold, stiffens the edge and significantly affects the quality of the float.

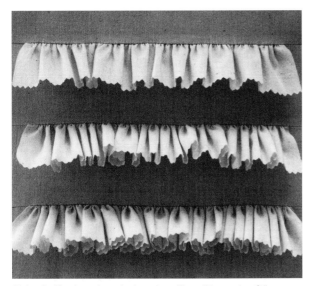

III-1—Ruffle chart that displays the effect of increasing fullness on muslin ruffles of identical width gathered to the same target measurement. (top) Ruffle gathered from a strip cut 200% longer than the target. (center) The ruffle strip was 300% longer than the target. (bottom) 400% longer. The pinked edge finish doesn't influence the float.

GATHERED SINGLE-EDGED
RUFFLES

III-3—Bias-cut ruffles applied in-seam and arranged in overlapping tiers. The top tier is gathered from a ruffle strip cut 150% longer than the target measurement; the ruffle strip cut for each successive tier increases 50% in length. A wavy edge finish on the bias strips contributes an extra flip to the float of the ruffles.

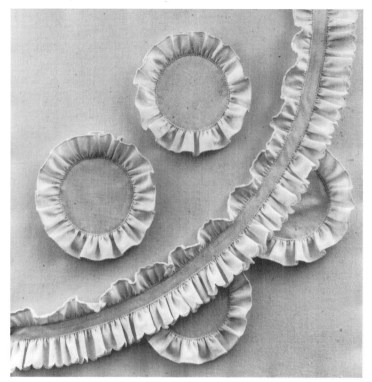

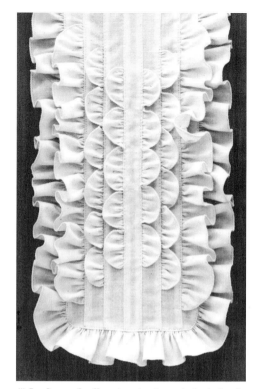

III-4—Narrow ruffles sewn around circles and to each side of a curved bias strip before edgestitched application. The floating edges of the ruffles bordering the curving strip are scalloped, the outer ruffle with satin stitching, the inner ruffle with a machine-stitched shell hem. A hairline edging finishes the ruffles surrounding the circles.

III-5—Rows of ruffles changing from single-shell ruffles in the center, to ruffles that taper out in-seam, to a bordering ruffle gathered extra tightly at the corner curves. A hairline edging finishes all ruffles.

III-6—Layered ruffles. The narrow ruffle on top, gathered from a strip cut two times the target length, was finished with a zigzagged flat hem. The wide ruffle underneath, gathered from a strip cut three times the target length, was finished with a faced, scalloped edge.

GATHERED
SINGLE-EDGED
RUFFLES

III-7—Puffed ruffles. (top) Three rows gathered from bias-cut strips folded to a 1″ (2.5cm) width. (bottom) Two rows gathered from straight-cut strips folded to a width of 2¼″ (5.8cm).

Gathered Double-Edged Ruffle

—a strip of fabric gathered to a smaller target measurement on centered stitching. Applied to a foundation with both edges free to float in variable, rolling folds, the top-stitched-and-gathered stitching in the center is a visible feature of double-edged ruffles.

Procedures

1. Choose an appropriate and effective finish for the floating edges of the ruffle. Each edge may have the same or a different finish. (Refer to "Edge Finishing for Ruffles" on page 43.) To determine the width of the ruffle strip: Set a finished width for the ruffle on each side of the centered stitching line; include, for each side, an allowance for the selected edge finish; total all measurements (Fig. 3-35).

2. Follow the procedures described for "gathered single-edged ruffle," steps #2 and #3, on pages 49–50.

3. Apply the selected finish to both long edges of the ruffle strip.

4. On the ruffle strip, mark the centered stitching line with a fabric-safe medium, or a pressed fold, or gauge the stitching distance from the right edge of the strip with a device on the bed of the sewing machine. Following the designated line, stitch and gather to the target measurement (refer to "Gathering Methods" on page 3). To deal with a lengthy ruffle strip gathered on pulled thread stitching, divide the line to be gathered into halves, quarters, or eighths; mark the divisions between segments with pins or chalk. Equate to similar but smaller divisions on a target gauge. Gather segment by segment to the target measurement. Distribute the gathers evenly.

5. With a fabric-safe medium, mark the foundation fabric with straight or curving lines that indicate the placement of the ruffle's gathered stitching. For easy accuracy, mark another line to the right for the right edge of the ruffle to meet (use chalk, disappearing pen, a row of pins, or a temporary, lightly pressed fold). Matching the ruffle to the guideline, topstitch over the gathering stitches to attach the ruffle to the foundation. Use straight or appropriately decorative stitching when sewing by machine (Fig. 3-36). Use the half backstitch for hand sewn applications.

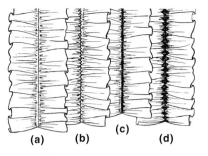

Fig. 3-36. Topstitched application for double-edged ruffles: (a) Straight stitching with gathering thread removed afterwards. (b) Zigzag stitching straddles the gathered stitching. (c) Satin stitching and (d) decorative stitching cover the gathering stitches.

Notes & Variations

Edge finish, gathering density, fabric characteristics, and ruffle width interact to generate the wavy dimensionality of the floating edges at the sides of double-edged ruffles. The standard double-edged ruffle is gathered with hand stitching, with straight or zigzagged machine stitching, or with automatic machine gathering using the gathering foot or ruffler attachment (refer to "Gathering Methods" on page 3), and it is gathered on a straight row of stitching centered between the edges of the ruffle strip.

Deviating from the standard, gathering expanded to two, three, or more parallel rows of stitching—the *spread-seam or shirred ruffle*—introduces a decorative band of confined folds between the loose folds released at the sides (Fig. 3-37). Other deviations: A ruffle gathered a little off-center or on a stitching line that curves. Applied to a foundation with the gathered stitching straightened out, the curving fluctuations that were present in the stitching line before gathering transfer to the silhouettes of the floating edges.

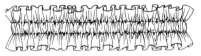

Fig. 3-37. Spread-seam ruffle with shirred folds between two rows of gathering. Add extra width for the expanded gathering area when cutting the ruffle strip.

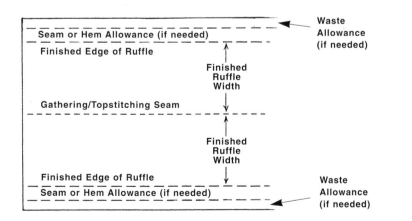

Fig. 3-35. Fabric strips cut for gathered double-edged ruffles must include measurements for finished ruffle widths on either side of the centered seamline, with measurements added to each floating edge if and as required for the chosen edge finish.

If the stitching to be gathered veers from edge to edge but is gathered until the stitching is straight, the floating edges assume shell-like formations. Patterns for the gathering that produces a *double-shell ruffle* have spaces enclosed by stitching lines. After marking the stitching line on the back of the ruffle strip, gather a double-shell ruffle by hand to regulate the shaping of the shells. Because of its unusual shaping, a double-shell ruffle may be easier to attach to a foundation with hand stitching (Fig. 3-38).

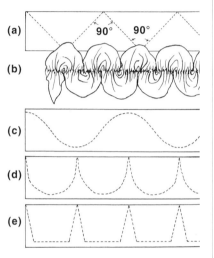

Fig. 3-38. (a) Stitch one 90-degree angle of this double-shell ruffle pattern, gather until the angled stitching line straightens, secure, and continue to the next angle. (b) Gathered double-shell ruffle. (c) Curvy version of (a). Ruffles gathered from patterns (d) and (e) have unequal side formations.

The flexibility of double-edged ruffles invites curving arrangements. Curving the ruffle alters the float of both edges: The floating folds on the inside edge of the curve increase while the folds on the outside edge decrease. If the side ruffles are wide and the curves steep, the floating edge located on the outer curve will stretch out and turn up unless the gathering at the source is especially tight—which will cause the fullness released on the inside of the curve to swell into bulging folds. Only narrow ruffles 1″ (2.5cm) or less from edge to edge are used for *ruffle designs*.

With moderate-to-generous gathering, they negotiate tight curves with unobtrusive straining and squeezing at opposite edges. Ruffle designs exploit the contrast between winding bands of ruffles with rippling edges and smooth background areas. A **scrolled ruffle design** conforms to a planned, repeating pattern of lines traced on the right side of the foundation fabric (Fig. 3-39).

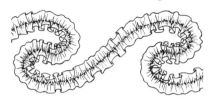

Fig. 3-39. Narrow, double-edged ruffle scrolled in a repeating wave design.

An **allover ruffle design** patterns the surface with a meandering, unplanned application of ruffles (Fig. 3-40).

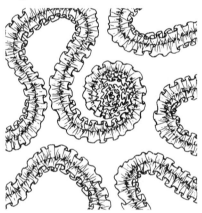

Fig. 3-40. Narrow, double-edged ruffles swirled over the surface in a design improvised while topstitching, with one end coiled to diversify the relief.

The foundation fabric disappears, or almost disappears, underneath *massed ruffles*. For **low massed ruffles**, straight or curving rows of double-edged ruffles are applied to a foundation with floating edges touching. The gathered-and-topstitched seams are a visible component of the re-designed surface (Fig. 3-41).

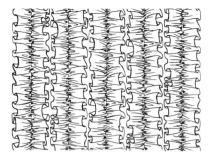

Fig. 3-41. Double-edged ruffles topstitched with edges touching, following application lines spaced a bit closer than two-ruffle-widths apart.

For **high massed ruffles**, rows of double-edged ruffles are topstitched together so closely that adjacent ruffled edges are forced upward to float about one-ruffle-width above foundation level, burying the topstitched-and-gathered seams (Fig. 3-42).

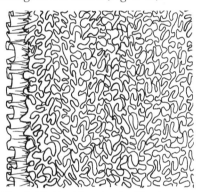

Fig. 3-42. Double-edged ruffles topstitched in congested rows re-surface foundation fabric with swirling edges elevated above shadowy depths.

Straight or slightly curving rows of ruffles can be massed and topstitched by machine: With previously attached ruffles off to the left of the presser foot, hold the edge of the closest ruffle away from the needle with a ruler while topstitching the new ruffle. A coiled application will need hand sewing, at least at the start. To prevent distortion, stiffen the foundation fabric with a temporary stabilizer.

Layered double-edged ruffles are stacked one over the other with their gathering stitches matched, and topstitched to a foundation as one (Fig. 3-43).

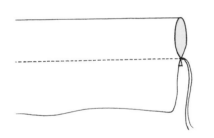

Fig. 3-43. Layered floating edges of two double-edged ruffles accumulate height, rising high above the top-stitched gathering.

A *puffed double-edged ruffle* must be cut and stitched from doubled fabric with unpressed folds (see "Edge Finishing for Ruffles" on page 44). After gathering and application, puff the side ruffles by pulling the layers apart (refer to "puffed single-edged ruffle" on page 52). **Variation:** Double-edged ruffle with one side puffed and the other side a standard, floating-edged ruffle (Fig. 3-44).

Fig. 3-44. Preparing a double-edged ruffle strip with the fabric on one side doubled for puffing after gathering and application.

Taper or fan the ends of double-edged ruffles that stop within the foundation fabric. Tapering involves folding the end of the ruffle strip on the stitching line with right sides facing and sewing a seam that gradually curves from the fold to the matched edges. Trim the excess, open the strip, gather to the tip, and topstitch to the foundation. To fan the end of a ruffle, sew the ends of the side ruffles together with edges matching and right sides together, open, pull down, and tack to the foundation (Fig. 3-45).

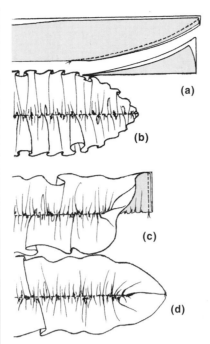

Fig. 3-45. Two ways to end a double-edged ruffle: (a) Taper the end of the strip (b) before gathering. (c) After gathering, join the ends of the side ruffles (d) and fan down to foundation level.

A *tucked ruffle* has three floating edges and one gathering seam. The overall width of the ruffle strip includes three ruffle widths, two at the sides of one doubled-fabric ruffle in the center (Fig. 3-46). The floating edge of the ruffle in the center is always on the fold. The gathering seam is stitched through two layers of fabric a ruffle's width from the fold. With the finished edges below the gathered stitching spread out into side ruffles, the ruffle sits on its seam, which is under the center ruffle (Fig. 3-47).

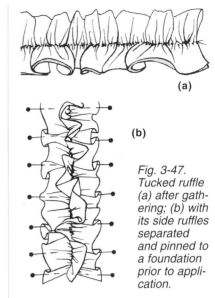

Fig. 3-47. Tucked ruffle (a) after gathering; (b) with its side ruffles separated and pinned to a foundation prior to application.

To attach to a foundation, topstitch next to the gathered seam with the side of a zipper foot up against the center ruffle, and then topstitch next to the other side of the gathered seam. By hand, sew over the gathered seam with stitches that alternate between a stitch on one side and a stitch on the other side of the center ruffle. Tucked ruffle options include enlarging or decreasing the width of the center ruffle, snip-fringing or puffing the center ruffle, and gathering the center ruffle over a cord inserted inside the fold.

Waste Allowance (if needed)

Seam or Hem Allowance (if needed)
Finished Edge of Side Ruffle
Finished Side Ruffle Width
Gathering Seam
Center Ruffle Width
Folded Edge of Center Ruffle
Center Ruffle Width
Gathering Seam
Finished Side Ruffle Width
Finished Edge of Side Ruffle
Seam or Hem Allowance (if needed)
Waste Allowance (if needed)

Waste Allowance (if needed)

Fig. 3-46. The fabric strip cut for a tucked ruffle must include measurements for side and center ruffle widths, with additional allowances on each side as required by the chosen edge finish.

A double-edged ruffle will have a perky appearance, whether it's applied horizontally, vertically, or multi-directionally, if ruffle fabric, ruffle width, and edge finishing are selected with that effect in mind. A vertically applied double-edged ruffle will drape from its topstitched-and-gathered seam if the width of the side ruffles becomes more than the fabric and the edge finishing can support, or when the ruffle fabric is soft and fluid. If applied horizontally, the ruffle above the topstitched-and-gathered seam will flop over the ruffle beneath.

Headed ruffles, double-edged ruffles gathered off-center between a wide ruffle and a smaller heading, are always applied horizontally. Calculate the width of the heading, as affected by fabric type and edge finish, so that it will stand up and float at the top (Fig. 3-48).

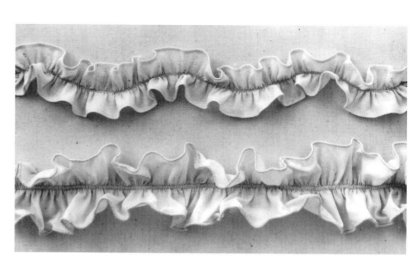

III-8—Two ruffles satin-stitched to a foundation. The curving ruffle has straight-stitched double-fold hems; the ruffle with the fanciful, twisty float has wired edges.

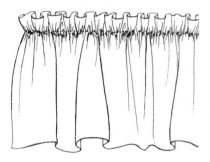

Fig. 3-48. Headed ruffle.

Headed ruffle options involve combinations with a spread seam, a puffed heading, and a tucked or layered ruffle. A **split headed ruffle** allows for differences, such as fabric, gathering density, or pleating, between the heading and the ruffle. Actually, a split-headed ruffle is composed of two single-edged ruffles with their gathered seam allowances butted. The wide ruffle and the narrow heading may be stitched to opposite sides of a band before topstitching to the foundation, or, after direct topstitching, the seam allowances may be covered with an edgestitched band or a double-edged ruffle.

GATHERED DOUBLE-EDGED RUFFLES

III-9—Ruffles, finished with hairline edging, applied in rows with edges touching (low massed ruffles).

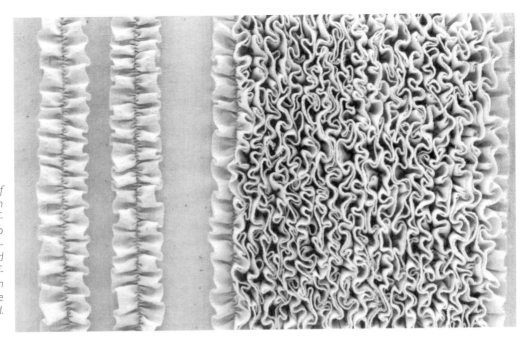

III-10—(left) Two rows of ruffles set apart from each other. (right) The same ruffles applied in rows so close together that adjacent edges are forced upward (high massed ruffles). The re-surfaced muslin is thick and heavy. All ruffle edges are overlocked.

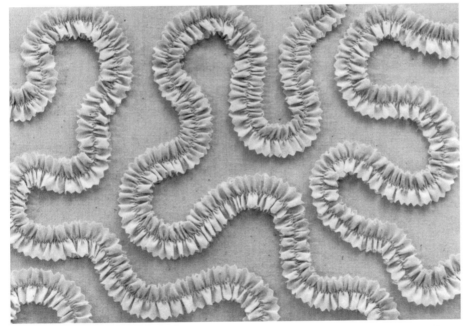

GATHERED
DOUBLE-EDGED
RUFFLES

III-11—Muslin patterned allover with a meandering, improvised design of pinked ruffles 3/4" (2cm)

III-12—Muslin ruffles applied in tight coils with edges finished (left to right) with straight-stitched double-fold hems; with hairline edging; with one edge pinked and one edge selvedge; with ravelled fringe.

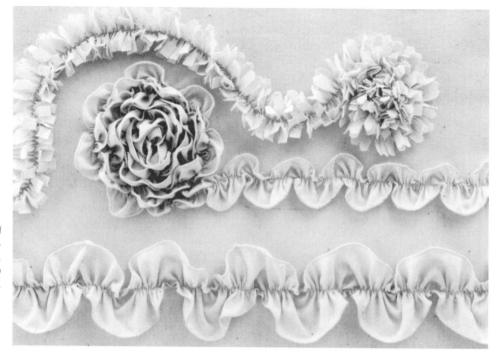

III-13—(top) A snip-fringed ruffle that ends in a coil. (bottom) Two double-shell ruffles, the smaller hand stitched into a tight, flower-like coil.

GATHERED DOUBLE-EDGED RUFFLES

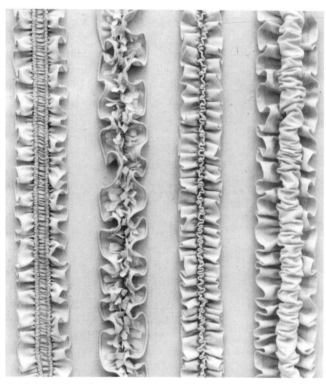

III-14—Four fanciful ruffles, all gathered from ruffle strips cut slightly longer than twice the target length. (left to right) Hairline-edged ruffle spread-seam gathered on two corded seams; snip-fringed ruffle layered over a ruffle with firm, double-fold hairline edging; tucked ruffle with a shallow ruffle centered between side ruffles finished with deep, single-fold hems; tucked ruffle with the center ruffle puffed and side ruffles finished with twin-needle-stitched, single-fold hems.

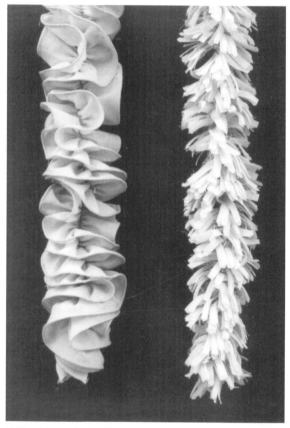

III-15—Unattached ruffles gathered into long, flexible, fluffy cylinders on seams zigzagged over string. For each cylinder, two ruffle strips that tripled the target length were gathered as one. (right) Snip-fringed edge finish. (left) Double-fold hairline edging.

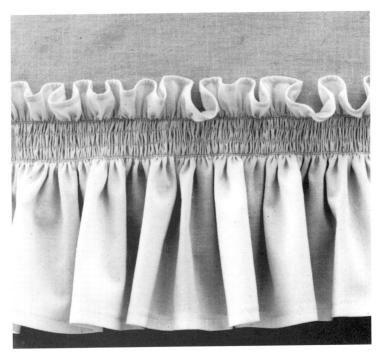

III-17—Headed ruffle with a band of shirring separating the heading from the ruffle. The edges were finished with straight-stitched, double-fold hems.

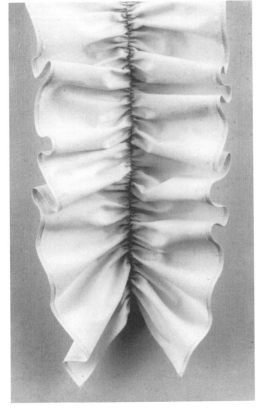

III-16—Side ruffles 4 ½" (11.5cm) wide pulled downward by the weight of the muslin.

GATHERED DOUBLE-EDGED RUFFLES

III-18—Split headed ruffle. The gathered seam allowances of the ruffles and the layered heading pad the edgestitched tape with their bulk.

PLEATED SINGLE- OR DOUBLE-EDGED RUFFLE

—a strip of fabric reduced in length by systematic folding anchored with stitching along one edge or down the center. The edge or edges of a pleated ruffle float in regular, orderly folds.

PROCEDURES

1. Choose a pleating arrangement for the ruffle (Fig. 3-49). Decide whether the folds will be pressed or unpressed.

2. Select an edge finish that will affect the folds at the float agreeably, or, if the pleats are to be pressed, an edge finish that will accept sharp creases (refer to "Edge Finishing for Ruffles" on page 43).

3. Determine the width of the pleated ruffle strip, including allowances for the selected edge finish: For a single-edged ruffle, refer to Fig. 3-22 on page 49; for a double-edged ruffle, refer to Fig. 3-35 on page 55.

4. To calculate the length required for a ruffle strip pleated to the target measurement: Make a folding gauge from a short strip of paper marked with dots spaced ¼″ (6mm) or ½″ (1.3cm) apart, as appropriate for pleating depth and implementation. The dots indicate pleat folds; the distance between dots equals pleat depth; count dots to regulate pleat spacing. Matching dots, fold into the chosen pleat arrangement. Apply the following formula:

[pre-folding length/paper
÷ after-folding length/paper]
x target measurement for pleated ruffle
= Estimated Length of Ruffle Strip

5. Cut ruffle strips to size on the straightgrain of the fabric, piecing strips together if necessary (refer to Fig. 3-23 on page 50). For a single-edged ruffle, apply the selected edge finish to one long edge of the ruffle strip; for a double-edged ruffle, finish both long edges.

6. Marking with a disappearing pen or chalk on the right side of the ruffle strip, space dots ¼″ (6mm) to ½″ (1.3cm) apart, as pre-planned, along the unfinished edge for a single-edged ruffle, or centered for a double-edged ruffle. Matching dots, pleat the ruffle strip, securing each fold with hand basting or machine stitching. If the ruffle strip is wide or the fabric limp, hand form, pin and hand baste the folds before machine stitching over the dots. For ruffle strips of manageable width and fabric, form the pleats while machine stitching (Fig. 3-50). For a pleated ruffle with sharply creased folds, press the folds from seam to finished edge.

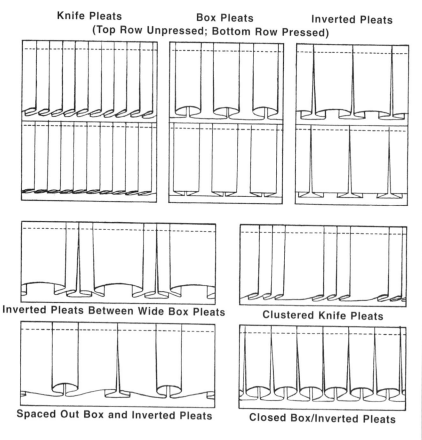

Knife Pleats   **Box Pleats**   **Inverted Pleats**
(Top Row Unpressed; Bottom Row Pressed)

Inverted Pleats Between Wide Box Pleats

Clustered Knife Pleats

Spaced Out Box and Inverted Pleats

Closed Box/Inverted Pleats

Fig. 3-49. Pleated ruffle arrangements.

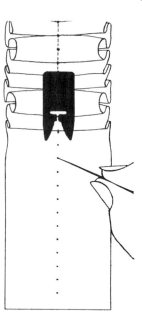

Fig. 3-50. To form pleats while machine-stitching: Prick a dot marked on the strip with the tip of a sturdy needle or pointed tool. Push it under or lift it over to make an outer fold that matches the correct dots. Grip the just formed fold with the pointed tip as the fabric slips under the presser foot.

7. To attach a pleated single-edged ruffle to flat fabric, conceal the seam allowance inside another seam, at a hem, or with suitable surface application (refer to Figs. 3-25, 3-26, 3-27, & 3-28 on pages 50–51). Topstitch a pleated double-edged ruffle to foundation fabric, sewing over the ruffle's seamline. Match the ruffle's seamline or the right edge of the ruffle to a guideline marked on the fabric (refer to Fig. 3-36 on page 55).

NOTES & VARIATIONS

Beneath the application seam, pleated ruffles are smooth with disciplined folds and underlayers. Compared to gathered single-edged ruffles, the seam allowances of pleated single-edged ruffles (same length, same target) are less bulky. At the float, pleated ruffles roll into rounded, repetitive folds or, if pressed, angle into creased, arranged folds. The type of pleat affects the float—inverted pleats remain close to foundation level while box pleats elevate. Pleating arrangements that feature localized fullness—pleats isolated in between unpleated segments of the ruffle strip—contrast bursts of folded fullness with areas of smooth ruffle fabric.

Pleat depth based on a folding gauge of dots spaced no more than ½″ (1.3cm) apart relates proportionally to most ruffle widths and applications. For pleat formation, consecutive dots indicate the outer fold, the inner fold, and the outer fold match point of one pleat, and, if the arrangement dictates, some dots are counted as spaces between pleats. To pleat wide ruffle strips, particularly if the pleats are to be pressed, mark the edge or edges with a duplicate of the dots on the seamline; match all the aligned dots when folding and pinning each pleat; and baste at the edge or edges as well as on the seamline. Locate pleat folds on the straightgrain of the fabric. Press lightly to hold the pleats, remove the basting at the edge or edges, and steam press thoroughly to produce a ruffle with crisp folds (don't move until cool and dry). To maintain the integrity of the folds, apply a pressed, pleated ruffle to the foundation in a straight line.

Like gathered ruffles, applications of unpressed pleated ruffles can be curved as much as the pleating will accept gracefully. The folds of a narrow *box/inverted pleat ruffle* adapt nicely to the sinuous curves of scrolled or allover ruffle patterns (Fig. 3-51).

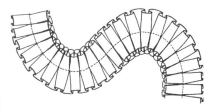

Fig. 3-51. The pleating of a narrow, inverted/box pleated ruffle alternately stretches and flattens on the outside, and condenses and heightens on the inside as it negotiates a tight curve.

The spread-seam ruffle, layered ruffles, low massed ruffles, and headed ruffles, variations described for gathered single- and double-edged ruffles, pertain to pleated ruffles as well. For applications that require quantities of pleated ruffles, use the ruffler attachment to convert ruffle strips into automatically knife-pleated and straight-stitched single- or double-edged ruffles. Simple adjustments change the attachment from gathering to pleating mode and regulate the separation between knife pleats by stitch count—a pleat every stitch, a pleat every 6 stitches, a pleat every 12 stitches. Stitch length regulates pleat depth. (Fig. 3-52).

Fig. 3-52. The ruffler, a sewing machine attachment, looks more complicated to operate than it actually is.

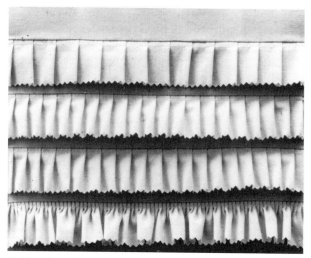

III-19—Chart of ruffles automatically knife-pleated with a ruffler attachment. (top) Ruffle pleated on every 12th stitch. (center) Two rows of ruffles pleated on every 6th stitch. (bottom) Ruffle pleated on every stitch with a floating edge that looks like the result of gathering.

III-20—Narrow ruffle strips automatically knife-pleated on every stitch, finished with hairline edging. (top) Band with a ruffle attached before edgestitching to the foundation. (bottom) Circles appliquéd over the seam allowance of a previously attached ruffle.

PLEATED SINGLE-EDGED RUFFLE

III-21—Four ruffles 1 " (2.5cm) wide: (from the top) knife-pleated and pressed; unpressed box pleats; box pleats with two unpressed knife pleats on either side; close knife pleating with the folds steamed to hold.

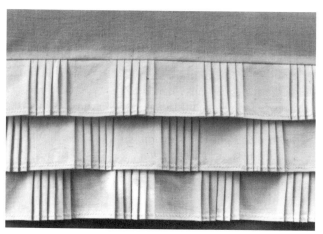

III-22—Three overlapping tiers of pressed, knife-pleated ruffles with a single-fold, twin-needle edge finish.

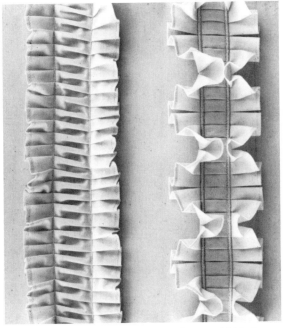

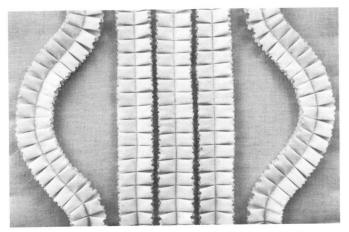

III-23—(left) Knife pleats with a band of centered folds that reverse direction between topstitched seams.
(right) Arrangement of box, knife, and inverted pleats with a centered ladder of folds between satin-stitched seams.

III-24—Box/inverted pleat ruffles 1 ½" (4cm) wide.

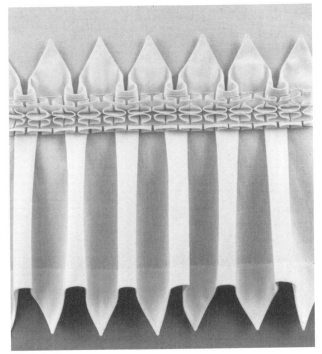

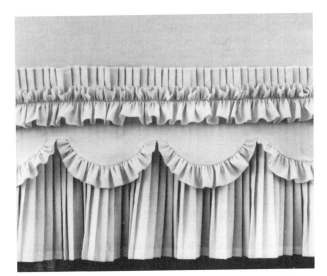

III-25—Headed ruffle with box pleats between deep points contoured into each faced edge. Two layers of box/inverted pleat ruffles, hairline edged, cover the application seam. The "boxes" of the ruffle on top are tacked together in the center.

III-26—Elaborate ruffle built over a headed ruffle knife-pleated on a Perfect Pleater. Gathered ruffles border the scalloped edge of the band that overlays the deep, pleated ruffle. A double-edged ruffle gathered off-center covers the split.

A *flounce* is a flowing attach-ment that gradually flares and swells from a smooth seam-line to a floating edge of rolling waves and folds. It starts as a curvilinear piece of fabric with one edge longer than the other. When its incurved shorter edge is straightened and stitched to a stabilizing fabric, the longer edge develops graceful fullness. As part of a whole, the flounce can be a solo addition, or flounces can be applied in rows that either partially or completely cover the base fabric.

FLOUNCES

4 Making Flounces

CIRCULAR FLOUNCE

—a circle of fabric with a round cutout in the center, split open, straightened out, and seamed to another piece of fabric along its inner, shortest edge. The longest edge floats in waves and folds.

PROCEDURES

1. A refresher vocabulary:

   Circumference—the distance around a circle.

   Diameter—any straight line passing through the center of a circle from one side of the circumference to the other.

   Radius—a straight line extending from the center of a circle to any point on the circumference.
   Radius of a curving section of a circle—radius of the circle which has the same curvature as the curving section at any point.

2. Choose between a flounce with maximum, moderate, or minimal flare as controlled by the radius of the round cutout in the middle of a circular flounce pattern, and the length of the flounce:

   ♦ The smaller the radius of the central cutout, the greater the flare at the floating edge of a flounce after it is applied (Fig. 4-1).

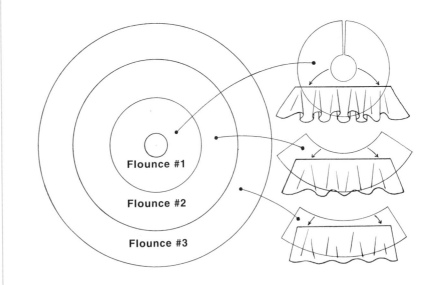

Fig. 4-1. Circle divided into three rings of equal depth to demonstrate the relationship between the flare at the floating edge and the radius of the circular curve that becomes the straightened edge of the flounce.

- Flounce depth as it increases also increases the flaring. As the difference between the circumference of the central cutout and the circumference of the floating edge increases, the folds at the edge become more voluminous (Fig. 4-2).

Fig. 4-2. Three flounces cut with identical circular curves at the top, but increasing in depth.

To evaluate a flounce, sample the effect of central cutouts that vary in size on a flounce that remains the same in depth and straightened length at the application seam.

3. To draft a circular flounce pattern, establish two measurements, one for the radius of the central circle and a second for the depth of the flounce:

a. Draw the central circle using a compass set to the radius measurement ((a) in Fig. 4-3). Adding a measurement for flounce depth to the radius, reset the compass and draw a second circle outside the first ((b) in Fig. 4-3).

b. To provide a seam allowance, draw a smaller circle inside the center circle. To include a hem allowance for a finish applicable to a curving edge (refer to "Edge Finishing for Ruffles" on page 43), enlarge the outer circle.

c. Indicate one or more side openings. Align side openings to a radius of the outlined circles ((c) in Fig. 4-3). Cut out the circular flounce pattern.

4. To estimate the fabric requirement for a particular circular flounce application (Fig. 4-4):

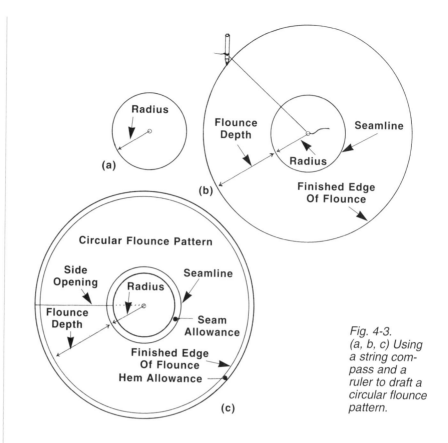

Fig. 4-3. (a, b, c) Using a string compass and a ruler to draft a circular flounce pattern.

a. Calculate the length of the circular seamline on the pattern:

[2 x radius] x 3.14 (π)
= whole circular seamline length

whole circular seamline length
− side opening seam allowances
= Circular Seamline Length

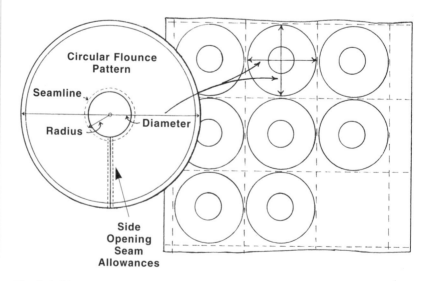

Fig. 4-4. After calculating the number of circular flounce pattern pieces a particular application will need, use the diameter of the flounce pattern to plan a cutting arrangement, and figure how much fabric will be required.

b. Figure out how many circular flounce pieces will be needed to cover the application's seamline(s):

total length of seamlines on application
÷ circular seamline length
= Circles to Cut

c. Determine how much fabric will be needed to cut the required number of circular flounce pattern pieces:

fabric width
÷ diameter of circular flounce pattern
= circles fitting crossgrain

circles to cut
÷ circles fitting crossgrain
= lengthgrain rows of circles
(a fraction counts as a row)

lengthgrain rows of circles
x diameter of circular flounce pattern
= Fabric Length Required

5. Cut each circular flounce from fabric following the perimeter of the paper pattern or its traced outline. Locate the side opening that cuts each circle apart on the straightgrain of the fabric. When sewing two or more circles together to extend the seamline length of a flounce, join with a reversible French or flat-fell seam, especially if the swing of the floating edge is likely to reveal both sides of the fabric (Fig. 4-5).

6. Apply the selected finish to the floating edge of each flounce.

7. Attach the flounce or flounces to the stabilizing fabric, sewing on the designated seamline. To enable straightening the curving seam allowance/seamline of the flounce to match the straighter seamline on the fabric with minimal strain, clip into the flounce seam allowance at regular intervals. Make as many clips as necessary, but never overclip (Fig 4-6). Conceal the flounce's seam allowance:

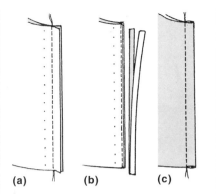

(a)　　　(b)　　　(c)

Fig. 4-5. French seam: (a) With wrong sides together, match the edges to be joined and sew down the center of the seam allowance. (b) Trim the seam allowances next to the seam. (c) Folding on the seam, turn inside out with right sides together, and sew on the stitching lines.

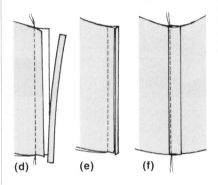

(d)　　　(e)　　　(f)

Flat-fell seam: (d) With right sides together, match the edges to be joined and sew the stitching lines together. (e) Trim one seam allowance by half; fold and press the untrimmed seam allowance over the trimmed seam allowance. (f) Open up the fabric, right sides down, and edgestitch next to the fold of seam allowance.

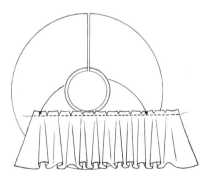

Fig. 4-6. Seam allowance of flounce clipped to straighten for the application seam.

• With an appropriate surface application—Using a fabric-safe marker, draw seamline and edge-matching guidelines on the foundation. Matching the guidelines, straight stitch the flounce to the foundation. Zigzag stitch over the edge of the seam allowance, or cover the seam allowance with an edgestitched band of fabric (Fig. 4-7).

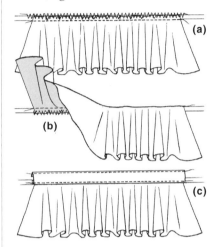

Fig. 4-7. To apply a flounce to a foundation: (a) When rows of flounces overlap the flounce below, sew each flounce right side up. (b) Sew a flounce wrong side up and flip it over its seam allowance. (c) Sew right side up and cover the seam allowance with an appliqué.

- Inside a seam—Matching edges, baste the flounce, right side up, to the right side of fabric #1. With right sides together, pin fabric #2 over both and sew through all layers next to the basting seam; or lap the turned edge of fabric #2 over the seam allowance of the flounce and edgestitch through all layers (Fig. 4-8).

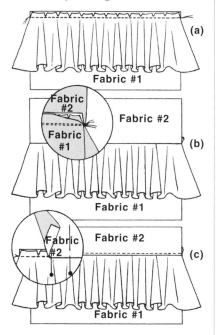

Fig. 4-8. In-seam applications for a flounce: (a) After machine-basting the flounce to fabric #1, (b) pin fabric #2 over both with right sides together, turn to the back, and machine-stitch; or (c) pin and edgestitch the turned edge of fabric #2 over all seam allowances.

- In a hem treatment—(a) Bind the edge when a flounce lies on top of the fabric to which it is attached. Sew a narrow strip of bias-cut binding, right side down, over the flounce; turn the binding over all seam allowances to the back, and hand stitch its turned edge to the fabric under the flounce ((a) and (b) in Fig. 4-9).

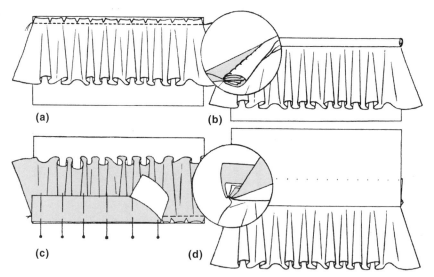

Fig. 4-9. (a) After machine-basting the flounce over the underlying fabric, (b) encase the edges inside a binding. (c) Pin a facing over a flounce basted to a fabric extension, sew through all layers, (d) turn the facing to the back, and slipstitch to the fabric.

(b) Face the edge when a flounce extends beyond the fabric to which it is attached. Sew a facing, right side down, over the back of a flounce which is basted to the right side of the fabric. Turn the facing to the back of the fabric and the flounce right side out; slipstitch the facing to the fabric above the flounce (see (c) and (d) in Fig. 4-9). A decorative facing is an option: Sew the facing, right side down, over the front of a flounce which is basted to the back of the fabric; turn the facing to the front and edgestitch over its turned seam allowance.

Notes & Variations

A circular flounce generates floating fullness by encouraging flare, and does it without bulking up the seamline. The circularity and depth of the flounce pattern, the fabric component, and the edge finish interrelate to produce maximum, moderate, or minimal waviness at the floating edge, but a smooth layer of flounce fabric at the seamline is a constant.

Since the grain on a circular flounce is constantly changing, a flounce application needs grainline balance if it is to hang the same way on either side of a central point. Place the straightgrain of a flounce in the center so that grainline changes move identically on the sides, or hang the true bias of the flounce in the center. For flounces applied in multiple rows, repeat the same balance.

Long rows and multiple tiers of flounces require the chaining together of many circles. For short rows of flounces with moderate to minimal flare, a segment of the entire circular flounce pattern may be all that's needed for one row. To balance the grainline on all rows and save on fabric as well, align the segments in rows on the fabric when cutting out the flounces (Fig. 4-10).

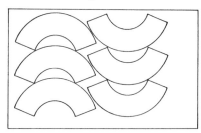

Fig. 4-10. Cutting guide that repeats the same grain alignment for each circular flounce segment.

Finishing an edge that continuously curves and changes grain is a challenge. When selecting an edge finish, consider ease of application, compatibility with the characteristics of the fabric, and how the finish will influence the quality of the float (refer to "Edge Finishing for Ruffles" on page 43). If both sides of the flounce will be visible when applied, the appearance of the back of an edge finish is as important as how it looks in front. A flounce that's completely lined converts both sides of the flounce into a right side, avoids problems caused by curve and weave, and enables edge contouring such as scallops or points. A faced or bound edge is also reversible. For other kinds of finish, staystitch next to the edge before application, keep hem folds tiny, and gently ease the fabric as it moves under the presser foot.

The application takes care of the sides of a flounce when a continuous flounce encircles a tubular foundation, or when both sides of a flounce are caught into cross seams. For situations where a flounce stops mid-fabric, the sides of the flounce need to be finished at the same time as the floating edge is finished, before the flounce is applied. Unless sides with dangling corners are appropriate, eliminate the corners by curving the floating edge into the seamline of the flounce before finishing the edge (Fig. 4-11).

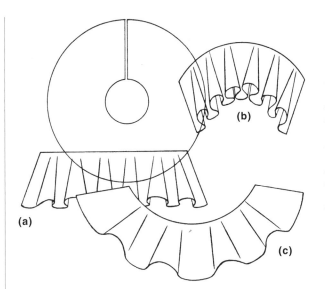

Fig. 4-12. Contrast the effect on the floating edge when the same circular flounce is applied (a) in a straight line, (b) to an inside curve, (c) to an outside curve.

Fig. 4-11. Circular flounce pattern with one side of the opening curved. After finishing the floating edge plus the curved and straight sides, the flounce, set into a vertical seam, falls in swinging folds from a curving top to a hanging point at the end.

When a flounce is lengthy from seam to hem, finish the edge *after* the flounce has been applied. Let it hang for 24 hours to allow the portions located on the bias to settle. Where the hemline droops, trim it evenly, and then finish the edge.

The flexible seamline of a circular flounce will follow curving as well as straight lines of application. The folds at the floating edge of a flounce sewn around an outward curve spread and diminish; sewing a flounce inside an inward curve squeezes and deepens the folds (Fig. 4-12). If the deviation between the seamline curve of the flounce and the application line is great ((b) in Fig. 4-12), clipping the seam allowance before stitching is a necessity. If the deviation is middling to slight ((c) in Fig. 4-12), attach the flounce without pre-clipping, stopping frequently while sewing to lift the presser foot and realign seamlines and edges before continuing.

After application, clip the seam allowance as the need to release any pull on the fabric dictates. Every clip into the seam allowance of a circular flounce weakens the seam: Less is always better and none before sewing is better still.

The floating edge of a *spiral-cut circular flounce* becomes less and less wavy as it moves out from the center of the circle. For an application where gradually diminishing waviness can be exploited, spiral-cut flounces save fabric. Draft a spiral-cut flounce pattern over a base of concentric circles spaced the depth of the flounce apart (slightly more for a flounce with a lining). Finish the edge with zigzag stitching or a lining before cutting out the flounce. Compared to a

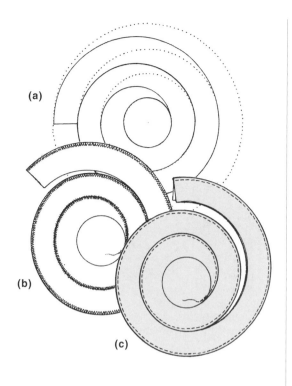

Fig. 4-13. (a) Spiral-cut flounce pattern. (b) Zigzag edge finish stitched over the outline before cutting on the outer needle holes of the stitching. (c) Sewing a lining, right sides facing, to the flounce by stitching just inside the outline before cutting out.

(a)

(b)

(c)

standard circular flounce, the seamline on one spiral-cut flounce goes a long way (Fig. 4-13).

A *layered circular flounce* consists of two or more flounces, stacked edge over edge, applied as one with all seamlines matching. If the fabric is crisp or firm enough to remain separated when the layers are pulled apart after flounce application, the flounce has an airy, fluffy appearance (Fig. 4-14).

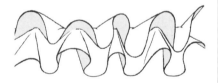

Fig. 4-14. Two-layered flounce.

Layered flounces cut from soft, supple fabric resist separation—the folds tend to nestle together—unless vertical application allows the folds to slip apart as they hang and sway.

There are two kinds of *tiered circular flounce* applications. (1) Rows of flounces are applied to a foundation with the floating edge of the flounce above concealing the applied edge of the flounce below.

(2) The rows of flounces are connected. The second flounce is attached to the floating edge of the first flounce, flounce #3 is sewn to the floating edge of flounce #2, and so on. The measurement around the top edge of each successive flounce increases significantly to the final floating edge which will be extravagantly enlarged, way beyond the flaring potential of flounce #1 even if its length were extended to the total length of the tiered flounces.

A *double-edged circular flounce* begins as two flounces sewn together with right sides facing before application. Opened and topstitched to a foundation, the double-edged flounce flares out into spreading folds at each side of the seamline both flounces share (Fig. 4-15).

Before joining the seamlines of the two flounces, piece extensions to each flounce together and finish the edges. If lining is the finish of choice, sew the lining to the flounce after sewing the two linings and the two flounces together (Fig. 4-16). Sew the lining to the flounce on one of the side openings before turning right side out; after turning, turn the seam allowances on the open end to the inside and stitch together—if the application requires such finishing.

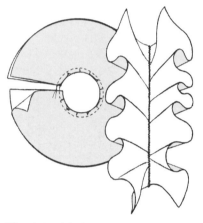

Fig. 4-15. (a) Two circular flounces sewn together (b) and applied with zigzagged topstitching over the joining seam.

For a *layered double-edged circular flounce*, baste the seamlines of two or more double-edged flounces together and topstitch to the foundation as one (fabric affects the separation of the layers, as described in a previous paragraph).

Applied in rows spaced less than the depth of one flounce apart, the floating edges of *massed double-edged circular flounces* stand upright because the seamlines are crowded together so closely.

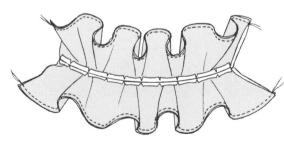

Fig. 4-16. Lined double-edged circular flounce before turning right side out.

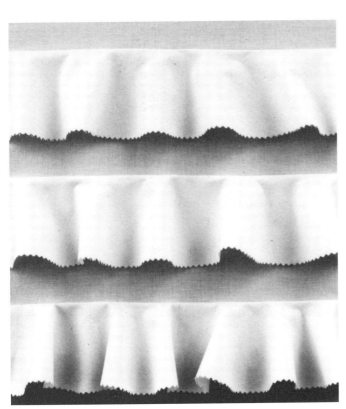

IV-1—Chart of muslin flounces, all 3" (7.5cm) deep. (top) Minimum flare at the floating edge of a flounce cut with an inner circle that has a 4 1/2" (11.5) radius; (center) moderate flare—a 3" (7.5cm) radius; (bottom) maximum flare—a 1 1/2" (4cm) radius.

IV-2—Flounces 2" (5cm) deep, cut around an inner circle with a 1 1/2" (4cm) radius. Above the four overlapping rows at the bottom, a continuous flounce reverses back and forth in rows that shorten as they angle upward.

CIRCULAR FLOUNCE

IV-3—Cut from circles with a 1" (2.5cm) inner radius, a flounce that spreads into deep, luxurious folds, bolstered with a double-fold hem.

IV-4—Two muslin flounces 4″
(10cm) deep fall into the swinging, alternating folds unique to
vertical applications. A hairline
edge finish, stitched twice, adds
body to the floating edge.

CIRCULAR FLOUNCE

IV-5—(top) A two-layer flounce
rises from a faced edge.
(bottom) Arched lines of application
and sturdy, double-fold hems inten-
sify the folds at the floating edges
of three moderately-flared flounces.

IV-6—Two spiral-cut flounces 2″ (5cm) deep, with a zigzagged edge finish, surround a pocket-shaped appliqué. The flare of each flounce gradually diminishes from maximum at the layered lower edge to minimum for the tiered rows on top.

CIRCULAR FLOUNCE

IV-7—Four double-edged muslin flounces, moderately flared and self-lined, with floating edges that stand in stately, sculptured waves when applied in close rows.

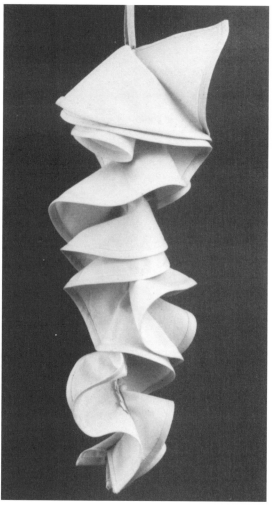

IV-8—Buoyant application of five double-edged muslin flounces set in slightly curving rows spaced very close together. The edges are finished with a single-fold hem.

IV-9—Flexible cylinder of swirling, encircling edges that spring from a two-layered, double-edged flounce. The bias-bound flounces taper from 3 1/2 " (9cm) to 1 1/2 " (4cm) in depth, measured around a center cutout with a 1 " (2.5cm) radius for maximum flare.

CIRCULAR FLOUNCE

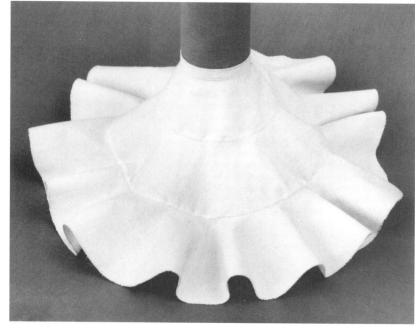

IV-10—Tiered flounces. The circumference at the floating edge is 10 times greater than the circumference of the binding at the top, although the top-to-hem measurement of the flounces is only 8 1/2 " (21.8cm).

CONTROLLED FLOUNCE

—a shaped piece of fabric designed to spread out into rolling folds at assigned positions on the floating edge when its incurved, shorter edge is straightened and seamed to a foundation.

PROCEDURES

1. Cut a target pattern that duplicates the size and shape of the area the flounce will cover when it's applied. If one side of the area is a mirror-image of the other side, or if the same contour repeats many times, make a pattern that includes one complete segment of the repeat (Fig. 4-17).

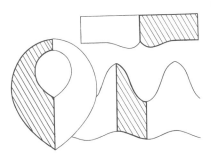

Fig. 4-17. Three target patterns, each representing an area to be covered with a controlled flounce. Shading marks the mirror-image segments that will be slashed-and-spread into patterns.

2. Decide whether deep folds, moderate waves, or slight ripples will be appropriate for the floating edge of the flounce to be developed from the target pattern:

a. At the location of each fold, wave, or ripple planned for the floating edge, pencil a line on the cut-out target pattern that connects the floating edge to the seamline and indicates the hang of the fold ((a) in Figs. 4-18, 4-19, and 4-20).

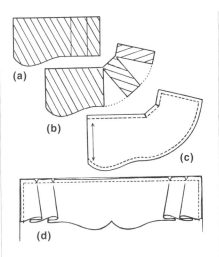

Fig. 4-18. (a) Target pattern with lines indicating fold locations (b) slashed and equally spread. (c) Final pattern with stitching line, clipping, and grainline notations. Note that one side must be matched to the fold of doubled fabric when cutting. (d) Controlled flounce made from the pattern.

b. Starting at the floating edge, slash each pencilled line, stopping about 1/16″ (1.5mm) from the seamline edge. Fan out each slash to enlarge the floating edge, and glue or tape the expanded target pattern to another sheet of paper. Relate the extent of each spread to the effect desired: For a softly rippled edge, open the slashes a little; for an edge with sweeping folds, open the slashes very wide. Estimate that one-half the spread at the floating edge will equal the height of a ripple or wave or the overlap of a fold. Use a compass to measure and duplicate the spread of a slash at the floating edge ((b) in Figs. 4-18, 4-19, and 4-20).

c. Draw a new floating edge that curves smoothly across the openings, always retaining the length set by the target pattern. Add a seam allowance to the seamline edge and a hem allowance to the floating edge for the chosen edge finish (refer to "Edge Finishing for Ruffles" on page 43). Add seam allowances to the sides, except for a side to be matched to the fold where a seam allowance is superfluous. Since every slash-and-spread location requires a clip in the seam allowance above to enable returning the flounce to its target seamline contour, note the apex of each opening with a mark inside the seam allowance that indicates a clip. Cut out the flounce pattern ((c) in Figs. 4-18, 4-19, 4-20).

3. Cut the controlled flounce from fabric following the perimeter of the paper pattern or its traced outlines. Match the lengthgrain of the fabric to a central and balanced position on the flounce. Sew the sections of the flounce together.

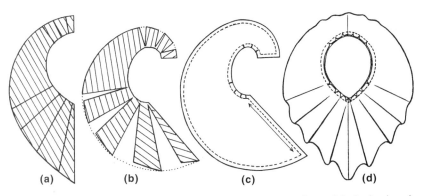

Fig. 4-19. (a) Target pattern with lines indicating fold locations, (b) slashed and unequally spread. (c) Final pattern with stitching line, clipping, and grainline notations. (d) Controlled flounce made from the pattern.

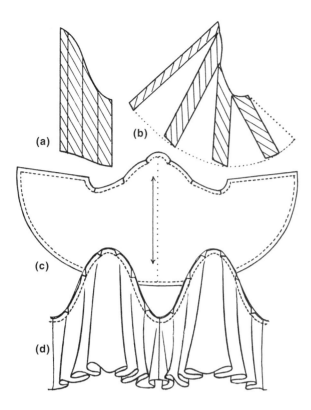

Fig. 4-20. (a) Target pattern with lines indicating fold locations, (b) slashed and widely spread. The half-width section on the left edge will be full size when seamed to a duplicate pattern piece. (c) Final pattern with stitching line, clipping, and grainline notations. (d) Controlled flounce made from the pattern.

4. Apply the selected finish to the floating edge (refer to "Edge Finishing for Ruffles" on page 43), but if the flounce is lengthy from seam to hem, finish the edge after the flounce is applied. Let it hang for 24 hours to allow the portions located on the bias to settle: Where the hemline droops, trim it evenly, and then finish the edge.

5. Sew the flounce to flat fabric, clipping the seam allowance where the pattern indicates to let the flounce seamline match the seamline on the application ((d) in Figs. 4-18, 4-19, 4-20). Conceal the seam allowance of the flounce in a manner appropriate for the application (refer to Figs. 4-7, 4-8, and 4-9 on pages 69–70).

NOTES & VARIATIONS

For situations where a circular flounce won't work, a controlled flounce can be custom-designed to fit and fill the special requirements of a particular application. Using the slash-and-spread technique of pattern development, a controlled flounce can be variably flared with deep folds for one part of the floating edge and delicate ripples elsewhere. With a controlled flounce, folds, waves, or ripples can be isolated to specific portions of the floating edge. The spacing between the folds, waves, or ripples can be regulated. A controlled flounce can be devised to fall with equal flare from all points of a convoluted seamline.

The amount of spread to allot to a slash involves informed guesswork. Parameters for the widening that will produce slight ripples, moderate waves, or lavish folds in the floating edge are expressed in generalities—a little, a whole lot, somewhere in between. Additionally, the characteristics of the intended fabric and the finish applied to the floating edge will affect the appearance of any amount of flared fullness. Test before finalizing a controlled flounce pattern.

To continue controlling the flounce after it is applied, arrange the flaring at the floating edge to reflect the intentions of the pattern while the flounce is hanging, or arrange and pin to a flat surface. Steam. Wait until the fabric cools and dries before moving.

Like circular flounces, controlled flounces may be *layered* (two or more flounces applied one on top of the other) and *double-edged* (two flounces flaring out to the sides from a shared seamline).

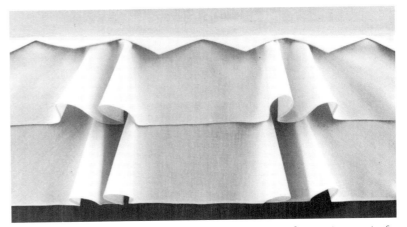

IV-11—Flounce designed to flare out into a pair of spreading folds at intervals that coincide with the sawtooth spacing of the lapped heading. A narrow, double-fold hem edges the tiered flounces.

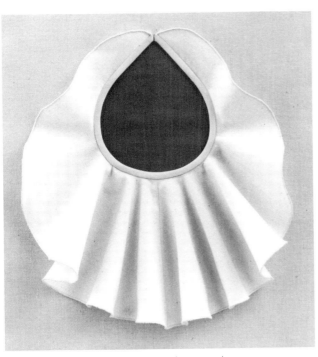

IV-12—Flounce that starts out flat at the top and gradually develops deep folds at the bottom of the circular opening. A satin-stitched, hairline finish supports the roll of the folds.

CONTROLLED FLOUNCE

IV-13—Elaborate flounce designed to spread into sweeping folds from an arched-and-tabbed seamline. A single-fold hem, zigzagged, finishes the floating edge.

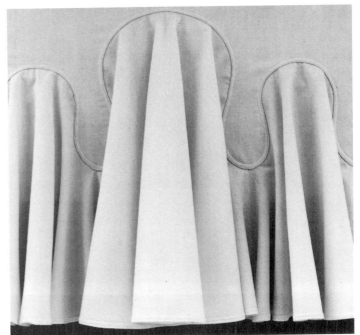

*G*odets are triangular inserts that inject flaring fullness into flat fabric. Used alone or in multiples, a godet starts at any selected mid-point within the fabric and ends at the lower edge which floats in waves or folds caused by the expansion. Slender godets sculpt fabric into a trumpet-like shape; medium-width godets swell into cone-shaped projections of fabric; wide godets burst out from the background fabric into a cascade of spreading folds.

GODETS

5 Making Godets

GODET

(pronounced go-day')—a section of a circle set into a seam or a slash within a piece of fabric to expand the floating edge at that place. A godet develops rolling waves or folds as it spreads.

PROCEDURES

1. For each godet, select a point inside the pattern or the fabric where the godet will begin its spread. The distance from point to lower edge equals the length of the godet, and includes a hem allowance.

    ◆ If the fabric is unseamed, connect each point to the lower edge with a straight slashline perpendicular to the edge.

Mark the pattern, then the wrong side of the fabric with slashlines that follow the grain, or mark directly on the fabric ((a) in Fig. 5-1).

    ◆ If the fabric has a vertical seam at godet location, position the point on the seam. The seam remains open to the lower edge for godet insertion ((b) in Fig. 5-1).

2. Using a mechanical or string compass set to the length of the godet, draft the godet pattern. Draw a circle or a portion of a circle. Estimate how much of the circumference the godet should add to the edge where it will be inserted to achieve the desired float. Isolate that amount by connecting the circumference to the compass point with two straight lines, establishing the width of the godet at the lower edge (note that after hemming the width will measure somewhat less). Add a seam allowance to the straight sides of the circular segment ((c) and (d) in Fig. 5-1). The pattern is ready to cut out and use.

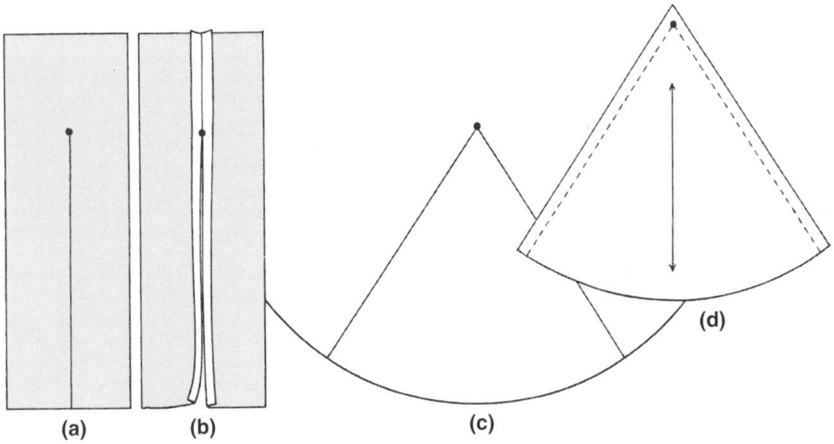

Fig. 5-1. (a) Slashline, or (b) seam opening, into which (c) this segment of a circle, the godet, will fit. (d) Godet pattern with stitching line, godet point, and straightgrain markings.

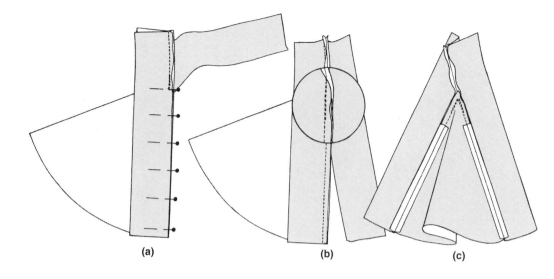

(a) (b) (c)

Fig. 5-2.
(a) One side of a godet pinned into an opened seam (b) and stitched.
(c) The inserted godet with seam allowances pressed.

3. Cut out the godet from fabric following the perimeter of the pattern or its traced outline. The center axis of a godet is always matched to the straightgrain of the fabric. On the godet's wrong side, mark the point where the side seamlines meet at the tip. For insertion into a slash, mark the side seamlines as well.

4. Insert the godet:

   ◆ Into a seam opened to godet length. With right sides together and edges matching, pin match the last stitch of the seam above the opening to the point of the godet, and pin one side of the godet to one side of the opening. Sew from the point of the godet to the lower edge, backstitching at the point. Attach the other side of the godet to the other side of the opening. When finished, the break between the godet seam and the seam above should be imperceptible ((a) and (b) in Fig. 5-2).

   ◆ Into a godet-length slash.

   a. Before slashing the fabric, indicate seamlines that angle from the lower edge to the godet's point on each side of the slashline. Hand baste a 2″ (5cm) or 3″ (7.5cm) square of organza or lining material to the front of the fabric behind the top of the slashline. Starting at the bottom of the square, machine stitch up to the point on one side; pivot on the needle; take a horizontal stitch across the point; pivot and sew down the other side to the bottom of the square. Stitch right beside the seamline with very small stitches ((a) and (b) in Fig. 5-3).

   b. Slash up to the horizontal stitch at the point. Remove the basting; pull the reinforcing square to the back; press the seam allowances toward the square. Treat the reinforcement as an extension of the seam allowance. With right sides together, pin match the horizontal stitch at the point of the reinforcing seam to the godet's point. *Matching seamlines,* pin and baste one side of the godet to one side of the opening; pin and baste the other side of the godet to the opening. Machine stitch and remove the basting ((c) and (d) in Fig. 5-3).

5. Press the godet's seam allowance toward the fabric at the top of the godet. About 1″ (2.5cm) to 2″ (5cm) below the point, clip and press the seam allowances open ((c) and (e) in Fig. 5-3).

6. Hem the floating edge of the godet and the fabric on the sides.

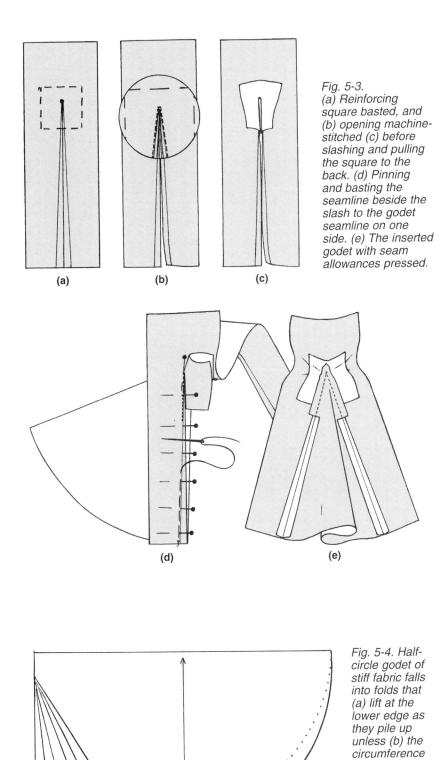

Fig. 5-3.
(a) Reinforcing square basted, and (b) opening machine-stitched (c) before slashing and pulling the square to the back. (d) Pinning and basting the seamline beside the slash to the godet seamline on one side. (e) The inserted godet with seam allowances pressed.

(a) **(b)** **(c)**

(d) **(e)**

Fig. 5-4. Half-circle godet of stiff fabric falls into folds that (a) lift at the lower edge as they pile up unless (b) the circumference of the godet pattern is gradually elongated to compensate.

(a) **(b)**

Notes & Variations

Although triangular godets are usual, godets as wide as a half circle and as large as a full circle are feasible when exceptionally lush, luxurious folds are the desired result. A wide godet of fabric with sufficient body to stand out and away from the insertion fabric will rise at the floating edge as it projects unless the lower edge is elongated when the godet is designed (Fig. 5-4).

If the godet is wide and long, hang the application for 24 hours before hemming to allow the bias of the fabric to settle. If the fabric is soft and loosely woven, the godet is liable to sag from its seams unless allowed to stretch out before insertion. Hang the godet from its point for 24 hours before sewing into the seam or slash. In either case, hem after trimming the overextended fabric evenly at the edge.

When planning a hem treatment for godets, consider the degree of curve at the floating edge of the godet, the characteristics of the fabric, and the effect of an edge finish on the sweep of the float. "Edge Finishing for Ruffles" on page 43 describes possibilities: For large-scale godets, add to those choices a deeper, single-fold flat hem, eased around the curve, perhaps with a suitable stiffening laid inside the fold.

The *handkerchief edge* is peculiar to godets. It starts as a square, usually of light, delicate fabric. One corner of the square becomes the point of the godet; each side of the square equals the length of the godet. For two sides of the square, select an edge finish that favors a soft, fluid float (Fig. 5-5). After insertion, the unattached corner of the square dips to a floating point in the center.

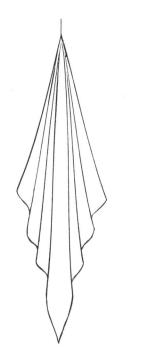

Fig. 5-5. Square godet creates a handkerchief edge. The floating corner and sides of the godet can be adjusted for length.

Insertion in a slash is more troublesome than godet insertion in a seam. Even with a reinforcing square, the miniscule seam allowance at the top of the slash makes neat insertion tricky. Tilting the seamlines farther away from the slashline helps. Cutting a very narrow V-shaped slash permits manageable seam allowances around the point, but places both slash and godet seamlines on different slants of the bias. That may cause stretch problems, a consideration before selecting this option (Fig. 5-6). Widening the slash to a narrow, arched cutout and rounding the point of the godet equalizes the seam allowances at the top, but also eliminates the vanishing point that is a distinctive feature of the triangular godet (Fig. 5-7).

Restricting godet openings at the tip with a stay in back forces godet fullness forward and prevents soft, slippery, godet fabric from sliding behind the insertion seams (Fig. 5-8).

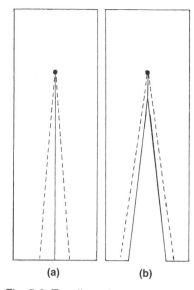

(a)   (b)

Fig. 5-6. To relieve the squeeze at the point of a slash, (a) move the seamlines farther away from the slashline at the lower edge, or (b) locate the seamlines beside a V-shaped cutout.

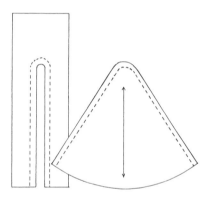

Fig. 5-7. The seam allowance around the curve of an arched cutout will need close clipping to accommodate godet insertion. The rounded tip of the godet matches the arch of the opening.

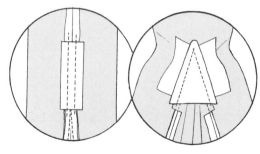

A *mock godet* converts an in-seam godet insertion into a one-seam construction. Instead of cutting a separate godet, one-half the intended godet is cut-in-one with the side fabric, trading two side seams for one centered seam that continues from the seam above (Fig. 5-9). Although a mock godet streamlines cutting and sewing procedures, it has a disadvantage: Both sides of a mock godet fall on the bias of the fabric, which may begin to sag from the firmer stitching in the seam.

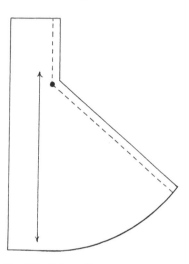

Fig. 5-9. A "cut 2" mock godet pattern has one seam down the middle. A circle (●) indicates the point where a true godet would have peaked.

Fig. 5-8. A stay stitched to the seam allowances: (a) Holds the top of an in-seam opening closed. (b) Restricts the opening at the top of an in-slash godet.

V-1. Three in-seam godets. Two shorter, triangular godets flank a tall, half-circle godet that projects, train-like, from its insertion seams.

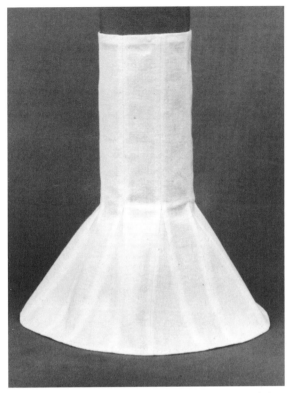

V-2. Eight slim godets inserted into eight seams shape a tubular muslin construction that suddenly flares where the godets start.

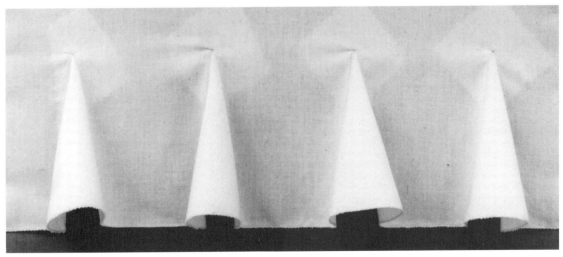

V-3. Four muslin godets inserted into slashes.

V-4—Five godets set into slashes stepped in length. Although each godet is cut from the same 50-degree section of a circle, hem measurements increase as the godets increase in length.

GODETS

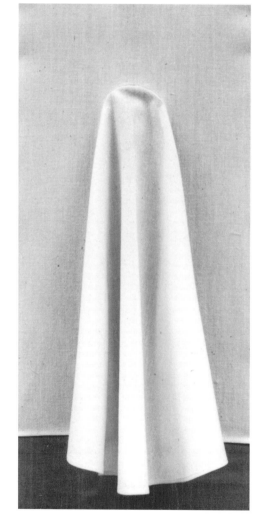

V-5—Quarter-circle godet with a rounded tip inserted into a slender, arched cutout.

Systematic
Folding

PART THREE

*P*leats are measured folds formed at the edge of a piece of fabric where they are secured with stitching. Beyond the stitching, pleats become loose folds that continue the arrangement set at the edge.

At the edge, pleat folds are either levelled or manipulated to project. The folds are released in sharply creased order, or they continue unpressed and modify into softly spreading rolls. After reducing fabric measurement at the source, the full extent of the pleated fabric becomes accessible where the folds are unconfined, all the way to an opposite edge that floats or another edge where the folds are again secured with stitching.

PLEATING

6 Pleating

Note: This chapter begins with BASICS, indicated by a gray band located underneath the relevant columns.

PLEAT BASICS

PRESSING PLEATS

At one time or another during the formation of pleated fabric, the iron becomes an essential tool. Sometimes heat, steam, and pressure are as much a part of pleat preparation as needle and thread. At other times, steaming finishes the job, preserving a careful arrangement of rolling folds.

There's more to pressing the folds of flat and partial pleats into sharp, lasting creases than proper setting of the controls on an iron. After basting the pleat arrangement, a gentle pressing with steam makes the preliminary creases. For the final, hard pressing, a broad surface is more efficient for large applications than the narrow surface of a regular ironing board. Prepare a table top with padding—layers of blanket or towels covered with sheeting, underlined with aluminum foil. If using a regular ironing board, back it up against a table or chair to support overhanging fabric.

To prevent imprinting, remove all pins and basting threads from the first group of pleats to be pressed. Arrange these pleats on the pressing surface, smoothing, straightening, and aligning into the correct position. To prevent the outer folds from leaving an impression on the fabric beneath, place a strip of brown paper, cut slighter wider than pleat depth and longer than pleat length, inside the underfold of each pleat to be pressed.

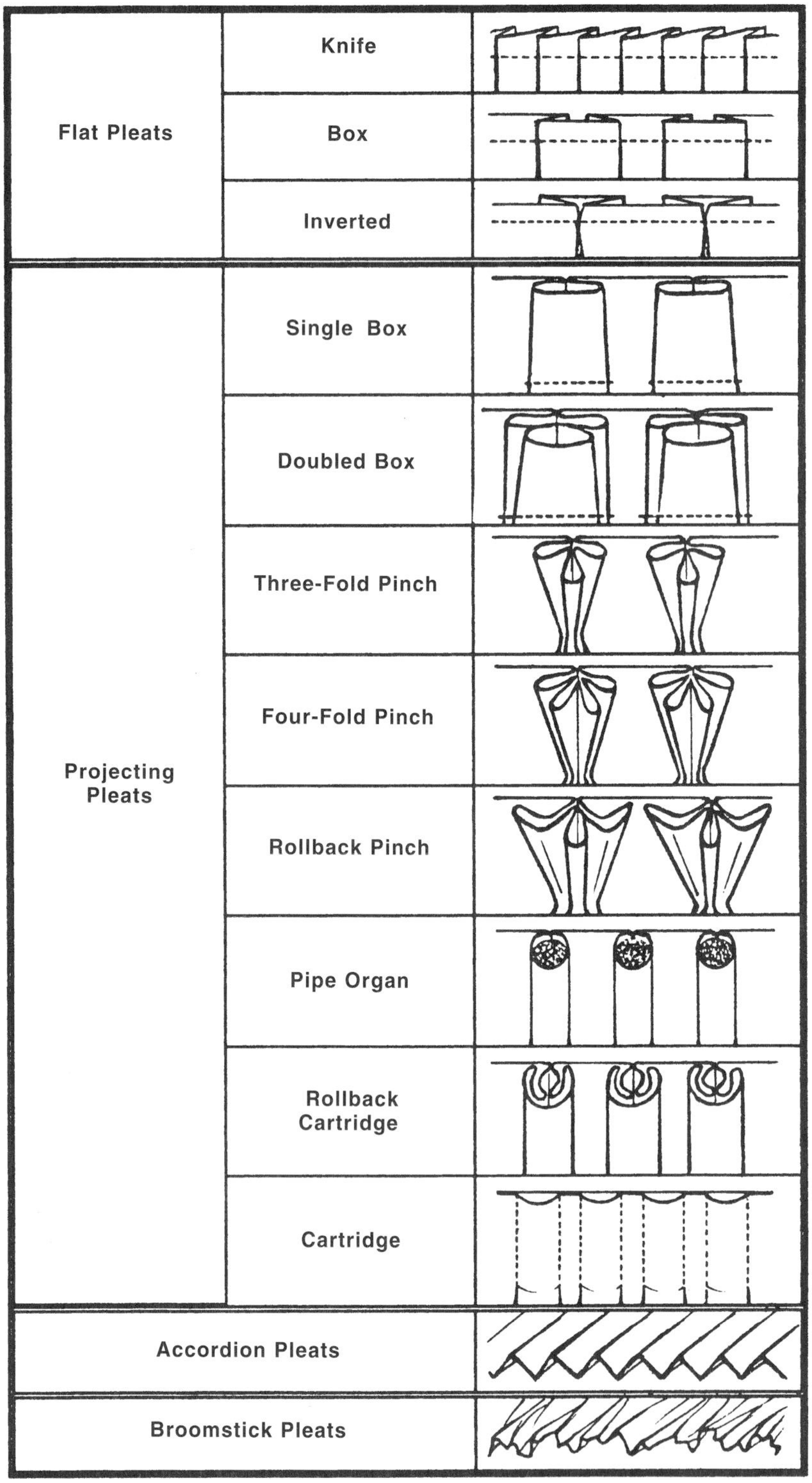

Flat Pleats	Knife	
	Box	
	Inverted	
Projecting Pleats	Single Box	
	Doubled Box	
	Three-Fold Pinch	
	Four-Fold Pinch	
	Rollback Pinch	
	Pipe Organ	
	Rollback Cartridge	
	Cartridge	
Accordion Pleats		
Broomstick Pleats		

Fig. 6-1. Pleat profiles.

Immerse a press cloth in water, wring it out, and spread the damp cloth over the pleats. Press with a hot iron until the cloth is dry, holding the iron firmly in place to send steam down through the folds underneath. Don't slide the iron; pick it up and re-position. Remove the dry cloth but let the fabric cool and dry thoroughly before moving on to the next group of pleats. Tailors use a clapper, a narrow, smooth hardwood block about 12″ (30.5cm) long, to pound the folds of the steamy-warm pleats until they cool. When all the pleats have been pressure-and-steam-creased, turn the fabric to the other side and repeat the process.

For extra setting power, dip the press cloth into a solution of one part white vinegar to nine parts water. Use two press cloths, one under the pleats and one on top.

To complete an application of unpressed pleats, tug the folds into an equalized arrangement while hanging, or arrange the folds while pinning the edges to a padded board, stab pinning interior folds, if necessary. Settle the arrangement by steaming with an iron or steamer moved slowly above the surface of the fabric. Allow to cool and dry before moving.

HEMMING FLAT & PARTIAL PLEATS

When pleating lengthy fabric, the seams that join two pieces of fabric are always situated unobtrusively. Unless the application and pleating arrangement make it unavoidable, never locate joining seams on an outer fold. When forming flat pleats, place joining seams on inner folds, or centered behind an inverted pleat.

Seams on the inner folds of flat and partial pleats present problems when hemming. There are two options when dealing with the seam allowances: (1) Press the inner-fold seam allowance open and flat from the lower edge to the depth of the hem. Turn up the hem and stitch. Clip the seam allowance at the top of the hem to free it from confinement, re-fold the pleat, and steam press the hemmed pleat fold. (2) Hem each piece of fabric first, then sew the pieces together, matching the hem folds exactly. Form the pleats with the joining seam aligned to an inner fold. Trim the seam allowances diagonally across the hem folds. Overcast the cut edges of the seam allowances to the depth of the hem (Fig. 6-2).

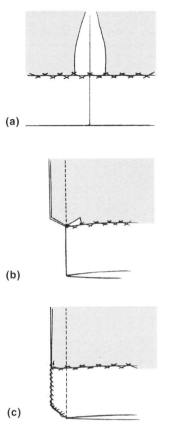

(a)

(b)

(c)

Fig. 6-2. To hem pleated fabric with seams located on inner folds:
(a) Press the seam allowances open, hem, and (b) clip above the hem.
(c) Hem the fabric. After sewing the hemmed sections together, overcast the angle-trimmed seam allowances.

To cope with the folds of edgestitched pleats when hemming the floating edge: (1) Hem the fabric first, then edgestitch the pleats. (2) Stop edgestitching at least 1″ (2.5cm) above the upper level of the finished hem. Hem the pleats. Finish the edgestitching, beginning with the needle in the last of the previous edgestitches. Leave about 3″ (7.5mm) of thread at the lower edge of the hem and tie the bobbin and needle threads together to secure the stitching. Insert both thread ends into a needle; at the final stitch, push the needle inside the hem fold and bring it out half-its-length away before cutting the threads.

Fold and steam press the hemmed pleat edge, allowing the fabric to cool and dry before moving.

FLAT PLEATS

—parallel folds lifted from the surface of the fabric and laid down smoothly to the side. The folds, arranged in a systematic fashion, are secured with stitching at the top and released below:

KNIFE (SIDE) PLEATS

—adjacent underfolds turned in the same direction.

BOX PLEATS

—adjacent underfolds of equal depth turned in opposite directions.

INVERTED PLEATS

—adjacent underfolds of equal depth turned to meet in the center.

(Refer to "Pleat Profiles" on page 90.)

PROCEDURES

1. Set a target measurement for the fabric to match after it is pleated.

2. Plan an arrangement of flat pleats that will fit within the target measurement: Use a strip of paper as long as the target measurement to indicate the position of each outer fold, or plot on a graph-paper reduction. Specify the type of flat pleat each fold position represents (Fig. 6-3).

3. Calculate the amount of fabric required for the desired number of pleats:

   a. Establish a depth, the measurement between outer fold and inner fold, for each fold indicated on the plan.

   b. The mathematics:

      2 x pleat depth
      = one pleat underfold

      one pleat underfold
      x number of pleats
      = total pleat underfolds

      total pleat underfolds
      + target measurement
      = Pleated Fabric Requirement

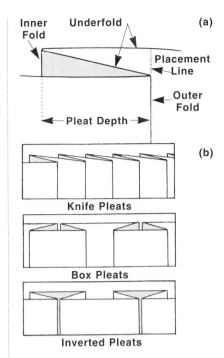

Fig. 6-3. (a) Anatomy of a flat pleat. (b) Types of flat pleats. Arrangements may consist of one type of pleat or a combination, and the space between pleats and pleat depths may vary.

4. Using another strip of paper as long as the pleated fabric requirement, or a graph-paper reduction, make a pleating pattern with measured underfold spaces separated by perpendicular lines. On consecutive lines, indicate an outer fold for every pleat fold marked on the original plan, next to an inner fold and a placement line for each pleat. Arrows connecting outer folds to placement lines, indicating direction, will prevent confusion. Also note "right side" on the pattern.

5. Add the desired length, including a hem allowance, to the pleated fabric requirement and cut the fabric.

6. Decide how the pleats will appear:
   - With folds unpressed and softly rolled.
   - With folds pressed and sharply creased.
   - With outer and/or inner folds edgestitched to hold a sharp crease permanently ((a) in Fig. 6-4).

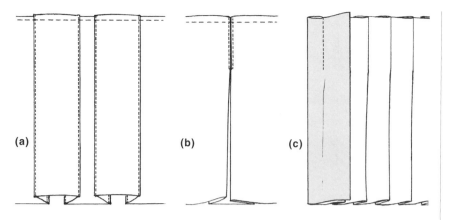

Fig. 6-4. (a) Two box pleats with outer and inner folds edgestitched.
(b) Inverted pleat with release point lowered visibly with edgestitching.
(c) Knife pleats with release points lowered invisibly.

♦ With a lowered release point: Pleats stitched from the top of the fabric down for a specified distance, either visibly by edgestitching next to the fold through all layers, or invisibly by sewing fold and placement lines together in back ((b) and (c) in Fig. 6-4).

♦ A combination of the above.

7. Mark the back of the fabric with pleating lines, reversing the pattern. The exception: Mark pleats to be edgestitched on the right side of the fabric. Using a long straightedge, indicate an outer fold and a placement position for each pleat (the inner fold is automatic). Begin with scissor-nip markings inside the seam allowances across the top and bottom edges of the fabric. Connect the nips directly opposite with lines, following the straightgrain of woven fabric. Differentiate between fold and placement lines with the markings:

♦ Broken and unbroken lines of a fabric-safe marker such as chalk, disappearing pen, or soap sliver ((a) in Fig. 6-5).

♦ Basting seams using two colors of thread.

♦ Basting seams using different stitch lengths ((b) in Fig. 6-5).

♦ Pin-marked lines, changing the head color of the pins.

8. Form the pleats:

♦ When working from the back of the fabric on a knife or box pleat arrangement, baste each outer fold line to its placement line, sewing through two layers of fabric. Turn the underfold to the appropriate side and pin. (Note that knife pleats marked and formed on the wrong side of the fabric open in the opposite direction on the right side of the fabric.) For inverted pleats, baste the outer fold lines on adjacent pleats together; center the shared placement line over the basted seam and pin the underfolds. To lower the release point of any pleat invisibly, machine stitch over the basting from the top to the designated release point below (Fig. 6-6).

♦ When working from the front of the fabric, fold each pleat on its outer fold line and bring the folded edge to the placement line; pin, and then baste through all three layers of each pleat. If the folds are to be edgestitched, distance the basting seams from the outer folds (Fig. 6-7).

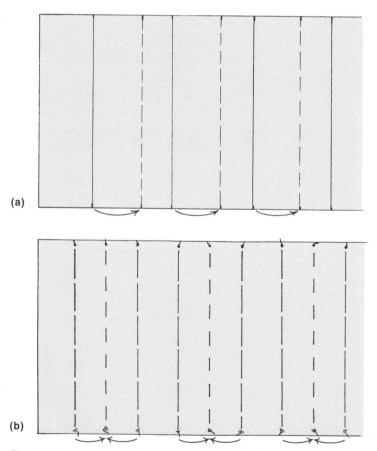

Fig. 6-5. Removable pleat markings: (a) For knife pleats—unbroken chalk lines for outer folds, broken lines for placement lines. (b) For inverted pleats—long basting stitches for fold lines, short stitches for shared placement lines.

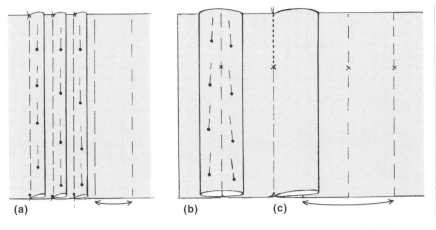

Fig. 6-6. Forming pleats on the back of the fabric: (a) Knife pleats with fold and placement lines basted together. (b) Inverted pleat centered and pinned after (c) basting the fold lines together and lowering the release point with machine stitching.

Fig. 6-7. Pleats formed on the right side of the fabric with basting holding all layers together.

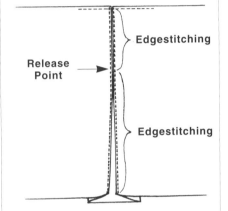

Fig. 6-8. Inverted pleat edgestitched 1/16″ (1.5mm) from the folds through three layers to lower the release point, and through two layers to crease the pleat folds permanently.

- Lightly steam press all folds that will be creased.

9. If desired, choose one of the following to edgestitch the pleat folds:

   - Starting at the top, edgestitch through two layers next to the outer fold, the inner fold, or both. (Refer to "Hemming Flat and Partial Pleats" on page 90.)
   - For pleats with edgestitched folds and release points also lowered with edgestitching: (1) Edgestitch each pleat fold, starting at the release point. (2) Edgestitch from the top to the lowered release point through all three layers, ending with the needle in the first of the previous edgestitches (Fig. 6-8).

   - Edgestitch from the top to the designated release points only.

10. Sew the pleats down across the top inside the seam allowance.

11. For all but unpressed pleats, steam press the folds into sharp creases (refer to "Pressing Flat and Partial Pleats" on page 89).

12. Hand or machine sew a single-fold flat hem into the floating edge (refer to "Hemming Flat and Partial Pleats" on page 90). Press again. Bind the top edge of the pleated fabric, or seam it to an extension (refer to "Stabilizing Gathered Stitching" on page 6 for applicable directions).

NOTES & VARIATIONS

Arrangements of flat pleats feature the repetitive, orderly organization of parallel folds that open when disturbed. Variations in pleat depth, in the spacing between pleats, and in the combining of knife, box, and inverted pleats are the design components of flat-pleat arrangements.

Groupings of knife pleats may be turned in opposite directions. Sometimes authorities define knife pleats as pleats 5⁄8″ (1.5cm) deep facing in the same direction, and pleats with a depth greater than 5⁄8″ (1.5cm) as side pleats. *Kilt pleats* are deep knife pleats with underfolds that overlap.

Pleat terminology in action may be easier to remember than pleat terminology from a diagram. From the side, push a ruler under the fold on top (the outer fold). When it is stopped by the fold hidden underneath (the inner fold), note the measurement on the ruler at the outer fold. That's pleat depth. Pleat depth, doubled, is the underfold. The spacing between pleats refers to the distance between two pleat folds on top.

When pleating, work on a surface that allows large sections of the fabric to be spread out from top to lower edge. Use a gridded cutting board to hold the fabric straight and assist when marking the pleat lines. Where lengths of fabric are joined, place the seam at the inner fold of a pleat unless the joining seam can be located on the placement line behind an inverted pleat.

Topstitching that crosses an arrangement of pleat folds controls pleat release in an unusually decorative fashion. *Pleat topstitching* patterns the area above the released pleats with a linear design that combines vertical rows of folds with horizontal rows of plain or fancy topstitching (Fig. 6-9). To prevent gapping, baste a stay underneath the pleating before topstitching. After topstitching, trim the stay where the topstitching stops.

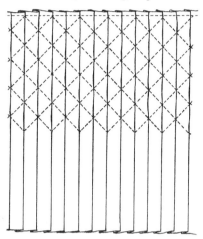

Fig. 6-9. Diagonal topstitching that lowers release points and becomes a design element in combination with the folds of the pleats.

Doubled or tripled pleating produces extravagant folded fullness at the floating edge. To double or triple a pleat, stack the underfolds, matching the layers in depth or graduating their size with the smallest on top (Fig. 6-10). Doubled or tripled pleating adds the bulk of many fabric layers to the top edge.

Underlays allow change in the fabric visible at the back of inverted pleats or in between two box pleats. An underlay is as wide as the space between two adjacent inner folds. Inserted into the fabric of the pleating, an underlay replaces the back of the underfolds removed between the inner folds (Fig. 6-11).

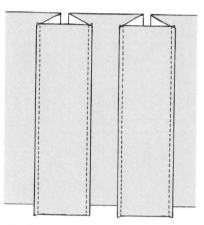

Fig. 6-11. Two inverted pleats with underlays replacing the back of the underfolds.

The *Perfect Pleater* is a simple but ingenious device that sets shallow pleats into a length of fabric without prior marking and basting. The fabric, pushed down into the spaces behind a succession of cloth-covered louvers, emerges knife or box pleated when steam pressed while in the pleater. Skipping louvers—pushing the fabric into the slot behind every second, third, or fourth louver—varies the spacing between the pleats. Although the pleaters will form continuous pleats in fabric of any length, the 11″ (28cm), 22″ (56cm), or 27″ (68.5cm) width of a pleater limits the width of the fabric it can conveniently pleat, and the pleaters restrict pleat depth to ⅜″ (1cm) or 1⅜″ (3.5cm). Within those boundaries, the Perfect Pleater is an easy-to-use and time-saving tool (Fig. 6-12).

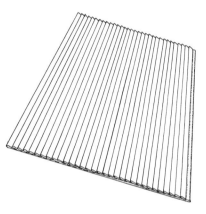

Fig. 6-12. A Perfect Pleater for knife pleats.

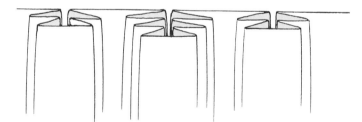

Fig. 6-10. Box pleats with the two side pleats doubled, the center tripled, and pleat depths staggered.

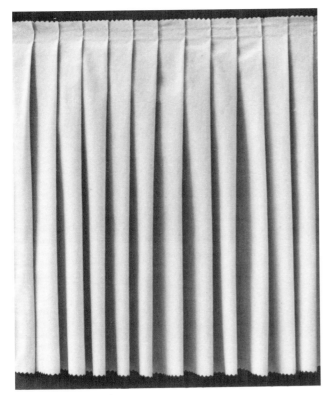

VI-1—Unpressed knife pleats.

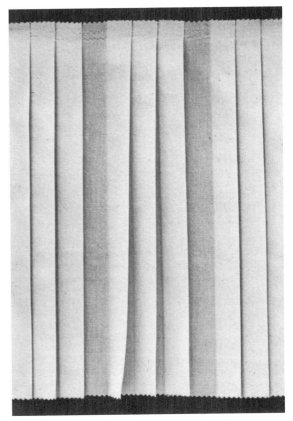

VI-2—Pressed knife pleats, clustered in groups of three.

FLAT PLEATS

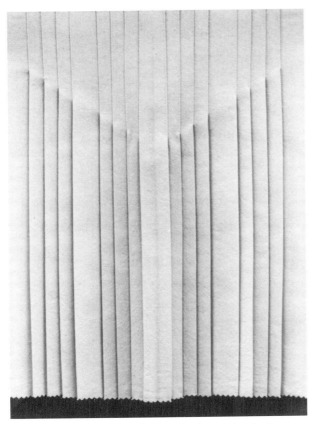

VI-3—Pressed knife pleats with lowered release points that reverse direction on either side of a central box pleat.

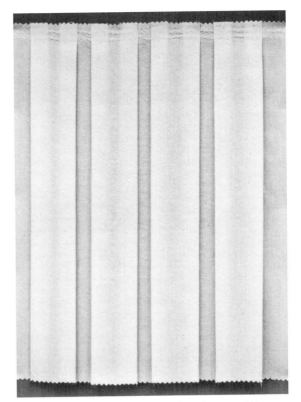

VI-4—Four box pleats edgestitched along the outer folds.

VI-5—Double-fold box pleats with the back pleats edgestitched and the front pleats unpressed.

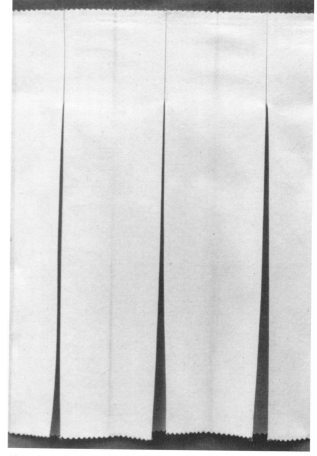

VI-6—Three inverted pleats with lowered release points and inner and outer folds edgestitched.

FLAT PLEATS

VI-7—Inverted pleats stacked three deep with all folds matching and unpressed.

VI-8—Knife pleats with lowered release points defined by top-stitched seams that cross the folds from side to side in a jagged, irregular manner.

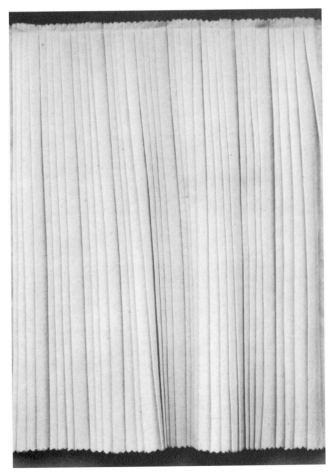

FLAT PLEATS

VI-9—Knife pleats formed on a Perfect Pleater.

PARTIAL PLEATS

—flat pleats that open below the top of the fabric with underfold layering removed above the release points. There are two kinds of partial pleats:

EXTENSION PLEATS

—**knife** or **box** pleats formed by sewing specially designed pleat sections together; **inverted** pleats formed by sewing underlays between specially designed pleat sections. Above the release points, pleat folds continue as seams.

SET-IN PLEATS

—inserts of **knife, box,** or **inverted** pleats stitched inside a segment removed from the lower portion of the fabric.

PROCEDURES

1. Draft patterns for the pleat sections:

   Knife or box extension pleats:
   Establish the following measurements to use when developing the pattern for one pleat section ((a) in Fig. 6-13):

(1) Pleat depth. (2) Space between pleats (pleat depth plus an additional amount for extra spread, if desired). (3) Length of a pleat from the top to the lower edge. (4) Length of a pleat from the top to the release point.

Inverted extension pleats:
Add a second pattern for an underlay that duplicates the underfold extensions at the sides of adjoining pleat sections ((b) in Fig. 6-13).

Set-in pleats:
(1) Draft a pattern for the shape to be cut out from the fabric. (2) Fold a length of paper, slightly longer and much wider than the cutout shape, into an arrangement of knife, box, or inverted pleats. (3) Position the cutout over the folded pleats; trace and cut on the outline. Open and pencil folding guidelines on the pleat insert pattern (Fig. 6-14). Avoid locating pleat underfolds too close to the sides of the cutout when tracing its shape on the folded pleats.

Fig. 6-14. (a) Cutout to be filled with a pleated insertion. (b) Pattern for the pleated insertion, cut from folded paper, that will be set into the cutout. Add seam allowances to final patterns.

(a)

Cutout

(b)

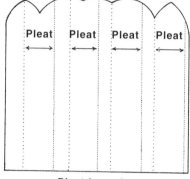

Pleat Insertion

2. Cut and sew the pleats:

   Knife or box extension pleats:
   (1) Cut as many pleat sections as required, cutting around the outline of the pattern or following a tracing of the pattern. (2) With right sides facing, sew the pleat sections together. Open and spread out. (3) Measure the depth of each pleat to assure a match when folding and turning the pleats in the desired direction. Baste each pleat through all layers. (4) After clipping seam allowances to the release points, press the seam allowances above the pleat extensions open and flat. Lightly press the pleat folds (Fig. 6-15).

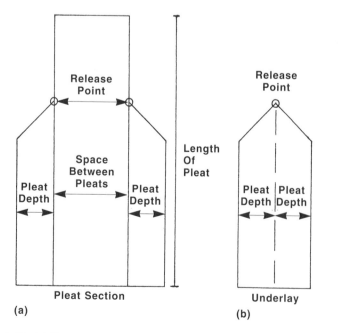

(a)

(b)

Fig. 6-13. (a) Pattern for a partial-pleat section. The side extensions are knife- or box-pleat underfolds. (b) Pattern for an inverted pleat underlay that duplicates a side extension, doubled. Add seam allowances to final patterns.

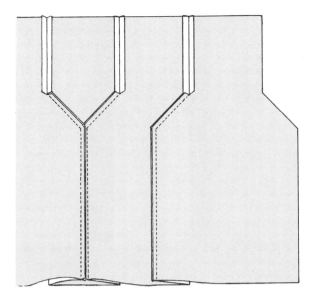

Fig. 6-15. Extension pleat sections seamed together, turned to form a box pleat on the left and a knife pleat on the right.

3. Secure the loose underlayers of extension pleats by topstitching through all layers from the release point to the edge of the underlayer extensions (Fig. 6-18).

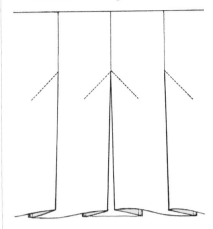

Fig. 6-18. Extension pleats finished with topstitching that secures the angled pleat extensions underneath.

4. Steam press creases into the pleats (refer to "Pressing Flat and Partial Pleats" on page 89).

5. Hand or machine sew a single-fold flat hem into the floating edge. (For extension pleats, refer to "Hemming Flat and Partial Pleats" on page 90.) Press again.

NOTES & VARIATIONS

Unpressed folds are an option for an application of set-in pleating. Other options include edgestitching the folds before insertion, layering the pleats two or three deep for additional fullness, and forming the pleats on a Perfect Pleater (as described on page 94). The shaping at the top of a cutout for set-in pleats can be curved, straight, or pointed, and the cutout can be wide enough for one pleat or a succession of pleats.

A stay that secures the loose tops of extensions and underlays invisibly, replaces the topstitched stabilizing which is visible in front. To prepare for stabilizing with a stay, draft patterns with underfold extensions that are straight instead of angled at the top.

Inverted extension pleats:

(1) Cut as many pleat sections and underlays as needed, cutting around the outlines of the patterns or following tracings of the patterns. (2) With right sides facing, sew two pleat sections together from the top to the release point. (3) Stitch an underlay between the two adjoining pleat extensions, sewing each side from the release point to the lower edge. (4) Press the seam allowances above the release point open and flat. Center the underlay beneath the converging pleat folds, baste, and press lightly (Fig. 6-16).

Set-in pleats:

(1) With a fabric-safe marker, trace the seamline (the outline of the cutout) onto the right side of the fabric. Cut out a seam-allowance-distance inside the seamline. Clip the seam allowance, turn it to the back on the seamline, and baste. (2) Cut out the pleat insert following an outline traced on the fabric. Mark the fold and placement lines. Fold, baste, and lightly press the pleats. (3) Pin and baste the pleated insertion behind the prepared opening. Edgestitch next to the fold around the opening (Fig. 6-17).

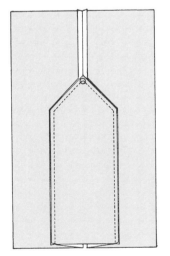

Fig. 6-16. Underlay seamed between two adjoining pleat extensions with inverted pleat folds centered in front.

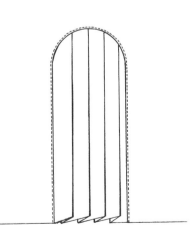

Fig. 6-17. Knife-pleated insert set into a cutout (see Fig. 6-14 for the patterns).

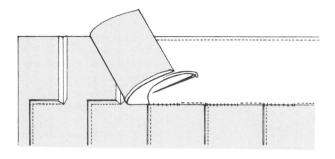

Fig. 6-19. Extension pleats stabilized with a stay, hand stitched to the underlayer extensions. To prevent stitches from showing in front, move between extensions with running stitches in the stay.

From lining material, cut a stay that will cover the joined pleat sections from side to side and top to release points, plus seam allowances. Turn and press the seam allowance on one long edge of the stay to the back. Working with the extension-pleated fabric wrong side up, baste the unturned edge of the stay to the top of the joined sections. Handstitch the turned lower edge of the stay to the seam allowances at the top of each pleat extension (Fig. 6-19).

Extension pleating is generally crisply pressed because the seams in the underfolds already function as if creased.

PARTIAL PLEATS

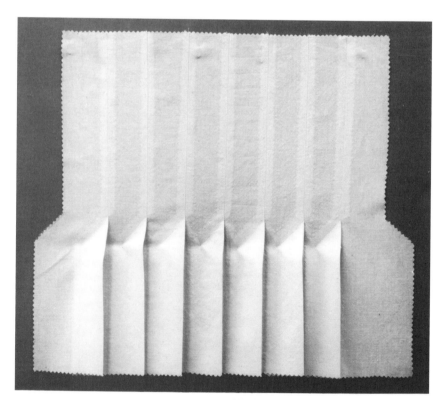

VI-10—Eight pleat sections with extensions that create seven knife pleats. If the sides of the sample were seamed together, another pleat would be formed.

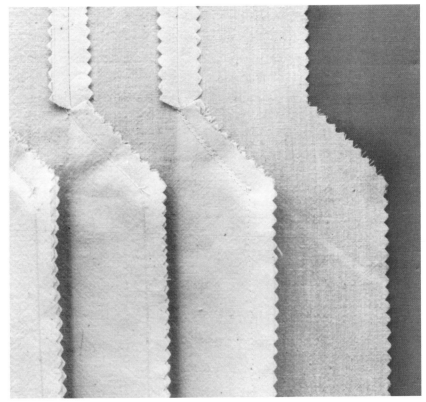

VI-11—The back of the knife pleating sample showing its seamed construction.

VI-12—Six pleat sections combined and folded into five inverted extension pleats backed with underlays. A continuous topstitched seam stabilizes the tops of the extensions.

VI-13—The back of the
inverted pleat sample
showing the underlays.

PARTIAL PLEATS

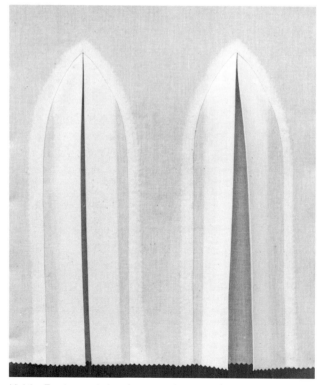

VI-14—Two inverted pleat inserts set into curved-top cutouts.

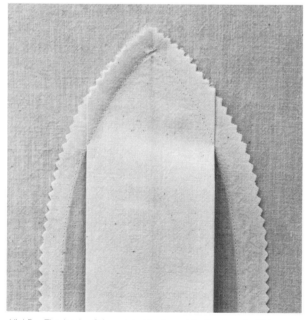

VI-15—The back of the set-in pleat sample. Pleat underfolds are
caught into the construction seam only at the top.

PROJECTING PLEATS

—folds lifted from the surface of the fabric and structured at the top, or head, into rolled arrangements that stand out from the fabric itself. Below the pleated, self-finished heading, the fabric falls in deep, regular, rounded folds to the floating edge. There are seven basic types of projecting pleats:

DOUBLED BOX PLEATS

—pleat allowances subdivided at the head into two tiers of outward facing folds.

SINGLE BOX PLEATS

—have a single pair of outward facing folds.

THREE-FOLD AND FOUR-FOLD PINCH (FRENCH) PLEATS

—pleat allowances subdivided at the head into fanlike arrangements of three or four smaller pleats.

ROLLBACK PINCH PLEATS

—have an additional turn on the outer pleats.

PIPE ORGAN PLEATS

—pleat allowances stuffed into cylinders at the head.

ROLLBACK CARTRIDGE PLEATS

—pleat allowances subdivided at the head into two smaller pleats covered with a rolled box pleat.

CARTRIDGE PLEATS

—pleat allowances arched over and seamed to a stay.

(Refer to "Pleat Profiles" on page 90.)

PROCEDURES FOR BOX, PINCH, PIPE ORGAN, AND ROLLBACK CARTRIDGE PLEATS

(Procedures for Cartridge Pleats start on page 106.)

1. Decide which type of pleat is the most appropriate for the project. Set a target measurement for the pleated fabric to match at the top.

2. Calculate the amount of fabric required for the pleating:

   a. Set a pleat allowance measurement for each pleat. As indicated by the individual instructions that follow, pleat allowance requirements vary with the type of pleat, and are influenced by the nature of the fabric, the scale of the application, and preference. Larger pleat allowances produce higher projections in the pleats that structure the heading, and release deeper, more spacious folds into the fabric below. Using a strip of fabric, pin test pleats constructed from different measurements before setting an amount for the pleat allowance.

   b. Establish a measurement for the space between two pleats, and decide how many pleats will be appropriate for the target measurement, using either of these methods:

      ◆ Pick a number for the pleats the target measurement can be expected to accommodate. Divide the target measurement by that arbitrary figure to get the space between pleats.

      ◆ Using a strip of fabric, pin test to find the most appropriate spacing for the pleats. Divide the target measurement by the space between pleats, adjusting the figure as needed to get a round number for the pleats that will fit within the target measurement.

   With projecting pleats, the width of the space between pleats as indicated by a number is deceptive. In actuality, the structured pleat folds spread out into the space between pleat seams to a greater or lesser degree, making the visible space between pleats appear smaller than the allotted measurement.

   c. Estimate the fabric requirement:

   pleat allowance
   x number of pleats
   = total pleat allowance

   target measurement
   + total pleat allowance
   = Estimated Fabric Requirement

   d. Add the necessary length, including measurements for the heading turnback and a hem, to the width of the pleated fabric requirement. Cut the fabric.

3. Prepare the heading and pleat allowances:

   a. Make a doubled pleat heading by turning the top of the fabric to the back; press. The pleat heading should be at least half-the-pleat-allowance deep. If needed to brace the structure of the particular pleat, stiffen the heading with interfacing.

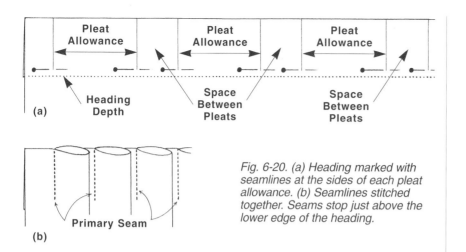

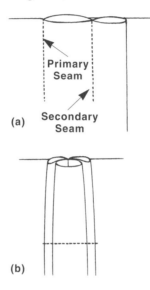

Single box pleat:
(1) For each pleat, flatten the pleat allowance, centering the fold over the primary seam.
(2) Topstitch straight across the base of the pleat where the primary seam ends, or tack the underfolds to the fabric behind with invisible stitches (Fig. 6-22).

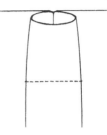

Fig. 6-20. (a) Heading marked with seamlines at the sides of each pleat allowance. (b) Seamlines stitched together. Seams stop just above the lower edge of the heading.

b. On the right side of the fabric, divide the heading across the top into pleat allowances separated by spaces between pleats. Marking with disappearing pen, chalk, a sliver of soap, or pins, measure and indicate the seamlines on either side of each pleat allowance with a line that extends straight down from the top to a point slightly above the lower edge of the pleat heading ((a) in Fig. 6-20).

c. With the right side outside, fold, pin match, and sew the seamlines on either side of each pleat allowance together. These primary seams establish the folds that will be structured into projecting pleats ((b) in Fig. 6-20).

4. Structure the pleat allowances:

Doubled box pleat:
(1) For each pleat, subdivide the pleat allowance into two parts with a secondary seam as long as, and parallel to, the primary pleat allowance seam. Equalize the parts or make the part next to the fold smaller than the part next to the seam.
(2) Collapse the pleat allowance, centering the secondary seam over the primary seam. At the top edge, tack the two seams together. (3) Centering the loose pleat allowance, secure with topstitching straight across all folds where the primary seam ends, or

tack the pleat underfolds with hand stitching invisible on top (Fig. 6-21).

Fig. 6-21. To form a doubled box pleat: (a) Stitch the secondary seam. (b) Re-fold the pleat allowance, centering seams. Topstitch across the base of the pleating.

Fig. 6-22. Single box pleat.

Three-fold pinch pleat:
(1) For each pleat, divide the folded pleat allowance into thirds, marking the third next to the fold with a row of pins that parallel the fold. (2) Pushing the pin-seam down to the primary seam, open and flare the pleat allowance below the pin-seam out to the sides, making three equal pleats, two on either side of the center pleat defined by the pins. At the top edge, tack the folded arrangement to the primary seam. Finger crease the folds of the three pleats before removing the pins. (3) At the base, secure the folding with machine stitching that crosses straight out from the end of the primary seam to the matched pleat folds, or hand tack the folds together (Fig. 6-23).

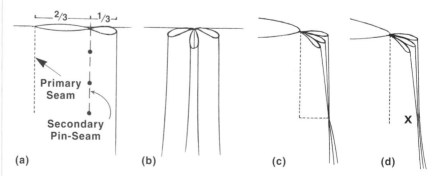

Fig. 6-23. To form a three-fold pinch pleat: (a) Establish a pin-seam. (b) Re-fold into three pleats and remove the pins. (c) Topstitch across the base of the pleating, or (d) hand tack at the x position.

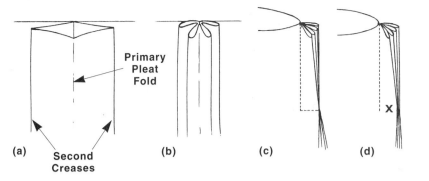

Fig. 6-24. To form a four-fold pinch pleat: (a) Center and flatten the pleat fold. Crease at the sides. (b) Turn the side creases inside to the primary seam, making four pleats. (c) Topstitch across the base of the pleating, or (d) hand tack at the x position.

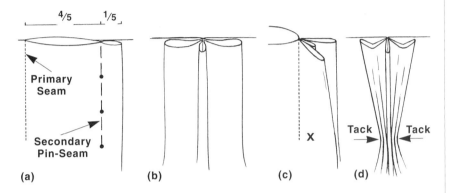

Fig. 6-25. To form a rollback pinch pleat: (a) Establish a pin-seam. (b) Re-fold into three unequal pleats, and remove the pins. (c) Tack all pleats at the x position and (d) tack the side folds to the primary seam at the base of the pleat.

Four-fold pinch pleat:
(1) For each pleat, flatten the pleat allowance, pin matching the center fold to the primary seam. Finger crease the two new folds created at the sides.
(2) Push each of the side creases inward to the primary seam, creating four equal-sized pleats. At the top edge, tack the three inside folds to the primary seam. Finger press the new outer folds.
(3) Secure as described for three-fold pinch pleats (Fig. 6-24).

Rollback pinch pleat:
(1) For each pleat, divide the folded pleat allowance into fifths. Mark the fifth next to the fold with a row of pins that parallel the fold. (2) Push the pin-seam down to the primary seam, spreading the pleat allowances between the pin-seam and the primary seam out to the sides. The pleats formed at the sides will be twice as deep as the

center pleat. At the top edge, tack the two inner folds to the primary seam. Finger crease all folds before removing the pins. (3) At the base, hand tack through all three pleats, catching the fold of the smaller pleat in the center. (4) Turning the folds of the side pleats down to the heading, tack each outer fold to the primary seam at the base of the pleat (Fig. 6-25).

Pipe organ pleat:
For each pleat, convert the pleat allowance into a cylinder by stuffing it with polyester fiberfill, or insert into the pleat allowance a roll of crinoline or other stiffening as long as the heading. To stabilize, tack the cylinder, at the top and base, to the fabric behind it for a short distance on both sides of the primary seam (Fig. 6-26).

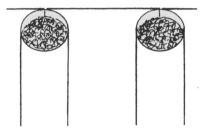

Fig. 6-26. Two pipe organ pleats.

Rollback cartridge pleat:
(1) For each pleat, finger crease the fold of the pleat allowance. Dividing the pleat allowance into thirds, mark the third closest to the primary seam with a row of pins that parallel the seam. (2) Holding the pleat allowance below the pin-seam upright, collapse the pleat allowance above the pin-seam, matching the finger-creased fold to the pin-seam. Finger press the new folds at the sides. (3) Remove the pins, releasing two interior pleats that form a support for the wide exterior pleat which curves around the interior pleats to the back. On both sides, slipstitch the outer folds of the surrounding pleat to the primary seam from the base to the top (Fig. 6-27).

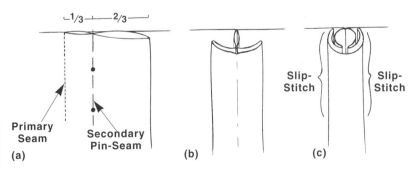

Fig. 6-27. To form a rollback cartridge pleat: (a) Establish a secondary pin-seam, and (b) stand the pleat while re-folding the upper pleat allowance. (c) Remove the pins, roll the surface pleat around to the heading, and slipstitch the outer folds beside the primary seam.

5. Finish the floating edge of the pleated fabric with a double- or single-fold hem. To hang, attach the pleated heading with suitable hardware to a rod or rigid surface, or slip a fabric extension underneath the heading and attach the base of each pleat to the fabric with invisible hand tacks.

NOTES & VARIATIONS

Comparing the projecting pleats, single box pleats are the least dimensional with doubled box pleats next to the least in dimensionality. Pipe organ pleats, particularly if closely spaced, present the most sculptural appearance. Rollback cartridge pleats, which look like small, neat, pipe organ pleats, conceal the surprising fullness they release inside a deceptively neat, plain heading. Doubled box pleats can be tripled for lavish fullness in the hanging fabric below the heading. Two or more types of projecting pleats can be combined in the same heading to vary the structured appearance at the top and the depth of the folds released by the different pleats.

Pinch pleats may be reduced to two folds or expanded to five folds. The pleat allowance can be subdivided into as many folds as the fabric will sustain, and the folds can be varied in depth as well. Stuffing changes three-fold pinch pleats into *goblet pleats.* With the two inner folds between the pleats unattached at the top, polyester fiberfill forces the pleats that rise from the pinch-pleated base to open up like a bowl (Fig. 6-28).

Doubled box, pinch, and pipe organ pleats may need additional tacking at the top, beside the primary seam, to prevent the pleat formation from flopping forward or wobbling from side to side. Finger pressing and steaming the structured folds settles their arrangement.

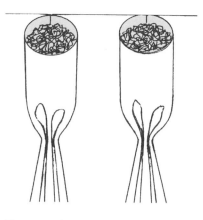

Fig. 6-28. Goblet pleats.

Unlike flat pleats with their pressed or unpressed options, projecting pleats fall unpressed from heading to floating edge. To control the spread of the folds, tug and stroke the folds between heading and hem into flowing regularity. Hold the arrangement temporarily with one or several strips of fabric loosely wrapped and pinned around the hanging fabric. Steam. When the fabric is cool and dry, remove the strips.

To be inconspicuous, seams joining lengths of fabric should fall on or next to the primary pleat allowance seams.

PROCEDURES FOR CARTRIDGE PLEATS

(For Rollback Cartridge Pleats, refer to "Procedures" on page 103.)

1. Set a target measurement for the fabric to match after it is pleated. Cut a strip of paper as long as the target measurement, or scale the target measurement down on graph paper. Divide it into spaces which limit the width of each cartridge pleat after structuring, separated by spaces between the pleats.

2. Calculate the amount of fabric required for the number of cartridge pleats planned for the target measurement:

   a. To determine the appropriate curving projection for each pleat, test by pinning a strip of fabric or paper to a pleat-width space. The length of the arched fabric between the pins is the pleat allowance measurement.

   b. Estimate the fabric requirement:

   pleat allowance measurement
   − width of pleat
   = difference per pleat

   difference per pleat
   x number of pleats
   = extra fabric needed for pleats

   extra fabric for pleats
   + target measurement
   = Pleated Fabric Requirement

   c. Add the necessary length, plus allowances for a heading turnback and a hem, to the width required for pleating, and cut the fabric.

3. Cut a narrow stay of stiff or stiffened fabric as long as the target measurement and as wide as the chosen depth of the pleat heading. On the pleating fabric, make a heading as wide as the stay by turning the top to the back; press. Stiffen the turnback with interfacing if the fabric needs support.

4. Outline a pleat-allowance space on the fabric for every pleat-width space on the stay, separated by spaces between pleats that match. With disappearing pen, chalk or a sliver of soap, mark perpendicular seamlines on the stay. Draw perpendicular stitching lines across the top of the fabric, stopping each line above the lower edge of the turnback (use an L-square or follow the fabric's grain) ((a) and (b) in Fig. 6-29).

5. Aligning the top edge of the fabric to the top edge of the stay, pin match each stitching line on the fabric to its corresponding line on the stay and sew together ((c) in Fig. 6-29).

6. Finish the floating edge of the pleated fabric with a double- or single-fold hem. To hang, attach the stay with suitable hardware to a rod or hard surface.

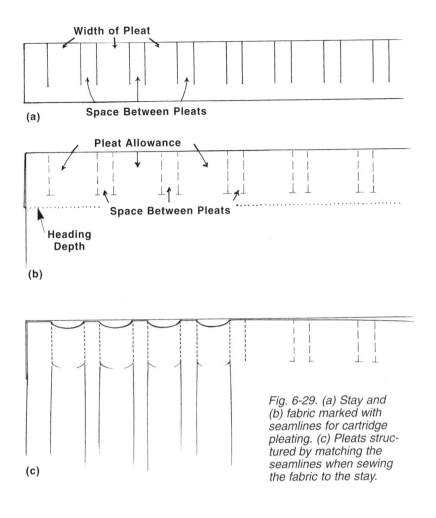

Width of Pleat

(a)

Space Between Pleats

Pleat Allowance

Space Between Pleats

Heading Depth

(b)

(c)

Fig. 6-29. (a) Stay and (b) fabric marked with seamlines for cartridge pleating. (c) Pleats structured by matching the seamlines when sewing the fabric to the stay.

NOTES & VARIATIONS

Instead of a stay aligned to the top of the pleated fabric, fabric may be pleated to the lower edge of fabric that extends above the pleated fabric. Because cartridge pleats can be designed to project a little or a lot, the stay is usually visible behind cartridge pleats. Stay fabric should be decorative as well as functional.

Soft cartridge pleats fall into a drape instead of projecting outward, exposing the stay above the loose folds of the drape. To drape, the fabric allowance per pleat must be much wider than the space allotted per pleat on the stay. The stay should be appropriately deep and decorative.

For *continuous cartridge pleats*, the space between pleats shrinks to the width of one seam that cuts a sharp valley between the bulging curves on either side ((b) in Fig. 6-30).

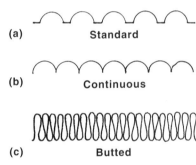

(a) **Standard**

(b) **Continuous**

(c) **Butted**

Fig. 6-30. Cartridge pleat profiles from the top.

Butted cartridge pleats seem like a misfit in the cartridge category. The pleats are formed on gauged gathering threads (refer to "Gathering Methods" on page 4),

creating a packed mass of folds with a thick edge ((c) in Fig. 6-30). Butted cartridge pleating requires a lot of fabric. To calculate the amount, pleat a test strip of fabric as directed in the following, and attach to a certain number of inches on a stay; measure the pleated fabric needed to cover that distance and compute accordingly. To form the pleats, (1) mark the top of the fabric on the heading turnback with two uniform rows of equidistantly spaced dots. The distance between the dots sets the depth of the pleats. (2) Run sturdy thread in and out of the dots in each row (Fig. 6-31) and gather, packing the fabric into densely layered folds. (3) Standing the pleats on end over a stiff, sturdy stay, tack the turn of each fold to the stay, first along the top, then at the bottom (Fig. 6-32).

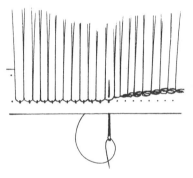

Fig. 6-32. Tacking the tops of butted-cartridge-pleat folds to a stay before tacking the bottom of each fold to the stay.

To equalize the spacing of the folds, mark the stay with two dotted guidelines, a dot for every stitch into a fold. Cartridge pleated fabric butted to a stay projects outward before falling in lavish folds to the floating edge. The silhouette is bell-like when the stay encircles a solid form. If the fabric is very stiff and the pleats fairly deep, butted cartridge pleats are self-supporting and stand upright or extend like a shelf from the stay.

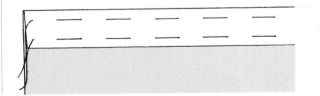

Fig. 6-31. Butted cartridge pleats are formed when rows of large, equally spaced hand stitches are gathered.

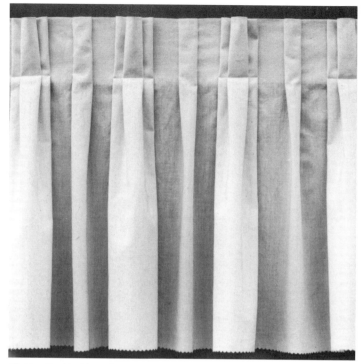

VI-16—Doubled box pleats alternating with single box pleats.

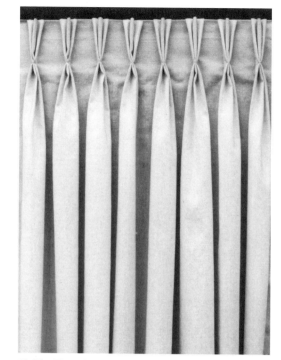

VI-17—Three-fold pinch pleats that fan out above over-the-fold tacking stitches at the base.

PROJECTING PLEATS

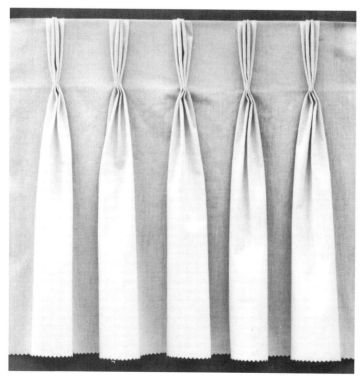

VI-18—Four-fold pinch pleats.

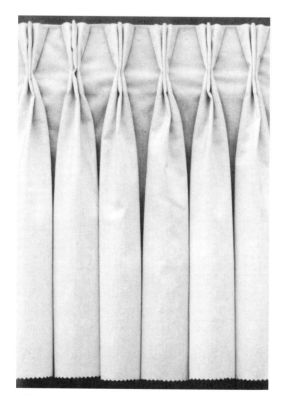

VI-19—The wing-like turnbacks of rollback pinch pleats require more fabric than three-fold pinch pleats, and the fabric falls in wider, deeper columns below the heading.

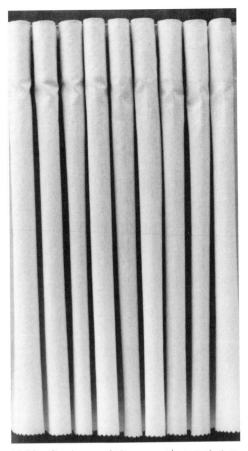

VI-20—Closely spaced pipe organ pleats project as much as the diameter of the tubular shapes in the heading.

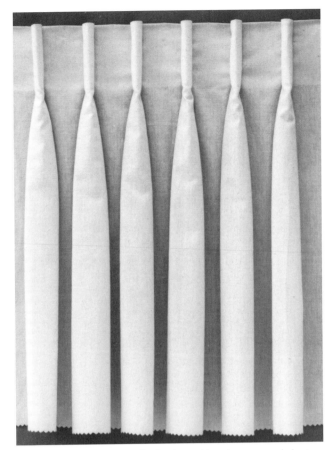

VI-21—The tidy structuring of rollback cartridge pleats, a rounded exterior concealing supportive pleats inside, releases unexpected fullness.

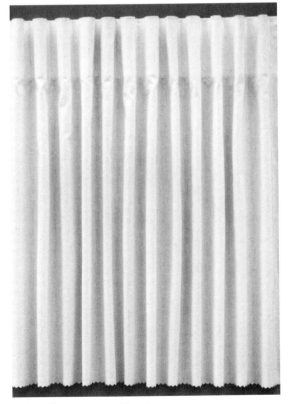

VI-22—Continuous cartridge pleats.

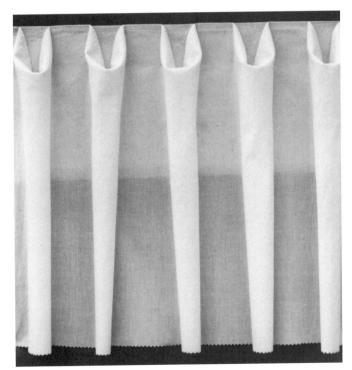

VI-23—Soft cartridge pleats sewn to a stay visible behind the draped arrangement of folds that head each pleat.

PROJECTING
PLEATS

VI-24—Butted cartridge pleating ⅜" (1cm) thick at the stitched edge shows the bell-like silhouette characteristic of this method of attachment.

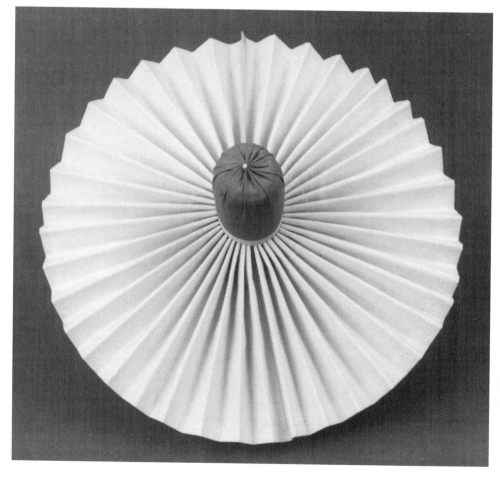

VI-25—Muslin stiffened with iron-on interfacing and cartridge-pleated on gauged stitching with one thick edge butted and tacked to a stay. The self-supporting folds project straight out when the construction is lifted above the surface.

ACCORDION PLEATS

—fabric folded alternately in and out with even spaces between the parallel folds, creating projecting pleats that resemble the bellows of an accordion in action and appearance. There are two kinds of accordion pleats:

HAND-FORMED ACCORDION PLEATS

folds spaced at least ½″ (1.3cm) apart, marked, formed, and steam pressed by hand.

MINI-ACCORDION PLEATING

folds spaced no more than ⅛″ (3mm) apart, mechanically formed on a smocking pleater.

(Refer to "Pleat Profiles" on page 90.)

PROCEDURES FOR HAND-FORMED ACCORDION PLEATS

(For Mini-accordion Pleating, refer to page 112.)

1. Set a target measurement for the fabric to match after it is pleated. Pick a pleat depth wider than ½″ (1.3cm).

2. Cover all or a portion of the target measurement with a strip of paper folded alternately in and out, equating the distance between folds to pleat depth. Spread the pleats equally as much as desired. Measure the test strip, and estimate the amount of fabric required for the pleating accordingly. Add the necessary length, plus allowances for a heading turnback and hem, to the width required for the pleating. Cut the fabric.

3. Head the top of the fabric with a turnback and hem the lower edge of the fabric.

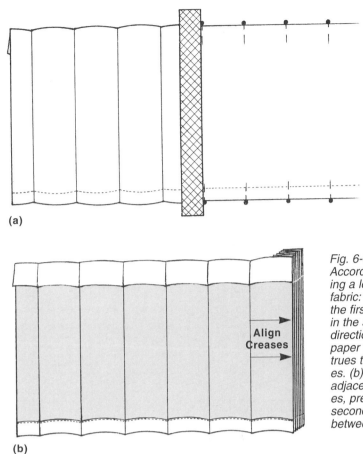

Fig. 6-33. Accordion-pleating a length of fabric: (a) Press the first creases in the same direction over a paper strip that trues the creases. (b) Matching adjacent creases, press the second folds in between.

4. Measure and mark a succession of fold indicators spaced *two pleat depths* apart. Insert pins perpendicular to the edges at the top and bottom of each fold position. On woven fabric, the fold lines in between should parallel the straightgrain.

5. Fold and press the pleats, using the straight edge of a stiff strip of paper cut longer than pleat length:

   a. Press the inward folds first. With the fabric right side up, align the edge of the pressing guide to, and between, the pins marking the first fold. Remove the pins, turn the fabric over the edge of the guide, and crease the fold with a steam iron and pressure. Open the fabric, move the guide to align with the pins marking the next fold, turn in the same direction as before, and press that crease. Continue setting every pin-marked fold in the same manner ((a) in Fig. 6-33).

   b. Turning the fabric over, form new folds between the previous folds. Matching the first two folds, steam press the new fold created in the middle. Align the third fold to the second fold, creating another new fold; steam press. Continue aligning folds and pressing, stacking pleat over pleat, until all in-and-out folds are sharply creased ((b) in Fig. 6-33).

6. Control the pleating:

   ♦ Stabilized but movable at the top: Hang the pleats from a rod, dowel, or cord inserted through loops or rings attached to the top between folds, or pushed through holes that perforate the heading between folds.

- Stabilized permanently at the top: Cut a narrow stay as long as the target measurement. Divide the stay into spaces, each as wide as the desired spread of one accordion pleat. Mark the spaces with perpendicular pins or lines. Matching the top of the pleated fabric to the top of the stay, tack each inward/back crease to the stay at the top edge, or machine stitch over each back crease, stopping before reaching the lower edge of the stay (Fig. 6-34).

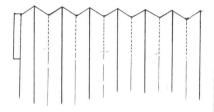

Fig. 6-34. Accordion-pleat spread controlled at the top when back creases are topstitched to a stay.

To hang the pleating, attach the stay with appropriate means to a firm surface. An option: Use the lower edge of a piece of fabric that extends above and beyond the pleated fabric as a stay.

NOTES & VARIATIONS

Steam creasing accordion pleats ½″ (1.3cm) or smaller in depth is tricky and trying to impossible: The greater the depth, the easier to pleat. During and after pressing, accordion pleats stack up one on top of the next with back creases and front creases aligned. To minimize the pressing complications that develop as the extra layers of fabric at the turnback and hem build up, use the selvedge for a hem, serge the edge or edges, or fold and sew the hem after pressing and re-set the pleats. Folds may be permanently fixed with edgestitching.

Accordion-pleated fabric is flexible in the direction of the folds, but the in-and-out folding imparts stiffness to the fabric in the other direction. The pleating "breaks" if forced to bend across the folds. If a stiff fabric is accordion-pleated, the result is close to inflexible across the creases. For self-supporting applications that stand or project, stiffen the unpleated fabric with starch or an iron-on interfacing. Butt the thick edge of the pleating to a stay and tack each fold to the stay with equidistant spacing (refer to "Butted Cartridge Pleats" on page 107).

Accordion pleating, tightly bundled at the heading or at a cross-section in the center, opens and spreads out to a floating edge or edges. To fan accordion pleats, run strong thread or cord run through the folds, pack the pleats into a solid mass, and fasten the ends securely (Fig. 6-35).

Locate a seam joining two pieces of fabric on a back crease.

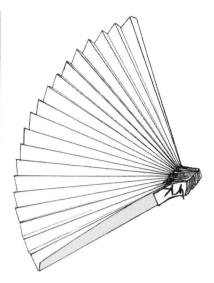

Fig. 6-35. Accordion pleats, tightly compressed at the heading, spread out to a curving edge.

PROCEDURES FOR MINI-ACCORDION PLEATING

1. Using a smocking pleater, pleat the fabric. (Refer to "Using a Smocking Pleater" on page 126.)

2. Stretch out the fabric on the pleating threads and press to smooth out the edge to be hemmed. Hem the floating edge, and the top edge, if required by the stabilizing method:

- For a pleated edge, fold on the final row of pleating thread. Make a tiny double-fold hem that fits inside the space before the next row of pleating thread (Fig. 6-36). Re-pleat the fabric on its threads, including the hem.

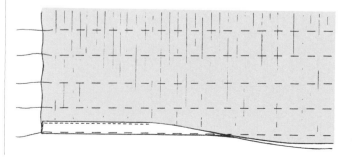

Fig. 6-36. Machine-stitching a hem into fabric spread out after mini-accordion pleating on a smocking pleater. The fabric will be re-pleated after hemming.

- For a frilly edge, hem just outside the last row of pleating thread. For a ruffled edge, hem a distance away from the final row of pleating thread. Re-pleat the fabric on its threads, excluding the hemmed edge. (For finishing options, refer to "Edge Finishing for Ruffles" on page 43.)

3. Pushing all the pleats together tightly on the pleating threads, steam with an iron held slightly above the surface of the pleats. Allow to cool and dry thoroughly before continuing.

4. To stabilize the pleats across the top, sew to plain fabric cut as long as the target measurement:

a. Cover the pleated seam allowance with an extension or binding. (1) Cut a temporary stabilizer, a strip of paper or a tear-away product. Spreading the pleats out evenly on the pleating threads, pin the edge of the pleating over the stabilizer. (2) Cut plain fabric for an extension or a binding. Matching edges, cover the pleating with the plain fabric, right sides together, and machine-stitch, squashing the pleats between the layers. The pleating will appear gathered at the top. (3) Remove the temporary stabilizer from the seam. An option: Use fabric for a permanent stabilizer. (Refer to "Stabilizing Gathered Fabric" on page 6.)

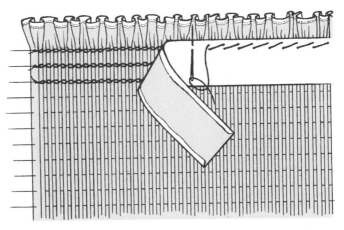

Fig. 6-37. Hand stitching a stay over the back of mini-accordion pleats stabilized with three rows of backstitching.

b. Expose the finished edge of the pleating, attaching it to an extension or stay slipped underneath the final rows of pleating thread.

- To retain the regularity and three-dimensionality of the pleats: (1) Turn the pleating over to the back. (2) Following the last row of pleating thread, catch the tip of each rib with a backstitch. Add one or more rows of backstitching. The tension on the thread controls the spread of the pleats, allowing some flexibility for adjustment. (3) Pin the extension or stay over the backstitched area and handstitch to the backstitching threads Fig. 6-37).

- An alternative method: Slip an extension or stay under the frilled or ruffled edge. Following the final row or rows of pleating thread, baste the pleating to the fabric underneath. Edge-stitch a length of ribbon or tape over the basted pleating, crushing the pleats under the stitching.

5. Remove the pleating threads.

NOTES & VARIATIONS

Estimate the fabric requirement for mini-accordion pleating as three to four times the target measurement, the general rule-of-thumb for applications that involve the smocking pleater.

Like hand-formed accordion pleats, fabric pleated with the three-to-four-plus pleats per inch that a smocking pleater produces acquires stiffness up and down the pleating, although it is more supple across the folds than fabric with deeper accordion pleats. Unlike hand-formed accordion pleats, which can usually be re-set by hand pressing, the folds of mechanically-formed mini-accordion pleating aren't renewable when use, dampness, or laundering destroys their definition.

Fabric can be mini-accordion pleated by hand following a grid of dots marked on the fabric, and the pleating can be stabilized across the top with a heading of decorative stitching worked from the front (refer to "English Smocking" on page 129).

VI-26—Hand-formed, sharply creased pleats spread out on a rod inserted through holes punched in the heading. The arrangement is movable and temporary.

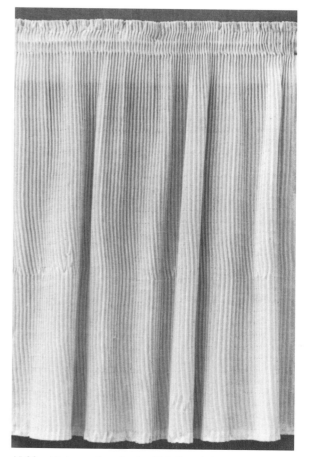

VI-28—Mini-accordion pleating ⅛". (3mm) deep, produced on a 24-needle Sally Stanley pleater, stabilized across the top with three rows of backstitching and a stay. The slight interruption in the regularity of the ribs about two-thirds of the way down reveals the mismatching that occurred when the fabric was pleated a second time to extend its length.

VI-27—Arrangement of hand-formed pleats permanently attached to a stay with a short seam over each back fold.

WRINKLED PLEATING

—irregular ridges and grooves set by bunching and scrunching damp fabric, securing it tightly, and letting it dry. There are two types of wrinkled pleating:

BROOMSTICK PLEATING

—damp fabric gathered up, rolled around a cylinder, and bound to hold until dry. When unwrapped, the wrinkled folds are one-directional.

(Refer to "Pleat Profiles" on page 90.)

CONTORTION PLEATING

—damp fabric twisted into a rope, coiled, knotted, and dried in a microwave oven. When opened out, the wrinkled folds are multi-directional.

PROCEDURES

1. Sew a narrow hem into one or more edges of the fabric, if and where the application requires.

2. Prepare the fabric for wrinkled pleating:

   Broomstick pleating:
   a. Gather the opposite sides of the fabric with large running stitches, pushing the gathers together tightly. Very wide, lengthy fabric may need interior rows of gathering as well.
   b. Wet the fabric thoroughly, wring it out, and roll in towelling to absorb excess moisture.
   c. Stretching between the gathering, roll the fabric around a broomstick, a length of plastic pipe, or any other sturdy, moisture- and rust-proof cylinder. Tie the fabric to the cylinder at the top, then bind with fabric strips 1" (2.5cm) to 2" (5cm) wide. Wind the strips tightly around and around until the rolled fabric is entirely covered (Fig. 6-38).

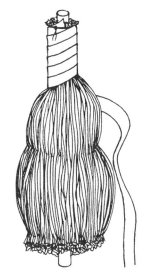

Fig. 6-38. Winding a strip of moist fabric tightly around a broomstick.

Optional preparation: Stretching and bunching, roll the damp, gathered fabric around itself. Shove it into the leg of a nylon stocking and bind at close intervals with nylon-stocking strips or cord.

Contortion pleating:
a. Immerse the fabric in water, wring it out, and roll in towelling to absorb excess moisture.
b. Fold the damp fabric into layers, turning it over repeatedly in one direction. Clamp one end of the narrow, layered fabric in a vise or ask another person to hold the end. Stretching the fabric taut, twist it so tightly that it spirals around itself when the ends are brought together.

Continue twisting and entwining until the fabric is contorted into a spherical knot (Fig. 6-39). Bind the knot with string or tie it inside the toe of a sock.

3. Dry the prepared fabric:
   ◆ In a warm, dry, well-ventilated atmosphere. Broomstick pleating will dry in a few days without mildewing, but air drying is not recommended for contortion pleating, unless only a small amount of fabric is involved.
   ◆ With consecutive cycles in an automatic dryer. Broomstick pleating prepared in a nylon stocking (the optional method) may be automatically dried. For contortion pleating, drying jump-started automatically can be completed in the air.
   ◆ A minute at a time in a microwave oven, until the moisture inside the oven evaporates. Microwave heat dries both broomstick pleating in a nylon stocking and contortion pleating thoroughly and quickly, but requires care and attention.

4. Untie, unwrap, open up, and spread out the fabric when it is completely dry. Remove any gathering threads.

Fig. 6-39. (a) Thick cord of tightly twisted, damp fabric, looped before releasing in the center to curl around itself. (b) Coiled, knotted ball of fabric.

5. To stabilize broomstick pleating, sew to plain fabric cut to a target measurement. Stabilize contortion pleating if and as the application requires. (For applicable directions, refer to "Mini-accordion Pleats," #4, on page 113.)

NOTES & VARIATIONS

Soft, thin, natural-fiber fabric, such as China silk and lightweight cotton, reacts best to wrinkled pleating methods. The amount of fabric required varies with the wrinkled fullness appropriate for the application, but three times the target dimension is a workable minimum.

After pleating, the sides of broomstick-pleated fabric are more or less straight, but the sides of contortion-pleated fabric will be as irregular and uneven as the interior pleating. The broomstick method produces ridges and creases that cross the fabric from one side to the other in a directional manner. With contortion pleating, one direction predominates—the direction that coincides with the original folded layering—but subsequent twists, bends, and knots introduce deflections and interruptions, resulting in a more complex configuration of wrinkles.

When dry and unwrapped, wrinkled pleating retains the imprint of its preparation. Modifications change the result. For example, when preparing damp fabric for broomstick pleating: Enlarge or reduce the size of the gathering stitches and increase the number of rows. Instead of thread-gathering, scrunch the fabric with fingers. Turn and twist while rolling the fabric around a cylinder. Leave sections of the rolled fabric unbound. Instead of binding, tie the rolled fabric at intervals with cord that bites into the bundled material. Add tying tightly with cord to the layering and twisting procedures of contortion-pleating preparation.

For maintenance, hand gather and twist broomstick or contortion pleated fabric into a roll and store inside a nylon stocking, or coil loosely and keep in a drawer or box. Moisture and heavy pressure will undo the creases of wrinkled pleating, but the pleats can be reset by repeating the preparation and drying procedures. The results will vary with every repetition.

VI-29—The variable, rugged pleating resulting from the broomstick process.

WRINKLED PLEATING

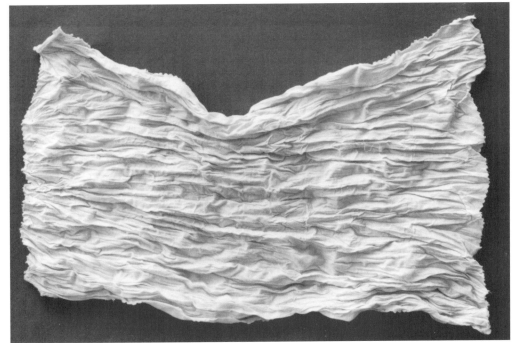

VI-30—Contortion-pleated square of muslin.

DOUBLE-CONTROLLED PLEATS

—pleats confined at both ends, with folds loose in the center. The stabilized pleat arrangements can be turned in any direction.

PROCEDURES

1. Select a pleat type that suits the purpose. Form the pleats on opposite sides of the fabric, following the procedures described for that type of pleating. (Partial pleats are inappropriate for double-controlled pleating.)

2. Stabilize the pleats at both ends. Either underline/stay the pleated fabric completely before binding or sewing the edges to another piece of fabric, or stabilize without underlining beforehand, as appropriate for the fabric and the requirements of the particular installation. Stabilizing and the type of pleating at the edges, in combination, affect the appearance of the folds in the middle:

Smooth folds:
Folds flow undisturbed between matching arrangements on opposite ends when the pleated fabric is stretched over a stiff underlining or held taut between stationary edges.

Turned folds:
Stretched out over a stiff underlining or held taut between stationary edges, the folds of flat pleats change direction when laid down in one direction on one edge and reversed on the opposite edge, or when pleat depth and the number of pleats, or the type of pleat, changes on each side.

Draped or puffed folds:
The folds in the center either drape of their own weight or rise up into puffs when the stabilized distance between the ends of the pleats is less than the length of the pleats. To drape, the folds of large-scale applications must be horizontal

with the vertical sides where the pleats originate stabilized rigidly. The folds of small-scale applications puff—with the cooperation of firm fabric—when basted to a full stay before finished application.

3. Settle the arrangement of folds by steaming with an iron moved slowly above the surface of the fabric. Allow to cool and dry before moving.

NOTES & VARIATIONS

There are two double-controlled pleating variations that require patterns: (1) Pleats formed on adjacent edges of the fabric, forcing the folds to converge at an angle in the center. (2) Pleats formed on one edge of the fabric with folds that dwindle out to nothing at the opposite edge. The pleating patterns are developed from target patterns that are slashed at pleat locations, following the intended direction of the folds from edge to edge, and spread to allow for a pleat underfold at every slash. (For directions adaptable to pleating, refer to "Single Edge Gathering," Notes and Variations, on page 12; and "Opposite-Edge Gathering," Notes and Variations, on page 17.) Pressed folds, accordion pleats, and wrinkled pleating are inappropriate for these variations.

The folds of *crossed pleats* puff up when they collide in the center. Using flat pleats, reduce each side of a square or triangle of fabric with the folds, then baste the pleated edges to a stay which is a smaller version of the square or triangle. The puffed fabric may be left as is, or it can be tacked down into a maze-like swirl of crests and grooves with furrowing (refer to "Furrowing" on page 9), or stuffed into biscuits (refer to "Biscuits" on page 258). **Variation:** Use pinch pleats for fabric reduction and topstitch the pleated edges to a foundation.

The folds of *fixed pleats* are stabilized into permanent, immovable arrangements. Without floating edges or loose folds, fixing pushes pleats in non-pleat-like directions. For exam-

ple: Fusing an arrangement of flat pleats to iron-on interfacing converts the pleat folds into unstitched, fake tucks. When the back-folds of cartridge or hand-formed accordion pleats are machine-stitched to a firm stay from one end to the other, the pleating enables self-supporting, sculptural constructions. Mini-accordion, broomstick, or contortion pleating, secured to a stay with tiny hand stitches spaced out and buried in the corrugations, suggest smocking. While stabilizing, shift the direction of the folds or wrinkles and vary the spacing between the ridges.

Needle-formed pleating is unique, a continuous arrangement of soft, flowing, rounded folds shaped with a needle and secured with hand stitches. Without previous markings or other preparation, baste the top edge of the pleating fabric to the top edge of a much smaller, stiffened stay. Working from the top down, pull up a fold with the point of the needle, hold with pins if necessary, and ground the fold to the stay with tiny, separated backstitches. Push and pull up another fold beneath the first fold; secure. Continuing row by row, maneuver subtle irregularities into the folds. Limit the length and change the drift of the folds with needle action and stitches. As pleat formation proceeds, the securing stitches recede into the grooves between succeeding rows. Needle-formed pleating may be adjusted to cover a stay with a modelled surface.

Solid mini-accordion pleating restructures fabric into a different, firm textile as thick as its pleat composition, with a finely ribbed surface texture. To build the solid pleating, accumulate pleater-formed pleats into a packed mass on the pleating threads. Extend the accumulation with more pleated lengths of fabric until it reaches the target measurement. The pleating threads, with ends tied together in pairs, remain in the textile for security. For additional texture, run fabric with wrinkles through the pleater. (Refer to "Using a Smocking Pleater" on page 126.)

VI-31—Unpressed knife pleats
that diminish and disappear
at the opposite edge.

VI-32—Unpressed knife pleats that
start and stop on adjacent edges.

VI-33—Knife pleats
stayed at both ends look
like horizontal louvers.

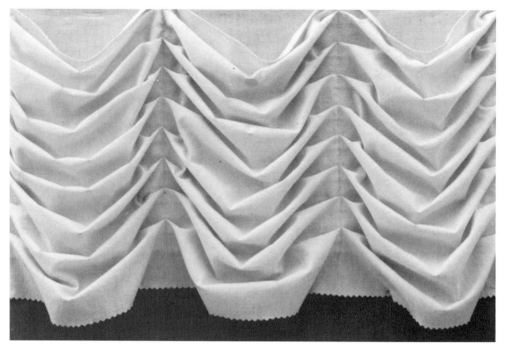

VI-34—Draped knife pleats.

DOUBLE-CONTROLLED PLEATS

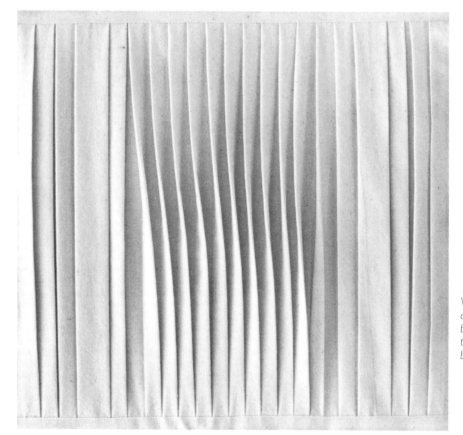

VI-35—Arrangement of inverted, box, and knife pleats vertically stretched between strips of fabric. The folds of the knife pleats in the center ripple because they change direction.

VI-36—Arrangements of knife, box and inverted pleats set into cutouts.

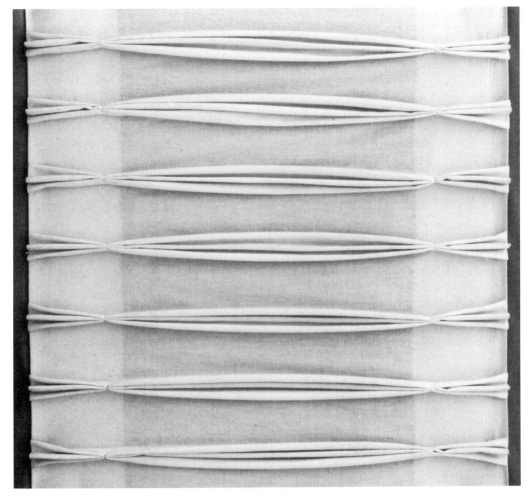

VI-37—Three-fold pinch pleats constructed and stayed at opposite ends of the fabric.

DOUBLE-CONTROLLED PLEATS

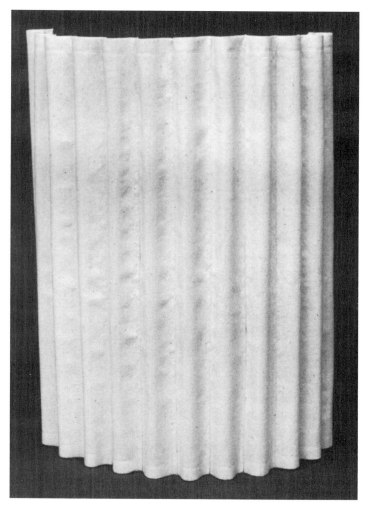

VI-38—Continuous cartridge pleats, seamed to a stiff stay from end to end, form a self-supporting, column-like structure.

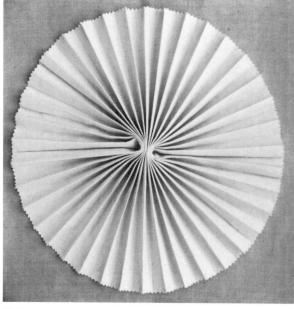

VI-39—Accordion pleats, firmly tacked through the center, spread out into a circle when the side pleats are seamed together. At the perimeter, the inside creases are secured to a stiff stay with tiny tacks.

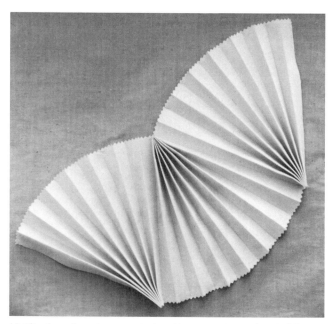

VI-40—Accordion pleats manipulated into a continuous band of fans and secured with tiny tacks to a stiff stay.

VI-42—Patchwork with crossed-pleat elements. The three largest squares and the rectangles are furrowed in the center.

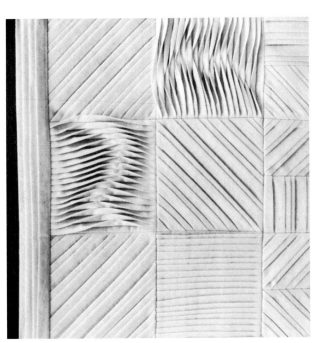

VI-41—Pleats formed on a Perfect Pleater, backed with iron-on interfacing, cut into squares, and assembled patchwork-style into a block. In two of the squares, the fold of each pleat, snagged by a stitch, was pulled back and tacked to the base of the pleat behind.

DOUBLE-CONTROLLED PLEATS

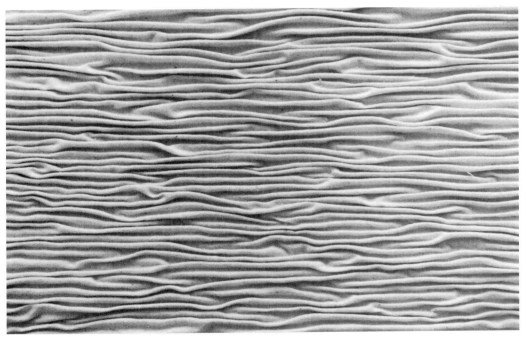

VI-43—Needle-formed pleating that looks like water rippled by a breeze.

*S*mocking secures and adjusts the folds of a finely pleated field of fabric with hand stitching. When the stitching is visible, it superimposes an ornamental thread design on the surface of the pleats, organizing and bending the underlying folds into cellular formations. When the stitching is invisible, the fluctuating movement of the folds becomes the decorative focus. Smocked fabric acquires the same thickness as its pleats, and loses flexibility across the pleating.

SMOCKING

7 Smocking

Note: This chapter begins with BASICS, indicated by a gray band located underneath the relevant columns.

SMOCKING BASICS

FABRIC REQUIRED FOR SMOCKING

Traditional wisdom advises three to four times the target width of the smocking as a basis for estimating the amount of fabric required for a smocking project. That's a fairly reliable guide for thin fabric prepared for English smocking on a pleater or hand pleated on dot-pickup stitches spaced ¼″ (6mm) apart, but inadequate when other factors apply.

- **Type of fabric.** When pleating a thicker fabric such as wool, each pleat fold will be more expansive, consequently, the pleating will match the target measurement with less fabric than the pleating of a fabric like batiste pleat-gathered on an identical grid.

- **Pleat depth.** Deeper pleats require more fabric for the same target measurement than shallow pleats. Widening the spacing of the dot grid followed for hand stitched pleating increases the fabric estimate. Stitched on the same grid, dot-in dot-out gathering requires more fabric than dot-pickup gathering.

- **Pleat density.** Smocking that features the patterning of massed pleat folds requires more fabric than other types of pleating. Shirred Italian smocking uses the most fabric, with contoured Italian smocking a close second, followed by English smocking.

• **Smocking construction.** While stitching an English or direct smocking design, a tight rather than light tension on the thread moves the tubes closer, increasing the amount of fabric needed. Direct smocking generally uses less fabric than English smocking worked on a similar grid. English, direct, and shirred Italian smocking shrink slightly along the length of the pleats. The multi-directional pull of North American and contoured Italian stitching reduces measurements in both directions significantly.

To estimate the fabric requirement accurately, make a small sample worked on a square of the chosen fabric, using the grid and stitching planned for the smocking project. Measure the fabric in both directions before and after smocking. Use those measurements in the following equation:

[sample measurement before smocking
÷ sample measurement after smocking]
x target measurement
= Fabric Requirement

For North American and contoured Italian smocking, use the equation for fabric length and then for fabric width.

When the fabric to be smocked requires piecing to extend its length, locate the seam inside a pleat channel. Because seams that cross the pleats add seam allowance bulk to the folds, the bulging band caused by the extra thickness will be obvious unless offset by pleat spread elsewhere.

USING A SMOCKING PLEATER

Mini-accordion pleating is the foundation for English smocking. Smockers have a choice: Form the pleats on rows of gauged hand stitches or use a smocking pleater, a nifty, hand-operated appliance that pleats yards of fabric quickly and easily.

Pleaters have gears that mesh together when turned, and a long, straight row of delicate needles that stitch thread through the pleats formed by the gears. Basic operation is simple. Thread the needles with sewing thread about 4″ (10cm) longer than the length of the fabric to be pleated. Tape the ends of the thread to the surface in front of the pleater. After trimming the selvedges, roll the fabric around a dowel. Insert the dowel inside the endplate openings on the pleater. Standing behind the pleater, turn the handle to move the fabric through the gears and onto the needles. When the needles fill up with pleats, push the pleats gently onto the threads. Continue until all the fabric has been pleated and pushed onto the threads. Cut the threads next to the needles to free the pleated fabric.

Smocking pleaters produce uniform mini-accordion pleats, at least ⅛″ (3mm) deep, that vary fractionally between three-plus to four-plus pleats for every inch of fabric, depending on the manufacturer of the pleater. Also depending on the manufacturer, the fabric width a pleater accepts varies from 5½″ (14cm) to 12″ (30.5cm). A second run through the pleater doubles the width of the fabric that can be pleated. Open and spread the pleated portion of the fabric on its

threads (knot one end of the threads) and steam press flat. Re-thread the pleater needles, but leave one needle at one end unthreaded. Re-roll the fabric on the dowel. Insert the dowel inside the endplate openings, matching the final row of pleating thread on the fabric to the position of the unthreaded needle on the pleater. Guide the fabric through the pleater with the unthreaded needle following the last line of pleating thread and, if possible, piercing the same holes. Cut the threads holding the fabric to the needles. Re-pleat the flattened fabric on its threads.

Unthreaded groups of needles create strips of gathering between bands of pleats. After pleating, spread the fabric on the threads and iron any folds out of the strips meant for gathering; re-pleat. For experimental pleating textures, send the fabric through the pleater deliberately rumpled or pulled off-grain.

When one piece of fabric isn't long enough, pleat the pieces separately. Matching the pleating threads, sew the pre-pleated sections together, locating the seam in a channel between two pleat tubes. Tie the pleating threads across the seam, push the pleats together and proceed.

When one piece of fabric has a seam down the middle, the seam allowance should be no wider than the distance between two adjacent needles on the pleater. During pleating, guide the seam to move between two needles. Angled or curved seam allowances must be basted down. The extra layer of fabric, and fabric that's too thick and heavy, tends to break needles.

Smocking Embroidery Stitches

For English and direct smocking, embroidery stitches have a functional as well as decorative purpose. After the pleating threads have been removed, the stitches hold the folds of English smocking together. For direct smocking, the stitches not only hold the folds together, they create the folds.

Each stitch also has a distinctive role to play in the overall decorative design on the surface of the pleating and in the patterning of the folds underneath. The stitches connect the tips of consecutive folds, or tubes, in a manner that arranges the tubes into cells between the rows of stitching. Every stitch follows its own path. (The arrows in the diagrams indicate starting points for a row made up of one particular stitch.)

The needle action of backstitching is the basis for most smocking embroidery stitches. For every backstitch in a straight row of *outline* stitching, hold the thread either below and under the tip of the needle as it emerges from a fold, or above and under the needle (Fig. 7-1).

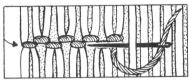

Fig. 7-1. Outline stitch.

Two abutted rows of outline stitching, with thread direction reversed for the second row, produce the *mock chain* stitch (Fig. 7-2).

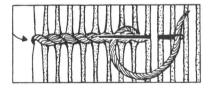

Fig. 7-2. Mock chain stitch.

Cable stitching is an outline-stitching variation. For each successive backstitch, alternate the thread position between below-and-under and above-and-under the tip of the needle (Fig. 7-3).

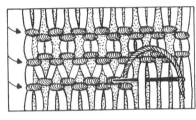

Fig. 7-3. Cable stitch.

Spaced rows of *double cable* stitching change the alignment of the tubes in one way if the stitches in successive rows are identical, and in another way if the stitches in successive rows alternate between up and down (Fig. 7-4).

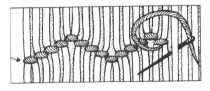

Fig. 7-4. Double cable stitch.

A cable-and-outline composite that moves diagonally up and down in close steps outlines a *wave*. On the way up, the thread remains below the angled needle; on the way down, the thread stays above the angled needle (Fig. 7-5).

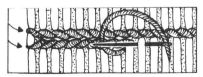

Fig. 7-5. Wave stitch.

Two rows of wave stitching, identical but reversed to meet at the end of a wave, combine into the *trellis* stitch (Fig. 7-6).

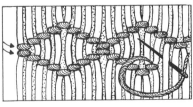

Fig. 7-6. Trellis stitch.

For *diamond* stitching, the needle alternates between moving up and across two tubes for a backstitch and moving down and across two tubes for a backstitch, with a cable-type anchoring stitch in between. Diamond stitching requires two rows of identical but reversed stitching that meet at every other cabled anchoring stitch (Fig. 7-7).

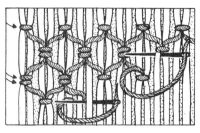

Fig. 7-7. Diamond stitch.

Double rows of honeycomb, surface honeycomb, and Vandyke stitching reorganize the tubes of the pleating into a substructure of diamond-shaped cells. Because the needle moves the thread up and down inside the tubes, one row of *honeycomb* stitching looks like two staggered rows of tiny, doubled, independent stitches that bind adjacent tubes together (Fig. 7-8).

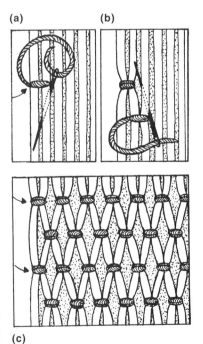

Fig. 7-8. (a) Moving down inside a tube. (b) Stitching two tubes together, and moving up (c) to create rows of honeycomb stitches.

For *surface honeycomb*, the thread wraps over the tube when moving up and down between the stitches that bind two tubes together (Fig. 7-9).

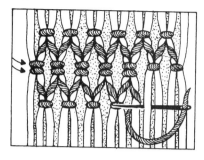

Fig. 7-9. Surface honeycomb stitch.

Like surface honeycomb, thread for *Vandyke* stitching wraps over the same tube as it moves up and down between binding stitches, but, unlike honeycomb, Vandyke is sewn from right to left. The binding stitches pick up two tubes with one stitch (Fig. 7-10).

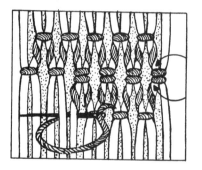

Fig. 7-10. Vandyke stitch.

Work *feather* stitching over horizontal pleating tubes. Picking up two tubes in a stitch, zigzag back and forth from right to left with the thread for each stitch forming a loop under the tip of the diagonally-pointed needle (Fig. 7-11).

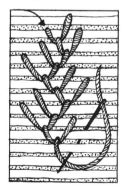

Fig. 7-11. Feather stitch.

Spool (Fig. 7-12) and *cable flowerettes* (Fig. 7-13) are spot stitches. Both bind tubes together in isolated locations.

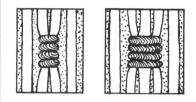

Fig. 7-12. Spool stitches.

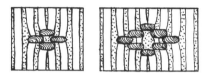

Fig. 7-13. Cable flowerette stitches.

MANAGING THE SMOCKING-PLEATED EDGE

The method used to finish and stabilize a smocking-pleated edge either flattens the tubes under a machine-sewn seam or preserves the stand of the tubes with hand stitching. Whether flattened or standing, maintain the arrangement of folds established by the final row of smocked stitching in the finishing of the edge.

CRUSHED & FLATTENED PLEATS

Leave a row of pleating thread inside the seam allowance of English-smocked pleating. For other kinds of smocking, prepare the edge with a row of gathering stitches or basting inside the seam allowance. With right sides together, sew the smocked edge to smooth fabric cut to size for an extension or binding. Locate the machine-stitched seam in between the pleating, gathering, or basting thread and the final row of smocked stitching (Fig. 7-14).

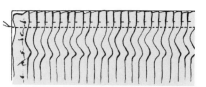

Fig. 7-14. Pleated edge of shallow English smocking machine-stitched to a fabric extension, right sides together. A row of gathering stitches remains inside the seam allowance.

Opened up, the smooth fabric extends beyond the smocking. Opened and turned over the seam allowances to the back, a strip of smooth fabric binds the edge. (Refer to "Stabilizing Gathered Stitching" on pages 6–7 for directions applicable to a smocked edge.)

To end the smocked pleating with a ruffle, locate the final row of smocking stitches a distance from the edge and hem the ruffle (refer to "Edge Finishing for Ruffles" on page 43). At the base of the ruffle, hold the smocking-pleated arrangement with a row of gathering or basting stitches. Slipping a fabric extension or narrow tape underneath the edge, topstitch with straight or decorative stitching over the stitches holding the arrangement (Fig. 7-15).

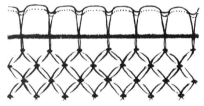

Fig. 7-15. Loose folds at the hemmed edge of directly-smocked honeycomb pleating, satin-stitched at the base to a fabric extension, open into a pleated ruffle.

An alternative: Stabilize the ruffle with narrow tape or ribbon topstitched across its base.

When the smocked fabric is thin and lightweight and the pleats shallow, even solid pleating can be crushed and flattened under a machined seam as previously described. But if the fabric is heavier and the pleating deep, or if the pleating was engineered with contoured Italian smocking, a standing edge is the better choice.

STANDING PLEATS

Before smocking the fabric, make a tiny double-fold hem in the edge next to the final row of stitches. After smocking, arrange the hemmed edge over a flat fabric extension and tack the groove of each pleat to the fabric underneath, continuing the pleat spacing established by the smocking (Fig. 7-16).

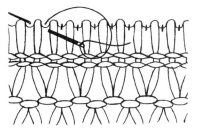

Fig. 7-16. To maintain the stand and arrangement of smocked pleats, hand stitch the turned-and-pleated edge over a fabric extension, catching the groove of each pleat with a tiny stitch.

To stabilize a ruffled edge and also keep the stand of the pleats, hand stitch a fabric extension or tape to the pleat folds in back, behind the final row or rows of smocking stitches (refer to Fig. 6-37 on page 113).

The erratic stitching paths of contoured Italian smocking force the edges of the pleated fabric into uneven curves. Either retain the shaped edge for its decorative effect, or start and finish the stitching far enough from the fabric's edge to allow for a straight seam or a straight trim.

ENGLISH SMOCKING

—a two-step procedure that involves structuring the fabric into shallow pleats with rows of stitching, and regulating the tubes of the pleats with rows of embroidery. Elasticity is an English smocking attribute.

PROCEDURES

1. To estimate the amount of fabric required, refer to "Fabric Required for Smocking" on page 125.

2. Pleat the fabric mechanically (refer to "Using a Smocking Pleater" on page 126). Skip steps #3, #4, and #5, continue with step #6.

3. To pleat the fabric by hand, mark the wrong side of the fabric with a grid of dots aligned to the straightgrain of woven fabric. The spacing between the dots in a row determines the depth of the pleating tubes. Choose an appropriate dot-marking method from the following:

   ◆ Place a smocking dot transfer sheet over the fabric. Transfer the dots to the fabric with an iron.

   ◆ Insert dressmaker's carbon between the fabric and a paper pattern of the dots. Use point pressure over each dot to transfer impressions to the fabric.

   ◆ Baste or pin a dotted tissue paper overlay to the fabric. (To stitch with a tissue paper overlay, handle overlay and fabric as one and gently tear the paper away when the stitching is done.)

   ◆ Use a fabric-safe marking tool to mark the fabric directly with a grid of dots:

      • Place a dot pattern under the fabric, using a light box for enhanced visibility, and trace.

      • Trace through a dot stencil placed on top of the fabric ((a) in Fig. 7-17).

      • Mark dots as directed by a saw-toothed template ((b) in Fig. 7-17).

      • Space and mark dots according to the measurements indicated on an L-shaped ruler aligned, row by row, to the straightgrain of woven fabric.

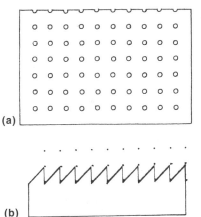

Fig. 7-17. (a) Stencil and (b) saw-toothed template used to mark fabric with rows of smocking dots.

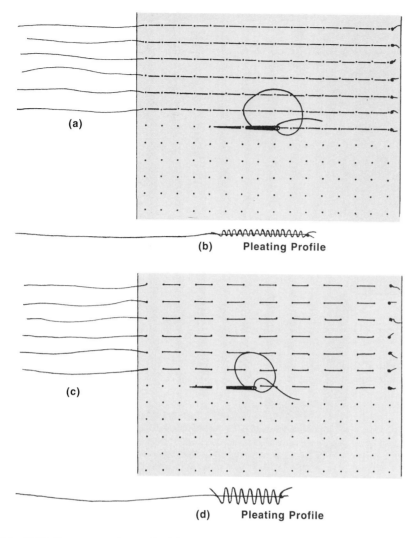

(a)

(b) Pleating Profile

(c)

(d) Pleating Profile

Fig. 7-18. To prepare dot-marked fabric for pleating, hand sew (a) with dot-pick-up stitching or (c) dot-in dot-out stitching. From identical grids, (b) dot-pickup produces two times as many shallow tubes as (d) dot-in dot-out with its deeper tubes.

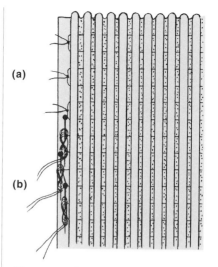

(a)

(b)

Fig. 7-19. After pleating, secure the seams (a) by tying adjacent threads together, or (b) winding pairs of threads, figure-8 style, around pins stuck into the fabric beside the last tube.

4. Hand sew each row of dots with running stitches using strong thread cut as long as the row plus 3″ (7.5cm), knotted at one end. The stitches in each row should line up exactly under the stitches of the row above.

   ♦ To make pleats with tubes one-half as deep as the space between dots, pick up each dot with a tiny stitch. The threads of dot-pickup gathering catch the tubes of the pleating at the base ((a) and (b) in Fig. 7-18).

   ♦ To make pleats with tubes as deep as the space between dots, push the needle into one dot and out of the next dot.

The threads of dot-in dot-out gathering, run through the center of the pleating tubes ((c) and (d) in Fig. 7-18).

5. Grasping the ends of the threads, push the fabric into itself, gathering it into pleats.

6. Pack the pleats together tightly, stretching lengthwise to straighten the tubes, and steam with an iron held just above the fabric's surface. After the pleating is cool and dry, spread the tubes of the pleats apart just enough to reveal the gathering threads between the tubes. Secure the loose threads at the ends of the seams, in pairs, by tying or winding around pins (Fig. 7-19).

7. With the pleated foundation right side up, arrange rows of ornamental and stabilizing embroidery stitches over the tubes. Use the gathering threads to gauge distance and keep the rows straight. Pass the needle through the peak of each succeeding tube as the particular embroidery stitch directs, maintaining a steady tension on the thread (refer to "Smocking Embroidery Stitches" on page 127). Follow a stitching pattern:

   ♦ Prepare a design on graph paper. Bisect the printed vertical lines, which represent the pleating tubes, with broken horizontal lines spaced out to indicate the gathering threads. Using another color or colors, outline the paths followed by the various stitches as they cross the tubes, drawing short, curvy lines to indicate the lay of the thread between stitches (Fig. 7-20). When stitching, count the tubes to copy the design. To center a balanced design on the pleating, baste the center tube, and tubes at counted intervals on each side, with colored thread.

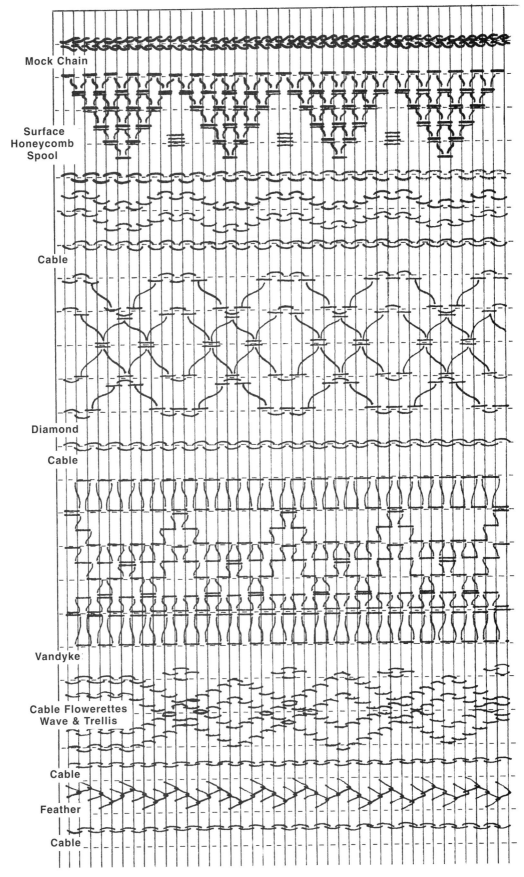

Mock Chain

Surface
Honeycomb
Spool

Cable

Diamond

Cable

Vandyke

Cable Flowerettes
Wave & Trellis

Cable

Feather

Cable

Fig. 7-20.
Traditional
English smock-
ing pattern with
ornamental
bands devel-
oped from com-
binations of
embroidery
stitches. Note
that tube-stabi-
lizing rows of
outline (mock
chain) or cable
stitching begin
and end the
design.

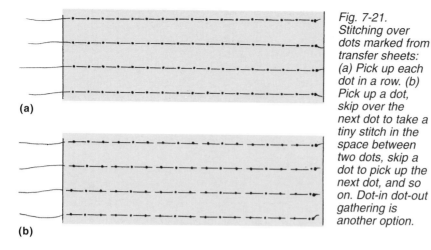

(a)

(b)

Fig. 7-21. Stitching over dots marked from transfer sheets: (a) Pick up each dot in a row. (b) Pick up a dot, skip over the next dot to take a tiny stitch in the space between two dots, skip a dot to pick up the next dot, and so on. Dot-in dot-out gathering is another option.

- ◆ Improvise a design while embroidering, using a variety of stitches.

8. Stretching gently to emphasize the structuring of the tubes, pin the edges of the smocking to a padded surface. Set with steam, moving the iron just above the fabric, and allow to cool and dry before moving. Remove all gathering threads.

9. For finishing options, refer to "Managing the Smocking-Pleated Edge" on page 128.

NOTES & VARIATIONS

Manufacturers determine the depth of the shallow pleats that smocking pleaters and dot transfer sheets produce. But in the real world of variables, the interpretation of "shallow pleat" should be relative to fabric and application. With hand-calibrated dot patterns and hand-sewn gathering stitches, pleat depth can be adjusted to suit any conditions. The distance between the rows of gathering stitches can be related to stabilizing the tubes sufficiently and having enough guidelines for the embroidery design. Dot-in dot-out stitching produces pleats with deeper tubes that are better stabilized because thread runs through the middle of the pleats.

The dots printed on transfer sheets reflect a rectangular grid with a ratio of 2 across to 3 down. To gather as if the dot grid were squared, a 3 to 3 ratio, and produce fewer and deeper pleats, stitch from dot to space to dot rather than the usual dot to dot (Fig. 7-21). Skip three or more rows of dots when stitching to introduce a band of irregular gathering into the repeats of orderly pleating.

Marking dots on the fabric is dispensable under two circumstances: (1) With evenly patterned ginghams, plaids, stripes, and spotted designs, follow a grid dictated by the design when stitching. (2) When the weave of the fabric to be smocked is pronounced, count threads in the weave to regulate the length of the stitches and the space between rows.

Because of its elasticity, a strip of English-smocked fabric can be steam set to curve slightly, but, for smocking meant to curve deeply or encircle—and remain flat—start the curving at the beginning. Cut the fabric on a curve and adjust the smocking dots to radiate outward from the row of dots around the inside curve. Slash a dot pattern marked on paper or a transfer sheet between rows of dots; spread the slashed pattern over the fabric, opening the slashes and increasing the distance between the dots from the inside to the outside curve (Fig. 7-22). Use the most elastic embroidery stitches—large wave, diamond, honeycomb, Vandyke—for the rows of smocking on the outside curve, saving outline and cable, the firmer stitches, for the inside edge.

Fabric smocked in the English manner is as thick as the depth of the pleats, although it loses some height when the pleats are spread. The smocked fabric remains flexible in the direction of the tubes, but resists such flexibility in the opposite direction. Allover smocking produces an ornamental textile. Partial smocking also manages fullness, releasing the fabric into spreading folds where the smocking stops.

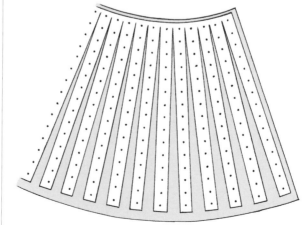

Fig. 7-22. Dot pattern slashed between the rows of dots up to the dots on the top row, and spread out equally at the cuts to adapt to curving fabric.

Traditional designs for smocking embroidery are formal, repetitive, and symmetrical, and sometimes include pictorial motifs and patches of solid stitching within the fretted bands that cross the pleats. Six-strand cotton embroidery floss which can be split into finer floss by removing strands, is generally used to stitch the designs.

Experimental smocking pushes the conventions of classic English smocking. It flaunts uneven pleating, inventive embroidery applications, unexpected thread textures, eccentric furrowed and cellular formations, and self-supporting constructions. The deviations from standard techniques that experimentalists exploit include gathering on irregular grids (Fig. 7-23), asymmetric embroidery stitch patterning, unusual embroidery stitches and stitch combinations, multiple tubes caught into a stitch, unequal and exaggerated carry-over distance between stitches, overlapping stitches, variable thread tensions, loose threads on the surface, objects attached with stitching, and so on.

With *reverse smocking,* the wavy profiles of the pleat tubes, controlled by invisible smocking stitches, are the decorative attraction. Reverse smocking is English smocking wrong side up. The smocking is worked on the back of the pleats. Each stitch and stitch combination produces a different effect on the movement of the pleats in front. (Honeycomb stitching, which requires thread passed underneath the fabric, is unsuitable for reverse smocking. Use surface honeycomb instead.) Reverse smocking and right-side smocking can be combined in the same piece.

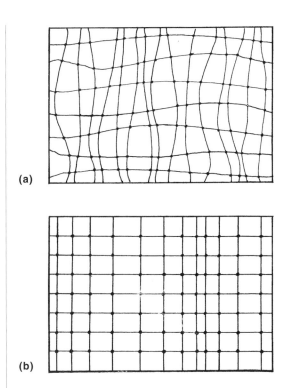

(a)

(b)

Fig. 7-23.
Experimental dot grids that gather into pleatings with uneven surface textures on dot-pickup stitching: (a) Randomly drawn grid. (b) Unevenly spaced grid.

Interior smocking is a variation of English smocking that doesn't seem like smocking at all. The pleating is secured to a stay with stitching laid down inside the grooves between the tubes. Straight embroidery stitches, such as running, back, stem, and chain, sewn along each groove from end to end, or cords couched within the grooves, attach the pleated fabric to a stiffened stay. For additional texture, thread carried over the top of a tube and pulled taut breaks the flow of a pleat. Because interior smocking requires a stay, it loses all elasticity.

Mock smocking combines shirring with embroidery. The irregular folds released by rows of gathered stitching replace the mini-pleating of real smocking. Decorative machine embroidery topstitched over the machine-stitched and gathered rows, with a permanent or temporary stay underneath, replaces the hand embroidery that structures the pleats of real smocking. Mock smocking is a popular counterfeit because it's fast—entirely machine produced, although some mock smockers hand embroider over the rows to suggest authenticity. (Refer to "Shirring" on page 31.)

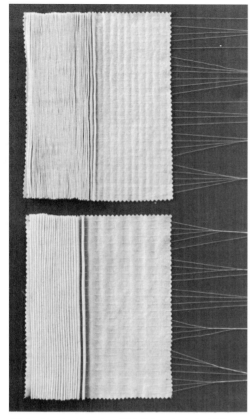

VII-2—Muslin as it emerges finely pleated from a Sally Stanley smocking pleater.

VII-1—Identical lengths of fabric hand stitched following identical dot grids: (top) Sample gathered on dot-pickup stitching has shallow pleats with thin tubes; (bottom) sample gathered on dot-in dot-out stitching has pleats twice as deep with broader tubes.

ENGLISH SMOCKING

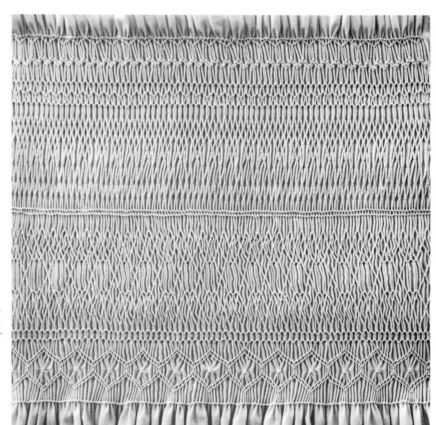

VII-3—Classic English smocking worked with three-strand embroidery floss on a foundation of machine-produced pleating.

VII-4—Honeycomb smocking on machine-made pleating, eased into a curve with the help of the pointed design and steam.

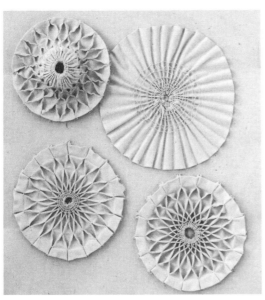

VII-5—Exercises in circular smocking over pleats gathered on similar radiating grids. (lower right) The most successful, a medallion smocked from a circle 8" (20.5cm) in diameter with a circular cutout in the center 4" (10cm) in diameter. The smocking in the other examples, on smaller circles with smaller central cutouts, is less effective. Smocking structured one of the circles (top left) into a cone.

ENGLISH SMOCKING

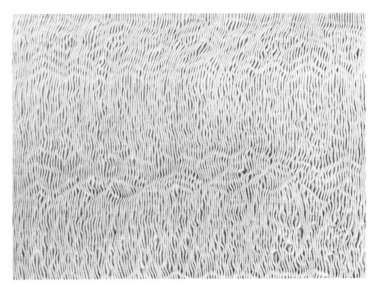

VII-6—Reverse smocking ripples the profiles of massed pleats. The smocking was improvised and irregular.

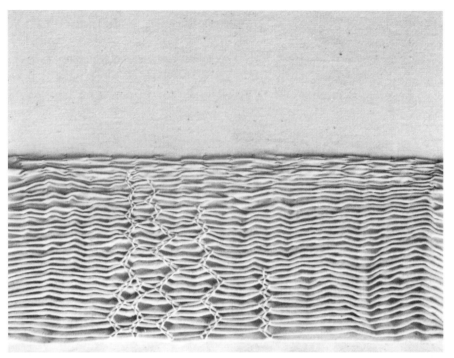

VII-7—Horizontal pleats that gradually decrease in depth, smocked with feather stitching on the surface and reverse-smocked with rows of outline stitching in back.

ENGLISH SMOCKING

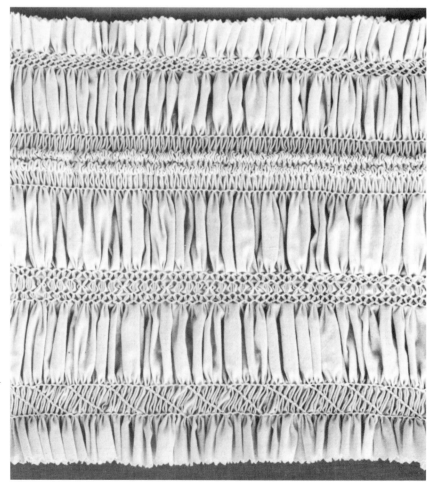

VII-8—A sample with strips of gathering between bands of smocking stitched through two pleats at a time. On one band of smocking, two rows of honeycomb stitching with the threads of the up and down stitches pulled tight, bunch the pleats into a raised relief.

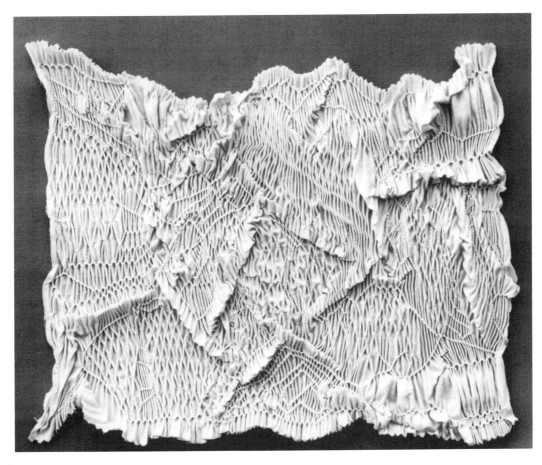

VII-9—Experimental, improvised smocking worked on a ground of machine-produced pleats textured with random folds as it was fed through the gears of the pleater.

ENGLISH SMOCKING

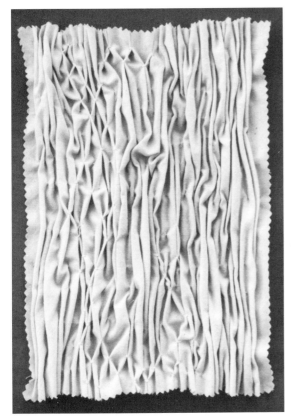

VII-10—Rugged pleating hand-gathered over a random grid, smocked in places with honeycomb stitching, with gathering threads assimilated into the informal structuring.

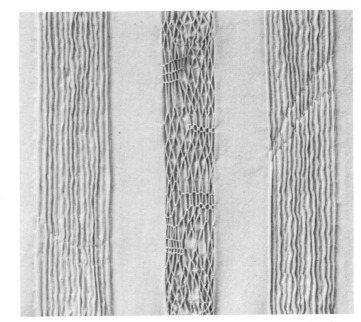

VII-11—One length of fabric with three separated strips of hand-gathered pleating. (center) Conventionally smocked pleats appear inset into the fabric. (sides) Stay-backed, interior-smocked pleating seems to sit on top of the fabric.

DIRECT SMOCKING

—stitching, worked on a grid-based pattern of dots, that draws the fabric into structured folds with pulled thread while creating a decorative pattern. Direct smocking mimics English smocking but accomplishes the effect with one stitching procedure rather than two.

PROCEDURES

1. Review the procedures for English smocking that begin on page 129.

2. On gridded paper, prepare a dot pattern to support the smocking embroidery stitches chosen to structure the fabric with pleats (refer to "Smocking Embroidery Stitches" on page 127). Each dot represents the peak of a future fold and will be picked up by a stitch. The space between dots becomes a fold when two dots are pulled together with stitches (spaces ¼″ (6mm) or ⅜″ (1cm) wide are usually appropriate). Straight horizontal rows of dots indicate stitching paths for honeycomb, surface honeycomb, Vandyke, outline, and cable stitches. Designs that include wave, trellis, and diamond stitches require staggered rows of dots. Align the dots vertically as well as horizontally (Fig. 7-24).

3. Mark the *right* side of the fabric with the dot pattern, aligning the rows with the straightgrain of woven fabric. Before choosing one of the following dot-marking methods, test on a scrap of fabric to make sure that the marking substance will wash out or completely disappear:

   ♦ Insert dressmaker's carbon between the fabric and a paper pattern of the dots. Use point pressure over each dot to transfer impressions to the fabric.

   ♦ With the dot pattern underneath, copy the dots showing through the fabric. Use a light box for enhanced visibility.

   ♦ Mark dots through punctures in a stencil placed on top of the fabric.

   ♦ Use an L-shaped ruler to spot straight rows of dots.

4. Picking up each dot as if it were the fold at the tip of a pleat, stitch across the fabric. Refer to the wavy lines on the pattern for direction. The stitches that connect two adjacent dots from the same row (outline and cable), or two-stepped but adjacent dots (wave and trellis), are pulled taut and together to create the tube-and-channel composition of the smocking. The stitches that move up and down between the pulled stitches (surface honeycomb, honeycomb, diamond, and Vandyke) remain slack to maintain dot separation (Fig. 7-25).

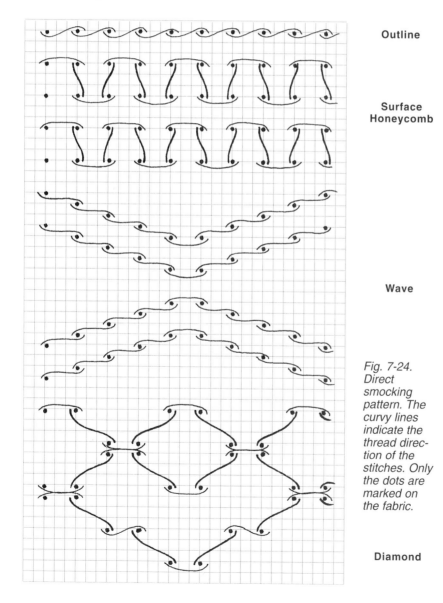

Outline

Surface Honeycomb

Wave

Fig. 7-24. Direct smocking pattern. The curvy lines indicate the thread direction of the stitches. Only the dots are marked on the fabric.

Diamond

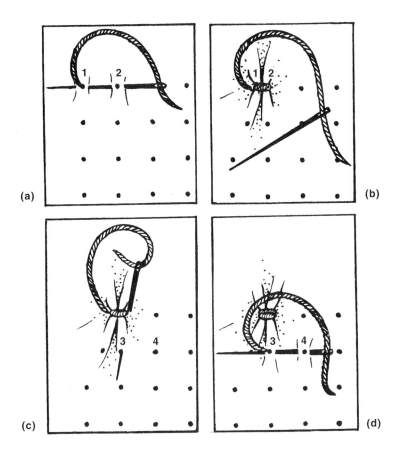

(a) **(b)** **(c)** **(d)**

Fig. 7-25. Honeycomb stitching interpreted for direct smocking: (a) Pick up dots 2 and 1 on the needle with two separate, tiny stitches. (b) Draw the dots together on pulled thread. (c) Insert the needle into the fabric at dot 2 and bring it out at dot 3 in the row below. Do not pull dots 2 and 3 together. (d) Pick up dot 4 and then 3 on the needle and draw dots 4 and 3 together on pulled thread. Continue moving up or down between rows of dots, alternating between taut and slack stitches.

NOTES & VARIATIONS

Direct smocking has an arrangement of folds under the stitches, an obvious difference when compared to English smocking with its unmistakably pleated substructure. Direct smocking is more flexible across the pleating than English smocking and, started from identical grids, doesn't finish as thick. Unlike English smocking, it is not elastic.

If the fabric is woven or printed with a grid-based pattern (ginghams, checks, spotted designs), smock by following evenly spaced points repeated on that grid.

The distinctive formation of folds produced by *reversed direct smocking* is much different in appearance than the rippled pleating of reversed English smocking. Reversed direct smocking is marked and stitched on the wrong side of the fabric. Because of thread visibility, avoid using the honeycomb stitch.

Experimental direct smocking is worked on a grid of unevenly spaced dots, which may or may not be marked on the fabric. The stitching changes and wanders as inspiration directs.

5. Pin the finished smocking around the edges to a padded surface, gently stretching it into shape. Steam with an iron held above the fabric, and allow to cool and dry before moving.

6. For finishing options, refer to "Managing the Smocking-Pleated Edge" on page 128.

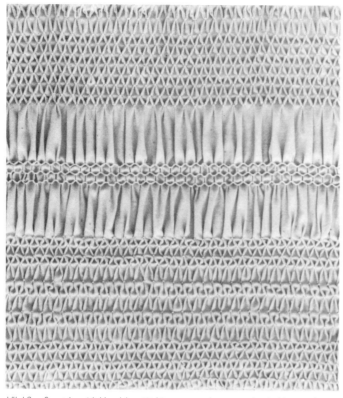

VII-12—Sample with Vandyke stitching on top, honeycomb stitching at the bottom, and cable stitching in the center, all smocked with three-strand embroidery floss.

DIRECT SMOCKING

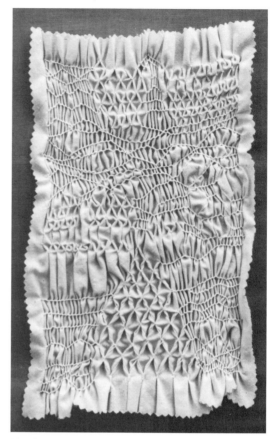

VII-13—Experimental direct smocking with outline, cable, honeycomb, and surface honeycomb stitching applied at random to an erratic grid.

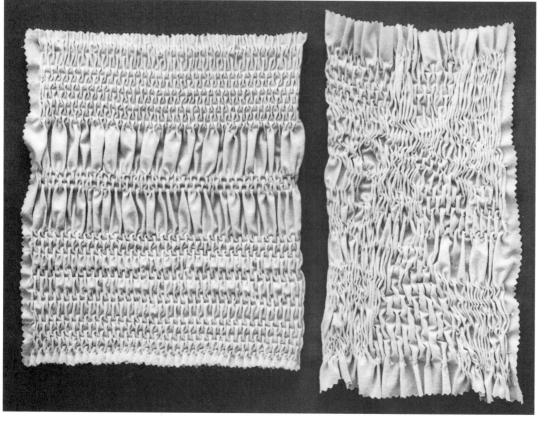

VII-14—The back becomes the front for reversed direct smocking.

NORTH AMERICAN SMOCKING

—a grid-regulated system of pulled stitches alternating with slack stitches that invisibly reshapes the fabric into an intricate composition of folds.

PROCEDURES

1. Select a pattern from the diagrams in Fig. 7-26. (Refer to "Fabric Required for Smocking" on page 125.)
2. Review the English smocking directions for marking dots on fabric, step #3 on page 129. Choosing an appropriate method, mark the wrong side of the fabric with an equidistant grid of dots. For the flower pattern only, dot the right side of the fabric with a previously tested, fabric-safe, washout or disappearing marker (the flower variation is stitched on the wrong side of the fabric).
3. Following the stitching path indicated for the pattern, smock row by row with sturdy thread, connecting pairs of dots with pulled stitches separated by slack, knotted stitches (Fig. 7-27). For the flower and the flower variation patterns only, connect four dots on one pulled stitch (Fig. 7-28).

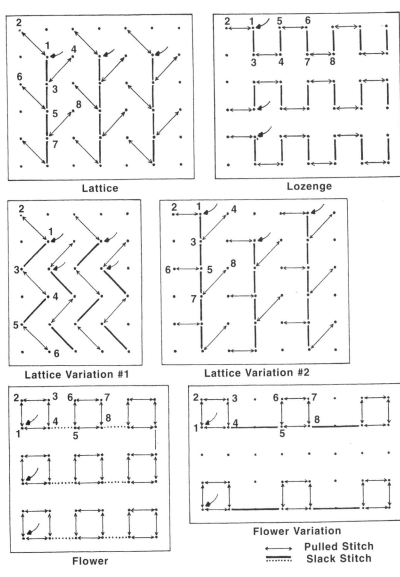

Fig. 7-26. North American smocking patterns.

Lattice

Lozenge

Lattice Variation #1

Lattice Variation #2

Flower

Flower Variation

⟷ **Pulled Stitch**
······ **Slack Stitch**

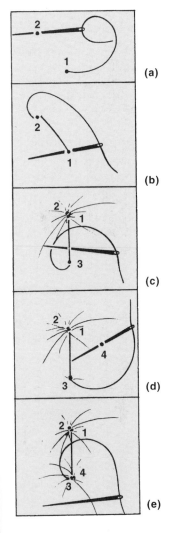

(a)
(b)
(c)
(d)
(e)

Fig. 7-27. To stitch the lattice, lattice variation, and lozenge patterns: (a) Bring the needle up at dot 1, pick up dot 2 and (b) return to pick up dot 1. (c) Pull dots 1 and 2 together. Pick up dot 3 and slip knot the thread to secure. (d) Pick up dot 4, (e) return to pick up dot 3, and pull dots 3 and 4 together. Continue, alternating between slack and slip-knotted, and pulled stitches.

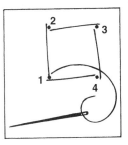

Fig. 7-28. To stitch the flower pattern, pick up dots 1, 2, 3, and 4 with stitches angled toward the center. Pull the dots together tightly and secure with a tiny, invisible stitch. Without pulling the connecting thread, carry the thread in back to the next group of four dots and repeat.

4. With right side up, pin the finished smocking around the edges to a padded surface, stretching gently while straightening the sides. Steam with an iron held just above the smocking. Allow to cool and dry before moving.

5. For finishing options, refer to "Managing the Smocking-Pleated Edge" on page 128.

NOTES & VARIATIONS

Fabric already patterned with a grid-based design of lines or spots cancels the need for marking with a grid of dots. Unlike English and direct smocking, North American smocking is supple in all directions. It is not elastic.

For *reversed North American smocking*, the wrong side is the intended right side, and the marking and stitching are done accordingly. Choose decorative thread because the slack, knotted stitches will be visible.

Experimental North American smocking involves playing with variations: Change from an equidistant or squared grid to a rectangular grid. Gradually increase/decrease the size of the grid. Combine flower-type stitching with the stitching for non-flower patterns. Devise original stitching paths.

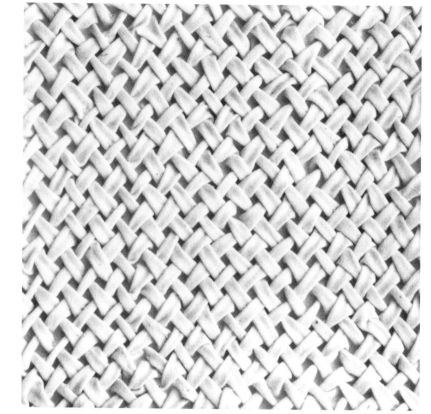

VII-15—The lattice pattern.

NORTH AMERICAN SMOCKING

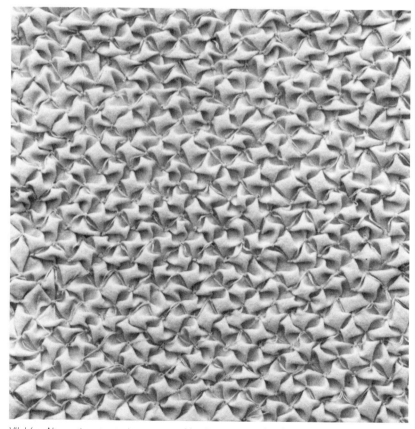

VII-16—Alternative structuring presented by the reverse side of the lattice smocking sample.

VII-17—The lozenge pattern.

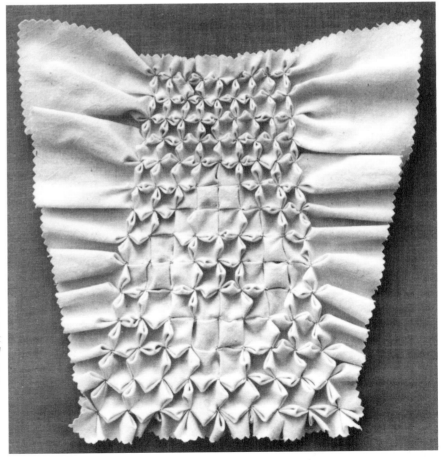

*VII-18—Flower pattern worked on a
gradually expanding grid of dots.
After smocking, all folds except
those outlining the central diamond
were pushed up to the surface,
creating the petal-like formations.*

ITALIAN SMOCKING

—fabric drawn up into close pleats on rows of gauged stitching with deviations that create patterned irregularities. There are two kinds of Italian smocking:

CONTOURED ITALIAN SMOCKING

—fabric gathered into pleats on rows of stitching that turn and angle, causing the pleats to bend and crumple where the stitching veers.

SHIRRED ITALIAN SMOCKING

—fabric gathered into pleats on rows of straight stitching with skipped stitches that form a delicate, puffy, raised design.

PROCEDURES FOR CONTOURED ITALIAN SMOCKING

1. Copy one of the designs in Fig. 7-29 on appropriately scaled, gridded paper. To avoid confusion, alternate between two differently colored pens for successive rows. Note that the short lines and the spaces in between are equal in size, and that their length equals the depth of the pleating formed when the stitches are gathered.

2. Mark stitching paths on the *wrong* side of the fabric. Matching the stitching lines to the straightgrain of the weave, place the pattern underneath the fabric. Trace the broken lines with a fabric-safe, fine-point, disappearing pen or pencil, alternating colors for successive rows. Use a light box for enhanced visibility. Carefully re-aligning the pattern, trace as many repeats of the design as necessary. An alternative to tracing: Use a tissue-paper overlay marked with the pattern.

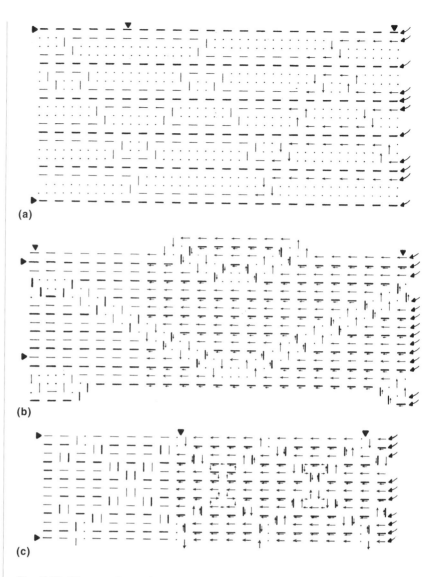

(a)

(b)

(c)

Fig. 7-29. Three patterns for contoured Italian smocking. The arrows on the right indicate where rows of stitching begin. Each short line represents a surface stitch. Stitches move in and out of the spaces between lines, and they do not follow a straight path. The large triangles (▲) mark the limits of one pattern repeat. (Dotted lines are gridline markings, not stitching indications.)

3. With strong thread as long as a row plus 3″ (7.5cm) for each end, stitch each row as marked, a surface stitch over every line. Do not secure or clip the threads at the ends of seams.

4. Grasping the ends of the threads two-by-two, push the fabric into itself on the stitched thread, gathering it into close pleats. To secure the pleating, tie the ends of the threads together in pairs and trim.

PROCEDURES FOR SHIRRED ITALIAN SMOCKING

1. Copy one of the designs in Fig. 7-30 on gridded paper appropriately scaled for the pleating. The space between two dots in a horizontal row becomes a pleat fold when the stitching is gathered.

2. Mark dots on the *right* side of the fabric, aligning the dot rows with the straightgrain of woven fabric. Choose fabric-safe marking substances that will wash out or disappear, having been previously tested on a sample of the fabric:

   ◆ Trace dot impressions from the paper pattern onto the fabric with dressmaker's carbon between both.

   ◆ With the pattern underneath, mark the dots that show through the fabric. Use a light box for enhanced visibility.

   ◆ Mark dots through punctures in a stencil.

   ◆ Use an L-shaped ruler to measure the separations and mark the dots.

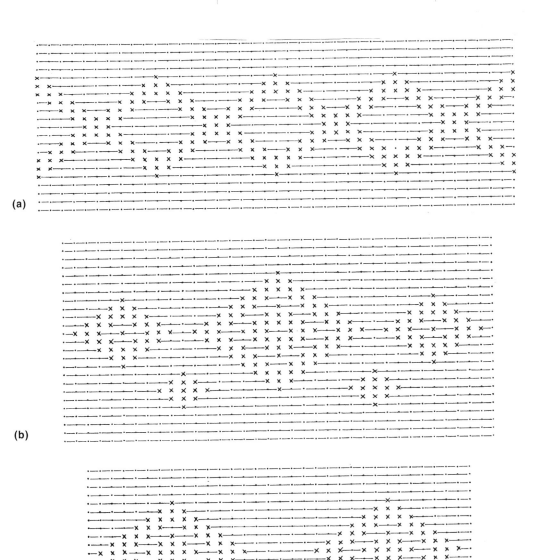

(a)

(b)

(c)

Fig. 7-30. Three designs for shirred Italian smocking.

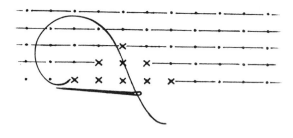

Fig. 7-31. Shirred Italian smocking is based on dot-pickup gathering, with the thread skipped underneath the x-marked dots. Groupings of x-marked dots are always in threes or fives.

- Counting dots from the top and bottom of the design, x-mark the dots that make up the motifs.

3. Use strong thread as long as a row plus 3″ (7.5cm) for each end. Without securing or clipping the threads at the ends of rows, follow the dots with dot-pickup stitching:

    a. Pick up each dot in the first row with a tiny stitch.

    b. For the second and all interior rows, pick up every other dot with a tiny stitch, but *alternate the dots picked up for adjacent rows.* Carry the needle and thread *behind* each grouping of x-marked dots (Fig. 7-31).

    c. Pick up each dot in the final row with a tiny stitch.

4. Grasping the ends of the threads two-by-two, push the fabric into itself on the stitched thread, gathering it into tightly massed pleats. Gather from one side to the center, then the other side to the center. To secure the pleating, tie the ends of the threads together in pairs and trim.

NOTES & VARIATIONS

Traditionally, the fabrics used for Italian smocking are soft and thin, but, for contemporary purposes, the techniques have been successfully applied to a variety of unconventional materials. In general, Italian smocking uses extravagant amounts of fabric (refer to "Fabric Required for Smocking" on page 125). For finishing options, refer to "Managing the Smocking-Pleated Edge" on page 128.

After gathering into pleats, Italian smocking designs contract into an abbreviated version of the design on paper. To offset this shrinkage, designs are always elongated sideways when planned. Shirred Italian-smocking designs become so compressed that they are planned on a grid with rows more closely spaced than the dots within the rows. Before developing an original pattern, understand the stitching process and how it works. Indicate stitching paths for several repeats of the design to make transfer to fabric easier. Stitch from the bottom of the fabric up after marking with chalky-type substances that easily rub off.

Using one thread to stitch two rows is efficient and secures one end of the pleating permanently. Cut a length of strong thread twice as long as needed for one row, plus 6″ (15cm). Thread one end into a needle and stitch one row, leaving a 3″ (7.5cm) tail of thread after the last stitch. Insert the long, dangling end of the thread into the needle and stitch the next row. Gather the two rows stitched on the same thread as one, pushing the pleating as it accumulates from one end to the beginning, and tie the ends to secure.

After stitching but before gathering, soak or wash out the dot markings for shirred designs and iron the fabric. Where appropriate to the application, tie the threads to secure the gathering—but don't trim the ends. The shirred smocking can be undone for future laundering and ironing, and re-pleated afterwards. Because the gathering thread for shirred Italian smocking becomes a visible part of the basket-weave pleating, the decorative as well as durable quality of the thread should be considered.

Fabric smocked in the Italian manner feels firm and solid. It is as thick as the pleats are deep and it is not elastic. Both types of smocking roll with the direction of the pleats but resist such flexing across the pleating. Because the pleats are gathered so tightly, shirred smocking is stiffer than contoured smocking.

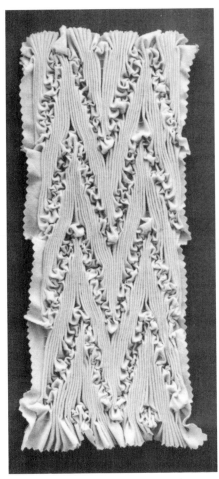

VII-19—Contoured design stitched as diagrammed in Fig. 7-29 (see (b)).

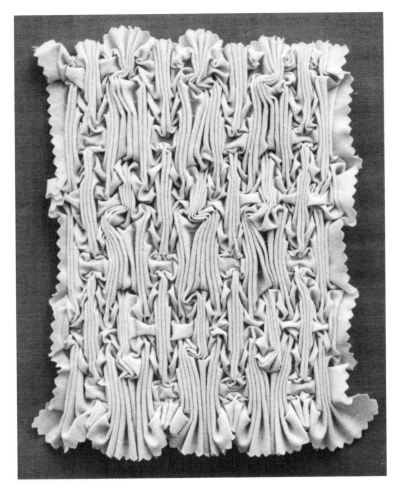

VII-20—Contoured design stitched as diagrammed in Fig. 7-29 (see (c)).

ITALIAN
SMOCKING

VII-21—Shirred design stitched as
diagrammed in Fig. 7-30 (see (c)),
with delicate, basket-weave pleating
around the raised motifs. The released
fabric falls into particularly full folds
because the pleats, which are only
1/8" (3mm) deep, are so compacted.

*T*ucks are slender folds lifted from the fabric and sewn at their base from end to end. The folds are either pressed into low relief or they are maneuvered to project with higher relief from their seamed foundation. Tucks vary in width from broad to tiny and pattern the fabric allover or in isolated bands. Tucked fabric is stable; from the back, tucks appear as seams. Tucks add self-thicknesses to fabric.

TUCKING

8 Tucking

Note: This chapter begins with BASICS, indicated by a gray band located underneath the relevant columns.

TUCK BASICS

EXTENDING THE TUCKING FABRIC

Tucks reduce fabric measurements in one and sometimes both directions. Before starting to tuck, it may be necessary to increase the length of the fabric with an addition. After tucking, extension-adding methods vary with the kind of tuck.

SEAMS COINCIDING WITH TUCKS

To join two pieces of fabric with a seam that parallels the tucks, hide the seam behind an unfinished tuck. Finish one piece of fabric with a folded but unstitched tuck, adding a seam allowance underneath. Lap the fold over the edge of the second length of fabric, pin together, and sew the tuck. Continue the tucking (Fig. 8-1).

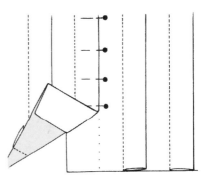

Fig. 8-1. To add fabric undetectably, sew the last tuck when it is lapped over the extension.

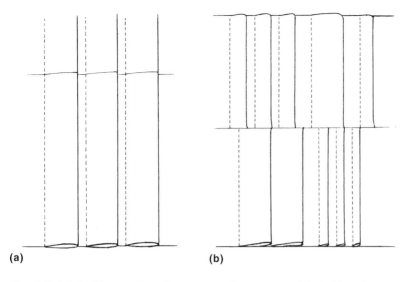

(a)   (b)

Fig. 8-2. (a) Tucking continued across previous seams. (b) Tucking pieced together after sewing the tucks.

SEAMS PERPENDICULAR TO TUCKS

After sewing two pieces of fabric together, fold and sew the tucks across the joining seam, unless there's a compelling reason to tuck first and join later (Fig. 8-2). Tucking first and joining later changes the vertical tucking pattern when both pieces of fabric were tucked with different arrangements, or when mismatching identically tucked pieces is intentional. Matching identically tucked pieces with finicky precision has a decorative purpose when the fabric changes, or when the intrusion of horizontal seamlines is a designer choice.

When finished tucks are pressed flat, attaching an extension to the tucked edge is simple: Sew the two together with right sides facing, or lap the turned edge of the extension over the tucking and edgestitch. When tuck folds project or cause the fabric to puff, the edge where the tucking ends needs preparation before adding the extension: (1) Flatten the tuck folds with basting in a manner that continues the pattern and direction of the folds, and (2) stabilize the seam allowances of cross-tacked and seamless tucks, and pattern tucking, with hand or machine stitching that also controls stretch and dimensions.

To maintain the stand of unpressed or projecting tuck folds when attaching an extension, press and stitch a single-fold hem into the fabric before stitching the tucks. Lap the hemmed edge of the tucking over the extension and attach with hand stitching (refer to Fig 7-16 on page 129), or zigzag or hemstitch by machine. Machine sew slowly, moving each tuck fold back and then forward to keep it between the stitches that straddle the edge (Fig. 8-3).

Fig. 8-3. Zigzag top-stitching that attaches tucked fabric with projecting folds to an extension.

(refer to Fig 7-16 on page 129)

STANDARD TUCKS

—parallel folds pulled up from the surface of the fabric and held by stitching from one end to the other. Standard tuck seams are straight and sewn at an equal or slanted distance from the folded edge through two layers of fabric. There are seven basic types of standard tucks:

PIN TUCKS

—narrow tucks that are sometimes only a pin's diameter wide but are never seamed more than 1/8" (3mm) from the fold.

SPACED TUCKS

—tucks that are identical in width and visibly spaced an identical distance apart.

BLIND TUCKS

—tucks without visible spacing in between because folds touch or overlap the seamlines of adjacent tucks.

GRADUATED TUCKS

—a series of tucks that progressively increase in width with the visible spaces between also progressively increasing, matching the width of the smaller of the adjacent tucks.

CENTERED TUCKS

—tucks with two folds made by centering each tuck over its seam.

DOUBLED-AND-CENTERED TUCKS

—are subdivided with secondary seams into two parts which, when centered with one seam over the other, form two tucks stacked one on top of the other.

TAPERED TUCKS

—tucks sewn with straight seams which move in an oblique rather than parallel relationship to the fold.

(Refer to Fig. 8-4.)

End of TUCK BASICS

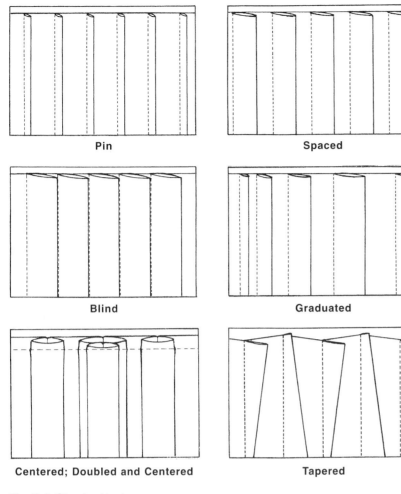

Pin

Spaced

Blind

Graduated

Centered; Doubled and Centered

Tapered

Fig. 8-4. Standard tucks

PROCEDURES

1. Estimate the amount of fabric required for tucking that will match a target measurement. Apply one of the following methods:

UNEQUAL DESIGNS

For designs with unequal tuck widths and spacing, fold paper to try out different arrangements. Measure a repeat of the chosen arrangement before and after folding, and calculate from that basis:

[before folding ÷ after folding]
x   target measurement
=   Fabric Requirement

UNIFORM DESIGNS

For uniform designs, use formula #1 or formula #2.

Formula #1:

a. Establish measurements for the *width* of a tuck (the space between tuck seam and tuck fold) and the *visible space* between one tuck and the next (Fig. 8-5).

b. Find out how many tucks will fit within the target measurement:

target measurement
÷   [width + visible space]
=   Number of Tucks

c. Figure the total amount of fabric required for the tucking:

tuck width x 3
=   fabric required for one tuck

fabric required for one tuck
x   number of tucks
=   fabric needed for tucks

visible space
x   number of tucks
=   total visible space

fabric needed for tucks
+   total visible space
=   Fabric Requirement

Formula #2:

a. Establish measurements for the *width* of a tuck (the space between tuck seam and tuck fold) and the *seam space* between two adjacent tuck seamlines (Fig. 8-5).

b. Find out how many tucks will fit within the target measurement:

target measurement
÷   seam space
=   Number of Tucks

c. Figure the total amount of fabric required for the tucking:

tuck width x 2
=   tuck width inside seams

tuck width inside seams
x   number of tucks
=   total tuck width inside seams

total tuck width inside seams
+   target measurement
=   Fabric Requirement

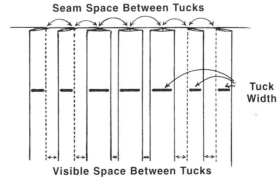

Seam Space Between Tucks

Tuck Width

Visible Space Between Tucks

Fig. 8-5. Tuck terminology demonstrated in a diagram with two spaced tucks on either side of three centered tucks.

Note: The width of a centered tuck, measured from fold to fold, is identical to its measurement from fold to seamline before centering. When centered tucks are doubled, their combined widths equal the width in the formulas (Figs. 8-5, 8-10, and 8-11).

2. Mark tucking guidelines on the right side of fabric that has been cut to size (refer to "Extending the Tucking Fabric" on page 149). Every tuck has a fold line centered between two stitching lines that are matched for seaming (Fig. 8-6)—but marking all lines is seldom necessary:

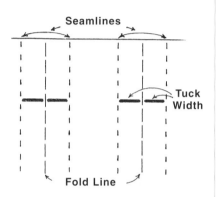

Fig. 8-6. Two tucks before sewing.

a. Using a long ruler, measure off fold positions for every tuck on the top and bottom edges of the fabric, marking with a fabric-safe disappearing pen, chalk, or scissor-nips. Connect opposite edge marks with the ruler and indicate fold lines with disappearing pen, chalk, or thread basting—or fold between the edge marks and crease with an iron (for centered tucks, crease very lightly). Align folds to the straightgrain of woven fabric.

b. Indicate stitching lines in the same manner but with different markings (another color, longer basting stitches, or narrow masking tape beside each seamline). Mark the stitching line to the left of the fold line—the line visible on top when the tuck is folded for seaming—if marking is necessary at all (Fig. 8-7). Seamline indications are optional when tuck width can be controlled with a sewing-machine device or a tucking gauge while hand sewing. Seamlines for pin tucks are never marked. Tapered tucks and unusually wide tucks need seamline indications. **Doubled-and-centered tucks** need two stitching lines (Fig. 8-11). For slippery fabrics, mark a stitching line on either side of each fold line, lines that will be matched to prevent fabric creep and assure accuracy when sewing.

3. Sew the tucks by hand or machine. If not done before, fold on the indicated lines with wrong sides together and crease the folds with an iron, or run the length of the tautly held fold over the edge of a table (crease centered tucks lightly). Pin the layers together and stitch each tuck from the side that will be seen. Turn previously sewn tucks away from the tuck seam in progress.

a. When stitching lines are not indicated, hand sew with an even running stitch and a cardboard tucking gauge (Fig. 8-8).

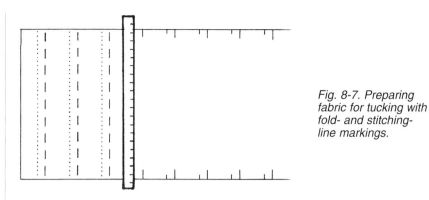

Fig. 8-7. Preparing fabric for tucking with fold- and stitching-line markings.

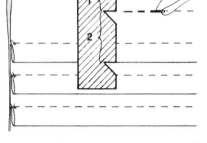

Fig. 8-8. Hand sewing tucks with a gauge notched to direct the seam in progress, and to indicate (1) the width of the tuck, and (2) the distance between the stitching line and fold of the previously sewn tuck.

For machine sewing, control needle distance from the folded edge by aligning the fold with markings on the needle plate of the machine, with a magnetic or screw-in seam allowance guide, with masking tape stuck to the bed of the machine, or by using the right edge of the presser foot as a gauge (Fig. 8-9).

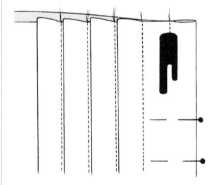

Fig. 8-9. For precise stitch formation, sew tucks with a straight-stitch foot and round-hole needle plate attached to the machine.

Specialized machine attachments that assist tuck sewing—an overedge foot, an edge stitcher, or an adjustable blindhem foot—keep pin-tuck seams from wandering and, for wider tucks, the tucker and the gauged presser foot save marking time and support precision.

b. Follow the stitching-line markings when sewing. If both stitching lines are marked, pin match and baste each tuck before starting to sew. Avoid snagging the marking or basting threads in the tuck seams. For **doubled-and-centered tucks**, sew a secondary as well as a primary seam (Fig. 8-11).

4. Press the tucks:

♦ For **all but centered tucks**, press in the wrong direction first, then press in the right direction, using a press cloth to protect the fabric. Turn the tucked fabric to the back and press again on a padded surface to preserve the dimensionality of the surface folds. If imprinting is a concern, insert strips of brown paper between the tucks and the fabric before pressing (refer to "Pressing Flat and Partial Pleats" on page 89).

♦ For **centered tucks**, center the tuck fold line over the seamline before pressing (Fig. 8-10).

For **doubled-and-centered tucks**, center the fold line over the secondary seamline, then center the secondary seam over the primary seam before pressing (Fig. 8-11). As a pre-pressing aid, push a dowel inside the tuck tube to open and spread it for centering.

5. Secure the tuck folds at each end with basting inside the seam allowances. Topstitch down the middle of **centered** and **doubled-and-centered tucks**, an option for centered tucks but recom-

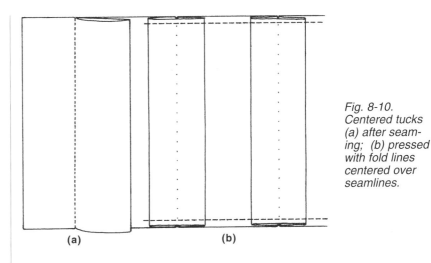

(a)   **(b)**

Fig. 8-10. Centered tucks (a) after seaming; (b) pressed with fold lines centered over seamlines.

mended for doubled-and-centered tucks. After topstitching, press again.

6 Refer to "Extending the Tucking Fabric" on page 149.

NOTES & VARIATIONS

The smooth symmetry that distinguishes standard tucking demands exact measuring and marking, accurate folding, and seams stitched plumb-straight a precise distance from the fold. These additional suggestions make a difference in the result:

Before marking, true the grain of woven fabric and steam press. Spread the fabric over a surface larger than its length and width and hold it taut while marking. Use a gridded cutting board for straightness control. Optional methods for fold-line marking that may be

appropriate in some instances: Draw out a thread from the weave of the fabric. Turn the fabric to the back and score with a blunt tapestry needle. Make rows of tailor tacks.

When creasing folds prior to stitching, fold and press over the straight edge of a strip of heavy paper aligned to the straightgrain between opposite position marks. Space the seamlines of adjacent tucks at least a presser-foot width apart, as measured from the needle to the left. For the final pressing, avoid excessive steam which may cause the fabric to pucker.

Align the folds of tapered tucks to the straightgrain of the fabric even though the tapering seams slant, either alternating direction from tuck to tuck (refer to Fig. 8-4), or moving in the same direction (Fig. 8-12).

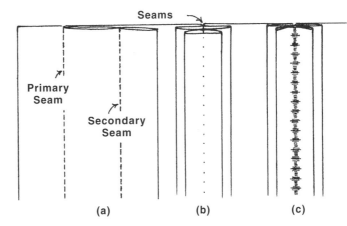

Seams

Primary Seam

Secondary Seam

(a)   **(b)**   **(c)**

Fig. 8-11. Doubled-and-centered tucks: (a) After sewing, and (b) pressed with the fold line centered over both seams. (c) Stabilized with decorative topstitching.

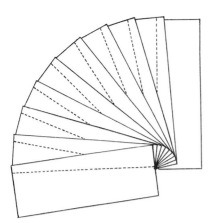

Fig. 8-12. Tapered-tuck seamlines, slanting in the same direction and meeting at the widest ends, re-shape the fabric like a fan.

The on-grain folds prevent the off-grain seams from stretching and snapping. For tucking applications purposely designed with off-grain folds and seams, choose firm fabric, limit the length of the tucks, and use strong thread to counter the stretchy bias. Bias-set tucks re-shape the contours of the fabric. When tuck folds and seams are parallel, a square, tucked diagonally, finishes diamond-shaped; a rectangle finishes as a parallelogram. When tucks are not parallel, the changes in the contours are unpredictable (Fig. 8-13).

Designer tucks interpret the standards freely, mixing and contrasting different kinds and sizes of tucks into individualized patterns. Plan designer-tucking patterns with

drawings on graph paper, and finally by folding paper. Indicate fold and stitching lines on the paper and transfer to the fabric.

Cross tucking embellishes fabric with intersecting rows of horizontal and vertical folds. If all the vertical tucks are stitched first, the crossover horizontal tucks will overshadow the levelled tucks underneath. When tuck stitching alternates back and forth between vertical and horizontal, the cross-tucked design appears interlaced. For either approach, press before changing direction. When stitching a new tuck over previous tucks, sew with the folds of previous tucks facing away from the approaching presser foot. Thick fabrics are not suitable for cross tucking.

Random tucking flaunts the rules. Working with unmarked fabric, tucks are casually folded and stitched. Unplanned and irregular, folds and seams tilt haphazardly and cross at unusual angles.

Mock pin tucking substitutes raised double-stitching, created with twin-needle machine sewing, for the folds of standard pin tucking. By tightening the thread tension or, on some machines, by running the bobbin thread through the hole in the finger of the bobbin case as well (Fig. 8-14), twin-needle stitching in back pulls close together, making a ridge in front.

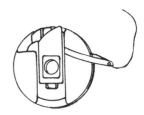

Fig. 8-14. Bobbin case for front-load machines with thread drawn through the hole in the finger, before inserting into the machine.

The space between the twin needles—1.6mm, 2mm, 2.5mm, 3mm, 4mm, 6mm—controls mock pin-tuck size and height. With a correlated pin-tuck foot on the machine, the spacing between parallel twin-needle tucks is easy to regulate (Fig. 8-15). Pin tucks formed with twin-needle stitching can follow lines that curve, twist, and cross as well as lines that are straight and parallel.

Fig. 8-15. Twin needle and the bottom of the 5-grooved pin-tuck foot it matches. Placing the grooves over previously sewn tucks regulates the distance between tucks.

The hand of fabric changes after it is tucked, becoming thicker by two layers, firmer, and less pliant across the tucking. Doubled-and-centered tucks weight the fabric with four layers. Cross-tucked fabric loses some flexibility in both directions.

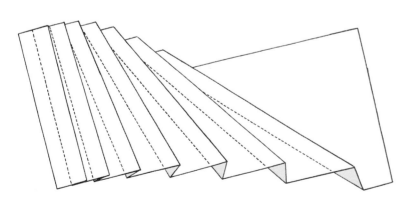

Fig. 8-13. Fabric re-shaped with tucks stitched parallel to the folds, and the space between folds greater at one edge than the other.

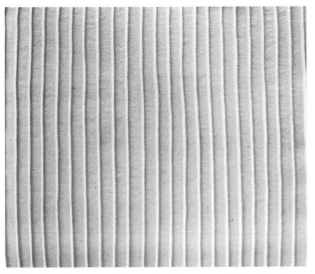

VIII-1—Pin tucks sewn with an edgestitcher to maintain uniformity.

VIII-2—Tucks of equal width visibly spaced the same distance apart.

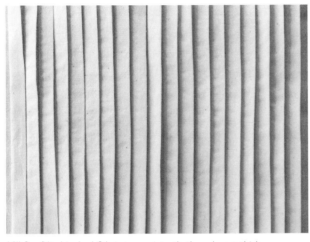

VIII-3—Blind-tucked fabric is consistently three layers thick.

STANDARD TUCKS

VIII-5—Centered tucks stabilized with zigzagged topstitching
alternate with tucks stabilized with seams across the ends.

VIII-4—Graduated tucks.

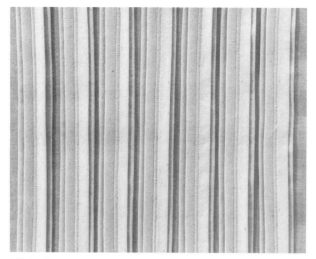

VIII-6—Doubled-and-centered tucks stabilized
with close zigzagging down the center.

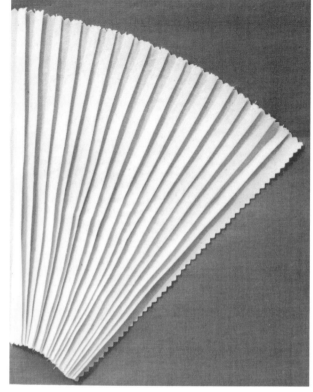

VIII-7—Tapered tucks with seams that slant in the same direction.

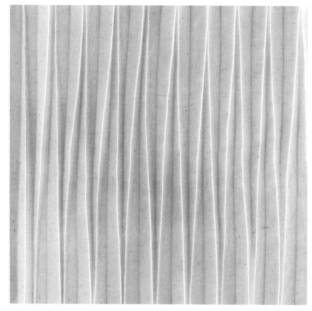

VIII-8—Tapered tucks with slanting seams that alternate direction.

STANDARD TUCKS

VIII-9—Designer tucking
that contrasts clusters of
pin tucks with wide tucks.

VIII-10—Cross tucking with horizontal tucks that appear to recede behind vertical tucks.

VIII-11—Cross tucking has a more complex over-and-under dimensionality when the sewing of horizontal and vertical tucks alternates back and forth.

STANDARD TUCKS

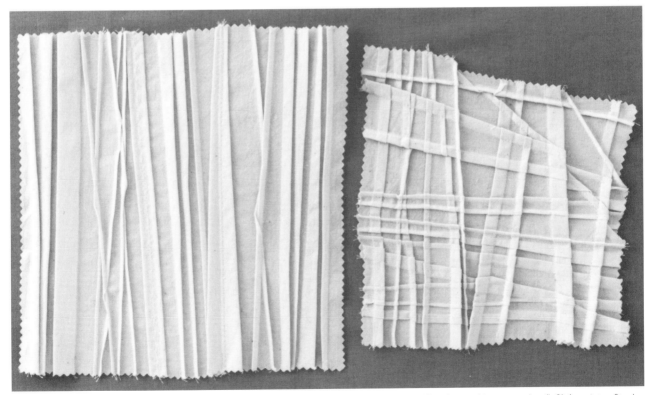

VIII-12—Random tucking examples: (left) A variety of tucks seamed asymmetrically in a generally vertical direction. (right) Tucks that criss-cross each other any which way.

STANDARD TUCKS

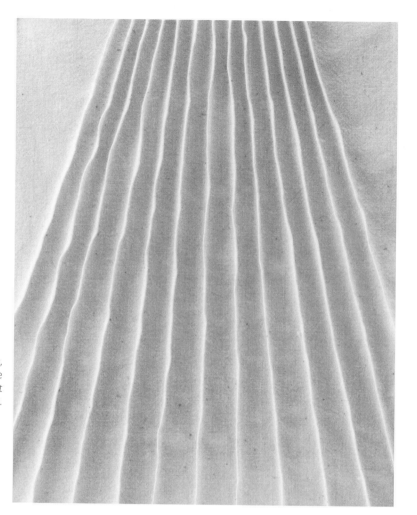

VIII-13—Pin tucks, unpressed, pattern the muslin with folds that stand up like ridges.

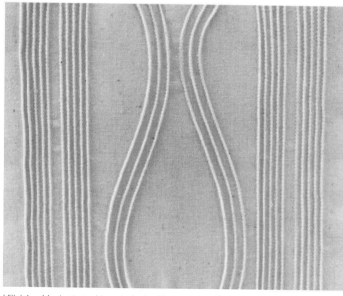

VIII-14—Mock pin tucking stitched with a twin needle and a grooved pin-tuck foot.

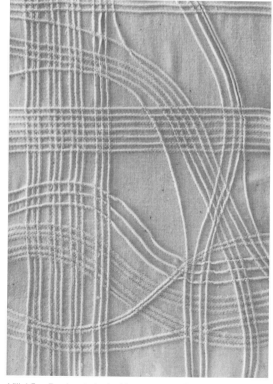

VIII-15—Freely stitched with a twin needle, mock pin tucks curve and cross and appear to weave over and under.

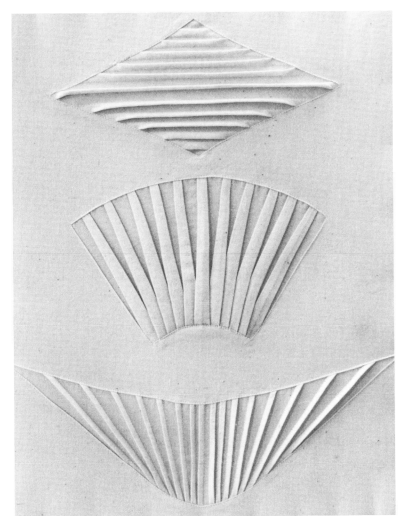

VIII-16—Tucked inserts: (top) Unpressed tucks diagonally stitched across a square. (center) Tapered-and-centered tucks. (bottom) Tucks with slanting folds.

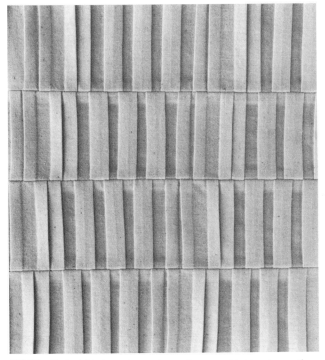

VIII-18—Two kinds of tucking cut into squares and reassembled into fabric patterned with tuck folds that change direction.

VIII-17—Tucked fabric cut into strips and reassembled to stagger the lines of the folds.

Curved Tucks

—blind, spaced, or graduated tucks that follow a curving path which usually parallels the curving lower edge of the fabric. Fabric flares below a curved tuck.

Procedures

1. Review the procedures for Standard Tucks that begin on page 150.

2. Plan an arrangement of curved tucks that conforms to the circular shaping of the fabric. To accommodate the tucks, add two times the width of each tuck to the length or radius of the fabric when cutting. If the fabric is cut in segments, seam the segments together before tucking.

3. For each tuck, mark a fold line and an upper and lower seamline by measuring down from the center of the circle or the apex of a circular segment, or by measuring up from the curving lower edge of the fabric (Fig. 8-16). Crease each fold line with the tip of an iron.

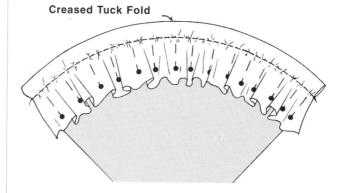

Creased Tuck Fold

Fig. 8-17. Curved tuck with the seamline underneath gathered to match the upper seamline.

4. Seam each tuck:

   a. Hand sew over the lower seamline with running stitches, or machine sew with large, loose stitches. With the tuck folded, gather and ease the stitching on the lower seamline, segment by segment, until it matches the upper seamline, which will be shorter. Steam press the eased stitching and pin or baste the tuck seamlines together (Fig. 8-17).

   b. Follow the upper seamline to sew the tuck.

   c. Remove any basting and steam press before proceeding to the next tuck.

Notes & Variations

The fabric between curved tucks should be pucker-free and will be if the difference between the lower and upper seamline of each tuck is eased smoothly. The flare of curving tucks is progressive; the amount of flare increases with the depth and number of the tucks. Flaring escalates even more when successive tucks gradually increase in width.

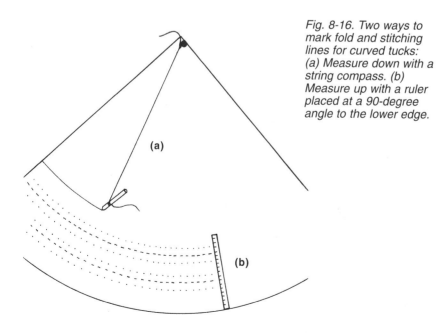

Fig. 8-16. Two ways to mark fold and stitching lines for curved tucks: (a) Measure down with a string compass. (b) Measure up with a ruler placed at a 90-degree angle to the lower edge.

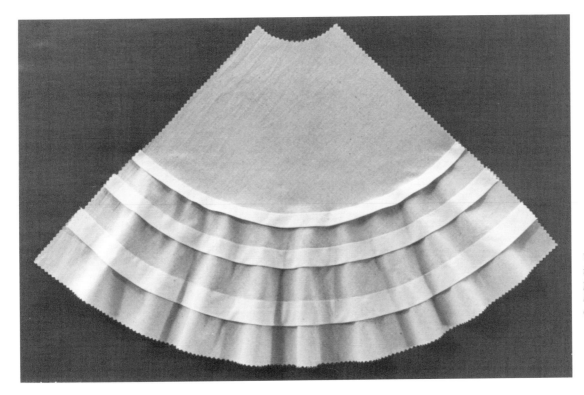

VIII-19—The tuck-produced flaring accumulates with successive tucks.

Note: Procedures for Shell Tucks begin on page 162.

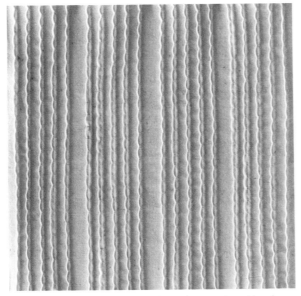

VIII-20—Tucks shell-scalloped while machine sewing with an overedge stitch.

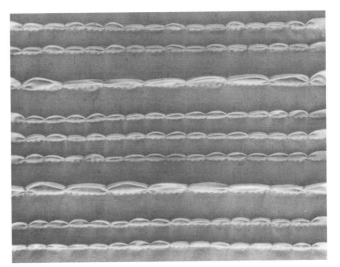

VIII-21—Hand-stitched shell tucking.

SHELL TUCKS

—narrow tucks with shell-like, scalloped edges shaped with thread carried over the folds at regular intervals and pulled taut. Shell tucks can be sewn by hand or machine.

PROCEDURES

1. Review the procedures for Standard Tucks that begin on page 150.

2. To make **machine-stitched** shell tucks:

   a. On a scrap of folded fabric, test machine-produced overedge stitching, guiding the fold so that when the needle swings to the right, it just misses the edge. Juggle stitch length with tightened tension until a pleasing shell edge results (Fig. 8-18).

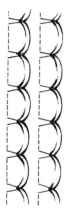

Fig. 8-18. Shell tucking shaped by machine with a tight overedge stitch.

   b. Taking the reach of the overedge stitch as the width of a tuck, plan an arrangement of spaced or blind tucks. After marking fold positions on the fabric, fold and then crease the folds with an iron.

   c. Machine stitch each tuck with overedge stitching as tested. Adding a straight-stitched seam beside the overedge stitching is an option.

3. To make **hand-stitched** shell tucks:

   a. Plan an arrangement of spaced or blind tucks ¼" (6mm) to ½" (1.3cm) wide. Mark the positions of seam and fold lines on the fabric. Fold where marked and then crease the folds with an iron.

   b. Hand sew each tuck with running stitches, stopping to bring the thread over the tuck fold from back to front at intervals spaced at least two times the tuck width apart. To determine the most satisfactory spacing, test on a scrap of fabric first. For even shells, mark overedge points with pins, chalk, or disappearing pen, or gauge by counting the running stitches in between (Fig. 8-19).

4. Stretch and pin the edges of the shell-tucked fabric, right side up, to a padded surface, and steam with the iron held just above the tucking. Allow to cool and dry before moving.

NOTES & VARIATIONS

The width of machine-sewn shell tucks is limited to what the machine can produce. However, wide tucks and graduated, centered, or tapered tucks can have shell-scalloped edges by overedge stitching after the tucks have been seamed into the fabric. Fabric shell-tucked by machine stiffens more crosswise than fabric shell-tucked by hand.

The directions for hand-stitched shell tucking are specific: Bring the needle and thread over the edge *from back to front*—which turns the fold forward to make the slight rim suggestive of shells. If the tuck is wider than ½" (1.3cm), the folds tend to roll over too much. Wide tucks may be scalloped with a few extra stitches running out to the fold, which helps to gather the tuck's width into the base seam. If the overedge stitches are too close together for the width of the tuck, the shells will drag the tuck from a level plane. Test to find the appropriate spacing.

(See photos of Shell Tucks on page 161).

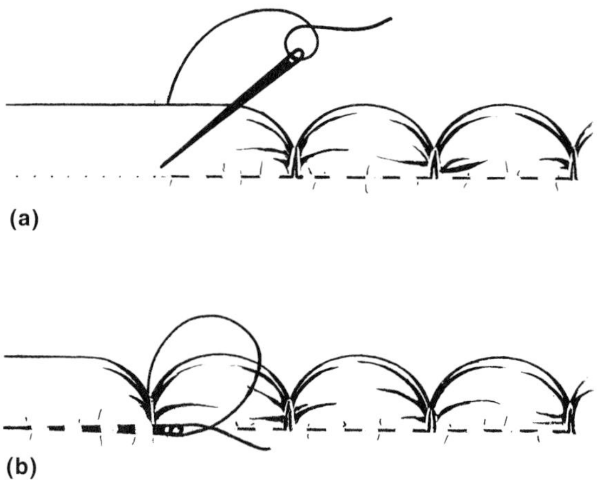

(a)

(b)

Fig. 8-19. To shell tuck by hand:
(a) Sew with running stitches. Stop at a pre-set point, draw the needle out in back and bring it over the fold to the front.
(b) Push the needle through the base of the tuck to the back, and pull the thread to crumple the tuck. Bring the needle forward again and resume sewing to the next crush-point.

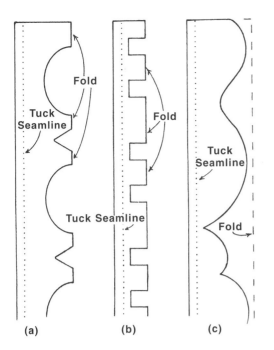

Fold

Tuck
Seamline

Tuck Seamline

(a)

Fold

Fold

(b)

Tuck
Seamline

Fold

(c)

Fig. 8-20.
Contoured-tuck pat-
terns: (a & b) With
cutouts separated
by intact portions of
the tuck fold.
(c) Contoured to
reshape the edge
completely. Patterns
do not include seam
allowances.

CONTOURED TUCKS

—spaced or blind tucks wider than
1/2″ (1.3cm) with folded edges that
have been reshaped to curve and
angle.

PROCEDURES

1. Review the procedures for
Standard Tucks that begin on
page 150.

2. Plan tuck width and spacing using
folded paper, testing different contours for the tucks. Estimate the
fabric requirement. Make a template for the contoured edge of the
tucks (Fig. 8-20).

3. Mark the right side of the fabric
for tucking:

    a. Using a long ruler, measure off
    fold positions for every tuck
    on the top and bottom edges
    of the fabric and mark with
    scissor-nips that are visible on
    both sides. Also indicate a
    seamline position to the left
    of the fold position (the seam-
    line that will be on top when
    the tuck is folded for sewing).

    b. Connect the opposite seam-
    line-position marks on the
    top and bottom edges of the
    fabric with a straight line of
    fabric-safe chalk, disappearing
    pen, or thread basting.

4. Contour the edges of the tucks:

    a. Turning the fabric to the back,
    connect the scissor-nip fold
    marks on opposite edges with
    a straight line of chalk, disap-
    pearing pen, or thread bast-
    ing. Fold each tuck on the
    line (the right side of the fab-
    ric will be inside), pin or
    baste, and crease the fold
    lightly with an iron.

    b. Using the template, trace the
    contoured seamline down the
    length of each tuck. Stitch
    each contour on the line, trim
    a seam allowance distance
    from the seam, and clip the
    seam allowance at inside
    curves and angles (Fig. 8-21).
    Turn the contoured edge of
    each tuck right side out and
    press.

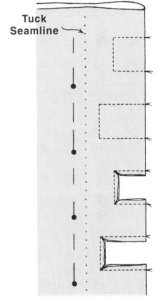

Tuck
Seamline

Fig. 8-21. Tuck contoured with seams
stitched on traced outlines. To prepare for turning right side out, segments inside seams are removed
and corners clipped.

5. Pin or baste, and then sew each
tuck by machine or by hand, following the marked seamline.

6. Steam press the tucked fabric.

Notes & Variations

When designing a contoured tucking pattern, consider the effectiveness of a design when it's repeated row after row. Testing with paper, vary the spacing between the tuck rows and overlaps, stagger the pattern, or turn pairs of tucks to face each other (Fig. 8-22).

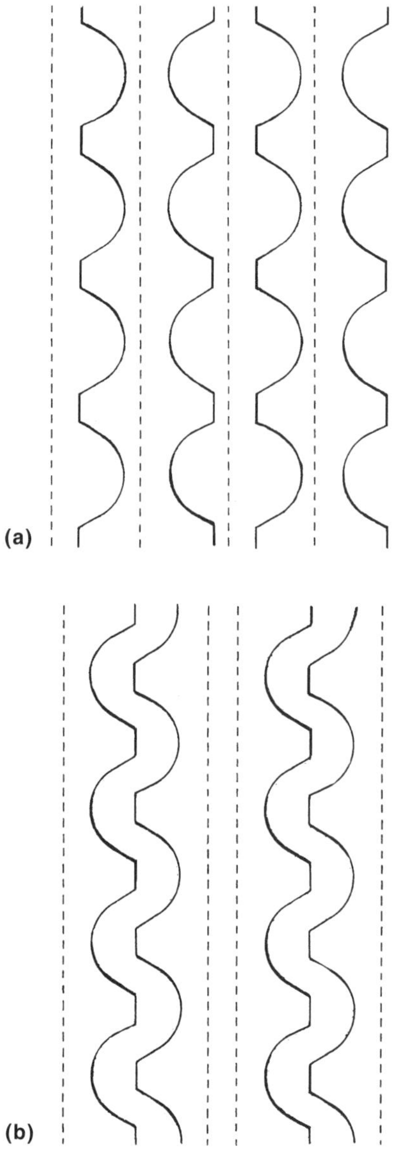

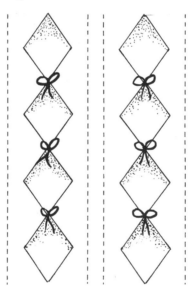

(a)

(b)

Fig. 8-22. Variations with a contouring pattern.

Combine different contouring patterns. When blind tucks are contoured, note that tuck seamlines will show unless the amount of overlap is increased to compensate for the depth of the contouring.

Keyhole tucks, which look as if openings were cut through a top layer of fabric to expose another layer underneath, are actually pairs of identically contoured tucks that meet in the center. Since keyholes require two tucks joined in the middle, the measurements for each combination must be exact: Two tucks of equal width after contouring, with seamlines spaced two times that width apart. Cut a keyhole tucking pattern on the fold of a strip of paper (the fold is where the tucks will meet); open the strip to see the keyhole design. After contouring the edges, stitching the tucks, and pressing the folds to face each other, hand sew the tucks together where they touch using decorative or invisible stitching (Fig. 8-23).

Fig. 8-23. Diamond-shaped keyholes created by bow-tying the points of two zigzag-contoured tucks together.

Satin-stitched contoured tucks are shaped after the tucks have been stitched. A border of thread prevents the cut edges of the fabric from fraying and also emphasizes the contoured profiles of the tucks. After tracing the contours onto the front of a finished tuck, cut out on the line and satin stitch over the cut edges with an overedge foot attached to the machine. The alternate method: Follow the traced outline with satin stitching; remove the fabric beyond the satin-stitched contours by cutting from needle hole to needle hole with small, sharp scissors, without snipping a thread (Fig. 8-24).

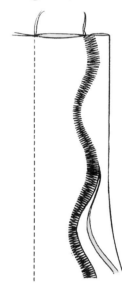

Fig. 8-24. Contouring the edge of a tuck with closely trimmed satin stitching.

Machines with a selection of decorative stitches can be programmed to satin stitch a suitably contoured seam for trimming afterward. Contoured-tuck edges may also be thread-bound with a serger.

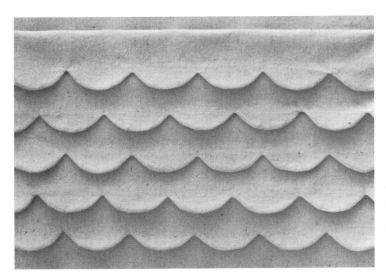

VIII-22—Wide blind tucks with edges scalloped on a turned seam. Tuck overlap was calculated to conceal the tuck seams.

VIII-23—Spaced tucks with sawtooth, satin-stitched edges.

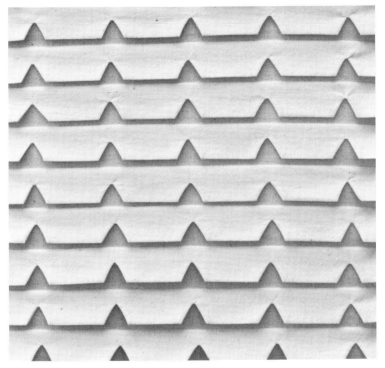

CONTOURED
TUCKS

VIII-24—Tucks with folds notched at regular intervals.

CONTOURED TUCKS

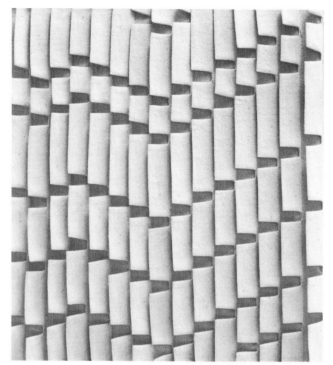

VIII-25—A pattern of notches, repeated but slightly staggered on succeeding tucks, creates a strong design that dominates the vertical lines of the blind-tuck folds.

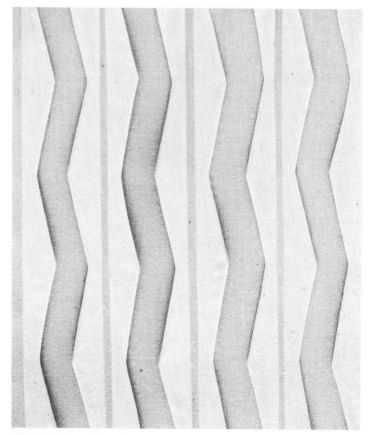

VIII-26—Facing tucks with a zigzag channel between zigzag-contoured edges.

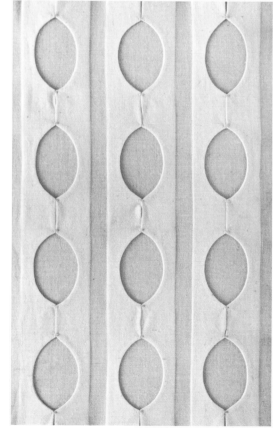

VIII-27—Keyhole tucks bar-tacked together where they touch.

Slashed Tucks

—spaced or blind tucks at least ½″ (1.3cm) wide cross-cut at regular intervals between fold and seam. There are two types of slashed tucks:

SHARK'S TEETH

—tucks slashed more than twice and folded under on either side of the cuts to create points between the slashes.

SNIP-FRINGED TUCKS

—tucks slashed into narrow loops.

Procedures

1. Review the procedures for Standard Tucks that begin on page 150.
2. Plan, mark, and sew a succession of spaced or blind tucks ½″ (1.3cm) wide or wider into appropriate fabric.
3. To make **shark's teeth**:
    a. With fabric-safe disappearing pen or chalk, mark the front of each tuck with slash lines between and perpendicular to the fold and seam of the tuck. Space the lines two times the width of the tuck apart, marking at least two slash lines per tuck (two slashes make one shark's tooth, three slashes make two shark's teeth, four slashes make three, and so forth). Relate the lines on adjacent tucks to an overall design. Slash where marked, cutting straight across from the fold right up to the tuck seam ((a) in Fig. 8-25).
    b. Turn the cut edges under, folding at a 45-degree angle to the tuck seam. Press, stroking the new folds into points midway between the slashes ((b) in Fig. 8-25).
    c. Re-sew the tuck seam with a zigzag stitch wide enough to catch and secure the cut edges hidden beneath the tuck ((c) in Fig. 8-25).
    d. Steam press with the shark's teeth face down on a padded surface.
4. For **snip-fringed tucks**:
    a. With chalk or disappearing pen, draw a line across the front of each tuck, indicating that the snips are to stop a "safe" distance from the tuck seam. The "safe" distance reserves a scant allowance between the base of the fringe and the seam.
    b. Snip each tuck closely, cutting straight in from the fold and stopping where indicated (Fig. 8-26).

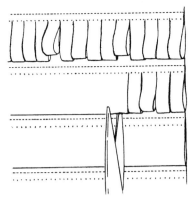

Fig. 8-26. Cutting into a tuck with uniform, closely spaced snips to create fringe.

Notes & Variations

Shark's teeth are easier to form when the tucks are wide, and easier to point if an extra bit of fabric is shaved from the sides of the cuts. Design options for shark's teeth include the obvious—identical tucks slashed identically to produce rows of shark's teeth with points in every row aligned, or, for more diagonal emphasis, identical tucks with slashes staggered in succeeding rows. Also, vary the amount of overlap or separation between tuck rows, change tuck widths, or space slashes more than two-times-tuck-width apart (Fig. 8-27).

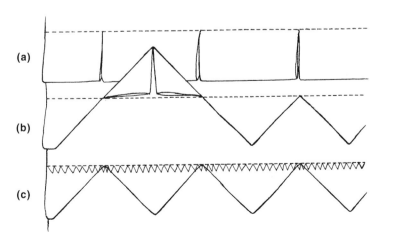

(a)

(b)

(c)

Fig. 8-25. To make shark's teeth: (a) Space slashes two-times-tuck-width apart. (b) Turn the edges of adjacent slashes to make angled folds. (c) Zigzag stitch to catch the edges.

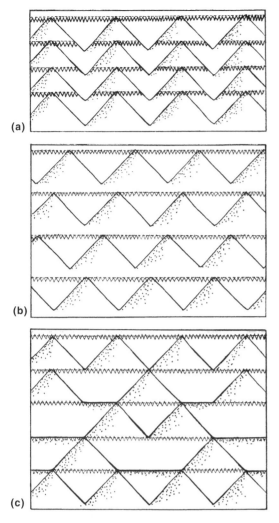

(a)

(b)

(c)

Fig. 8-27. Varied shark's-teeth designs set into
(a) overlapping blind tucks,
(b) spaced tucks, and
(c) blind tucks.

Fabric can be pile-textured all over with snip-fringed tucks. Cover the fabric with very closely spaced, unpressed blind tucks. Fringe the tucks and, if the fabric is a woven, automatically wash and spin dry to jumble and soften the snipped-fringe pile.

Ravelled-fringe tucks are split into thread-fine loops without slashing. One at a time, on tucks with folds aligned to the straight-grain, threads are picked and pulled out of the weave of the fabric with the help of a long needle or pin. Before unravelling, divide lengthy tucks into manageable sections with clips perpendicular to the seam. After fringing, stabilize with a seam of narrow zigzag stitching across the base of the fringe to prevent more unravelling (Fig. 8-30). Tucks may be fringed to the seam if the tucked fabric is strengthened with lining or press-on interfacing to prevent the seams from pulling out. Ravelled-fringe tucks are particularly effective set into fabric woven with thick thread or yarn. Many wovens have a different warp and weft; test for the most attractive fringing direction.

Vary with shark's teeth obtusely pointed: Space slash points more than two-times-tuck-width apart, remove V-shaped wedges of fabric from the tuck, and fold as usual (Fig. 8-28). Instead of zigzagging, choose a suitably wide decorative stitch.

Fig. 8-28. Slashing with notches to shape shark's teeth that point at angles greater than 90-degrees.

A construction variation for shark's teeth: After slashing, poke the cut edges *inside* the tuck tube to form the angle (Fig. 8-29). Ladder stitch the folded edges together, taking care to prevent fabric threads from escaping at inside angles, or machine stitch around the points of the folds with a narrow zigzag.

Slashes may stop short of the tuck seam, and the angles of the points may vary.

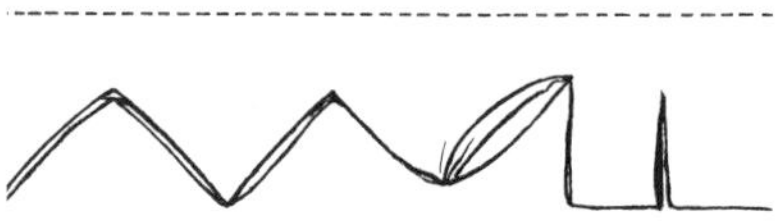

Fig. 8-29. Shaping shark's teeth by pushing the slashed edges inside the tuck tube.

Non-woven materials are particularly appropriate for snip-fringed tucks. Graduated, tapered, even centered tucks seamed down the middle may be snip-fringed. Cutting the tuck apart at the fold before snipping alters the fringe from looped to layered. If the fabric is a woven, repeating washings will fuzz and fray the fringe.

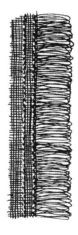

Fig. 8-30. Ravelled-fringe tuck.

VIII-28—Five wide blind tucks shaped into shark's teeth, above a border of smaller shark's teeth.

VIII-29—Blind tucks that increase in size with three shark's teeth centered in each tuck.

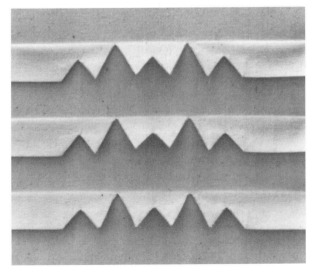

VIII-30—Shark's teeth, shaped by pushing the cut edges inside the tuck tubes, that vary in angularity and depth.

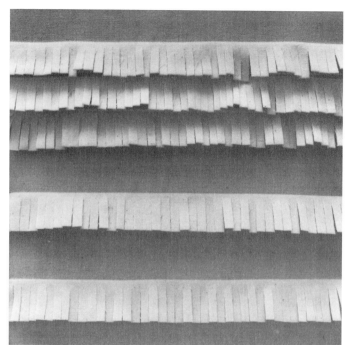

VIII-31—Snip-fringed tucks.

SLASHED TUCKS

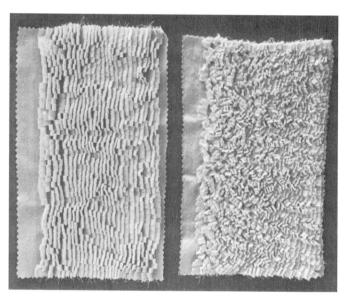

VIII-32—(left) Muslin re-textured with closely spaced unpressed tucks, snipped into loops. (right) A duplicate sample after automatic washing and spin drying made it more pliant and soft, and jumbled the looped texture.

VIII-33—Ravelled-fringe tucks in muslin with a 78 x 78 thread count. To enable the fringing, the tucks were cut apart at the folds.

CROSS-STITCHED TUCKS

—tuck folds forced to elevate between crossover stitching that holds the tucks down. There are two types of cross-stitched tucks:

UNDULATING TUCKS

—tucks that ripple back and forth between crosswise stitching that forces the tucks to change direction.

BOW-TIED TUCKS

—centered tucks with folds tacked together midway between the crosswise stitching that levels the folds.

PROCEDURES

1. Review the procedures for Standard Tucks that begin on page 150.
2. Establish a base of tucked fabric:
   - For **undulating tucks**, choose pin, spaced, or blind tucks.
   - For **bow-tied tucks**, use centered tucks.
3. Topstitch across the tucks, stitching parallel rows that follow straight, regularly spaced guidelines marked with fabric-safe chalk or disappearing pen:
   - For **undulating tucks**, alternate the direction faced by the tucks with every cross-stitched row. Allow sufficient space between adjacent rows of cross stitching for the tucks to reverse direction without dragging up the fabric (Fig. 8-31).

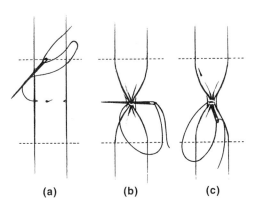

(a)   (b)   (c)

- For **bow-tied tucks**, provide enough space between the rows of crossover stitching for the folds of the centered tucks to be pulled up and tacked together without drawing up the fabric as well.
4. Convert segments of the centered tucks into **bow-tied tucks**. Midway between the crossover stitching, tack the folded edges together (Fig. 8-32).
5. Stretching gently, pin the perimeter of the tucked fabric to a padded board. Set the projecting tucks with steam from an iron held just above the fabric. Allow to cool and dry before unpinning.

Fig. 8-32. To hand tack bow-tied tucks: (a) Insert a needle into the tuck tube and bring it out at the left midpoint. (b) Catch the midpoint fold directly opposite with a stitch and pull the folds together. Secure with a second stitch. (c) Insert the needle inside the tuck tube, bring it out half-the-needle's-length away, and cut the thread.

NOTES & VARIATIONS

The wider the tucks, the wider the space needed between the rows of topstitching to keep the fabric flat. Undulating tucks reach a height where they change direction that equals the depth of the tucks. The height of a bow-tied tuck is a little less than half the width of the centered tuck.

Always locate rows of crossover topstitching inside the seam allowances at the ends of the tucks. To make the crossover topstitching a more dominant element in the overall design, use a decorative stitch when sewing. Unevenly spaced crossover rows that wander from the strictly parallel and rigidly straight, effectively pattern informal, looser applications of cross-stitched tucks.

Instead of tacking the folds together inconspicuously as directed above, tie centered tuck folds together with bow-ties of ornamental thread or cord and allow the ends to dangle. For a design in two layers, make bow-ties of the tucks on the top of doubled-and-centered tucks.

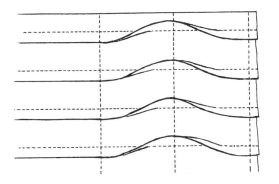

Fig. 8-31. Undulating an array of tucks with crossover rows of stitching that change the direction of the folds.

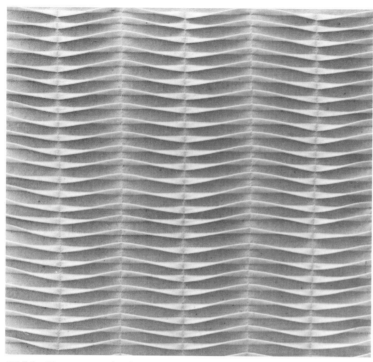

VIII-34—Narrow, spaced tucks undulated with crossover rows of topstitching.

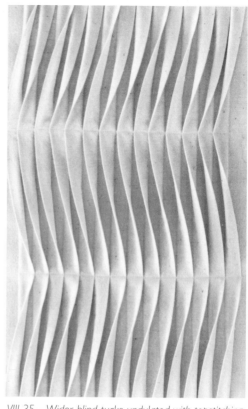

VIII-35—Wider, blind tucks undulated with topstitching.

CROSS-STITCHED TUCKS

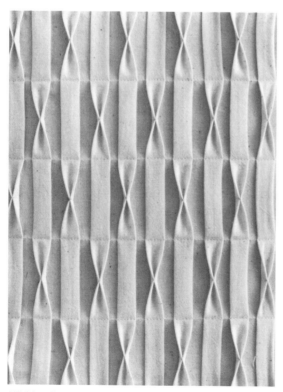

VIII-36—Centered tucks cross-seamed at regular intervals with bow-ties in every other segment.

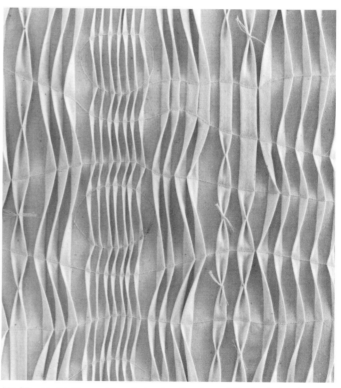

VIII-37—Undulating and bowtied tucks of various widths levelled with meandering rows of zigzag stitching.

CROSS-TACKED TUCKS

—centered tucks with folds hand-stitched together at intervals. There are two kinds of cross-tacked tucks:

BUBBLE TUCKS

—centered tucks that split open between stitches that squeeze the folds together.

CABLED TUCKS

—centered tucks that are spread open and secured with tacks, midway between other tacks that bind the folds together.

PROCEDURES

1. Review the procedures for Standard Tucks that begin on page 150.

2. Stitch a succession of centered tucks into a length of fabric.

3. Mark the surface of each tuck with spaced tacking points using pins, a fabric-safe disappearing pen, or chalk. Test for spacing first, applying the selected technique to a scrap of tucking. With needle and thread, tack the opposite folds of the tuck together at the marked points:

   a. Alternate hand-stitching techniques for **bubble tucks**:

   • For tucks that swell out between tacks: (1) Bring the needle out at the tuck's seam, underneath the tuck. (2) Carry the thread over the tuck to the other side and push the needle under the tuck and out at the seam. Pull the thread tight, crushing the tuck. (3) Repeat once more, secure the thread in back and clip—or carry the thread to the next tacking position ((a) in Fig. 8-33).

Fig. 8-33. Bubble tucks: (a) Crushed under pulled over-the-tuck stitches. (b) With folds tacked together and anchored to the tuck seam underneath.

   • A flattened version for wider tucks: (1) Insert the needle into the tuck from the seam in back, running it through the tuck and out the left fold. (2) Catch the fold directly opposite with a stitch and pull the folds together. (3) Tack again, then push the needle through the center of the tuck and out the back, pulling the tacked folds down. (4) Secure and cut the thread—or carry the thread to the next tacking position ((b) in Fig. 8-33).

   b. For **cabled tucks**, tack the folds together and, in between, tack each fold to the fabric behind (Fig. 8-34). The two tacks in between, located just inside the folds, allow the edges to curl up.

NOTES & VARIATIONS

Appearance governs the spacing between bubble-tuck tacks. Bubble tucks may be tied on the surface with decorative thread or narrow ribbon, leaving the cut ends dangling, and they are particularly effective when ribbon or cords are tacked inside the channels.

Cabled tucks need sufficient space between tacking points to prevent the pull on the tuck from bowing the fabric after it is cabled. The stand of a cabled tuck equals a little less than half the width of the centered tuck.

For both kinds of cross-tacked tucks, start and finish with tacks in the seam allowances at the beginning and end of a tuck. Both bubble and cabled tucks can be worked on the top layer of centered-and-layered tucks. Cross-tacked tucking stiffens the fabric up and down the length of the tucks.

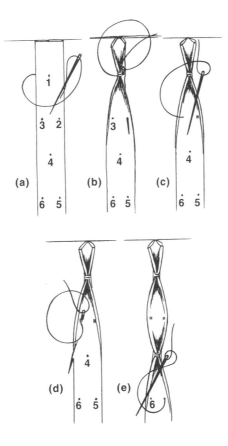

Fig. 8-34. To cable a centered tuck: (a) Bring the needle up through the tuck seam, into the tuck tube, and out the left fold at dot 1 level. (b) Catch the fold directly opposite with a stitch, pull the folds together, and tack again. Insert the needle into the right fold of the tuck and bring it out at dot 2. (c) Make two tiny stitches through to the back of the fabric, move to dot 3, and (d) make two tiny stitches. Insert the needle inside the tuck and bring it out of the left fold, level with dot 4. (e) Tack the folds together and continue to dots 5 and 6 as before.

CROSS-TACKED TUCKS

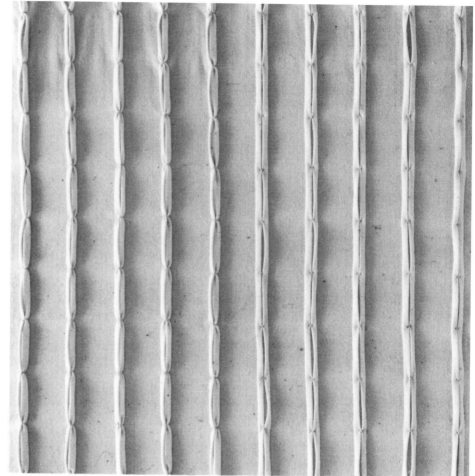

VIII-38—Bubble tucks (left) with folds crushed under over-the-tuck stitches; (right) with folds joined and anchored to the seam underneath.

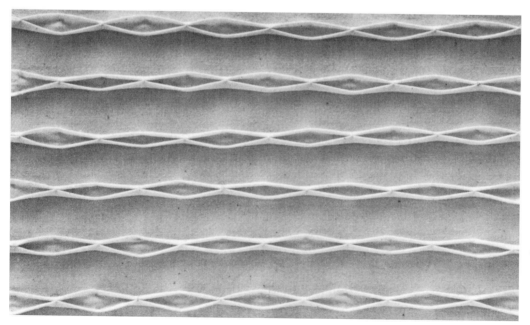

VIII-39— Cabled tucks.

PARTIALLY SEAMED TUCKS

—tucks stitched with seams that are deliberately incomplete. There are two types of partially seamed tucks:

RELEASED TUCKS
—parallel tucks with portions of their seams unstitched, releasing loose folds from the seamed folds.

INTERRUPTED TUCKS
—crossed tucks with unstitched intersections, creating puffs of fabric between the seamed folds.

PROCEDURES

1. Review the procedures for Standard Tucks that begin on page 150.

2. Plan an arrangement of partially seamed tucks on graph paper, outlining the seam/fold positions:

   ◆ For **released tucks**, draw parallel lines to indicate the pin, spaced, blind, graduated, centered, or tapered tucks that will open into unseamed folds at designated points ((a) in Fig. 8-35). Specify the type of tuck, tuck width, the space between tucks, and fold-pressing directions on the plan.

   ◆ For **interrupted tucks**, outline a cross-tucking pattern. Indicate the points where tuck stitching will be suspended ((b) in Fig. 8-35). Translate the plan into a full-sized tucking pattern, spread out to include space for the tuck folds, with tuck seamlines noted beside the centered fold lines. *Limit tuck width for an interrupted-tuck design to ¼″ (6mm) at the most.*

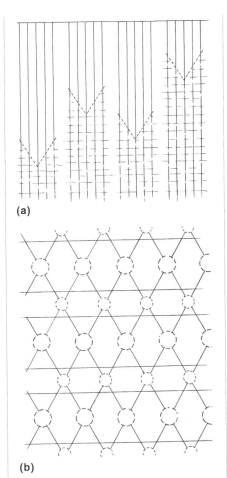

(a)

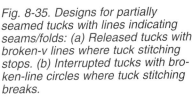

(b)

Fig. 8-35. Designs for partially seamed tucks with lines indicating seams/folds: (a) Released tucks with broken-v lines where tuck stitching stops. (b) Interrupted tucks with broken-line circles where tuck stitching breaks.

3. Using a fabric-safe, vanishing or removable, marking substance, mark the right side of the fabric with fold lines and seamlines as specified on the planned arrangement. Mark the points where tuck seams stop and start. For **released tucks**, expand the paper plan by adding measured tuck widths beside the fold lines. For **interrupted tucks**, trace fold lines from the pattern; trace seamlines if needed.

4. Fold and sew the tucks by machine, stopping and resuming where indicated. When a seam ends or begins inside the fabric, pull the end of the surface thread to the back and tie the needle and bobbin threads together before trimming the threads. If it

can be done inconspicuously, backstitch or stitch in place to secure the seam. Hand sewing may be easier than machine sewing for cross-tucked patterns.

5. Press the folds of **released tucks** flat in the direction specified on the original plan, with the released portions of the tucks continued as pressed or unpressed folds. For unpressed released-tuck applications and **interrupted tucks**, stretch and pin the edges of the tucking to a padded board. Steam with an iron held just above the surface of the tucks, and allow to cool and dry before moving.

6. Refer to "Extending the Tucking Fabric" on page 149.

NOTES & VARIATIONS

Released tucks are not purely decorative; they function somewhat like pleats to create and control fullness in the untucked sections of the fabric. The fullness can be isolated at one or on both ends of the discontinued tucks, or the fullness can be centralized. Either the tucked side or the seamed side of released tucks can be selected for the right side. When the seamed side is outside, the tucks in back are pressed flat.

Unlike released tucks, fabric patterned with an interrupted tucking design remains stabilized throughout and the result is more dimensionalized. Tuck folds stand, and the puffs that replace the intersections where tucks would otherwise cross project even more. The elevation of the puffs is determined by the number and depth of the tucks that discharge the puff. Since paper planning for an interrupted tucking design can't fully predict the cloth result, test first.

PARTIALLY SEAMED TUCKS

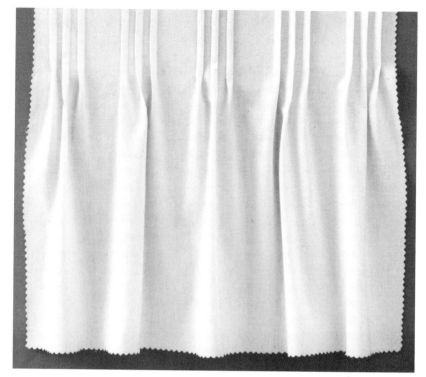

VIII-40—Parallel tucks in clusters of three release loose folds where the tucks stop.

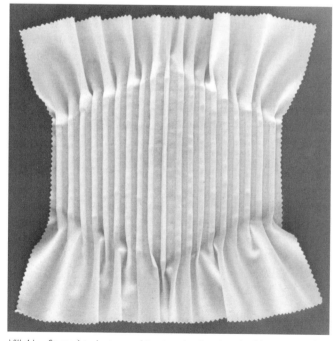

VIII-41—Spaced tucks, pressed in opposite directions beside a centered tuck in the middle, release loose folds above and below the tuck seams.

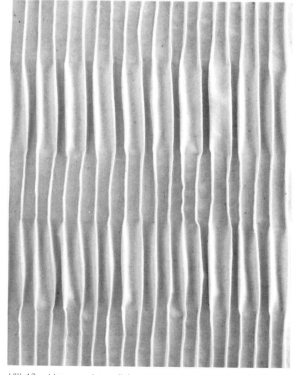

VIII-42—Unpressed, parallel, narrow tucks release bands of loose folds where tuck stitching stops.

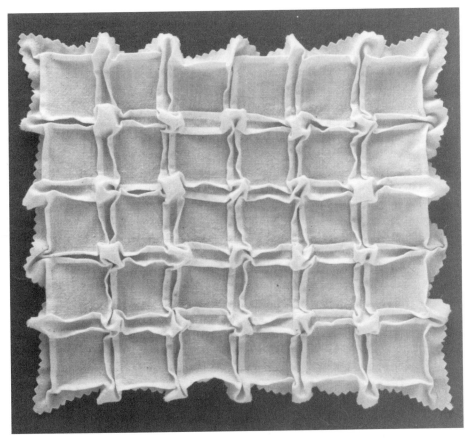

VIII-43—An interrupted cross-tucking design, pin-tucked.

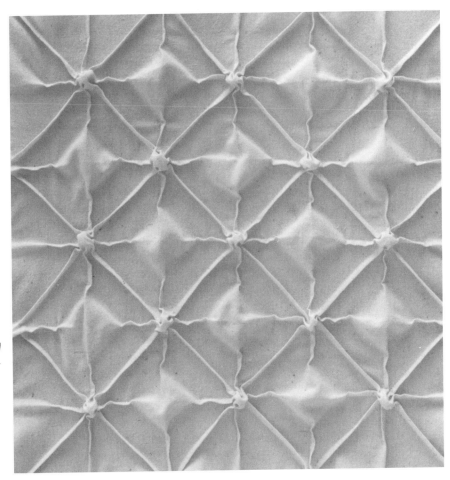

VIII-44—Another interrupted cross-tucking design.

SEAMLESS TUCKS

—tucks formed and secured with hand stitches at separated points along their length. There are two kinds of seamless tucks:

CLUSTER TUCKS

—three or more fanned tucks assembled at regular intervals with hand stitches connecting the base of the folds. Cluster tucks stand up from the surface of the fabric.

TIED TUCKS

—tucks shaped solely with ties that enclose and crush the tuck fold at intervals. Tied tucks puff up from the surface of the fabric.

PROCEDURES FOR CLUSTER TUCKS

1. Plan the number of tucks in a cluster, and the standing width of each tuck in the cluster. Decide how many clusters to include within the target measurement for the tucked application. To figure the space between clusters, divide the target measurement by the total number of clusters. Estimate the fabric requirement:

standing tuck width x 2
= total tuck width

total tuck width
x number of tucks per cluster
= width of one cluster

width of one cluster
x total number of clusters
= total cluster width

total cluster width
+ target measurement
= Estimated Fabric Requirement

2. On the wrong side of fabric that has been cut to size, measure and mark vertical rows of dots:

a. Start with horizontal lines of dots across the top and bottom edges of the fabric. Mark one dot for the back fold of each tuck in a cluster, plus one—four back folds for three

tucks, five back folds for four tucks, etc. Each tuck will be one-half as wide as the space between two back-fold dots. Separate the dot clusters with measured spaces.

b. Connect the back-fold dots on opposite edges with vertical rows of dots, identically spaced. Because each dot is a stitch location, gauge the distance between vertical dots by the need to assure the stability of a cluster along its length from edge to edge ((a) in Fig. 8-36).

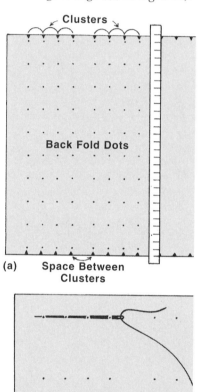

(a)

Space Between Clusters

(b)

Fig. 8-36. To make cluster tucks: (a) Mark the fabric with rows of dots aligned vertically and horizontally. (b) Pick up the dots in each horizontal row in a cluster, on tiny stitches, before pulling the stitches together on the thread.

3. Working from the back and using sturdy thread in a long needle, pick up each of the horizontal dots within a cluster with a tiny stitch, and pull the stitches together tightly on the thread. Repeat, then secure and cut the thread. Continue to connect each succession of horizontal dots in a cluster with stitches, moving down along the length of the cluster tuck ((b) in Fig. 8-36).

4. Stretching the cluster tucks along their length, pin the ends to a padded surface and steam with an iron held above the fabric. Allow to cool and dry before moving.

PROCEDURES FOR TIED TUCKS

1. Plan a repeating, full-sized tucking pattern on graph paper, using two dots connected with a line to indicate one tie (Fig. 8-37). The spacing between dots controls the amount of fabric that will be enclosed and crushed by a tie, and the spread and puff of the tuck between ties. Test the pattern on a square of fabric. Measure the fabric before and after the test and use those measurements as a basis for estimating the fabric requirement for a tied-tuck application:

[measurement before testing
÷ measurement after testing]
x target measurement
= Fabric Requirement

2. With a fabric-safe pen or pencil, mark fabric that has been cut to size with pairs of dots to be tied together. For surface ties, dot the right side (the technique will obscure the dots); for reverse ties, dot the wrong side. Puncture the pattern with holes to use as a dot-marking stencil, or trace dots with the pattern under the material.

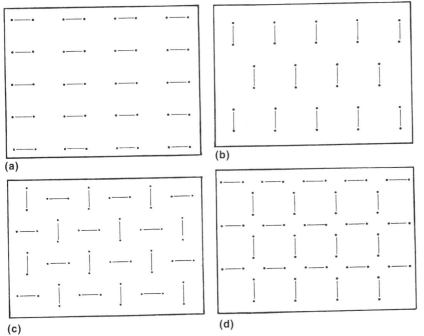

(a)

(b)

(c)

(d)

Fig. 8-37. Examples of grid-based tied-tuck patterns: (a) Identical rows of dots shape vertical tucks when pairs of dots are tied together. (b, c, d) Rows of dots with staggered spacing and changes in the direction of dots to be tied together release folds that restructure the fabric into non-tucklike formations.

3. With strong thread in a needle, connect each pair of dots: Insert the needle into one dot and bring it out at the other dot. Leaving a tail of thread, repeat the stitch (Fig. 8-38).

Fig. 8-39. A square knot. Trim the ends of the thread about ½″ (1.3cm) from the knot.

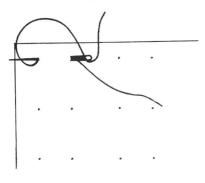

Fig. 8-38. Preparing to tie a tuck by connecting a pair of dots with repeated stitches.

Pull the dots together on the thread, crushing the fabric of the tuck. Tie the ends securely with a square knot (Fig. 8-39).

- When surface tying in front, don't let the crushed fabric slip under the pulled stitch to collect in back. The ends of the clipped thread become part of the surface texture.

- For reverse tying, draw the dots together with the crushed fabric pushed through to the right side. The ends of the clipped thread will remain hidden in back.

4. Stretching gently, pull out and pin the edges of the finished tucking to a padded board. Steam with an iron held just above the surface of the tucks. Allow to cool and dry before removing.

NOTES & VARIATIONS

Refer to "Extending the Tucking Fabric" on page 149.

When cluster tucks are reversed, the back folds of the clusters peep out between the gaps in the pulled stitches, and fan out more when stretched or pushed. For *reversed cluster tucks*, reduce the standing width of the tucks to minimize bulk underneath. Conceal the starts and stops of the thread in back, or secure the ends with decorative ties in front.

Besides following grid-based patterns, tied tucks can dimensionalize designs with lines that curve, diverge, converge, and disappear, outlining with tucks that vary in size and dwindle down to nothing. Patterns for *meandering tied tucks* are linear rather than dotted. They start on paper with lines that not only describe the design, but also indicate the center point between pairs of ties that raise the design from the fabric's surface. (1) Make a line drawing of the meandering design. Convert the drawing into a pattern, spreading the lines apart to allow for the fabric that will be drawn up into tucks when the design is tied. (2) Trace the pattern onto the right side of the fabric with fabric-safe disappearing pen or chalk, onto the wrong side of the fabric with a fabric pencil, or, for a design to include surface as well as reverse tying, outline the design with thread basting. (3) Gauging by eye or measuring, stitch in and out on either side of a line and knot the thread as previously described. Vary the distance between ties to accommodate the curves and deviations of the design. (4) When finished, pin the fabric around the edges to a padded board, stretching to smooth out the areas between the tucks and accentuate the relief of the design. Steam block, and allow to cool and dry before unpinning. (5) Because meandering tied tuck designs change the edges of the fabric from straight and true to distorted, trim the fabric back to shape. If needed, stabilize with underlining.

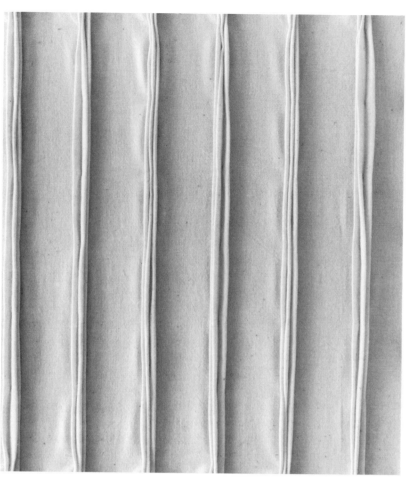

VIII-45—Bands of triple cluster tucks.

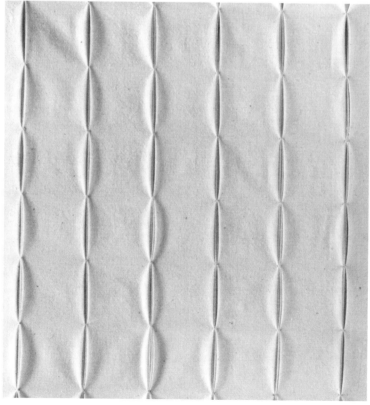

VIII-46—Reversed cluster tucks.

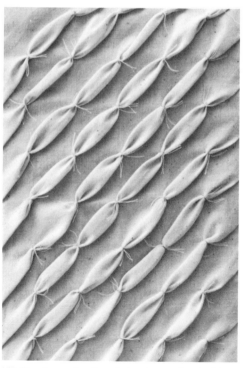

VIII-47—Rows of surface-tied tucks crossing the bias
of the muslin, basted to a lining.

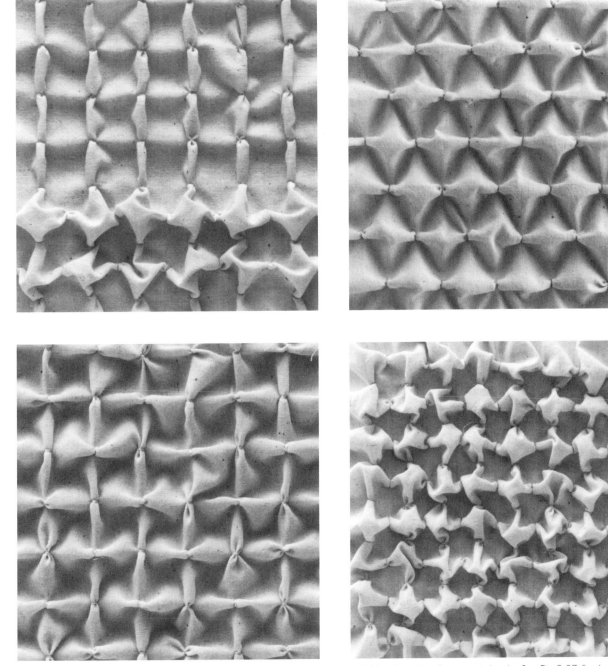

VIII-48—Samples of reverse-tied tucks. See Fig. 8-37 for the patterns used: (above left) see (a) and (d); (above right) see (b); (below left) see (c); (below right) see (d).

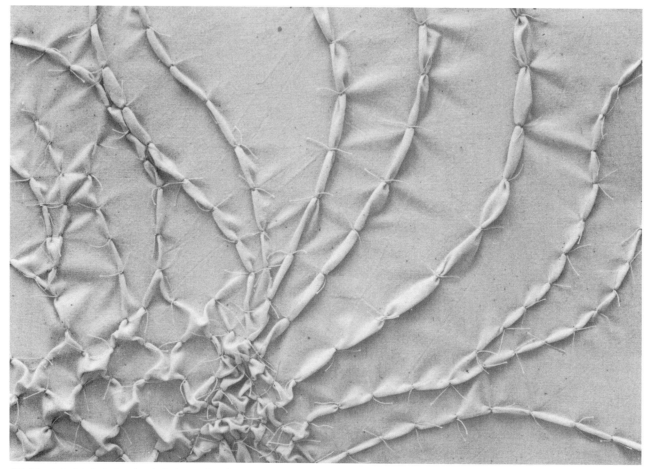

VIII-49—A tied tuck design that includes curving, diverging, converging, disappearing, crossing, and scrambled lines.

PATTERN TUCKING

—hand-stitched pin tucking that dimensionalizes designs with curving and angular as well as straight lines. Amid the ridges of the pin tucking, pattern-tucked fabric shifts between smooth and puckery.

PROCEDURES

1. Draft a full-size linear design on paper, expanding the space between lines to compensate for the loss that occurs after the lines are pin-tucked. To prove the design, test with a square of fabric. Measure the fabric before and after the test and use those measurements as a basis for calculating the fabric requirement, or work with fabric cut approximately 1¾ times larger in both directions than the target measurement for the finished tucking.

2. Trace the design onto the right side of the fabric with fabric-safe chalk, disappearing pen, or thread basting:

   - Pin the fabric over the paper pattern and place on a light box or window during daylight to expose the lines of the pattern distinctly enough to copy.

   - Trace the pattern onto tissue paper or tear-away stabilizer. Pin the pattern over the fabric. Following the lines of the pattern, thread baste through both, and then gently tear the pattern away.

3. Hand sew the design:

   - Running-stitched pin tucks. To sew straight lines and slight curves, fold on the traced line just ahead of the needle and sew with tiny running stitches no more than 1/16″ (1.5mm) from the fold. For tight curves and designs that continually curve, alternate between a surface stitch on one side of the line and a surface stitch on the other side of the line. After six

or more stitches, pull the thread to raise the pin tuck (Fig. 8-40). Negotiate steep curves with smaller stitches on the inside of the curve and larger stitches on the outside.

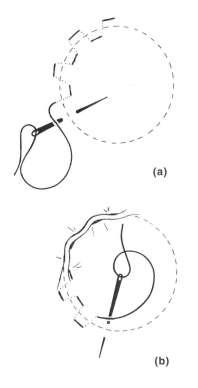

Fig. 8-40. To pin tuck a curving design with alternating running stitches: (a) Insert the needle 1/16″ (1.5mm) from one side of the line and bring it out 1/16″ (1.5mm) from the line on the side directly opposite. Moving forward slightly, take a tiny stitch back to the other side. Continue back and forth. (b) After six stitches, pull the thread taut to bring up the tuck, and proceed.

   - Pin tucking with overcast stitching. Make pulled stitches 1/8″ (3mm) wide that move under a line with the needle always crossing from the same direction. Overcasting with thread embosses the design with tiny ridges that have a rope-like edge (Fig. 8-41).

Fig. 8-41. To pattern tuck with overcast stitching: Bring the needle up a scant 1/16″ (1.5mm) to the left of the line. Moving forward across the line, take a stitch under the line to the side directly opposite, staying a scant 1/16″ (1.5mm) from the line on either side. Moving forward across the line, make another stitch in the same direction. After several stitches, pull the thread taut before continuing.

4. Stretching the pattern-tucked fabric gently, pin around the edges to a padded board. Steam with an iron held just above the surface of the tucks, and allow to cool and dry before moving.

5. Refer to "Extending the Tucking Fabric" on page 149.

NOTES & VARIATIONS

Pattern tucking is surprisingly versatile. It can follow lines that meander, converge, angle, split, cross, and stop and start anywhere. After a little experience with the technique, fabric can be tucked with a pattern improvised while stitching.

Given the curvilinear, atypical patterning of the folds raised from the fabric, finishing with a fabric that lies flat overall requires stitching drawn up just enough to create the tucked ridge—but never so much that the fabric begins to gather beyond the puckering characteristic of the technique. An exception: If the design includes circles within circles or squares within squares, the outer motifs may need some gathering to maintain a level fabric. Always, the tuck itself should be tiny.

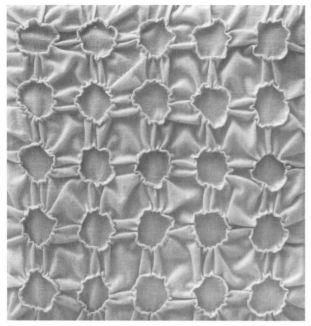

VIII-50—Rows of circles pin-tucked with ladder stitching.

PATTERN TUCKING

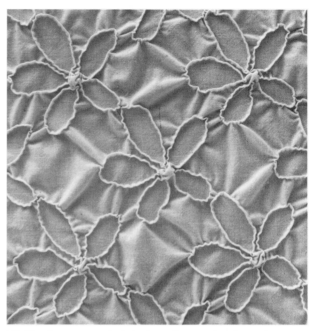

VIII-51—A running-stitched floral motif repeated in diagonal rows.

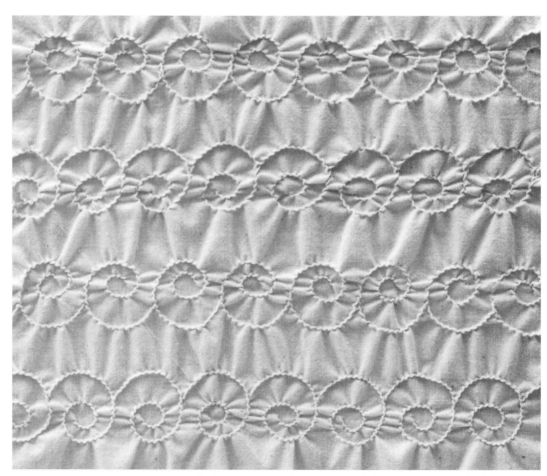

VIII-52—Shallow overcast stitching outlines a spiral design with twisty-edged pin tucking.

Filled Reliefs

PART FOUR

*C*ording raises linear designs from the surface of the fabric. Inserted inside channels stitched into doubled fabric, cord brings elaborate, interlaced compositions up from the surface with low-relief modelling. Encased inside tubes stitched into single fabric, cord lifts parallel rows of rolls from the surface in high-relief arrangements.

Besides elevation, cord adds its own substance to the fabric. Fabric has more weight and firmness after cording than before, and its flexibility is affected by the thickness and closeness of the cords and the tightness of their fabric wrapping.

CORDING

9 Cording

Note: This chapter begins with BASICS, indicated by a gray band located underneath the relevant columns.

CORDING BASICS

CORDS FOR CORDING

Select a cord for its quality in hand and in conjunction with the fabric, for its suitability to the cording technique, for its size in relation to the channel or tube, and for its practicality.

To bring complex, hand-sewn designs into relief, the soft, puffy, resilient, lightweight qualities of acrylic yarn make it the contemporary favorite. Threaded into a needle's eye, insertion into narrow channels is relatively easy, even when two, three, or four strands are combined to increase the filler bulk of the yarn. Fabric corded with yarn remains supple.

The more solid substance of cable cord offers the resistance needed for hand-stitched single-fabric cording, and for machine stitching with a zipper or cording foot next to the covered cord. Before acrylic yarn, cable cord was the raising element inserted into the channels of intricate designs, and it is still the choice when sturdy roundness is the desired result.

A loose twist of many plies of black or white cotton or polyester thread, cable cord is pliable and stable, and manufactured in a wide range of sizes identified by numbers that jump between #6 and #300 as diameters increase. Cable cord firms up when tightly encased in fabric. One hundred percent cotton cable cord tends to shrink when washed.

For thick, fat, surface cording, either connected or detached, welting cord is available in diameters that exceed the largest cable cord. Welting cord is made from cotton fibers shaped into a roll and contained inside a netting of thread.

Consider crochet cotton, heavy string, macramé cord, and rattail for twin-needle or zigzag cording, for delicate cording in narrow channels or tubes, and for cords brought to the surface. When additional texture is appropriate, novelty cords manufactured with uneven, nubby surfaces, or string or twine textured with crochet, knots, and twists, impart their irregularities to thin, snug fabric coverings.

Hand-Sewn Corded Quilting

—two layers of fabric covering cords confined within stitched channels, a combination that embosses an interlacing design into the surface fabric.

Procedures

1. Draft a full-size pattern for a design that uses, as the linear device, two parallel, evenly spaced lines. The lines define channels that follow curving, angular, entwining paths that appear to weave over and under one another. Where the double-line channels cross, one channel stops the progression of the other, and each channel alternates between proceeding over and disappearing under the channels it crosses. Because of the constant interruptions, channels are divided into short segments (Fig. 9-1). The safe width for the parallel lines is ¼″ (6mm) or less.

2. With a fine-line, fabric-safe marker, trace a faint but distinct copy of the design onto the inner lining or the surface fabric, both cut to the desired size (refer to "Transferring Designs" on page 205):

   ◆ For running-stitched corded quilting, trace a mirror-image of the design onto the inner lining.

   ◆ For back-stitched corded quilting, trace the design onto the surface fabric using a vanishing or easily removable marking substance.

   Baste the inner lining to the surface fabric.

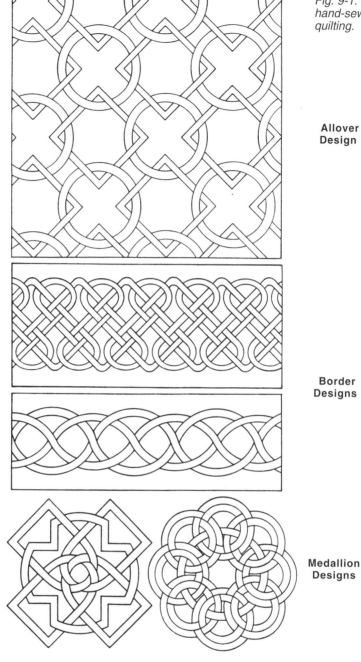

Fig. 9-1. Designs for hand-sewn corded quilting.

Allover Design

Border Designs

Medallion Designs

3. Cover the traced lines of the design with tiny, uniform stitches. At points where cross-over channels interrupt the line being stitched, move the needle between the fabric layers to the other side of the channel where the line continues, taking a tiny backstitch on each side of the interruption.

◆ When sewing with running stitches, periodically check the regularity of the stitches from the front.

◆ When backstitching, stretch the fabric in a hoop to prevent thread tension from pulling on the fabric.

4. Fill the stitch-outlined channels of the design with cord, either cable cord or acrylic yarn (refer to "Cords for Cording" on page 187), pulled through the channels with the aid of a tapestry needle or bodkin:

a. With the inner-lining side up, force the cord-threaded needle or bodkin into one end of a channel, piercing a hole through the lining only. Push the needle or bodkin through the channel until its forward movement is halted by a turn or a seam. Bring the needle or bodkin out of the channel through a hole punctured in the lining. Draw the cord through the channel, leaving a scanty tail exposed at the beginning.

b. If the needle or bodkin is stopped by an angle or curve it can't negotiate, bring it out to the surface, re-insert it into the same hole, and continue shoving it forward through the channel until it is stopped again. Push the needle or bodkin out of the inner lining at that point and pull the cord through the channel, but leave a tiny loop exposed at the angle or curve. When filling a long channel unimpeded by abrupt turns, break out of the channel at intervals to leave outside loops for slack to relieve the tension accumulated in the pulled cord.

c. When a seam crossing the channel blocks further progress, bring the needle or bodkin out of the inner lining, pull the excess cord through the channel, and cut the cord a short ¼" (6mm) from the lining where it emerged (Figs. 9-2 and 9-3).

d. Tug the fabric along the length of the corded channel to stretch out any constrictions caused by the drag of the cord. As the cording readjusts, the tails and loops retreat inside the channels.

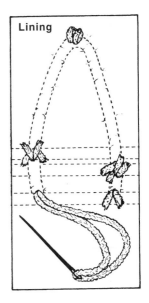

Fig. 9-3. Cording with doubled yarn.

5. Stretch and pin the corded quilting to a padded surface. Steam with an iron held above the fabric, and allow to cool and dry before moving.

6. Line the corded design. If needed, tack the outer lining to the inner lining inconspicuously at intervals. Cover the edges with binding or sew to an extension fabric, trimming bulky cords from the seam allowances if they interfere.

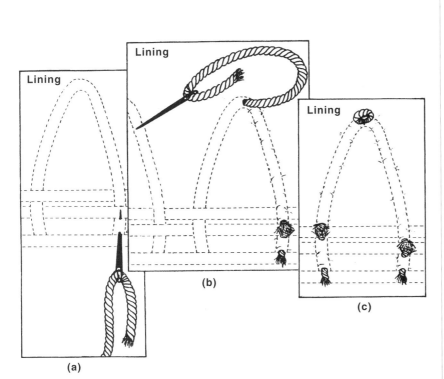

Fig. 9-2. Cording with cable cord: (a) Poke and wiggle the needle into and out of the inner lining. (b) At sharp turns, push the needle out, re-insert into the same hole and move forward. (c) Leave short tails where channels begin and end, and tiny loops at re-direction points.

Notes & Variations

After cording, the fabric between the cord-filled channels should be smooth and flat. For this result, channels ¼" (6mm) wide are safe. If the surface fabric has sufficient give, it will absorb the relief of elaborate cording through wider channels without disturbing the evenness of the intervening fabric, but test before application.

Number 50 cable cord or two strands of 4-ply acrylic yarn provide ample filler for a ¼" (6mm) channel. One strand of yarn will fill a channel ⅛" (3mm) wide. Comparing a ¼" (6mm) channel filled with #50 cable cord to a ¼" (6mm) channel filled with two strands of 4-ply acrylic yarn, the cable-corded channel has a more rounded, pronounced relief than the flatter, yarn-corded channel. Cable-corded fabric is firmer in hand than yarn-corded fabric.

Cable cord enters and exits a ¼" (6mm) channel as doubled cord, although a single cord remains inside, and requires larger openings and more effort to pull through the channels than doubled yarn. Doubled yarn enters and exits through smaller holes because pressure compresses its bulk, but, once inside, it expands to the same bulk that stays in the channel. A channel must have enough play to allow the interior movement of cord or yarn without jerking, but if the channel is too loose around the cord, the finished design will lack definition (Fig. 9-4). Choose a tapestry needle or bodkin with an eye just big enough to accept the cord or yarn that must be threaded through it. Relate the size of the shaft to the puncture the needle or bodkin needs to make in the inner lining. A puncture, preferably worked by pushing aside threads in the weave, should be barely large enough for the cord to pass through.

Fig. 9-4. To fit channel width to the cord, pin the cord between scraps of fabric and lining; test the slide of the cord. Remove the cord and measure the distance between pins.

Carefully done, yarn-corded designs are reversible. If entry and exit holes are poked through the lining without breaking threads in the weave, if the tails and loops left outside the openings are tugged, pushed, and teased back inside the channels, and if the weave distorted to make the openings is restored by scratching with a fingernail and needle, there won't be any procedural evidence to conceal underneath an outer lining. The inner lining becomes the outer lining. Select a loose weave for the one and only lining fabric.

String-guided yarn cording eliminates oversized entry and exit holes. Thread both ends of doubled string into a large-eyed needle with a long, slender shank. Work the needle into, through, and out of a channel segment. Loop doubled yarn through the loop at the end of the string. Pull on the string to lead the yarn into and through the channel until the yarn butts up against the seam at the end. Holding on to the string, stretch out the corded channel and cut the yarn at the beginning. Leave scanty tails to work into the channel and provide slack to relieve any strain on yarn stretched by pulling. If the channels are short and straight, the tails can be minimal. Remove the string (Fig. 9-5). John Flynn developed the string-guided method for cord insertion. He cords intricate designs from the top.

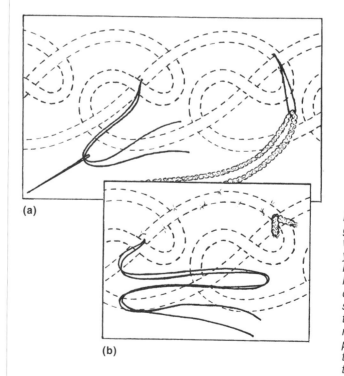

(a)

(b)

Fig. 9-5. String-guided cording with doubled yarn: (a) Yarn looped into the loop at the end of a doubled string run through a channel. (b) Yarn pulled through the channel on the string.

When corded quilting is integrated with stuffed quilting to raise designs that include shapes as well as lines, the combined techniques are called *trapunto*.

With an outer lining over an inner lining, cable-corded designs and non-reversible yarn-corded designs finish as three-layer textiles. To lighten the layering, use a gauzy inner lining for allover patterns, and cut away the uncorded lining around borders and isolated motifs.

For *single-fabric cording*, thread crossing over the cord in back substitutes for an inner lining. Particularly suitable for medallion-type motifs or abbreviated border designs, single-fabric cording is hand stitched with the fabric stretched in a frame or hoop large enough to expose the entire design. Trace the design on the right side of the fabric. With one hand, hold a length of cable cord underneath the channel to be corded. With the other hand, backstitch over both lines, alternating between a stitch on one side and a stitch on the other side, always scooping the needle down and up over the cord underneath. Pull the stitches against the sides of the cable cord, enclosing the upper half snugly with the fabric (Fig. 9-6).

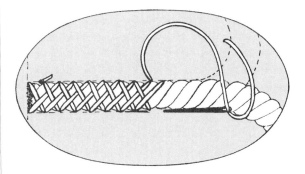

Fig. 9-7. Working on the wrong side of the fabric, use the closed herringbone stitch to oversew the cable cord.

Cut the cord where a channel segment begins and ends. Maintain an even channel width throughout. Adjust backstitching lengths around curves, taking longer stitches on the outside of the channel matched to shorter stitches on the inside. At outside angles, change to alternating the backstitches diagonally across the corner when alternating between the outside and inside of the channel is no longer possible; at the tip, turn to the back and tack the outer corner to the inside angle with stitches that aren't visible in front. Lining is optional. An alternate technique: Hand sew single-fabric cording from the back using a closed herringbone stitch to contain the cord (Fig. 9-7).

The channels of cord-quilted designs outlined with running stitches have a soft, blurry appearance. Backstitching, which outlines the channels with continuous, unbroken lines of thread, sharpens the design. Designs raised with single-fabric cording have the strongest definition. Cording, especially when elaborate and extensive, tends to shrink the fabric.

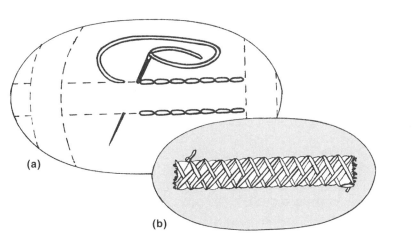

Fig. 9-6. (a) Using the alternating backstitch to secure cable cord underneath the fabric. (b) In back, crossover thread holds the cable cord in place.

HAND-SEWN CORDED QUILTING

IX-1—Running-stitched, cable-corded design.

IX-2—Duplicate designs with channels running-stitched on the left and backstitched on the right.

IX-3—Reverse side of the running-stitched design showing the ends and loops of the cable-cord filler.

IX-4—Single-fabric cording back-stitched over #50 cable cord.

IX-5—Reverse side of the backstitched design reveals the crossover thread that holds the cable cord.

MACHINE-SEWN CORDED QUILTING

—two layers of fabric covering cords confined within stitched channels, a combination that patterns the surface fabric with rounded ridges arranged in parallel rows.

PROCEDURES

1. Prepare a striped design composed of straight, wavy, or angled bands using equidistant double lines as the linear device. The most practical designs for machine-sewn corded quilting have parallel double-line channels that twist and turn, that touch but don't cross, and that continue uninterrupted by stops and re-starts where sewing thread must be secured (Fig. 9-8). The safe width for the double lines is ¼″ (6mm) or less, although straight, striped patterns will tolerate wider channels.

2. With a fine line, fabric-safe marker, trace a faint but distinct mirror-image copy of the design onto the lining (refer to "Transferring Designs" on page 205). Baste the lining to the surface fabric.

3. Sew by machine, covering the traced lines with straight stitching. If the design requires stopping a seam to start again a distance away, secure the stitching unnoticeably by tying the ends of the thread in back: (1) Pull the needle thread up and out on the lining side. (2) Tie the needle thread to the bobbin thread with a square knot. (3) Insert both threads into a hand-sewing needle; push the needle into the lining at the last stitch of the seam; bring it out half-the-needle's length away, and cut the threads at that point. (4) Steam press to set the stitching.

4. Fill the stitch-outlined channels of the design with cable cord or acrylic yarn, following procedures described on page 189, step #4, for "Hand-sewn Corded Quilting" (also refer to "Cords for Cording" on page 187). Most machine-sewn designs have channels with ready-made openings at the edge of the fabric. An elaborate, machine-sewn design may have closed interior channels as well.

5. Stretch and pin the corded quilting to a padded surface. Steam with an iron held above the fabric. Allow to cool and dry before removing the pins.

6. To prepare the edges of corded fabric for finishing or extension, remove stiff, bulky cord from the seam allowances. Measure the corded fabric from side to side across the center of the corded channels. Use that measurement when cutting the fabric that will be sewn to the edges of the cording and when cutting an outer lining for the corded design, if there are exposed cord ends to conceal. Ease the edges emptied of cords to match the fabric extension when sewing the two together.

NOTES & VARIATIONS

Review the Notes and Variations about "Hand-sewn Corded Quilting" that begin on page 190.

The most efficient designs for machine-stitched cording require sewing that moves down the fabric from top to bottom without any need to stop and re-position for a sharp turn or the ending/beginning of a seam. With the design traced on the lining, the bobbin side of the seam shows in front. Before sewing, test the balance between tension and stitch length on scraps, paying particular attention to the appearance of the bobbin stitches.

Straight-line channels may be stitched from the front when the width of the presser foot is the guide followed to gauge channel width and the spacing between channels. For solid cording, adjacent channels share the same seam, which can be widened with satin stitching or twin-needle seaming. Lead the cord through straight channels of moderate length with a tapestry needle or bodkin; or pull the cord through the channels with a piece of stiff wire, slightly longer than a channel, bent into a hook or loop at one end.

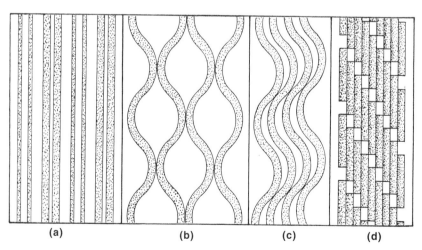

(a) (b) (c) (d)

Fig. 9-8. Continuous-line designs for machine sewing: (a, b, c) Designs with parallel, uninterrupted channels. (d) Design for solid cording with segmented channels. To stitch, sew the straight lines first, then the stepped lines that angle down and across, and oversew portions of the straight lines.

MACHINE-SEWN CORDED QUILTING

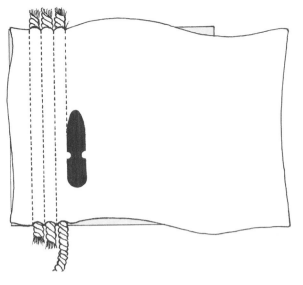

Fig. 9-9. Sewing the channel and the cord into the channel in one operation.

Twin-needle cording outlines narrow channels with two rows of stitching in front and interlaced stitching in back. Select a firm cord that fits between the twin needles, use a presser foot with a groove in the base, and choose a thin fabric that wraps the cord easily (Fig. 9-11).

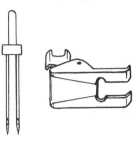

Fig. 9-11. Twin needle sizes—1.6mm, 2mm, 2.5mm, 3mm, 4mm, 6mm—indicate the space between needles, and that limits the width of the cord the stitching will be able to wrap. The groove on the base of the presser foot makes a passageway for the stitched cord.

Another option for straight-line patterns eliminates cord insertion as a separate activity. Channel stitching and cord insertion are simultaneous. (1) Start with a stiffly stabilized lining cut to size. Cut the surface fabric as long as the lining and corded channels, but wider than the lining to compensate for the curving of the surface fabric over the cords. Pin the edge of the surface fabric to the lining on one side. (2) With the surface fabric up, sew the first seam. (3) Insert a firm cord, such as cable cord, between the surface fabric and lining, pushing it up against the seam. With a zipper or cording foot, sew next to the cord, enclosing it inside a channel. (4) Continue adding corded rows, one against the other, or with uncorded separations to vary the design (Fig. 9-9). Indicate measured spacing between the cords with thin, faint guidelines marked on the surface fabric. If the surface fabric is bias-cut and cautiously eased or stretched as sewing proceeds, the cord can be stitched into rows that curve.

The humped ridges caused by the cord underneath are more pronounced when cord is stitched inside the channels rather than inserted after the channels are seamed (Fig. 9-10). Using either method of insertion, the embossed surface will have more texture if the cord inside the channels is rough with knobs and twists that show through the fabric. **Floaters** of cord deliberately brought out to the surface in certain places contribute the texture of cut, brushed-out ends to the overall relief.

With *single-fabric machine-stitched cording*, a network of thread encloses the cord. Twin-needle or zigzag stitching substitutes for the lining.

Increase the machine's top-tension setting to tighten the thread that crosses over the cord in back. Test the raised result of various settings on a scrap of practice fabric. Start stitching with the cord located under the fabric and between the lowered needles. Guide the cord under the presser foot as stitching progresses (Fig. 9-12).

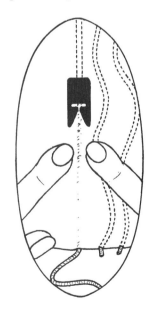

Fig. 9-12. Place a forefinger on either side of the cord underneath the fabric to centralize it as it moves toward the presser foot between the twin needles.

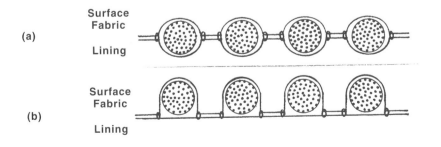

(a) Surface Fabric / Lining

(b) Surface Fabric / Lining

Fig. 9-10. Profile diagram illustrates the difference in surface elevation between (a) cord inserted after sewing the channels and (b) cord inserted while sewing.

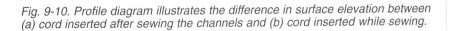

Single-fabric machine-stitched cording will follow straight or curving paths. Mark the design on the fabric with faint, temporary, single lines; use the presser foot to regulate the spacing between rows; or improvise a pattern while sewing.

The **zigzag cording** process is similar to twin-needle cording but the stitching in front is different. Stitched thread crosses back and forth over the ridge created by the cord underneath. Select a firm cord and choose a zigzag stitch width that straddles the cord closely. Zigzag stitching also attaches cord to the surface of the fabric, embellishing the fabric with cord that's visible between the crossover threads, or, with stitch length reduced almost to 0, with cord that's invisible under a solid covering of satin-stitched thread. **Floaters**, loops and ends of cord released from the covering thread, add loose texture to the surface. To interrupt a line of zigzag cording with loops of cord to the sides, stop stitching with the needle down, loop the cord back and forth in front of the needle, zigzag across the center of the loops, zigzag back for security, and continue forward (Fig. 9-13).

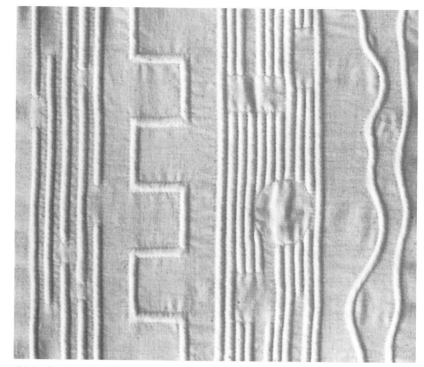

IX-6—Sampler of machine-sewn patterns with channels cable-corded after stitching.

MACHINE-SEWN CORDED QUILTING

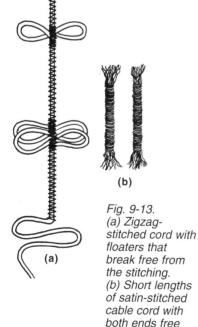

Fig. 9-13.
(a) Zigzag-stitched cord with floaters that break free from the stitching.
(b) Short lengths of satin-stitched cable cord with both ends free and untwisted.

IX-7—Two sizes of cable cord tightly encased as the seams were stitched.

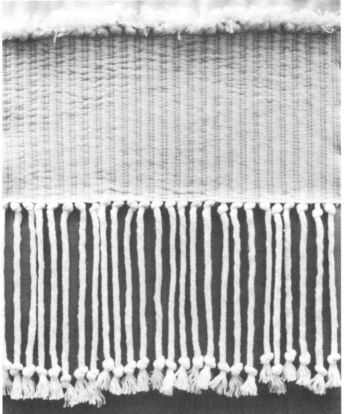

IX-8—Muslin textured by the cord inside the channels: (from the top) yarn, plastic beads, knotted twine, single-crocheted cord, knotted and twisted plastic strips.

IX-9 —Close cording that emerges from the channels as knotted fringe.

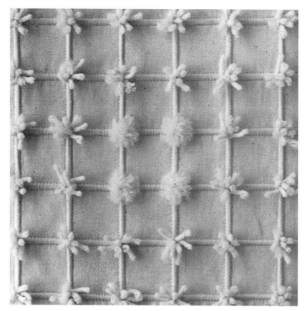

IX-10—Channels corded with yarn floaters brought to the surface where the grid of channels intersects. Yarn ends in the center were brushed out.

MACHINE-SEWN
CORDED QUILTING

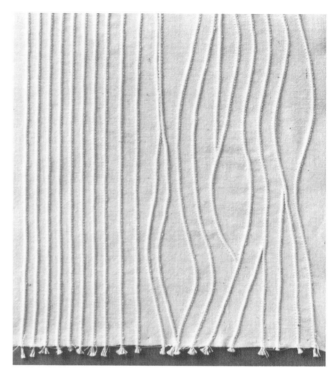

IX-11—Twin-needle single-fabric cording over heavy crochet cotton.

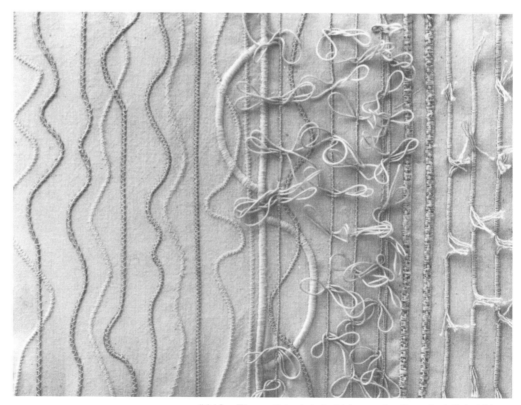

IX-12—Zigzag-stitched single-fabric sampler: (from the left) Invisible and visible zigzag cording; satin-stitched cord; looped cord; single-crocheted, satin-stitched cord; short lengths of satin-stitched cord with loose ends frayed.

SURFACE CORDING

—parallel tubular casings, raised and stitched into the fabric like tucks, that round out over the foundation when filled with cord.

PROCEDURES

1. Decide how much fabric to allow for a tubular casing for the selected cord (refer to "Cords for Cording" on page 187). Pin the cord inside a scrap of the chosen fabric, remove the pins and cord, and measure the distance between pinholes:

   ◆ For cording to be stitched into folds, confine the cord snugly with pins.

   ◆ For cording to be inserted after the casings are sewn, ease the covering to make room for cord movement inside (Fig. 9-14).

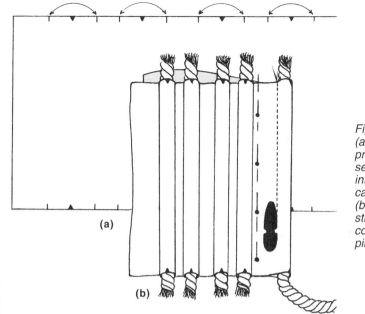

(a)

(b)

Fig. 9-15.
(a) Fabric prepared for sewing cord into tubular casings.
(b) Machine stitching a cord into a pinned fold.

Fig. 9-14. Testing the fit of a tubular casing around a cord to set the fabric allowance.

2. To estimate the amount of fabric required for a surface-corded application: (1) Multiply the amount of fabric needed to encase one cord by the rows of cord pre-planned for the target measurement, and (2) add that total to the target measurement for the application. Cut fabric for cording to size up and down as well as across the cords.

3. With a fabric-safe marking tool or scissor nips, mark the top and bottom edges of the cording fabric, right side up, with measured spaces for each cord casing and measured separations in between:

   ◆ For cord inserted-and-stitched in one operation, add a center point in between the seamline positions marked across the top and bottom edges of the fabric (see (a) in Fig. 9-15). Separations between the casings must be more than, or at least equal to, the width of the machine's cording or zipper foot.

   ◆ For cord inserted after stitching, the minimum separation between casings equals the overlap of adjacent, encased cords (Fig. 9-16). For each casing, indicate seamline positions across the top and bottom edges of the fabric, and connect the position marks opposite each other with faint but distinct lines up and down the fabric (see (a) in Fig. 9-17).

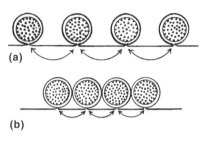

(a)

(b)

Fig. 9-16. Profile views of surface-corded channels demonstrate:
(a) The difference between the actual space between seams and the space that's visible between the sides of the corded tubes.
(b) The minimum space between seams for adjacent corded tubes that touch.

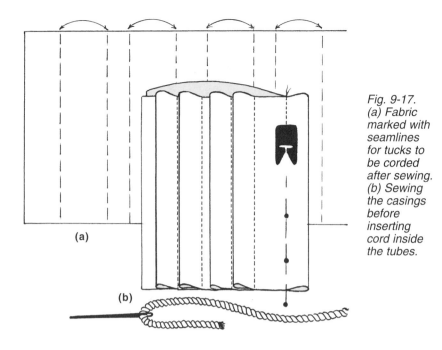

Fig. 9-17. (a) Fabric marked with seamlines for tucks to be corded after sewing. (b) Sewing the casings before inserting cord inside the tubes.

ric with cording spaces and separations, sew the ends of the fabric together, matching the markings. Stitch-and-cord each tube in one operation, butting the ends of the cord where they meet, or sew the tubular casings and leave an opening in each seam for cord insertion afterwards.

Unlike hand-sewn and machine-sewn corded quilting, surface-corded channels manage cords of any diameter (refer to "Cords for Cording" on page 187). Patterns are limited to straight rows varied with cording that differs in size.

Covered cords that are separated from the fabric can be curved and coiled during application. *Detached cording* is made from strips of bias-cut fabric wide enough to be folded lengthwise around the selected cord (Fig. 9-18). The cord is machine-stitched inside the casing with a zipper or cording foot.

4. Stitch and cord the tucks:

- To stitch-and-cord in one operation: (1) Fold between the edge marks that indicate the center of a casing space and pin away from the location of the seam. (2) Insert cord inside the pinned fold. (3) Pushing the cord against the fold, stitch next to the cord with a cording or zipper foot attached to the machine (see (b) in Fig. 9-15).

- To stitch the casing and insert the cord afterwards: (1) Pin match the seamlines that enclose a casing space. (2) Sew the seamlines together, removing each pin at the approach of the presser foot. (3) Threading the cord into a tapestry needle or bodkin, or using a hooking or clamping tool, work cord inside the tubular casings (see (b) in Fig. 9-17).

5. Remove cord from seam-allowance areas to prepare the edges of surface-corded fabric for finishing or extension. Center each flattened casing over the seam underneath and baste within the seam allowance.

NOTES & VARIATIONS

When a surface-corded application encircles, the corded tubes must be continuous. After marking the flat fab-

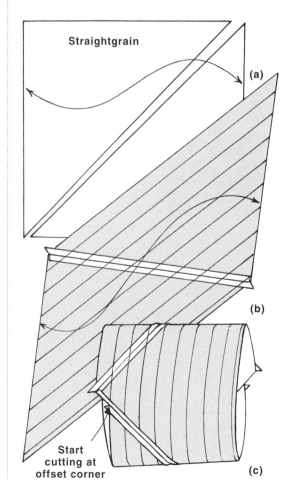

Straightgrain

(a)

(b)

Start cutting at offset corner

(c)

Fig. 9-18. To cut a continuous length of bias strip: (a) Cut a square on the straightgrain of the fabric. Cut in half diagonally. Sew the straight-cut edges of the triangles together as the arrows indicate. (b) Mark the wrong side of the pieced fabric with appropriately spaced parallel lines. Sew the opposite edges of the fabric together as the arrows indicate, (c) but offset one corner to match the first line, and match all succeeding lines to the overhanging end.

For **piping or welting**, fold a strip cut wide enough to include two seam allowances around the cord, with right side out, and machine stitch. Prepare piping/welting with seam allowances appropriate for sewing into a seam joining two pieces of fabric, or laying over a foundation in overlapping rows (Fig. 9-19).

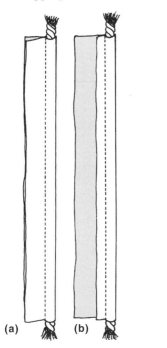

Fig. 9-19. (a) Piping/welting for in-seam application. (b) Piping/welting for laid-on application.

To sew piping/welting into a seam, baste it to the right side of one piece of fabric with all edges matching. If the seam is circular, stop sewing about 2″ (5cm) from the meeting point; open the piping/welting casing and sew the ends together; re-fold, and finish the basting (Fig. 9-20). Sew the second piece of fabric to the first with right sides facing and the piping/welting in between.

Piping/welting intended for laid-on application needs to be fabricated with unequal seam allowances, one scanty and one at least twice as wide as the diameter of the covered cord (see (b) in Fig. 9-19). Lay the covered cord on the foundation with the short seam allowance underneath; sew to the foundation by stitching over the cording seam. Place the corded edge of the next row up against the cording of the row just

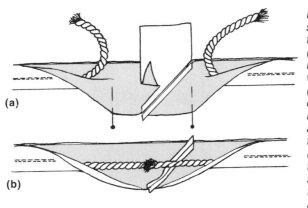

Fig. 9-20. To join in-seam piping/welting that surrounds: (a) Stop sewing and remove all piping/welting stitching 2″ (5cm) on either side of the meeting point. Make angled folds and trim the ends of the strips as shown. (b) Sew the ends together. Re-fold the seamed strip over the butted cord, align all edges, and resume the interrupted stitching.

applied; sew to the foundation, catching the wide seam allowance of the previous row in the seam. To start or stop a row internally, fold the end of the strip diagonally to the back, removing cord from the fold-back (Fig. 9-21). For a coiled application, the wide seam allowance may need clipping, particularly at the start, but avoid clipping deeply.

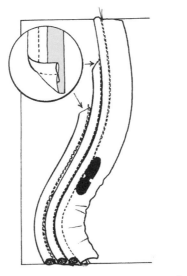

Fig. 9-21. Machine sewing rows of piping/welting laid over a foundation.

Seam allowances are inside **corded tubing**, another type of detached cording. To make corded tubing: (1) Cut a strip with two moderate seam allowances. Fold lengthwise around a cord with the wrong side outside. The cord should extend beyond the fabric strip by a duplicate length. (2) Using a zipper or cording foot, stitch next to but not tightly against the cord. At the end of the strip, pivot on the needle and stitch across the cord several

times. Trim the seam allowance close to the stitching (Fig. 9-22).

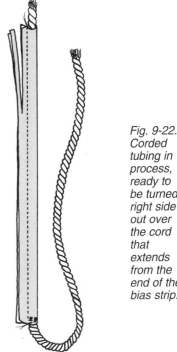

Fig. 9-22. Corded tubing in process, ready to be turned right side out over the cord that extends from the end of the bias strip.

(3) Holding the top of the cord, push the casing down and over the second half of the cord until it is covered with fabric right side out. Cut off the first half of the cord. (4) Hand stitch corded tubing with its seam against the foundation fabric. Working from the front, slip-stitch the tubing to the foundation, or, working from the back, stretch the foundation in a hoop and back-stitch into the tubing as it is pushed up against the fabric from underneath. Corded tubing is an appropriate medium for scrolled designs.

IX-13—*Tubes that sit on top of the same muslin that wraps the cable cord stitched inside.*

SURFACE CORDING

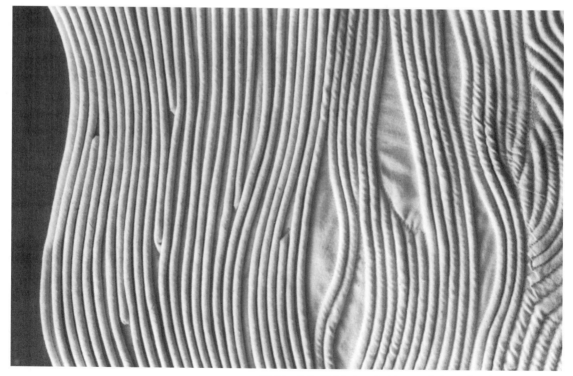

IX-14—*(left side) Strips of piping applied to a foundation in curving rows. (right side) Corded quilting with the cords stitched underneath muslin cut on the bias to accommodate the curving arrangement.*

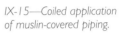

IX-15—Coiled application of muslin-covered piping.

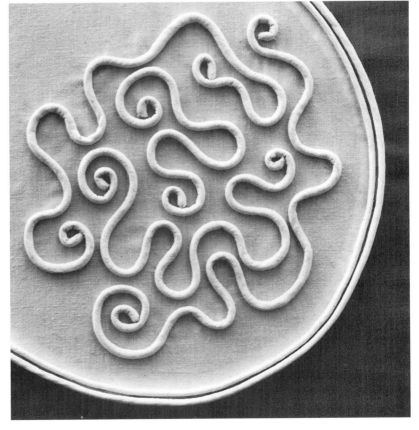

IX-16—Fabric embellished with corded tubing applied in a serpentine design and edged with a double row of piping/welting.

*F*unctionally, *quilting* is stitching that fastens three layers of fabric—a top, a batting, and a lining—into a stable textile that becomes more than the sum of its parts. Decoratively, quilt stitching indents a design into the soft thickness of the layered textile with interrupted or continuous lines of thread. Hand-stitched lines of thread have a different effect on the padded surface than thread lines sewn by machine.

A quilted textile has the bulk and warmth of its fabric components, and a substance in hand influenced by the kind and amount of stitching applied overall.

QUILTING

10 Quilting

Note: This chapter begins with BASICS, indicated by a gray band located underneath the relevant columns.

QUILTING BASICS

TRANSFERRING DESIGNS

Hand quilted or machine quilted, the type of design, the size of the top, and the quilting procedure are considerations when deciding whether to copy the design onto the fabric before the top is basted to the batting and lining, or afterwards, just prior to quilting. Copy before basting when intricate allover designs cross large areas of the surface, when the small size of the top makes it easy to trace the lines beforehand, or when the top/batting/lining will be hand quilted in a frame. Localized designs involving repeated shapes may be marked as quilting proceeds. Improvised patterns require little or no marking at all.

Mark lines on the right side of the top after the fabric has been pressed smooth. Immobilize the fabric to prevent it from moving during tracing. Use a fabric-safe substance that marks fine lines, barely distinct enough to see when stitching, durable enough to last until they are quilted, and preferably coverable by the stitching. If the lines will be visible after quilting, they must be completely removable by brushing, erasing, washing, or any other method compatible with the quilted textile. Chemicals in the marking substance should do no harm in the future. *To avoid unpleasant surprises, always test a marking substance on the fabric of choice before using extensively.*

TRACING METHODS

- Placing the design underneath the top, use a light box to expose the lines that need tracing. If the top is small, daylight shining through window glass will reveal the design to be traced.

- Place dressmaker's carbon between the design and the top. Trace over the lines of the design with a tracing wheel or an empty ballpoint pen.

- Heat press to automatically transfer a fresh photocopy of the design to the top (the image will be reversed) or, using a transfer pencil, trace the design onto paper and heat press the transfer copy of the design onto the fabric.

- Make a perforated stencil by machine sewing with a large needle and no thread over the lines of the design traced onto light cardboard or acetate. Pounce the design onto the top by forcing a harmless powder, such as cinnamon or talc, through the punctures; or define the design with dots marked on the top through the holes.

- Place a commercial or hand-cut slotted stencil made from soft plastic on the top and draw lines, guided by the channeled openings, to reproduce the design.

- Tape nylon net over the design-on-paper and trace the design on the nylon filaments with an indelible pen. Pinning the net to the fabric, follow the indications on the netting to mark the top with a broken line that describes the design.

- Trace around templates moved from place to place on the top. A template could be a teacup, a glass, a cookie cutter, or another suitably shaped household object; or it could be a cutout of cardboard, sandpaper, acetate, heavyweight non-woven interfacing, or lightweight plastic.

- Using a firm, straight edge long enough to reach across the top, trace straight lines on taut fabric. Use an artist's tool called a flexible curve, which stays bent into serpentine shapes, to trace repeated, curvy lines.

- To quilt long, straight lines without pre-marking, stitch next to one or both edges of masking tape stuck to the surface. The width of the masking tape—¼" (6mm), ½" (1.3cm), ¾" (2cm), 1" (2.5cm)—controls the spacing between lines. Do not leave masking tape on the top between quilting sessions.

- Stitch around the edges of a flexible, sticky template cut from adhesive-backed Contac paper or pressure-sensitive labels. Sticky templates have limited re-use and should be removed from the top after the outline is quilted to prevent residue from permeating the fabric.

- For echo quilting, guide the needle by using a thumb or forefinger to measure the distance between outlines.

When tops are large and elements in the design are continuous and aligned, divide the fabric into halves, quarters, and even eighths with guideline folds or basting; hold the fabric taut and keep the weave on grain; use a pattern with straight edges that can be matched to the straightgrain of the fabric; and measure frequently to check the position of motifs in balanced, symmetrical designs.

BATTING

Batting is manufactured from natural or synthetic fibers which have been mingled together, spread out into sheets, and treated to adhere. For stability and durability, batting requires a covering of fabric fastened with stitches. To the fabric that covers it, batting imparts warmth, body, and a softness receptive to the imprint of the stitch. The fiber content of the batting affects its utilization.

Cotton batting is valued by many quilters for its pleasing acceptance of hand-held needle action. Its thinness and softness invite fine quilting and elaborate, overall patterns, which make a decorative asset of a necessity. Cotton batting must be quilted every 2" (5cm) at the outside, preferably closer, otherwise it shifts and separates with use and becomes lumpy and ropey when washed. Gentle pre-washing is advisable because it tends to shrink. When quilted, a textile padded with cotton batting has less relief than a textile with polyester batting inside.

For many contemporary quilters, the primary attraction of polyester batting is its resistance to tearing and shredding, which allows lines of quilting to be spaced 4" (10cm) to 6" (15cm) apart. Variety and versatility are two of the other reasons for its popularity: Low-loft, regular-loft, and high-loft thicknesses; bonded or needlepunched finishing; differences in suppleness and resilience; and availability in standard, mattress-related sizes as well as by the yard. The disadvantage of polyester batting is a phenomenon called "bearding." A static-caused migration of batting fibers through the weave of top and lining fabrics, especially after washing, bearding leaves a fuzz on the surface that is particularly noticeable on fabric of a different color. To control this reaction, manufacturers bond the polyester fibers in battings with thermal or resin processing, finishes that

variously affect the hand and needle receptivity of a batt and its bearding resistance. Bearding is a definite problem when polyester batting is combined with fabrics that have a polyester content, and when the batting has been cheaply manufactured. Bearding is not a major problem when good quality batting is combined with closely woven, natural fiber fabrics.

Blended battings have a mix of cotton and polyester fibers. An effort by batting manufacturers to eliminate the problems while preserving the best of both fiber-worlds, blended battings offer the thinness and coolness of cotton with the quilting spaciousness of polyester and high resistance to bearding.

When cotton flannel or cotton knit fabrics substitute for batting, the barely padded fabric is supple and thin and the quilting lines may be widely spaced without creating washability problems, but the unique texture of the quilting is noticeably diminished.

Wool batting is soft, warm, resilient, and quilts like cotton. One manufacturer claims its 100% wool batting is washable and withstands 3" (7.5cm) stitching separations. Silk fibers make a featherweight, luxurious batting, most appropriate, obviously, for use with silk fabrics. Because it is expensive and unusually small in size, silk batting is generally confined to medium- and small-sized projects. Unlike cotton and polyester, wool and silk battings suffer the inconvenience of limited availability.

To choose a batting suitable for a specific project from the many brands on the market, ask to feel a sample and test its crushability and drape. Before beginning the project, test the batting with the chosen fabrics: (1) Quilt a small square of top/batting/lining in the intended manner with lines that are closely and widely spaced. (2) Measure the quilted sample. (3) Pull, twist, rub, wash, and dry the sample.

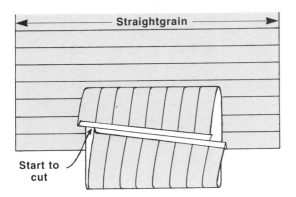

Start to cut

Fig. 10-1. To cut a continuous strip on the straightgrain, mark the back of the fabric with lines spaced a strip-width apart. Match the lines—but set off by one spacing—and sew the ends together. Cut on the line.

(4) Measure and compare with the original dimensions. Evaluate the condition of the batting between stitching lines, and the texture and loft of the quilted surface. (5) Make adjustments accordingly.

THE DOUBLE-BINDING EDGE FINISH

Binding frames a quilted textile with a smooth, narrow, protective edging. A doubled binding also increases the firmness and durability of the edge.

If the quilted textile is rectangular or square, *take length and width measurements across the center* to estimate the amount of binding required, and to cut the binding for each side. Pre-measured binding based on center measurements equalizes opposite sides. With the quilted textile smoothed out flat, use a tape to measure curving edges for binding length.

To bind straight edges, cut binding strips on the straight of the fabric, piecing the strips together as needed (refer to Fig. 3-23 on page XX), or cut continuous straight-grain binding (Fig. 10-1). For edges that curve, cut the strips on the bias (refer to Fig. 3-24 on page XX and Fig. 9-18 on page XXX). The width of a doubled-binding strip equals four times the width of the finished binding in front, plus two seam allowances. *Finished binding width equals the seam allowance around the edge of the quilted top at the least, and any batting that extends beyond the edge to fill a wider binding at the*

most. Cut a binding strip for each straight edge, adding two seam allowances and an extra amount to the length of strips that will be mitered at the corners. Cut one extended binding strip with two seam allowances for edges that curve. Fold the binding strips in half lengthwise and press.

Stabilize the quilted edges with machine basting inside the seam allowance. Mark long, straight edges at half and quarter points; mark the binding for those edges at half and quarter points, and mark the pre-measured length of the

binding at each end. Match and pin the cut edge of the binding to the edge of the top, one edge at a time, with the extra binding for mitering extending beyond each corner.

Sew the binding to each quilted edge, starting and stopping at the points where the seam allowance on the quilt turns corners. Long quilted edges may need gentle easing to match the pre-measured length of the binding. Ease the binding around curves. Miter the binding at corners. Turn the binding over the edges to the lining side of the quilted textile. Blindstitch the already-folded edge of the binding to the lining, concealing the machine-sewn seam under the fold (Fig. 10-2). A doubled binding should feel as thick all the way to its edge as the body of the quilted textile.

To bind entirely by machine, sew the binding to the lining side of the quilt, turn the folded edge to the front, and edgestitch through all layers to secure.

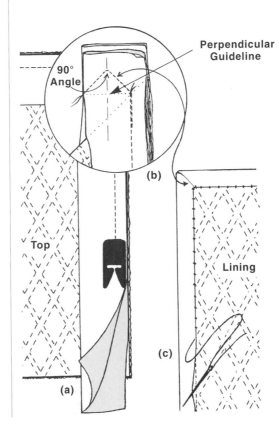

Perpendicular Guideline

90° Angle

(b)

Top

Lining

(c)

(a)

Fig. 10-2. (a) Sewing doubled binding to a quilted edge. (b) Do not sew through the quilt's seam allowances at corners to be mitered: Fold the quilted textile diagonally to match adjoining edges and binding overlaps. Mark a guideline perpendicular to the end of the seam; draw a 90-degree-angle seamline and sew the binding overlaps together as shown. Trim next to the seam. (c) Blindstitch the binding's folded edge to the lining.

Chapter 10   QUILTING   207

JOINING MODULAR UNITS

Choose one of the following methods to assemble pre-quilted modules into a larger construction.

CONCEALED CONNECTIONS

One of the two edges to be joined must be free from all quilting for a breadth equal to two seam allowances at least. For example, stop quilting ½″ (1.3cm) from the edge if the seam allowance is ¼″ (6mm); stop quilting 1″ (2.5cm) from the edge if the seam allowance is ½″(1.3cm). Pin the lining and batting of that edge back and out of the way, exposing the reverse side of the top. With right sides together, pin and sew the exposed top edge to the edge (all layers) of the second module. Spreading both modules out flat, trim the unattached batting to abut the seamed batting. With the seam allowance turned under, blindstitch the folded edge of the loose lining to the lining of the second module (Fig. 10-3). Finish quilting as needed to complete the design.

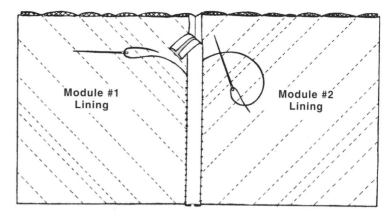

Fig. 10-4. Taped connection: Sew two modules together. Cover the seam allowances with blindstitched tape.

TAPED CONNECTIONS

Cut a strip of lining fabric four seam-allowances wide and as long as the modules to be joined. From the strip, make a tape with the seam allowances on each side pressed underneath. With right sides facing, sew the edges of two modules together, stitching through all layers. Picking apart any quilting seams, cut the batting out of the seam allowances and trim the lining seam allowances by half. Spread both modules out flat and finger press the seam allowances open. Cover the seam allowances with tape blindstitched to the lining on both sides (Fig. 10-4).

STRIPPED CONNECTIONS

Cut two strips, one for the top and one for the lining, each as wide as the desired spread plus two seam allowances, and as long as the modules to be joined. Sandwich the edge of one module between the two strips, right sides facing, and sew through all layers. With right sides together, sew the strip of top fabric to the second module. Spread both modules out to the sides of the connecting strip. Cut a length of batting wide enough to fill in the gap behind the top strip; hand sew the edges of the batting to the abutting seam allowances with large, loose stitches. Smooth the lining strip over the seam allowances and batting insert; with the seam allowance turned under, blindstitch the folded edge of the lining strip to the lining of the opposite module (Fig. 10-5). Add quilting to the stripping.

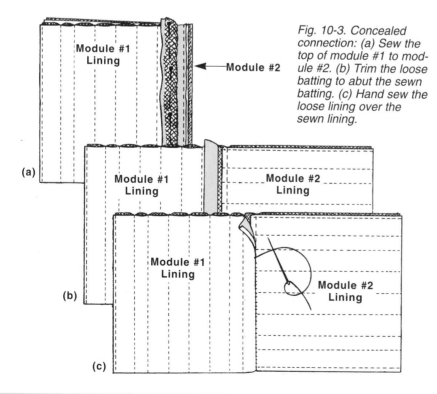

Fig. 10-3. Concealed connection: (a) Sew the top of module #1 to module #2. (b) Trim the loose batting to abut the sewn batting. (c) Hand sew the loose lining over the sewn lining.

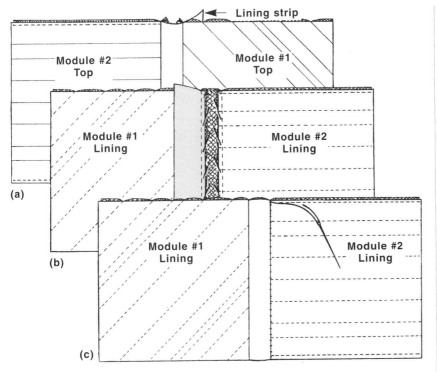

Fig. 10-5. Stripped connection: (a) Join modules to strips, leaving one edge of the lining strip loose. (b) Fill the space behind the top strip with batting tacked to the seam allowances. (c) Hand sew the folded edge of the lining strip to the adjoining module.

- Figurative motifs that are repeated in an orderly manner, or single motifs that are the focus of attention (Fig. 10-6).
- Patterns that fill in the backgrounds within outlined shapes and between figurative motifs, that connect figurative motifs to borders, and inner borders to outer borders. Background fillers are also used allover to cover the fabric without interruption from edge to edge (Figs. 10-6 and 10-7).

HAND QUILTING

—lines of running stitches designed to adorn and secure an impressionable top fabric to the soft batting and lining that are layered underneath.

PROCEDURES

1. Develop a design that will cover the full extent of the fabric with lines to be inscribed with running stitches. The stitched lines must be close enough to merge the three layers of top, batting, and lining into a single, stable textile (refer to "Batting" on page 206). Contrast in the direction, spacing, and density of the lines exploits the bas-relief potential of padded fabric. The simplest quilting design is an allover pattern with or without a border. Complex quilting designs combine:

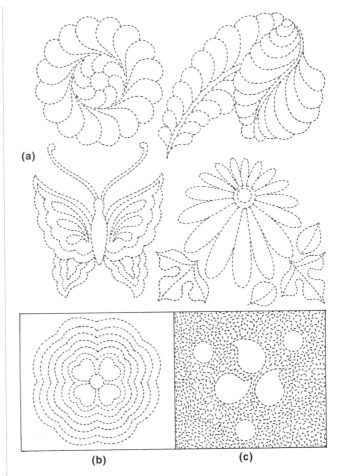

Fig. 10-6. Hand quilting designs: (a)Traditional figurative motifs. (b) Echo quilting and (c) stippling are specialty fillers that force surrounded motifs to stand out from closely quilted backgrounds.

Fig. 10-7. Designs for background fillers.

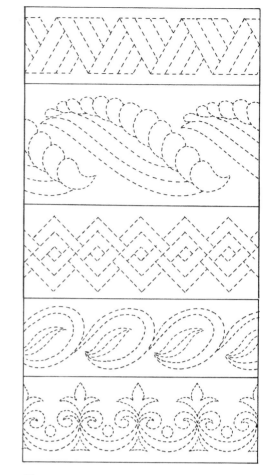

Fig. 10-8. Traditional border patterns.

- Outer borders that frame the interior quilting, and inner borders that enclose a portion of the greater design (Fig. 10-8).

2. Transfer the design onto the right side of fabric that has been cut to size for the top (refer to "Transferring Designs" on page 205). With fabric-safe markings, make faint but visible lines durable enough to survive the necessary handling prior to stitching. Fillers and motifs that are gauged by eye or improvised while quilting do not require marking, such as:

- Echo quilting ((b) in Fig. 10-6) mimics the contours of figurative shapes with a succession of ever-widening outlines spaced ¼″ (6mm) to ¾″ (2cm) apart.

- Stipple quilting ((c) in Fig. 10-6) surrounds figurative shapes with meandering, wavering, running stitches spaced at the most ¼″ (6mm) apart.

- Designs stitched as inspiration directs.

3. Cut the batting and lining slightly larger than the top. If the top is big (e.g., adult bed-covering size), cut the batting and lining 4″ (10cm) larger all around. For smaller tops, reduce the increase accordingly.

4. To baste the top, batting, and lining together, clear a firm surface large enough to support all or most of the fabric (a clean floor or utility table), or use a frame the size of the lining (Fig. 10-22). With the right side down, spread, square off, smooth, and

immobilize the lining by taping the edges to the surface or attaching the edges to the sides of the frame. Center the batting over the lining and smooth it out. Center and smooth the top over both. Hold the layers together temporarily with rows of long, straight pins while basting with thread or safety pins:

- Thread extra-long lengths of thread into a long, straight needle or a curved needle. Sew with running stitches about ½″ (1.3cm) long underneath and 1½″ (4cm) long on the surface. Baste in straight rows, spaced 6″ (15cm) apart or closer, that grid the surface or radiate from the center to the edges. Finish by basting around the outside edges inside the seam allowance (Fig.10-9).

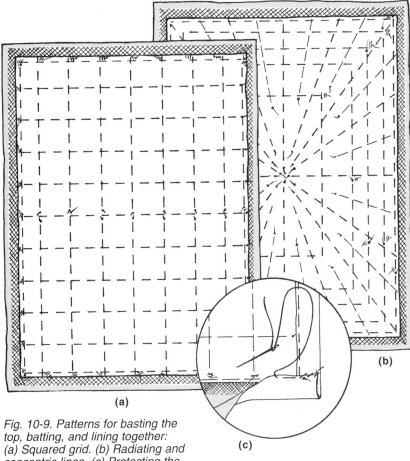

(a)

Fig. 10-9. Patterns for basting the top, batting, and lining together: (a) Squared grid. (b) Radiating and concentric lines. (c) Protecting the edges by folding and basting the extra lining to the seam allowance around the top.

(b)

(c)

◆ Pin with brass or nickel-plated steel safety pins, size 00, 0, or 1. Start at one end of the top/batting/lining. Smoothing outward constantly, insert rows of safety pins spaced 4″ (10cm) apart. Use a grapefruit spoon to help in closing the pins. Baste the outside edges with needle and thread (Fig. 10-10).

Roll large quilts as rows of basting are completed, reaching over the roll to continue basting. If the quilting design is already marked on the top, try to baste between the lines.

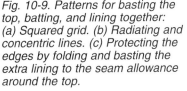

Fig. 10-10. Basting with pins.

5. Follow the lines of the quilting design with small, even, running stitches. Using sturdy quilting thread inserted into a short, strong, quilting needle called a between, sew through all the layers using a needle action that produces stitches which look the same in back as they do in front. Maintain a steady, moderate tension on the thread, pulling the stitches into the padded fabric to inscribe the design into the surface (Figs. 10-11, 10-12, and 10-13).

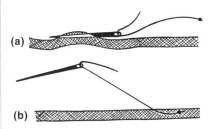

Fig. 10-11. (a) To start quilting, make a small knot in the end of an 18″ (46cm) length of quilting thread. Insert the needle into the top ½″ (1.3cm) from the outline where stitching will begin; run the needle through the batting and out at the starting point. (b) Tug on the thread to pop the knot through the top, to lodge in the batting.

(c) An alternative to buried knots utilizes thread 36″ (91.5cm) long. Use half the thread to quilt in one direction; use the other half to quilt in another direction.

While quilting, place the basted top/batting/lining in a frame or hoop, allowing some slack in the stretch to accommodate the quilting technique; or lap quilt without using stretching hardware:

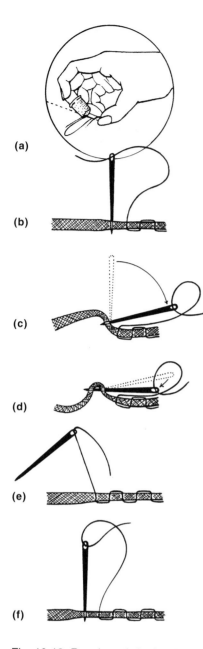

(a)

(b)

(c)

(d)

(e)

(f)

Fig. 10-12. Running-stitched quilting:
(a) The third finger of the sewing
hand, wearing a thimble, pushes and
rocks the needle through the top/bat-
ting/lining which is pinched toward
the needle by the thumb.
Underneath, the second or third finger of the other hand pushes the
point of the needle back up to the
surface. (b, c, d) The action of the
needle as it takes one stitch.
(e) Pulling the thread out and
(f) starting another stitch with a perpendicular needle. The needle can
take two or three stitches at a time
before pulling out the thread.

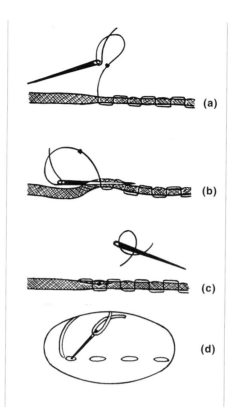

(a)

(b)

(c)

(d)

Fig. 10-13. To secure quilt stitching
when thread runs out, or at the end
of a quilting line: (a) Knot the thread
1/2" (1.3cm) from the surface. (b)
Insert the needle as if taking another
stitch but turn it backwards. Weave
the needle through the batting and
around the threads of previous stitches; bring it out half-its-length away.
(c) Tug the knot into the batting. Cut
the thread where it emerges. (d) To
secure with a pierced backstitch: End
with a tiny backstitch. Stab the backstitch with the needle, run the needle
through the batting, bring it out half-
the-needle's length away, and cut the
thread at the surface.

Fig. 10-14. Quilting frame
with the basted top/bat-
ting/lining rolled around
long rails to expose a
reachable section for
quilting. The material will
be unrolled and re-rolled
to move unquilted sec-
tions into view. For additional stability, pin the
sides to strips of muslin
tacked to the stretcher
bars at each end.

a. Quilting frames expand to
   expose the entire width of a
   large-sized quilting project,
   and maintain the basted
   top/batting/lining in ready-to-
   quilt position until the quilting is finished (Fig. 10-14).
   A quilting frame requires floor
   space, a top marked with the
   design before basting and setting into the frame, and dex-
   terity with the needle because
   the quilter sits facing the
   design from one direction.
   Frame quilting stabilizes the
   top/batting/lining for the
   duration of the quilting, so
   close basting isn't necessary
   and quilting can begin anywhere on the surface.

b. Quilting hoops are round,
   oval, or half-round, available
   in diameters from 10"(25cm)
   to 29"(73.5cm), and have
   deep rings with butterfly-
   screw clamps to cope with
   heavy, padded fabric
   (Fig. 10-15).

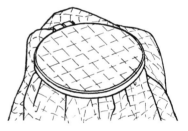

Fig. 10-15. Top/batting/lining
clamped into a 29"(73.5cm) hoop.
Change to a half-circle hoop when
quilting the outer edges, or baste
extra fabric to the edge to continue
stretching in the round hoop.

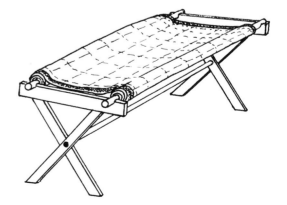

Hoop quilting is portable and flexible, allowing access to a selected portion of the design from any direction. To prepare for hoop quilting, baste extensively and protect the edges. If basted with safety pins, remove pins that interfere with clamping. Prop one side of the hoop on the edge of a table. Support the opposite side close to the body in a comfortable manner to facilitate the stitching activity. If the design isn't already outlined, trace the design on the top when the top/batting/lining is stretched tight in the hoop, before relaxing the stretch to begin quilting. For hoop quilting, designs are stitched from the center out to the edges. To prevent wrinkles, remove the top/batting/-lining from the hoop between quilting sessions.

c. Lap quilting needs the preparation of very close basting to be successful, but it is the most easily maneuverable of all the methods. Instead of quilting with one hand above and one hand underneath, use one hand to grasp and manipulate the fabric in front of the needle, which is maneuvered by the other hand. Lap quilting always moves from the center of the design outward. To provide an area of tension, sit in an upholstered chair and pin the top/batting/lining to the cloth on the arm, or wear denim jeans and pin to the cloth covering a knee, and quilt away from the anchor. Lap quilting is particularly suitable for small projects, and for large projects that have been divided into smaller modules.

6. When the quilting is complete, remove all basting thread except the thread inside the seam allowances at the edges. Trim the edges of the batting and lining flush with the trued-up edge of the top. Assemble quilted modules together using one of the methods described in "Joining Modular Units" on page 208. Cover the edges of a finished quilt or quilted item with machine-sewn, doubled binding (refer to "The Doubled-Binding Edge Finish" on page 207), or include the quilted piece within a larger construction of unquilted fabric.

NOTES & VARIATIONS

Novice quilters often feel clumsy trying to coordinate the movements of the hand above with the hand below when frame or hoop quilting. A little practice normalizes the activity, but it takes dedicated experience to achieve the tiny, even stitches—12 or more to the inch (2.5cm), counting only the stitches on top—that characterize traditional hand quilting. Thin, soft batting layered between thin, soft fabrics, a combination supple in the hand and easy for the needle to slip through, is the necessary base for fine hand quilting.

For many contemporary purposes, small quilting stitches aren't a part of the aesthetic. Uniformity and pictorial suitability are the standards. Sometimes contemporary hand quilting approaches the decorative appearance of embroidery.

Stabstitched quilting looks like running-stitched quilting but the needle action is different and preferred by some quilters. It's an ambidextrous activity: With the top/batting/lining in a frame or hoop, the hand above pushes the needle straight down through the layers. The hand below pulls the needle out and, moved forward by a stitch, re-inserts the needle into the lining, pushing it straight up for the hand above to retrieve, and so on.

Stabstitching tends to look sloppy in back until practice perfects the return stitch.

Backstitched quilting, an alternate to running stitching, covers a line with uninterrupted stitches, therefore it doesn't produce the puckery texture that distinguishes running-stitched quilting. Rarely used as the only quilting stitch today, backstitched quilting functions as an outline that emphasizes. By contrast with the running stitches used to quilt the majority of a design, backstitching will accent selected parts of the design.

Whatever the quilting technique, control when pulling the thread is essential. Correct thread tension indents the stitches into the padded surface; too much thread tension shrivels the quilted fabric. Some shrinkage, particularly when the quilting is extensive and includes stippling, is inevitable. If a certain finished size is important, add a safety measurement for shrinkage when cutting the fabrics and batting.

Designs with short, close lines that mean constant stops and starts for the stitching are easy for hand quilters to negotiate. Analyze the design to track the most long-running quilting path. If the line being stitched ends before the thread runs out, scoot the needle through the batting to a nearby line reachable by the needle and resume stitching at that point. End one line and begin the next with a tiny backstitch for security.

Never quilt long, straight lines with lengthy threads that could snap under future strain. Stitch a short span of the line and then veer off onto a crossing line, or move to a line nearby. Other quilting negatives include uneven stitches, stitches that waver instead of following each other smoothly, wrinkles trapped in the quilting stitches, noticeable knots and tails of thread, and design markings that are visible after stitching. Never press finished quilting.

Quilting can be isolated to a portion of the top fabric. The batting that pads the area should be thin and/or pulled and shredded around the edges to dwindle out gradually, otherwise the line where it stops may show as a ridge on top. Back the particular area to be quilted with lining, or line the entire top, and baste as previously described.

Unlike other edge-finishing methods, the *envelope edge* is applied at the beginning rather than the end of the quilting procedure. It's comparatively simple to do and adaptable to wandering contours and mini-sized as well as moderate-sized projects. Start with a same-size top, batting, and lining. (1) Matching edges, smooth the lining, face up, over the batting. Attach the two together with enough thread or safety-pin basting to prevent the batting from rumpling and stretching during turning. (2) With the edges aligned, pin the top, with its right side facing the lining, to the lining/batting. Machine sew around the edges, turning the corners with two or three diagonal stitches. Leave an opening large enough for turning on one straight side. Staystitch the lining/batting side of the opening on the seamline, press lengthy seam allowances open, trim all corners diagonally, and clip the seam allowances where necessary (Fig. 10-16).

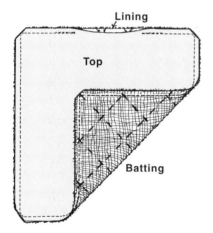

Fig. 10-16. Top/batting/lining prepared for an envelope edge.

(3) Pull the envelope right side out. With the seam allowances turned inside, close the opening with ladder stitching. (4) Thread baste the smoothed top to the lining/batting, or

re-pin if the first basting was safety-pinned. (5) Carry the quilting design to the edge of the batting inside the seam allowance and outline-quilt next to the batting's edge—or trim the batting from the seam allowance before turning. (Refer to Fig. 10-32 for assembly suggestions.)

For *flat hand quilting*, procedures and techniques are the same with one exception: The top and lining are quilted together without a layer of batting in between. As a result, the crinkly relief of the running-stitched line is minimal.

Tying is a quick and easy way to fasten the top, batting, and lining together into a stable unit. Spaced out in a gridlike manner, detached stitches with ends secured by tying the ends into a visible knot dot the surface. Tying is associated with fat, puffy, high-loft batting, either the extravagantly thick kind available for comforters or several layers of thinner batting. (1) Prepare the top, batting, and lining with safety-pin basting. (2) With the width of the top/batting/lining spread out on a table or set up in a frame, start measuring, marking, tacking, and tying at one end. Use a template with holes to spot the locations of the ties. Six inches (15cm) apart is a prudent distance for tying. (3) For the stitches and ties, thread perle cotton, embroidery floss, crochet cotton, yarn, or narrow ribbon, single or doubled, into a large-eyed needle. Always holding the needle perpendicular to the surface, make two stitches a scant ¼″ (6mm) wide, one on top of the other, leaving a tying tail at the beginning (with yarn or ribbon in the needle, make a single stitch). The ends can be tied, cut ½″ (1.3cm) or more from the knot, and left loose to garnish the top, or the ends can be tied in back, in which case the top will be dimpled with pulled stitches (Fig. 10-17).

The *lining-binding* is an uncomplicated edge finish appropriate for a tied textile. (1) Trim the batting flush with the edge of the top. Turn the excess lining over the edge to the front; trim evenly for binding. (2) Prepare the

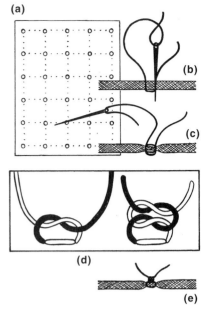

Fig. 10-17. (a) Tying template. (b & c) Making a double stabstitch with tying ends. (d) Tying the ends together with a square knot. (e) Profile view of a tie.

corners with a diagonal fold at the point and trim a seam-allowance distance from the fold. Re-fold with edges matching and right sides facing, and sew each corner miter on the fold line. (3) Pin the lining-binding to the front. With the seam allowance turned under, edgestitch by machine through all layers to secure the binding (Fig. 10-18).

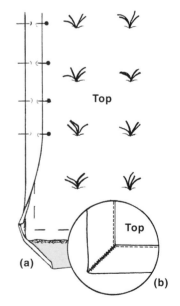

Fig. 10-18. (a) Lining-binding prepared for machine sewing with a diagonally folded corner. (b) Quick way to secure miters: Stop straight stitching at each corner to zigzag stitch over the butted folds.

X-1—Designs indented with running stitches: (from the top) Border design with ovals interrupting a straight-line filler; the feather, a classic quilting motif; flowing lines improvised while stitching; florals.

X-2—Running-stitched design centered around a floral that stands out from a stippled background. The edge is finished with doubled binding.

Chapter 10   QUILTING   215

X-3—Two circular windows emphasized with backstitched quilting, set in a field of running-stitched echo quilting. Inside, the window to the left is quilted with a grid-based diamond pattern; the window to the right with an improvised diamond pattern.

HAND QUILTING

X-4—Embroidery-floss ties used to quilt thick batting. In the center, crossed stitches indicate the ties that were knotted in back.

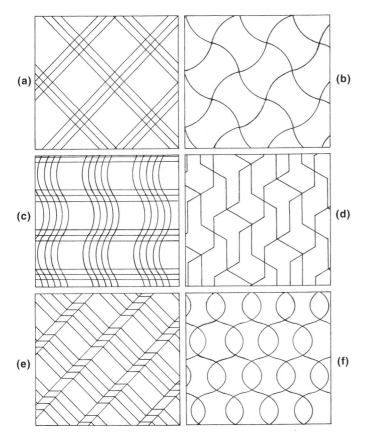

Fig. 10-19. Background or overall designs for machine-guided quilting: (a, b, c) Straight and slightly curving lines are the easiest to follow. (d, e, f) Angled and deeply curved lines require constant stops for re-direction.

Fig. 10-20. Border designs: (a, b, c) Machine-guided quilting. (d, e) Free-motion quilting.

MACHINE QUILTING

—two layers of fabric with batting in between held together with machine-sewn seams that follow a decorative pattern. The seams impress lines of continuous thread into the padded surface.

PROCEDURES

1. Create a linear design that will enhance the padded surface when inscribed with stitching by machine. Continuous lines that start and stop at the edges, and lines that describe or fill with a minimum of internal stops and re-starts, are the most efficient to machine stitch. Diversity in the spacing between the lines brings bas-relief contrast to the machine-quilted surface, but if the spaces become too large, the layers will be inadequately stabilized (refer to "Batting" on page 206.) Machine-quilting designs are divided into background (Fig. 10-19), border (Fig. 10-20), and figurative (Fig. 10-21), and subdivided into designs for machine-guided and free-motion stitching.

2. Cut fabric to size for the top, adding an allowance for shrinkage after quilting. Trace the design onto the right side of the top with a fabric-safe marking tool and a faint but visible line. Outline the entire design, those portions of the design that are figured and repeated, or important guidelines. For some designs, marking after basting and immediately before stitching may be appropriate. Improvised machine quilting requires little or no marking. (Refer to "Transferring Designs" on page 205.)

3. Cut the batting and lining slightly larger than the top. If the top is big (e.g., adult bed-covering size), cut the batting and lining 4″ (10cm) larger all around; for smaller tops, reduce the increase accordingly.

4. Baste the top, batting, and lining together:

   a. Spread the lining out, right side down, on a clean floor or utility table large enough to support all or most of the fabric. Square it off, *pull it smooth and taut across the crossgrain and lengthgrain of the fabric, and secure the stretch* by taping the edges with wide masking tape, or clamp the lining to the edges of the table with bulldog paper-binding clips.

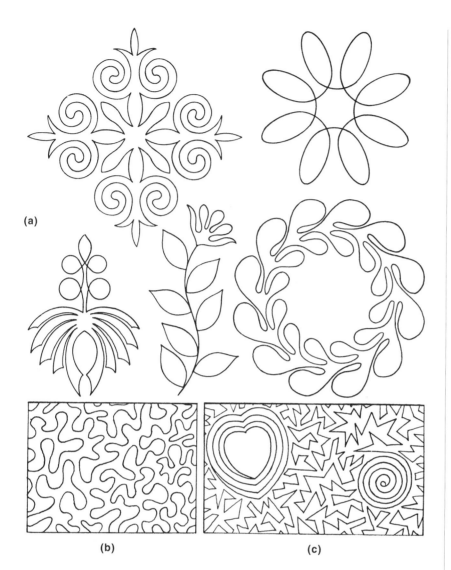

(a)

(b)　　　　　　　**(c)**

Fig. 10-21. Designs for free-motion quilting: (a) Figurative motifs for stitch-tracing without stops and re-starts elsewhere. The flower on a stem with leaves is the most forgiving to stitch because irregularity is built into the design. (b) Improvised meander stitching for filler. (c) Echo-quilted spiral and heart shape, with improvised meander-stitching filler.

As an alternative, use a frame as large as the lining, attach the edges of the lining to the four sidebars of the frame, and stretch between sidebars C-clamped together at the corners (Fig. 10-22).

b. Center the batting over the lining and smooth it out. Center and smooth the top, right side up, over the batting. Thread baste using a long or curved needle to crisscross the surface with rows of large stitches spaced at most 6″ (15cm)

apart (refer to Fig. 10-9), or fasten the layers together with safety pins at 4″ (10cm) intervals (Fig. 10-10). For small projects, basting with long quilting pins is an option.

Avoid basting where quilting lines are marked or intended. If the table top is smaller than the entire lining/batting/top, baste in sections, repeating the stretching and securing procedures described in step 4.a. for each section.

5. Machine quilt the design planned for the top. Relate the machine-stitching method to the demands of the design. Stitch with machine action automatically moving the top/batting/lining under the presser foot, or with hand action directing the movement of the top/batting/lining under the driving needle.

a. Overall, background, and border designs with straight lines, broad curves, and shallow angles are the most suitable for **presser-foot machine quilting**:

(1) Choose a presser foot that doesn't interfere with seeing the quilting line; that measures distance, if such spacing is required; and that feeds the layers evenly, particularly when quilting lines are lengthy (Fig. 10-23).

(2) Adjust the machine's upper tension to sew a seam that bites into the padded surface. Balance needle and bobbin tensions to interlock threads within the batting. Eight to 12 straight stitches per inch are acceptable parameters for stitch length.

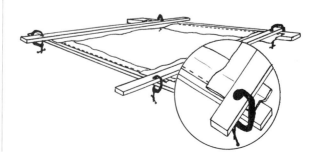

Fig. 10-22. Basting frame made from four lengths of lumber with strips of fabric stapled to the edges, C-clamped together with right-angled corners.

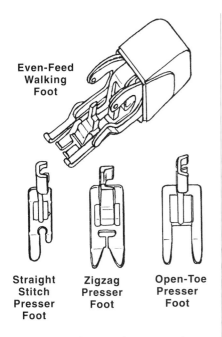

Even-Feed Walking Foot

Straight Stitch Presser Foot

Zigzag Presser Foot

Open-Toe Presser Foot

Fig. 10-23. Choices for presser-foot machine quilting.

(3) Analyze the quilting design for the easiest approach: As an example, quilt centralized pattern lines first to stabilize the basted top/batting/lining and divide it into sections. Next, quilt the anchor lines of the pattern, starting in the center and moving outward to the right. Finally, quilt subsidiary lines that parallel and mimic the anchor lines (Fig. 10-24). Sew overall patterns from one edge of the fabric to the other, or from one end of a line to its finish (Fig. 10-25).

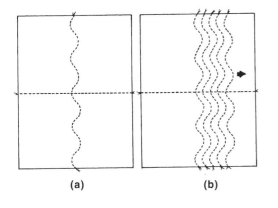

(a)   (b)

Fig. 10-24. To quilt overall patterns: (a) Stitch lines across the center first. (b) Stitch other pattern lines from the center out in each direction.

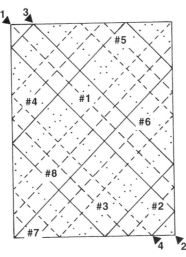

Fig. 10-25. Ernest B. Haight, a pioneer machine quilter, developed a sequential-line system of quilting that keeps the bulk of the top/batting/lining to the left of the presser foot. Outline a diagonal grid with lines that converge at the outer edge. Start quilting at arrow 1. At the end of line #1, swivel the fabric until line #2, which angles off to the left, is in stitching position. Quilt line #2. At the end, swivel to the left to quilt line #3. Repeat until there's no line to the left to quilt. Start over again at arrow 2, following the same "quilt to the left" path. The number of paths to follow before all lines are quilted varies with the size and shape of the rectangle.

(4) Unless the presser foot in use is a walking foot (Fig. 10-26), reinforce the smooth, basted alignment of the layers with extra straight pins beside the seamline, and gently ease the top layer only to compensate for presser-foot creep. Never pull or stretch in front and back of the needle. Expect to stitch with slow to moderate speed.

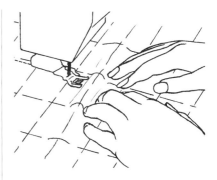

Fig. 10-26. Pushing the top/batting/-lining in front of a walking presser foot to assist the action of the dual feed dogs.

b. Use **free-motion quilting** for localized, intricate designs that require major and constant changes of direction:

(1) Lower the feed dogs or cover them with sticky tape. Choose a straight stitch with length set at 0. Fit the machine with a darning foot, a darning spring, or a spring needle (Fig. 10-27).

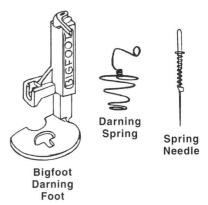

Bigfoot Darning Foot

Darning Spring

Spring Needle

Fig. 10-27. For free-motion quilting, machine attachments that hold the fabric down while the stitch is formed.

(2) Position the top/batting/lining on the bed of the machine. Select a single motif or limited area as the immediate focus for quilting activity. *Lower the presser bar lever!* Start by bringing the bobbin thread to the surface. Reproduce the locking action of extremely tiny stitches by moving the fabric slowly while running the machine.

(3) To quilt, grip the top/batting/lining with fingertips spread out on either side of the needle, preparing a flat, taut stitching space about 3" (7.5cm) to 4" (10cm) wide (Fig. 10-28).

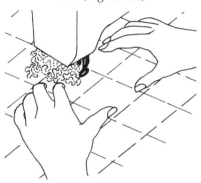

Fig. 10-28. For free-motion quilting, hands direct the top/batting/lining under the needle stitching the design. Tips cut from rubber gloves help fingers to get a better grip.

Coordinating a constant, moderate-to-fast needle speed with steady, fluid hand movements, operate the machine while steering the fabric under the needle as it follows the lines of the design. Quilt smooth lines with stitches that are equal in length. Don't watch the needle; concentrate on the line ahead of the needle. Move the top/batting/lining sideways, diagonally, forward, and backward without altering the straightforward position of the design. Keep enough slack in the surrounding fabric to maintain maneuverability.

(4) When quilting activity progresses beyond the flat, taut space controlled by the fingers, or if the fabric begins to jump up and down with the needle, stop with the needle down, reposition the hands, and start again.

(5) Finish a quilted line by bringing the movement of the fabric to a gradual stop, making ever-tinier locking stitches. Relocate to another part of the design without cutting the threads, but lock the threads before continuing to quilt. Clip all threads when the free-motion-quilted top/batting/lining is removed from the machine.

c. When a line of machine-guided or free-motion quilting begins and ends inside the fabric:

(1) Start by holding on to the end of the needle thread and hand-turning the fly-wheel to lower the needle through the top/batting/lining. Bring the needle back up to its highest position and tug on the needle thread to raise a loop of bobbin thread. Snag the loop with a pin and pull the bobbin thread out. Finger-grounding both strands of thread behind the needle, lower the presser bar lever and lock the thread by stitching into the same needle hole several times with stitch length set at 0. *Gradually* increase stitch length to the desired size.

(2) To end a line of quilting within the fabric, *gradually* decrease the stitch length to 0 and stitch into the final needle hole several times. Cut all locked threads at the surface.

6 To manage large, bulky, machine-quilting projects in the limited space available between the needle and the head of the machine on the right, and also control drag on the needle:

a. Enlarge the area in back and to the left of the machine with extensions, preferably level with the bed of the machine.

Unless the top/batting/lining has support, its weight will hinder the progressive movement of the fabric and distort the stitching.

b. Package the top/batting/lining before quilting interior lines. Make a tight roll of the fabric to the right of the quilting line; secure the roll with many bicycle clips or safety pins. Fold the fabric to the left of the quilting line, isolating a quilting channel between the roll and the folds. Accordion fold the rolled and folded top/batting/lining to the place where quilting is to begin. At the machine, hold the accordion-folded bundle in the lap, feeding it out with enough slack to prevent drag as stitching progresses down the channel (Fig. 10-29). Re-package as quilting proceeds outward to the edge on the right.

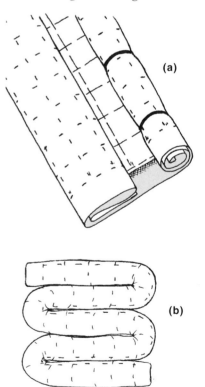

Fig. 10-29. (a) Large top/batting/lining rolled and clamped with bicycle clips to the right and folded to the left, exposing a long channel for quilting. (b) Top/batting/lining accordion-folded into a package to hold in the lap.

c. Subdivide large projects into two or three sections, or into smaller, modular units, to limit the bulk that complicates movement at the machine. Develop a quilting design that can be localized without losing its allover cohesiveness.

- For **installment quilting**, divide the batting into halves or thirds, or cut the entire top/batting/lining in half. Baste and quilt the first layered section of the partitioned top/batting/lining. If only the batting was divided: (1) Spread the next section of batting over the lining; (2) handsew the butted edges of the batting together with large, loose stitches; (3) baste the layers together; and (4) quilt. If the entire top/batting/lining was cut apart: (1) Baste the second half of the batting to the lining; (2) sew the batting/lining and top to the section already quilted, and trim the batting from the seam allowance; (3) baste the top over the batting/lining, and (4) quilt (Fig. 10-30).

- Modular quilting can be divided into halves, quarters, eighths, and more if necessary. Cut a top, batting, and lining for each module, adding seam allowances to the top and lining. Baste the layers of each module together, and quilt in the desired manner. Assemble the modules using one of the methods explained in "Joining Modular Units" on page 208.

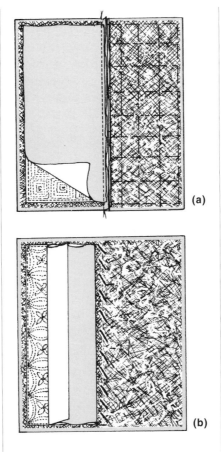

(a)

(b)

Fig. 10-30. Installment quilting: (a) Divide the top, batting, and lining into two sections and join together after quilting the first section. (b) Cut the batting into halves (or thirds) and insert between the top and lining after quilting the first section.

7. After finishing the quilting, clip any dangling thread ends that escaped previous notice. Remove all basting thread except the thread inside the seam allowances around the edges. Trim the edges of the batting and lining flush with the trued-up edge of the top. Cover the edges of the quilted textile with machine-sewn, doubled binding (refer to "The Double-Binding Edge Finish" on page 207), or include the quilted piece within a larger construction of unquilted fabric.

NOTES & VARIATIONS

"Test" and "practice" are the golden rules of machine quilting. On a square of top/batting/lining prepared for that purpose, test the operating condition of the machine, the size of the needle, the tension setting, the length and appearance of the stitch in front and back, and the strength and visual contribution of the thread. Test different presser feet. Allow ample practice time for free-motion quilting. Machine-guided quilting requires less practice because it resembles plain machine sewing.

Although certain kinds of design are recommended for either one mode of machine quilting or the other, the size of the basted layers makes a difference in applicability. A design with deep curves and acute angles is suitable for machine-guided quilting if the project is small enough to be pivoted without a struggle when the needle is down and the presser foot up. With frequent ups and downs of the presser foot and patient top/batting/lining readjustments, a figurative motif can be stitched into a module 12" (30.5cm) square. Lengthy lines that move from edge to edge are machine-guided designs, but skilled free-motion quilters are able to compose straight-line fillers between figurative motifs spaced a short distance apart. It's acceptable practice to quilt over a previous line when moving from one stitching line to another nearby, as long as the double stitching is precise.

To isolate a quilted design within a larger expanse of unquilted fabric: Baste a lining and thin batting under the area. Use a machine-embroidery hoop (Fig. 10-31) to prevent the stitching from shrinking the quilted section in relation to the unquilted part of the fabric. Thin out the cut edge of the batting or enclose it inside lines of quilting to prevent the edge from showing as a ridge on the surface.

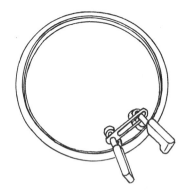

Fig. 10-31. Machine-embroidery hoops are 10″ (25cm) in diameter or smaller, and shallow enough to slip under a raised presser foot. Place the fabric over the outer ring and push the inner ring inside, forcing the fabric down to be level with the needle plate on the machine.

There are two other methods for securing an interior line of quilting stitches at the beginning and end that may be preferable at times: (1) Sew backward with microscopic stitches for ⅛″ (3mm) before starting and after stopping. (2) On the top or lining side, tie the ends of the bobbin and needle threads together with a square knot. Insert both ends into a hand-sewing needle. Push the needle into the last needle hole of the seam, through the batting, and out half the length of the needle away. Tug the knot under the fabric before clipping the threads. Make it a habit to deal with loose thread ends promptly. Forgotten ends snarled in subsequent stitching are difficult to pick out.

Obvious starts and stops are machine-quilting taboos, as are visible markings, wrinkles caught into stitches, and twisted surface fabric between lines of stitching. Stitch-length consistency is an attribute of good machine quilting. After washing, batting depressed by presser-foot pressure springs back to enhance the quilted texture. Close machine quilting stiffens a three-layered textile. Because machine quilting doesn't unravel like hand quilting, a machine-quilted textile may be cut apart and contoured for assembly into a larger application.

Similarities between machine-guided and free-motion quilting end at the sewing machine when entirely different working techniques take over. The free-motion quilter needs to establish a personal working relationship between the rhythmic movement of the hand-guided fabric, the speed of the needle, and the eye. Also, the free-motion quilter must learn to stop, readjust to a new finger grip on the fabric, and resume stitching without visible glitches betraying the break. The reward, for the practice required to master this interaction, is an energizing freedom while stitching that can't be replicated with machine-guided quilting.

A minor technicality—forgetting to lower the presser bar lever—is a major irritant to the enjoyment of free-motion quilting, aggravated by having to pluck out the thread mess that results. For free-motion quilters, symmetrical, repetitious motifs and long, unbroken lines are the most challenging to trace without wobbly deviations. Some free-motion quilters feel that framing a motif in a machine-embroidery hoop increases control (Fig. 10-31). A free-motion quilter needs to be resourceful when coping with bigness and weight, which constrain the flowing movements essential to stitching the designs and affect stitch consistency.

Straight-stitched machine quilting impresses a texture into the padded textile that's recognizably different from the relief made by hand-sewn running stitches. When the features built into contemporary machines are introduced, the machine-quilted line has a unique effect on the patterned and texturized surface. As a medium for visual expression, *art quilting* includes all kinds of quilt stitching and takes full advantage of the sewing machine's capabilities. To develop an individualized art-quilting style: Experiment with the textures of zigzag quilting, all widths, from spread in length to satin stitching.

Quilt with a twin needle. Explore the decorative stitches. Invent combinations of straight, zigzag, and decorative stitches. Improvise meander and filler patterns. Use reverse stitching for informal filling with machine-guided quilting. When free-motion quilting, unbalance the tensions to create distinctive thread variations. Break the rules to make discoveries.

Where it's appropriate, pre-finishing medium-sized projects or modular units with an **envelope edge** (refer to Fig. 10-16) saves time at the end. For modules with envelope edges, the means of assembly, either ties or tabs, may be sewn into the seams joining the top to the basted lining/batting (Fig. 10-32). Mini-modules for the openwork or tabbed constructions described below are too small for anything but a pre-finished envelope edge.

Fig. 10-32. (a) Ribbon ties and (b) tab connectors basted to the right side of a module's top before sewing to the lining/batting. Turned right side out and quilted, modules are pre-finished with an envelope edge and ready (c) to tie or (d) snap together.

Openwork mini-modules are small, quilted shapes hand-sewn together in arrangements with gaps that become part of the design. Using the same pattern, cut tops, lining, and batting for the mini-modules. Sew each set together, turn right side out, and hand sew the opening closed.

Machine quilt. Sew the mini-modules together where they touch, from the back, catching only the lining/ batting with the tacking stitches (Fig. 10-33).

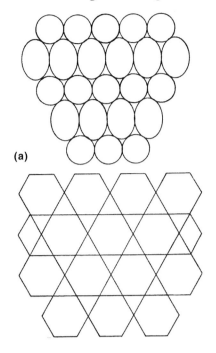

(a)

Fig. 10-33. (a) Openwork designs. (b) Sewing, (c) quilting, and (d) tacking two mini-modules together. (e) Assembled mini-modules with completed quilting that crosses from module to module, strengthening the connections.

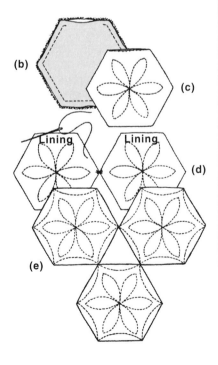

Use openwork compositions to create borders, insertions, or entire constructions.

Tabs are small, quilted, modular shapes that hang loose from a foundation in overlapping rows. The tops, batting, and lining for tabs are cut from the same pattern. Sew each set together, leaving the top edge open. Trim the batting from the seam allowance at the top and turn right side out. Machine quilt. Sew the tops of the tabs to a padded or sturdy foundation, closing the openings in the process (Fig. 10-34). Use tabs for borders or small constructions.

With *pressed quilting*, the indented appearance of seams and folds replaces lines of stitched thread. The top is cut up into strips which are sewn together and quilted to the batting/lining in one operation. For practical reasons, pressed quilting is a modular activity. (1) Plan a design for strips of fabric. (2) For each module, cut a lining and batting slightly larger than the finished dimensions, and baste the two together. (3) Cut strips of the required width plus two seam allowances. (4) Starting centrally or at the left edge, lay the first strip, trimmed to size, right side up on

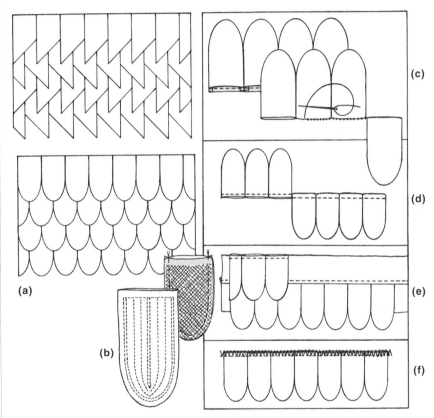

Fig. 10-34. (a) Designs for tabbed constructions. (b) Sewing and quilting a tab before application to a foundation. The seam allowance at the top of the tabs is either (c) turned inside while hand stitching, (d) enclosed under top-stitching, (e) caught into seams, or (f) covered with zigzag stitching.

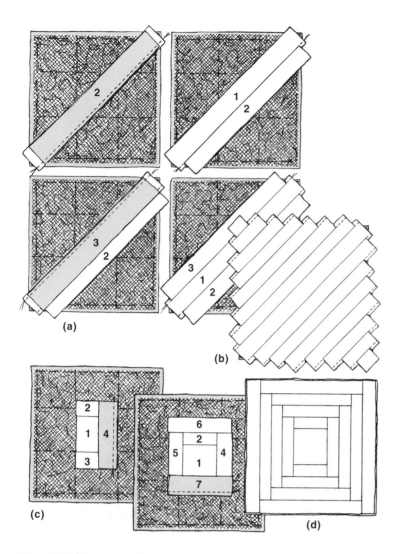

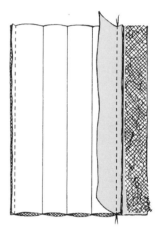

(4) Place top strip #3 over the second top strip and lining strip #3 over the second lining strip, and sew the four fabric strips and batting together. (5) Open, press, and repeat the procedure until the design is complete. Note that, with the exception of the strips that start the construction, all strips of batting are cut to the finished width plus one seam allowance only (Fig. 10-36).

Fig. 10-36. For reversible pressed quilting, strips of lining and top fabric, and batting, are assembled with stitching that is concealed on both sides.

Fig. 10-35. Pressed quilting sewn to a batting/lining foundation: (a) Strips of top fabric arranged diagonally. (b) Finished module before trimming. (c) "Logs" of top fabric arranged around a central square. (d) Finished "log cabin" module.

top of the batting. Place the second strip, also trimmed to size, right side down over the first strip. Matching the edges to be seamed together, stitch through all layers. (5) Open the second strip and lightly press the seam. (6) Continue adding strips and pressing each seam until the batting/lining is covered with a seam-patterned top (Fig. 10-35). (7) Trim the modules to size, assemble using one of the methods described in "Joining Modular Units" on page 208, and finish the edges with doubled binding (refer to "The Double-Binding Edge Finish" on page 207).

Reversible pressed quilting is built entirely from narrow strips—strips for the top, strips of batting, and strips of lining—all cut to size before stitching. (1) Begin by basting the first of the three-layered strips together around the outside edges. (2) With right sides facing, lay top strip #2 over the first top strip and lining strip #2 over the first lining strip. Sew the matching edges of all four fabric strips and the batting together. (3) Open and press the second strips to the side. Insert a strip of batting, butting the inside edges.

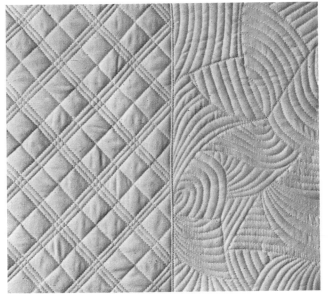

X-5—Two allover patterns, straight-stitched and machine-guided.

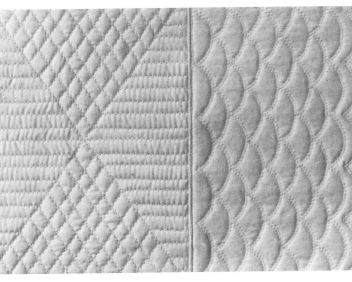

X-6—Two allover patterns, zigzag-stitched and machine-guided.

X-7—Delicate, fanciful, machine-guided quilting surrounds a heart outlined and filled with hand-sewn backstitching.

X-8—Designs traced with free-motion stitching above a border fashioned from machine-guided stitch combinations.

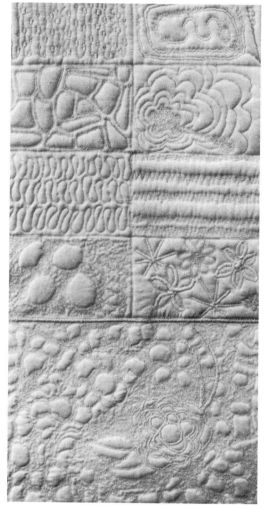

X-9—Panel of eccentric experiments in improvised free-motion quilting.

MACHINE QUILTING

X-10— A chain of openwork mini-modules inserted between quilted bands. The outer edge is finished with corded piping.

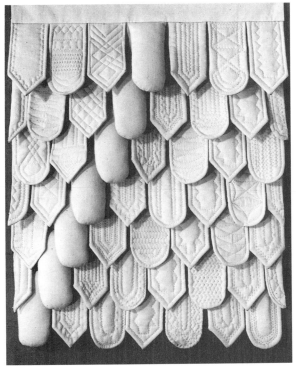

X-11—Overlapping arrangement of quilted tabs with a descending row of stuffed tabs for contrast.

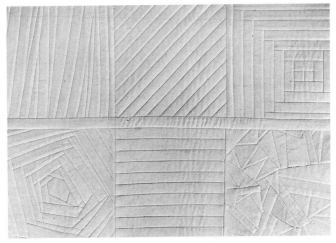

X-12—Six blocks of pressed quilting. The crazy-patched block in the lower right corner shows the occasional hand stitching required to piece and quilt oddly shaped scraps.

X-13—The reverse side of the pressed quilting sampler reveals the assembly methods: Concealed at the top, taped at the bottom, with a stripped connection between the two rows.

I nserted between two layers of fabric and confined within seamed boundaries, *stuffing* supports elevation. An adaptable fiber material that yields to the touch, stuffing upholds a bas-relief surface configured with low- or high-relief elements that were cut and stitched into specific shapes.

Where stuffing adds height, it subtracts flexibility. The higher the stuffed area, the less flexible it is. Maximum flexibility is restricted to the seams that ground the stuffed structuring. Stuffing also adds weight and bulk to its fabric environment.

S T U F F I N G

11 Stuffing

Note: This chapter begins with BASICS, indicated by a gray band located underneath the relevant columns.

STUFFING BASICS

STUFFING

Stuffing is both a noun and a verb. As a noun, stuffing is a loose, soft, airy accumulation of natural or synthetic fibers. It is used to fill up containers of fabric.

Before synthetics, stuffings of cotton and kapok (fibers that collect around the seeds of the tropical ceiba tree) were used to fill cloth casings. Polyester fiberfill is today's stuffing of choice, and it is the stuffing recommended for the manipulation techniques that follow. It is clean, resilient, non-allergenic, pleasant to handle, resistant to unwanted clumping, and washable. Packaged under numerous brand names, polyester fiberfill is widely available, but variable in quality. Good quality fiberfill is fluffy and consistently fine in texture, without fibers that shed or clot together.

As a verb, stuffing is the act of inserting stuffing, the noun, into stitched casings. The techniques described in this chapter indicate stuffing through temporary openings left in seams or through slits cut into linings or foundations. When slits are necessary, use small, sharp scissors to cut neatly through the backing fabric only. At a central location inside the seamed boundaries, cut the opening across the bias of the fabric to prevent the edges from fraying out with the friction of repeated stuffing insertions. Several slits may be needed to stuff around peekholes or meandering quilted or appliquéd shapes.

To guide "pulls" of stuffing through small openings into larger interiors, use the blunted or rounded tip of a slender tool long enough to reach the limits of the particular casing, such as a length of dowel or coathanger wire, a chopstick, a screwdriver with rounded corners, a blunted knitting needle or skewer, or a straightened paper clip or hairpin. Relate the size of the pull of stuffing to the size of the area being filled—wispy bits to work into tips and corners or to stuff a small, round appliqué; larger pieces to stuff a fat roll or plump biscuit. Begin by pushing stuffing against the seamed perimeters, especially into corners. Continue adding stuffing, always blending the new stuffing into previous stuffing, working toward the center of the shape and the opening. Distribute the stuffing evenly throughout. Model high-relief forms (elevated appliqué, rolls, biscuits, peaks and valleys) with finger pressure on the outside as well as stuffing pressure from the inside.

When stuffing from underneath, check results from the front. To stuff quilted or appliquéd shapes or half-rounds softly and evenly, hold work-in-progress up to the light to check for consistent stuffing distribution throughout the casing. Stuff every shape full enough to reach the intended elevation and substantially enough for the elevation to survive subsequent use. Stop before stuffing too fully, indicated by the undesirable distortions that develop.

Close in-seam openings as technique directions indicate. Close the openings cut into linings or foundation fabric with hand sewing (Fig. 11-1).

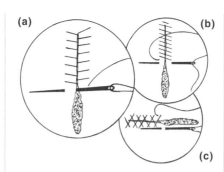

Fig. 11-1. Closing cut openings after stuffing: (a) Darning the edges together with over-and-under stitching. (b) Overcast and (c) herringbone stitching, two alternate but less desirable methods.

Afterwards, stuffing can be redistributed to fill out minor depressions previously overlooked, or to pull stuffing into points or corners that need attention. Use the tip of a sturdy needle inserted inside the area to move adjacent stuffing into the empty spot.

STUFFED QUILTING

—two layers of fabric fastened together with a stitched design containing enclosed shapes that are heightened with stuffing.

PROCEDURES

1. Draft a design with lines that include enclosed spaces appropriate for emphasis with stuffing (Fig. 11-2).
2. With a fine-line, fabric-safe marker, trace a faint but distinct copy of the design onto the right side of fabric that has been cut to size (refer to "Transferring Designs" on page 205). Baste the marked top fabric to lining fabric identical in size. An option for a design that will be running-stitched: Trace a mirror-image copy of the design onto the lining before basting it to the unmarked top.

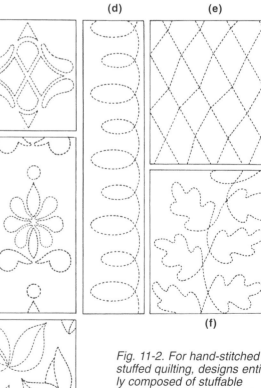

Fig. 11-2. For hand-stitched stuffed quilting, designs entirely composed of stuffable shapes: (a) Border. (b & c) Allover. For hand and machine stitching, continuous line designs that include enclosed shapes: (d) Border. (e) Gridded allover. (f) Wandering leaf.

End of STUFFING BASICS

3. Sew over the marked outlines:

- Hand sew with tiny, uniform, running or back stitches. If handsewing over outlines traced onto the lining, monitor the appearance of the running stitches from the front, checking for regularity.

- Machine sew, covering the lines with straight or satin stitching regulated by presser foot/feed dog action or with free-motion stitching, whichever is the most appropriate for the design (review the procedures discussed in "Machine Quilting" on page 218).

- When hand stitching or free-motion machine stitching, stretch the fabric in a hoop to prevent thread tension from drawing up the fabric.

4. Cut small slits into the lining inside the outlined shapes. Push wispy bits of stuffing through the openings, elevating each shape with soft, evenly distributed stuffing. To deter overstuffing, a problem with larger shapes, stretch the stitched fabric, lining side up, in a frame or hoop large enough to expose the design (Fig. 11-3). Hand sew the openings closed. (Refer to "Stuffing" on page 229.)

5. Stretch and pin the stuffed quilting to a padded surface. Steam with an iron held above the fabric. Allow to cool and dry before lining the stuffed quilting to conceal and protect the openings. Tack the outer lining to the inner lining at frequent intervals.

NOTES & VARIATIONS

Outlines that are hand-sewn with running stitches have a distinctively crinkly, pricked appearance which tends to blur intricacies in the contours of shapes. Smoothly flowing contours without finicky details are the best for running-stitched outlines. Use continuous-thread stitching, either hand-sewn backstitching or machine stitching, to outline shapes with detailed contours.

As shapes increase in size, the amount of stuffing the interior can accommodate expands, and so does the temptation to overstuff. Too much stuffing produces distracting waves and stresses in the surrounding fabric. The stuffed quilting goal: Raise the design without disturbing the level fabric between the stuffed shapes. Stretching the design in a frame or hoop discourages over-stuffing, but prevents it only if the stuffing is moved into position with gentle pressure, and if the total amount of stuffing inserted into a shape is moderated. With control, small-figured designs may be stuffed without stretching beforehand, especially if satin-stitched by machine. The dense-thread outline of satin stitching acts as a kind of stabilizer to the fabric.

When a design is too large for the size of an available hoop, stretch a portion of the design and stuff the exposed shapes. Without closing the hoop over anything previously stuffed, frame up another section of the design, stuff, and continue until hoop stretching is no longer possible. Maintaining the same density, stuff the leftover shapes.

With an outer lining over an inner lining that is underneath the top, a stuffed-quilting textile finishes with three layers of fabric. If the stuffed elements are separated by borders, fillers, or other designs not intended for stuffing, the inner lining can be limited to the areas where it's needed. After stitching those portions of the design designated for stuffing, trim the lining ¼" (6mm) from the stitching that surrounds the stuffed shapes.

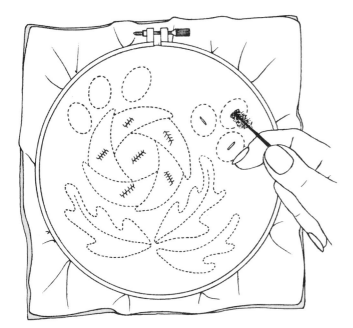

Fig. 11-3. Stuffing a design, outlined with running stitches, through slits cut into the lining.

Fig. 11-4. Design with stuffed elements inside an unstuffed border. Stitch and stuff the underlined inner circle first; then line the entire design and stitch the border scroll.

Add the outer lining and fasten it to the top by stitching those portions of the design not meant to be stuffed (Fig. 11-4). If it's practical, an isolated figure or motif can be outline-stitched to a trimmed lining, stuffed, and left at that.

Three alternative stuffing methods eliminate cuts into the lining and the need for an outer lining:

1. The first method requires a loosely woven lining fabric. Push the threads of the lining apart to create tiny openings through which wisps of stuffing can be inserted. After stuffing, tease the threads back together with a needle and fingernail scratching ((a) in Fig. 11-5). In the past, quilters relied on shrinkage after washing to tighten the weave of the lining behind their stuffed work—a useful strategy if lining shrinkage coordinates with the shrinkage of the top.

2. The second method requires a plan of approach to the stitching, which must be done by hand. Each shape is stuffed through an accessible opening in the outline stitching, before the stitching is completed. To shorten the path the stuffing needs to travel, the lining and top—separately—are rolled up close to the shape ready for stuffing ((b) in Fig. 11-5).

To utilize this method efficiently, proceed from the center of the design outward. Gauge the best location for each stuffing opening. Stitch shapes with neighboring edges and openings at one time, using different needles. Push stuffing on the end of a long tool, between the rolled-back top and lining, into the stitched enclosure. When filled to satisfaction, finish the outline stitching. Stop frequently to smooth and re-align the top and lining, pinning with safety pins.

3. The third method uses loosely spun, fluffy, acrylic yarn to fill small shapes. Each shape is stuffed with rows of yarn laid next to each other inside the stitched outline. Thread doubled yarn into a tapestry needle. Enter and exit the lining through holes forced into the weave by the guiding needle (avoid breaking threads in the fabric with a needle that's too large). Trim the ends of the yarn close to the surface where they disappear. Coax the ends inside by stretching the fabric and nudging with the point of a needle inserted into the interior. Close the holes with gentle scratching. Hold the yarn-stuffed shape up against strong background light to check the evenness and closeness of the strands inside ((c) in Fig. 11-5). With care, shapes can be padded from the front using the string-guided method of yarn insertion (refer to Fig. 9-5 on page 190).

Stuffed quilting and corded quilting are complementary techniques. When shapes for stuffing and narrow channels for cording are included in the same design, the technique combination and the result are called *trapunto*. Stuffed quilting and corded quilting can be worked over a lining padded with thin batting, and surrounded with regular quilting.

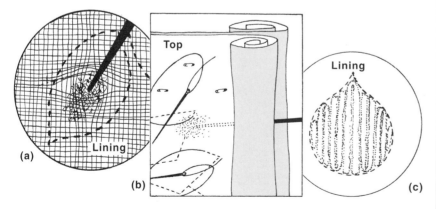

Fig. 11-5. To stuff stitching-outlined shapes undetectably: (a) Stuff through openings forced between threads in the weave of the lining. (b) Pause to stuff between the layers while stitching; finish stitching after stuffing. (c) Pad with rows of acrylic yarn.

Reversed stuffed quilting is outline-stitched around cutouts of padding. Cut the shapes from batting, fleece, felt, terry cloth, or other thick material, and arrange on the wrong side of the lining. After setting the arrangement with dabs of fabric glue or basting, baste the top over the lining. The top fabric needs to ridge over the edges of the cutouts with enough clarity to indicate a path for the hand-stitched outlining that follows. If the top fabric is sheer enough to expose not only the outlines but also the colors of the cutouts, reversed stuffed quilting is called **shadow quilting**.

Figures with foreground and background components benefit from *layered stuffed quilting*, a bas-relief technique that accentuates advancing forms (Fig. 11-6).

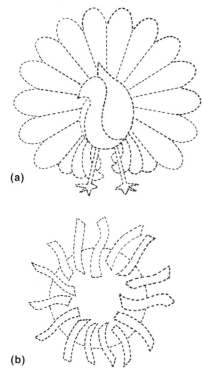

Fig. 11-6. Layered stuffed quilting advances designs with distinct foreground elements: (a) The head/neck and the legs/feet of the peacock. (b) The squiggles that overlap the circle.

(1) To prepare the original design, number the foreground shapes "#1." After stuffing, these shapes will appear on top or in front. Number the middle-ground shapes

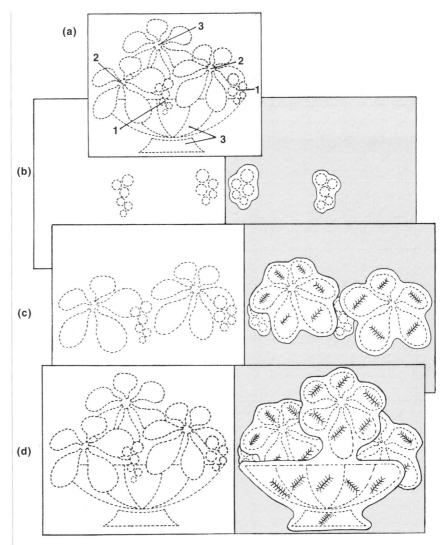

Fig. 11-7. (a) Design for layered stuffed quilting with areas numbered in advancing order. (b) Circles in layer #1 stitched and stuffed while stitching. (c) Layer #2, when stuffed, pushes layer #1 forward. (d) After stuffing, layer #3 recedes behind previous layers.

"#2." After stuffing, these shapes will appear to be behind the foreground shapes. The middle ground may be split into two levels, or omitted altogether. Number the background shapes "#3." After stuffing, these shapes will appear to be in back of all the other shapes in the design. (2) Trace the design on the right side of the top. (3) Pin thin lining cut larger than all the #1 shapes underneath the design. With running or back stitching, outline the #1 shapes. Stuff through cuts in the lining or through openings left before finishing the outline stitching. Trim the excess lining around

the shapes. (4) Cut and pin another piece of lining, larger than the #2 shapes, under the top. Outline the #2 shapes. When stitching an outline interrupted by a foreground shape, turn to the back and continue stitching through the lining only until the outline in front resumes. When stuffing, extend the stuffing behind foreground shapes that have already been stuffed to create the appearance of distinct foreground/background levels. Ease the stuffing out behind the hump of larger foreground shapes. Trim the lining around the #2 shapes. (5) Repeat for the #3 shapes (Fig.11-7).

XI-1—Running-stitched border design that includes a looped row of corded quilting between the stuffing-raised figures (trapunto).

STUFFED QUILTING

XI-2—Straight-line design straight stitched by machine with certain spaces in the grid selected for stuffing.

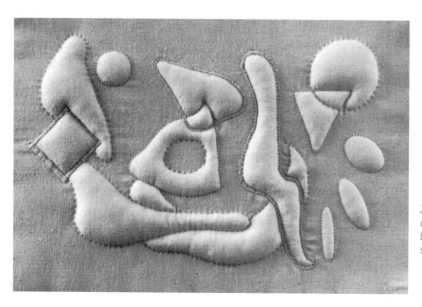

XI-3—Composition with shapes outlined by hand with running and backstitching, and by machine with straight and satin stitching.

XI-4—Reversed stuffed quilting outlined with running stitches (from the top) around cutouts of latex foam, around cutouts of batting, and around a felt cutout for the continuous border.

XI-5—Design backstitched and stuffed in three layers. The quilted seams that bisect the largest and lowest layer limit bulkiness.

XI-6—Floral design backstitched and stuffed in three layers, set over a stuffed background divided into nine squares. The center of the large flower was indented with needle modelling. A border of running-stitched flat quilting surrounds the stuffed design.

STUFFED APPLIQUÉ

—fabric cutouts stitched to a foundation with stuffing inserted between the layers.

PROCEDURES

1. Create a design composed of shapes with simplified outlines suitable for cutouts (Fig. 11-8). With a fabric-safe marker, trace faint but distinct outlines of the entire design onto the right side of foundation fabric that has been cut to size. For designs that require extensive stitching and stuffing, stabilize the foundation temporarily, choosing a stabilizing method appropriate to the stitching method.

2. Cut apart a copy of the design to make patterns or templates for each shape that will be appliquéd. With a fabric-safe marker, trace a faint but distinct outline for each appliqué onto the right side of the appropriate appliqué fabric and cut out:

   ◆ For appliqués that will be hand-stitched or machine-stitched with zigzag stitching or hemstitching, add a seam allowance around the traced outline.

   ◆ For appliqués that will be satin-stitched by machine, cut on the traced outlines, adding seam allowances only to those edges that will be slipped underneath adjoining appliqués.

3. Stitch the appliqués to the foundation, matching the appliqué outline to the foundation outline. Before turning an appliqué's seam allowance to the back, clip, notch, or trim the seam allowance at all curves and angles (Fig. 11-9).

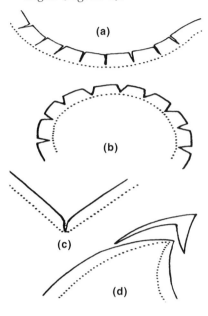

Fig. 11-9. To turn non-straight seam allowances smoothly: (a) Clip concave curves and (b) notch convex curves at intervals, stopping short of the fold line. (c) Clip inside angles to the fold line. (d) Taper-trim to the tip of an outside angle.

When two or more appliqués share a common outline, attach the background appliqué first, but don't stitch the shared edge. Then apply the foreground appliqué, covering the loose seam allowance of the background appliqué with the edge of the foreground appliqué (Fig. 11-10).

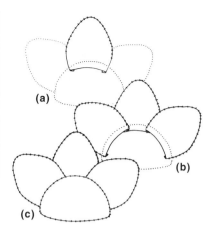

Fig. 11-10. (a, b, c) Motif applied in three stages. Each successive appliqué covers the loose edge of a previously attached appliqué.

a. **Hand sew** appliqués with blind or ladder stitching: Baste the appliqué in place, or pin from the back so that sewing thread won't snag on projecting pins in front. Turn under and pinch crease a small portion of the appliqué's seam allowance, concealing the traced outline on the fold. Stitch that portion to and over the matching outline traced on the foundation (Fig. 11-11). Continue to pinch crease ahead of the stitching, using the needle's tip to tease stray threads and reluctant folds into place, particularly at outside corners and inside angles.

b. **Machine sew** with the needle straddling the edge of the appliqué as it swings back and forth, piercing the appliqué and then only the foundation right next to the appliqué's edge (Fig.11-12). Stabilize the foundation with typing or freezer paper, a commercial stabilizer, or stretch the foundation in a hoop. Cover the traced outline on the foundation with the edge of the appliqué:

Fig. 11-8. Designs for stuffed appliqué have enclosed shapes to cut out and re-apply with stuffing underneath.

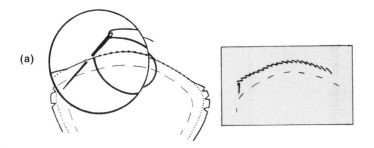

(a)

Fig. 11-11.
(a) Blindstitching an appliqué thread-basted to the foundation. In front, tiny tacking stitches straddle the fold. In back, the stitching thread moves forward.

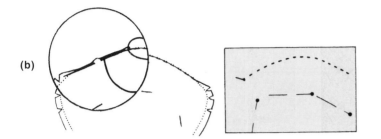

(b)

(b) Ladder stitching an appliqué pin-basted to the foundation. In front, the needle takes tiny stitches through the fold, alternating with tiny stitches through the foundation. In back, ladder stitching looks like running stitches.

- To prepare an appliqué for zigzag stitching or hemstitching, turn under, pinch crease, and heat press the seam allowance, concealing the traced outline on the fold. Pin or baste the appliqué to a foundation.

- For satin stitching, baste the appliqué in place with straight stitching next to the cut edge. Satin stitch over the straight stitching and the edge (Fig.11-13).

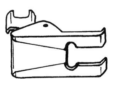

Fig. 11-13. For satin stitching, a presser foot with a groove in the base arches over the buildup of thread.

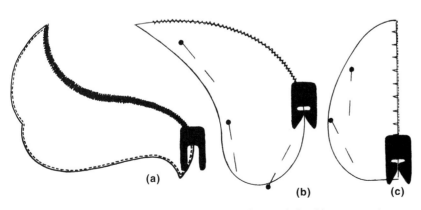

Fig. 11-12. Options for machine appliqué: (a) Satin stitch with an open-toe embroidery foot. (b) Stitch with a narrow zigzag. (c) Hemstitch. Use an embroidery foot if the zigzag foot hampers visibility.

To satin stitch a corner or angle, stitch up to the point, stop to pivot with the needle in the foundation, and continue stitching when the next side is in position. When satin stitching a curve, pause frequently with the needle down to turn the appliqué a little at a time (Fig. 11-14).

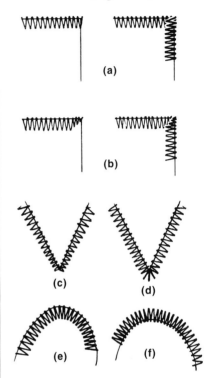

Fig. 11-14. Choices when satin stitching an appliqué: (a) Turn corners without changing stitch width. (b) Decrease to narrow when approaching and increase to wide when leaving a corner, or (c) an inside angle. (d) Hand guide the needle to fan out stitches around an inside angle, always returning to a common pivot point in the foundation. (e) Swivel with the needle in the foundation for outside curves, (f) with the needle in the appliqué for inside curves.

4. Stuff the appliqués softly (refer to "Stuffing" on page 229):

   - Interrupt the stitching to stuff an appliqué before enclosing it with stitches. Stuff a background appliqué before applying the foreground appliqué over the outline they both share ((a) in Fig. 11-15).

◆ After stitching, stuff an appliqué through a slit cut into the foundation behind the appliqué ((b) in Fig. 11-15). Hand sew the opening closed. If the foundation has been temporarily stabilized with paper or a commercial product, don't remove it, but cut an enlarged opening in the stabilizer to get at the cloth.

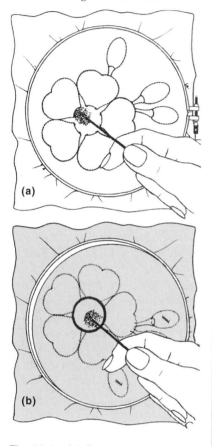

Fig. 11-15. (a) Stuffing appliquéd petals through openings to be closed when the center circle is appliquéd. (b) Stuffing the center circle through a slit cut into the foundation.

5. Remove the temporary stabilizer. Stretch the foundation and pin around the edges to a padded surface. Steam with an iron held above the fabric, and allow to cool and dry before moving. Line a stuffed-appliqué design that was stuffed from behind.

NOTES & VARIATIONS

Shapes for appliqué may be as delicate and intricate as the stitcher's technique can manage successfully. Sharp, slender points and deep, narrow angles with minute seam allowances present the greatest challenge. Simplified shapes with adequate seam allowances all around are the easiest to appliqué.

To make the appliqué process even easier, visualize frayed edges as desirable surface texture. For *frayed-edge stuffed appliqué*, trace simple, preferably straight-edged shapes onto fabric with a loose weave, and enlarge all around when cutting out. Machine sew each appliqué to the foundation or hand sew with straight stitching, following outlines traced on top. Before stuffing, brush out the edges or machine wash and dry the entire foundation to encourage fraying. Another option, not as fast as frayed-edge appliqué but less fussy than standard appliqué: Attach appliqués prepared with turned edges to the foundation with machine-sewn edgestitching, or hand sew next to the fold with straight stitching.

For appliqués with seam allowances, *freezer-paper preparation* assures turned edges that are smooth and accurate. For each appliqué, trace the outline of the pattern onto freezer paper and cut out on the line. Heat bond the freezer-paper shape, shiny side down, to the wrong side of the appliqué fabric. Cut out, adding a seam allowance around the edge of the paper. Folding over and against the edge of the paper, turn the seam allowance to the back and press firmly. For appliqués to be stuffed, remove the freezer paper before stitching to the foundation.

Standard stuffed appliqué is perfectly executed when the finished product duplicates the original design on paper, curve for curve and point for point; when all traced outlines are invisible; when threads from the weave, seam allowances, or stuffing are securely confined underneath the neatly stitched edges of the appliqués; and when the foundation around the softly stuffed appliqués remains smooth and level, and retains its original dimensions. If an appliqué is too large, the soft stuffing inside may shift or clump when extensively handled. After sewing a large appliqué to the foundation, divide it into smaller segments with seams topstitched by hand or machine, and stuff the segments.

Easing an appliqué to match a slightly smaller outline on the foundation results in a little more interior space to stuff; therefore, *eased stuffed appliqué* is somewhat loftier than the same appliqué would be if it weren't eased. Enlarge the pattern for an eased appliqué about ⅛" (3mm) all around, even less if the shape is very small. Because bias-cut edges absorb easing better than straightgrain edges, cut as much of the appliqué's edge on the bias as possible. When sewing to the un-enlarged outline on the foundation, work a bit of the excess into each stitch. After stuffing, the appliqué should be smooth and without any ripples at the seam to betray the easing.

For *stacked and stuffed appliqué*, cutout shapes are stitched one on top of the other in graduated sizes, with the largest anchored to the foundation (Fig. 11-16).

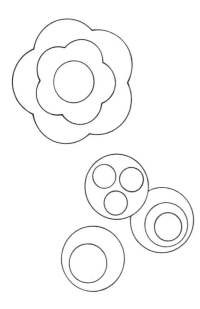

Fig. 11-16. Designs for stacked and stuffed appliqué.

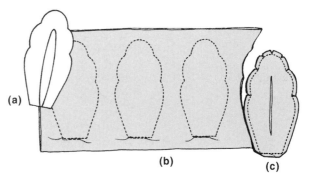

Fig. 11-18. (a) Loose appliqué pattern with topstitching outline indicated. (b) Pattern outlines stitched when sewing the lining to the appliqué fabric. (c) Cut-out appliqué ready to turn right side out through a slash in the lining. The slash will be enclosed inside the topstitching that attaches the stuffed appliqué to a foundation.

When machine sewing, start stacking the appliqués from the top: (1) Stitch the smallest appliqué to a medium-sized appliqué and stuff the smallest appliqué; (2) stitch the medium-sized appliqué to the largest appliqué and stuff the medium-sized appliqué; (3) stitch the largest appliqué to the foundation, and stuff it. The order of assembly is optional for hand-sewn stacks; either start at the top, as for machine sewing, or start at the base and proceed upward to the smallest appliqué, stuffing through openings in the stitching. Note that stacks of more than three layers tend to enlarge too much at the base, ending as a pillow that bulges below the level of the foundation as much as it rises above the foundation, unless the base appliqué is subdivided and stuffed in segments.

The unattached edges of *loose stuffed appliqué* spring up from the foundation, adding more elevation to shapes that are already puffed with stuffing. Loose stuffed appliqués are faced and lightly stuffed before they are centrally and visibly stitched to the foundation (Fig. 11-17).

Fig. 11-17. Designs for loose stuffed appliqué include internal topstitching/appliqué seamlines.

(1) Trace the outline of each pattern onto the wrong side of the lining. (2) Place the lining over the top fabric with right sides together and sew on the traced outlines. (3) Cut outside the seams (Fig. 11-18). Turn right side out through a slash cut into the lining. (4) Trace faint but distinct stitching lines on the top with a fabric-safe marker. Stuff lightly before sewing to the foundation with decorative hand or machine stitching. **Padded loose appliqué** is thickened with batting placed underneath the top when it is stitched to the lining, and plain **loose appliqué** is not filled at all.

XI-7—Hand-appliquéd design with satin-stitched veining for the leaves. Stuffing distinguishes between foreground and unstuffed background elements.

STUFFED APPLIQUÉ

XI-8—Design appliquéd with blindstitching by hand and satin stitching by machine. The two lower petals of the flower and the central circle at the base were eased for greater elevation.

XI-9—Hand-stitched, stacked, and stuffed design with the largest shape at the base reduced by stitching the shape above through to the foundation. The pointed shapes that appear to drape were stitched and stuffed when the other layers were finished.

XI-10—Design machine-appliquéd and stuffed from the top down. The fourth layer was outlined with top-stitching to reduce the size of the hexagon at the base. The corners of the triangle were needle modelled.

XI-11—(left) Batting-padded loose appliqués. (right) Floral executed in loose stuffed appliqué with one unstuffed leaf.

ELEVATED APPLIQUÉ

—small fabric shapes, supported with stuffing, that rise above the foundation to which they are stitched:

GATHER-ELEVATED APPLIQUÉ

—appliqués, lifted from the foundation by gathering, that stuff into softly rounded forms with puckery sides.

GUSSET-ELEVATED APPLIQUÉ

—appliqués, boosted above foundation level on a perpendicular fabric insertion, that stuff into smooth, boxy, flat-topped forms.

PROCEDURES

1. Develop an appliqué design with elements that are compatible with heightened relief. Simplify the contours of the shapes selected for elevation (Fig. 11-19). Cut apart a copy of the design to isolate the elements that will be elevated with gathering or a gusset.

Fig. 11-19. Arrangements of streamlined shapes for elevated appliqué.

2. To draft a pattern that elevates **all sides** of an appliqué:

With gathering:

Enlarge the appliqué all around by an amount equal to one-half the desired elevation. When enlarging an appliqué with a concave edge or an inside angle, slash and spread the enlargement of that edge to enlarge it even more, so that it will surpass the measurement of the original curved or angled edge enough to be gathered (Fig. 11-20).

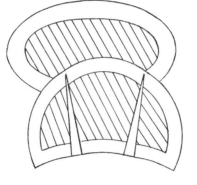

Fig. 11-20. Two shapes enlarged all around to create patterns for gather-elevated appliqué. The concave edge of the lower shape was slashed-and-spread to expand the gathering length of that edge.

With a gusset:

a Measure all around the shape to be elevated.

b. Draft a straight gusset with two parallel lines, each as long as the total measurement around the original shape, and as wide apart as the desired height of the elevation. Connect the parallel lines with perpendicular lines at the ends (Fig. 11-21).

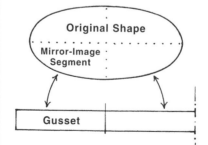

Fig. 11-21. Gusset that will surround and elevate an oval shape, drafted from the measured length of one mirror-image segment of the oval's contour. The gusset shown was drafted "on the fold."

3. To draft a pattern that elevates **all but one side** of an appliqué:

With gathering:

Enlarge the selected sides of the appliqué by an amount equal to the desired elevation. Gradually curve the enlargement into the original shape at the points (the ends of the side) where the enlargement ends (Fig. 11-22).

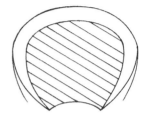

Fig. 11-22. Tapered enlargement that will elevate all but one side of an appliqué with gathering.

With a gusset:

a. Draw two parallel lines, each as long as the total measurement of the sides to be elevated, spaced as wide apart as the desired height of the elevation. Divide the space between the lines into segments with each segment equal to the length of the side it will elevate. Taper the elevated line into the baseline within each of the segments at the end.

b. Measure the tapering line. Compare with the baseline measurement for the same segment, which will be shorter, and subtract to find the difference.

c. To compensate for the increase caused by the tapering, cut the original shape apart between the sides that will be sewn to the tapered edge of the gusset. Spread at the cut to increase the length of each side by the difference (Fig. 11-23).

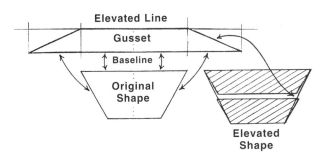

Fig. 11-23. Drafting a gusset that elevates three sides of a shape with four sides. The gusset is divided into segments, each one matching one of the three sides in length. The edges of the slashed and spread shape intended for elevation have been re-drawn to smooth out.

4. To draft a pattern that elevates **two opposite sides** of an appliqué:

With gathering:

a. Divide the appliqué in half, cutting straight across between the sides to be elevated.

b. Spread the parts to include an expansion as wide as the amount of the desired elevation.

c. Extend each of the sides to be elevated by an amount equal to the desired elevation.

d. Curve the extensions into the original shape at the corners (Fig. 11-24).

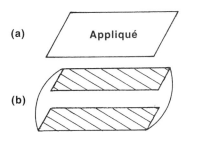

Fig. 11-24. (a) Appliqué to be elevated on opposite sides with gathering. (b) Appliqué slashed and spread to include the desired elevation, and curved outward at the slashed ends by the amount of the desired elevation.

With a gusset:

a. Draw two parallel lines, each as long as the measurement of one of the sides designated for elevation, and as wide apart as the desired height of the elevation. Taper the elevated line into the baseline at each end.

b. Measure the elevated line to the baseline. Measure the baseline, which will be shorter, and subtract to find the difference.

c. Cut straight across the original shape, bisecting the sides to be elevated by the gusset. Spread the cut by the amount of the difference, assuring a match when sewing the gusset to the elevated shape (Fig.11-25).

5. To draft a pattern that elevates **one side or two adjacent sides** of an appliqué:

With gathering:

a. Slash the appliqué, cutting straight across from the edge(s) to be elevated to the opposite side, stopping 1/16″ (1.5mm) from the opposite edge

b. Fan out the cuts to expand the side(s) to be elevated by a total amount equal to the desired elevation.

c. Enlarge the outline of the expanded side(s) by an amount equal to the desired elevation. Curve the enlargement into the original shape at the points where the enlargement ends (Fig. 11-26).

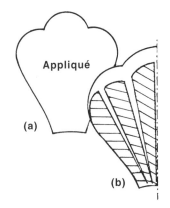

Fig. 11-26. (a) Appliqué to be elevated with gathering on one curvy side. (b) Appliqué slashed and spread, and curved out at the slashed edge with a line that echoes the original contour. The pattern was drafted "on the fold."

With a gusset:

a. Draw two parallel lines, each as long as the measurement of the side(s) to be elevated, and as wide apart as the desired height of the elevation. Taper the elevated line into the baseline at each end.

b. Measure the tapering line to the baseline. Measure the baseline, which will be shorter, and subtract to find the difference.

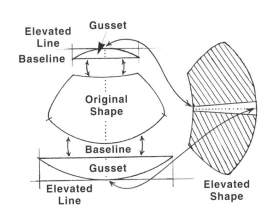

Fig. 11-25. Drafting patterns for two gussets that will elevate two opposite sides of a shape unequally, and the elevated shape that will be sewn to the gussets.

c. Slash the original shape, cutting straight across from the side(s) to be elevated to the opposite side, stopping 1/16″ (1.5mm) from the opposite edge. Fan out the cuts to expand the side(s) to be elevated by an amount that equals the difference—to assure a match when sewing the gusset to the elevated shape (Fig. 11-27).

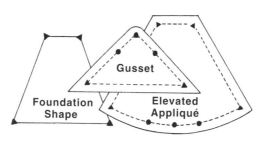

Fig. 11-29. Patterns for an appliqué that will be elevated on one side with the insertion of a triangular gusset. On the gusset, match-point symbols (● where sewn to the elevated appliqué, ▲ where sewn to the foundation), with corresponding match points on the foundation and the appliqué, indicate where to insert the gusset.

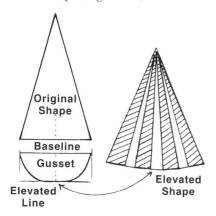

Fig. 11-27. Drafting a gusset that elevates one side of a triangle, then slashing and spreading that side of the triangle to match the elevated edge of the gusset so that the two can be sewn together.

6. To make **final patterns or templates** for elevated appliqués:

Gather-elevated appliqué patterns:

Make patterns without seam allowances. Use the original appliqué for the pattern to be traced on the foundation. As a gathering aid, indicate match points on the gathered appliqué pattern that correspond to match points on the foundation pattern (Fig. 11-28).

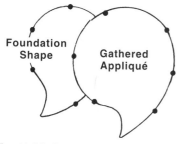

Fig. 11-28. Patterns for a gather-elevated appliqué with match point indications. The appliqué's outline is its fold and stitching line.

Gusset-elevated appliqué patterns:

Add seam allowances to each gusset and appliqué pattern. Use the original shape for the pattern to be traced on the foundation. For accuracy while stitching, indicate match points on the foundation shape that correspond to match points on the baseline side of the gusset. Indicate different match points on the elevated side of the gusset that correspond to similar match points on the elevated appliqué (Fig. 11-29)

7. With a fabric-safe marker, trace faint but distinct outlines of the entire design onto the right side of foundation fabric that has been cut to size. Indicate match points for the shapes to be elevated.

8. With a fabric-safe marker, **trace a faint but distinct outline** for each appliqué and gusset on the appropriate fabric. Mark all match points.

Gather-elevated appliqués:
Trace appliqué outlines onto the right side of the fabric. Cut out, adding a seam allowance around the outlines.

Gusset-elevated appliqués:
Trace appliqué and gusset outlines onto the wrong side of the fabric (optional: trace the seamlines as well). Cut out on the outlines.

9. Sew the elevated appliqués to the foundation:

Gather-elevated appliqués:

a. For each appliqué, turn the seam allowance under and pinch crease or heat press, concealing the traced outline on the fold.

b. Stitching next to the fold, gather the edge from one match point to the next, matching that section to the corresponding position marks on the foundation. Secure the gathering and continue to the next match point, and so on.

c. When the appliqué has been gathered to fit the outline, blindstitch to the foundation, matching the match points (Fig. 11-30, and also refer to Figs. 11-9 and 11-11).

Fig. 11-30. To appliqué a hand-gathered edge with blindstitching, distribute the gathers evenly and tack each furrow to the foundation. Remove the visible gathering thread when finished.

Gusset-elevated appliqués:

a. Prepare a gusset that elevates all sides of an appliqué by stitching the ends together with right sides facing.

b. With right sides facing, sew the elevated edge of the gusset to each appliqué, clipping the seam allowance of the straighter edge to enable edge alignment, and matching the match points.

c. Fold under and pinch crease the seam allowance at the baseline edge of the gusset, and on the un-elevated sides of the appliqué. With the right side outside, matching all match points, blindstitch the gusset/appliqué to the outline on the foundation (Fig. 11-31, and also refer to Figs. 11-9 and 11-11).

Fig. 11-31. Gusset with seam allowance clipped to allow sewing to the edges of a circular appliqué. The turned and pressed seam allowance at the baseline edge of the gusset is ready to stitch to the foundation.

10. Stretch the foundation in a hoop or frame large enough to expose the design. Stuff the elevated appliqués through slits cut into the foundation (refer to "Stuffing" on page 229).

11. Stretch and pin the edges of the foundation to a padded surface. Steam with an iron held above the fabric; allow to cool and dry before unpinning. Line the appliqué design, tacking the lining to the foundation at points where the stitches will be invisible in front.

NOTES & VARIATIONS

The choice between gathered elevation and gusset elevation is a matter of designer preference, influenced by which type of elevation would be the most appropriate for the design. Two other factors to consider: Sewing small gussets between a small shape and the foundation tests skill and patience. Gussets allow controlled variations in the stuffed shape, and gathering produces simple, rounded forms.

Gather-elevated appliqués often stuff higher than the anticipated elevation, particularly if the stuffing is mounded in the center. An appliqué gathered all around will stuff into a rounded form. To keep the middle as flat as possible, push the stuffing toward the elevated sides. The puckering at the edges that denotes gathering becomes more obvious as the elevation of the appliqué increases, although stuffing modifies the puckering somewhat. To subdue the puckering, replace hand gathering with bobbin-thread gathering: Machine stitch over the outline on the appliqué, gather, fold on the gathering stitches, and hand sew to the foundation.

To preserve the boxy definition of a gusset-elevated form, push the seamed edges and corners up and out with stuffing, pinch them after stuffing, and flatten and smooth the top and sides with outside pressure—or fill up a flat-topped form with a stack of batting and finish with stuffing underneath. Use the foundation shape to cut enough batting pieces to stack to the height of the elevation. Tack the layers together loosely with needle and thread. Stitch the gussetted appliqué to the foundation with the batting stack inside. To banish slack in the surface fabric, push stuffing beneath the batting through a slit cut into the foundation.

Gusset concepts are more difficult to understand than theories for gathered elevations, but they are worth knowing. To restate: When an elevated line changes direction at both ends to connect with a baseline, the elevated line will be longer than the baseline. Therefore, the edge of a shape that matches the baseline won't match the elevated line—unless the edge is adjusted. Slash the shape to spread out the edge so that it will match the increased length of the elevated line. Gussets can be drafted that will elevate an appliqué on a slant, or into a peak or arch, with predictable results.

To measure the perimeter of a shape with curving contours, follow the contour with a tape measure standing on edge; or stand a narrow strip of paper on edge, mark the length of the contour on the strip, and measure the distance between marks.

For small, low-relief appliqués or appliqués with at least one un-elevated edge, stuffing through an opening in the stitching that attaches the appliqué to the foundation is an alternative, but, in general, it's easier to distribute the stuffing evenly and control the shaping of an elevated form by stuffing it through a central slit cut in the foundation. A design with many elevated appliqués becomes top-heavy and needs a sturdy, substantial foundation for a base, such as stiff, heavy fabric; a batting-padded lining; or fabric secured in stretched condition.

Elevated piecework applies the concept of gathered or gussetted forms to pieced patchwork designs. Selected elements of a design are elevated with gathering or gussets, with each elevation basted to a lining before the pieces are sewn together in the usual, right-sides-facing fashion (Fig. 11-32). After assembly, the elevated elements are stuffed through slits cut into their linings.

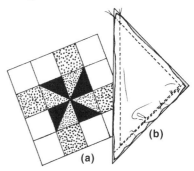

Fig. 11-32. (a) Patchwork design with triangular elements suitable for elevation. (b) Triangle with one side gathered and basted to a lining, prior to assembly into the block.

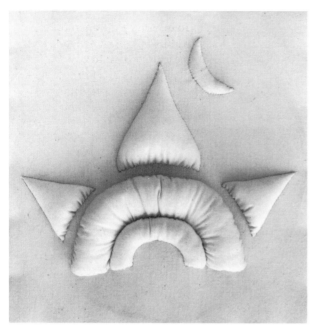

XI-12—Puckers and roundness characterize gathered forms. The moon at the top is simple stuffed appliqué.

ELEVATED APPLIQUÉ

XI-13—Pieced design with selected triangular elements elevated on one side with gathering.

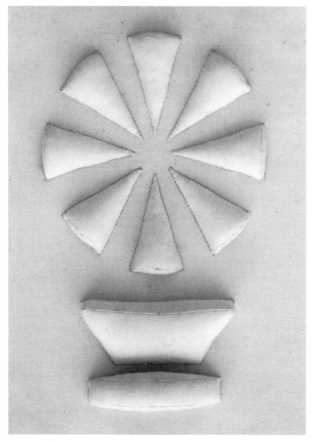

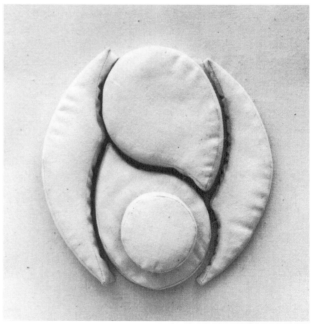

XI-15—Gusset-elevated shapes filled with stacks of batting.

XI-14—(from the top down) Appliqués gusset-elevated on one side only, on three sides, and on opposite sides. The tops of the two lower forms were stiffened with press-on interfacing.

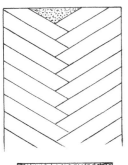

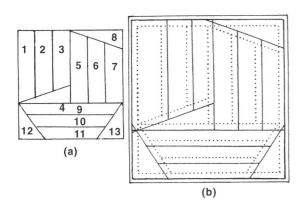

Fig. 11-33. Half-round designs meant to be continued or repeated to a larger size. The shaded areas will not be stuffed.

HALF-ROUNDS

—long, slender strips of fabric stitched side by side to a foundation with stuffing enclosed between the layers and seams.

PROCEDURES

1. Create an arrangement of narrow bars that are parallel, interrupted, overlapping, or skewed. Add triangular and tapered elements, and unstuffed areas, for variety and contrast (Fig. 11-33). Number the parts to indicate the sequence of application (the next half-round applied covers the seam allowance of the previously applied half-round, or half-rounds). Enlarge the design to actual size.

2. For the foundation, cut a piece of lining fabric slightly larger than the design unit requires.

   a. Stabilize the lining with freezer paper heat-bonded to the back, with typing-weight paper or commercial stabilizer machine-basted to the back around the edges, or by heavily starching the fabric.

   b. With a fabric-safe marking tool, trace the enlarged design onto the foundation—these lines are the seamlines. With a marker of another color, outline the edge of one seam allowance beside each seamline, generally the seam allowance to the right, as indicated by the order of application. These are the edge-matching guidelines (Fig. 11-34).

3. To determine the appropriate width for half-round fabric strips, measure the width of a strip on the foundation, add enough for two seam allowances, and include an extra amount equal to the desired height after stuffing. The amount added for stuffed height should not be more than one-third the foundation width of the strip. Measure and cut fabric strips for the half-rounds, continuing to cut more as needed while sewing proceeds.

4. Draft patterns for any tapered or triangular elements included in the design. Estimate the height after stuffing at the widest point of the element. Slash a cutout of the element from its widest to its narrowest point, stopping about $\frac{1}{16}''$ (1.5mm) from the narrow end. Spread the slash to equal the estimated height after stuffing. Re-draw the split outline generously; add a seam allowance (Fig. 11-35).

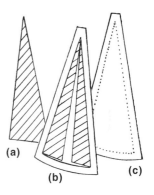

Fig. 11-35. (a) Cutout of triangular elements #4 and #8 in the design sketched in Fig. 11-34. (b) Cutout slashed and spread to include an allotment for height after stuffing, with seam allowance added. (c) The half-round pattern.

Use the pattern/template to trace and cut as many tapered or triangular half-rounds as the design requires.

Fig. 11-34. (a) Half-round design with components numbered in sewing order. (b) Design enlarged and outlined on the foundation. Dotted lines indicate seamlines; the cut edges will be matched to the solid lines.

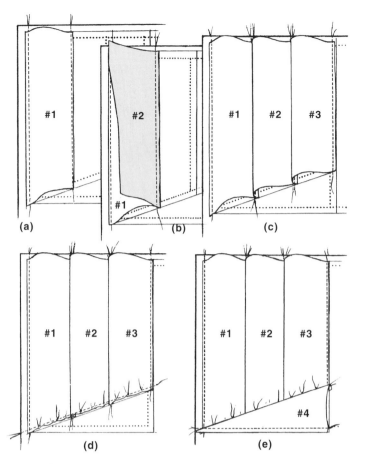

Fig. 11-36. To sew half-rounds to a foundation marked as shown in Fig. 11-34: (a) Baste strip #1 in position. (b) Sew strip #2 over the edge of strip #1. (c) Sew one edge of strip #3 over the edge of strip #2 and the other edge to the foundation. (d) Ease fullness at the ends of the strips into the basting seam. (e) Sew triangular half-round #4 in place.

5. To sew half-rounds, adapt the following steps to the needs of the specific design:

a. Cut enough from a half-round strip to cover the first half-round outlined on the foundation. Matching the edges of half-round #1 to the edge-matching guidelines marked on the foundation, machine stitch both of the long sides to the foundation with seams just inside the seam allowances. Trim the ends of the half-round to correspond with the guidelines on the foundation ((a) in Fig. 11-36).

b. Cut enough from a half-round strip for half-round #2 as outlined on the foundation. Place it right side down over half-round #1. Matching the edges, sew one long side of half-round #2 to half-round #1 on the seamline they both share. Turn half-round #2 right side up; trim the ends to correspond with the guidelines on the foundation. Baste the remaining long side to the foundation, matching the edge to the guideline and stitching inside the seam allowance; or sew half-round #3 to half-round #2 on their shared seamline without basting #2 first. Continue adding half-round strips, following the numbered sequence of application ((b) and (c) in Fig. 11-36).

c. To baste the ends of a half-round to the foundation, ease the excess fabric into the stitches as sewing proceeds, or gather with hand stitching first and baste over the gathering. Sew just inside the seam allowances ((d) in Fig. 11-36).

6. Stuff the half-rounds *softly* (refer to "Stuffing" on page 229), using either of the following methods:

♦ Leave one or both ends of a half-round or a group of half-rounds open during construction. Push stuffing through the open ends. Mound the soft stuffing in the center, thinning it out toward the side seams and ends. Close the ends by easing or gathering the excess fabric into seams (Fig. 11-37).

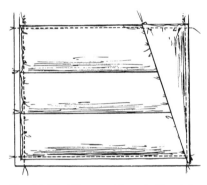

Fig. 11-37. After pushing stuffing into half-rounds through the open ends, ease-and-sew or gather-and-sew the ends to the foundation.

♦ Stuff while sewing each half-round to the foundation. (1) Sew the first side of the half-round in place. (2) Ease the fullness at the upper end of the half-round while sewing it to the foundation; at the corner, pivot with the needle down and sew the opposite side of the half-round, pause frequently to insert stuffing. At the lower corner, turn with the needle down and stitch across the end to enclose the stuffing, easing the fullness into the stitches (Fig. 11-38). Sew all seams inside the seam allowance.

Fig. 11-38. Simultaneously sewing and stuffing a half-round.

7. Remove the temporary stabilizer. Assemble as many half-round units as overall size requires. Line the construction of half-rounds, sewing the lining to the foundation at intervals and at the seamlines that connect the units.

NOTES & VARIATIONS

Theoretically, the foundation width of a true half-round is its diameter, so adding half the diameter (the radius) to the half-round strip would permit stuffing into a real half-round. Actually, that much elevation is too much for a half-round construction, unless it's part of a design featuring half-rounds that gradually increase to that height. When sewing half-rounds with more than ¼ the foundation width added to the half-round strip, cut the ends of the strips in an outward curve to allow more internal space next to the seam, room for stuffing to build up in height.

The seams between half-rounds bring the elevations on either side down to foundation level. Add a topstitched seam to expand the slim crevice created by the construction seam into a broader channel. After sewing the first side of a half-round in place, use that seamline/foldline to gauge a distance for the topstitching.

Confine the excess half-round fabric to the space between the topstitched seam and the seam that secures the second side to the foundation (Fig. 11-39).

A stabilizer prevents distortion during sewing and discourages overstuffing, but doesn't prevent it. Half-rounds are stuffed too full when the underside of the foundation begins to bulge and curl up between seams. To stuff while sewing, half-rounds are filled with too much stuffing when the stuffing impedes stitching with a regular presser foot on the sewing machine. For stuffing while sewing, use a straight-stitch sewing foot, or de-center the needle to the left if using a zigzag sewing foot.

Raised stripping is a low-relief version of half-rounds. It is similar to half-rounds in all respects but one: An amount for height after stuffing is not added to the strips or triangles stitched to the foundation. Raised stripping is very lightly stuffed during the sewing process.

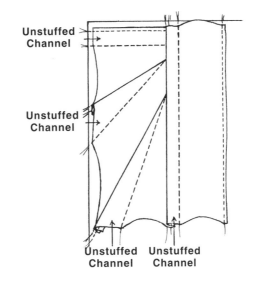

Unstuffed Channel

Unstuffed Channel

Unstuffed Channel   Unstuffed Channel

Fig. 11-39. Adding top-stitched channels to a half-round construction.

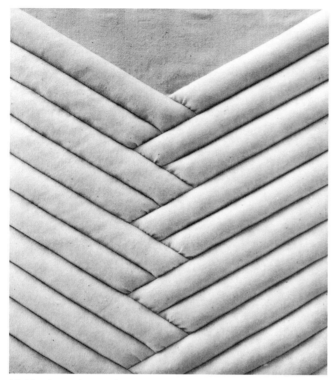

XI-16—An application that appears to weave underneath itself.

HALF-ROUNDS

XI-17—Topstitched channels separate most of the half-rounds in a design that zigzags between half-round borders at the sides.

XI-18—Traditional log cabin pattern with two sides of the design elevated by half-rounds and two sides unstuffed.

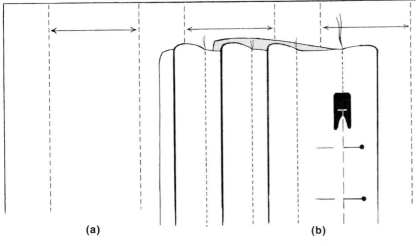

Fig. 11-40. (a) Pattern for a group of rolls with arrows connecting seamlines that will be sewn together. (b) Sewing pin-matched seamlines together.

CONNECTED ROLLS

—long, plump, stuffed cylinders that sit in parallel rows on top of the fabric in the background, from which they are constructed like tucks.

PROCEDURES

1. Set a diameter larger than ⅝″ (1.5cm) for each roll. On a scale diagram or actual-size pattern, allocate a narrow section for the casing for each roll. Each casing section should be three times wider than the chosen diameter for the stuffed roll, and as long as the length of the fabric. The lines that border the sections reserved for each casing will be seamlines ((a) in Fig. 11-40). Separate the seamlines of adjacent roll casings with background spaces:

   ◆ For an arrangement of rolls that touch one another, allow a space one diameter wide between two rolls of equal diameter. If adjacent rolls have different diameters, add one-half the diameter of one to one-half the diameter of the other and allow that much space between the two rolls.

   ◆ For an arrangement with channels of background fabric visible between rolls, add one-half the diameter of each adjacent roll to the width of the space to be visible between the two rolls.

2. Using a fabric-safe marker, draw the seamlines for each roll casing on the right side of the fabric. Start by measuring and marking seamline positions across the top and bottom edges of the fabric, and connect opposite position marks with a straightedge to trace the lines.

3. With the right side of the fabric facing up, fold and pin match the seamlines that enclose each casing; machine stitch over the line on top ((b) in Fig. 11-40). For very long rolls, leave 1½″ (4cm) stuffing openings in the seams, spaced 9″ (23cm) to 12″ (30.5cm) apart. Rolls shorter than 12″ (30.5cm) are stuffed through the open ends of the stitched tubes.

4. Push stuffing into the tubular casings through the openings in the seams or at the ends (refer to "Stuffing" on page 229). Stuff until the roll is round and smooth while retaining the degree of flexibility appropriate for the application. Reduce the amount of stuffing next to the ends, leaving a generous seam allowance empty. Close the openings in the seams with hand-sewn ladder stitches.

5. To close the end of a stuffed-roll casing in preparation for finishing the edge with binding or an extension:

   ◆ Pleat or gather the empty casing to match the roll's stuffed diameter. Center the empty casing over its own construction seam. Baste to the background fabric by hand or machine, stitching within the seam allowance.

   ◆ Flatten the empty casing without reducing width, center, and stitch it down (Fig. 11-41).

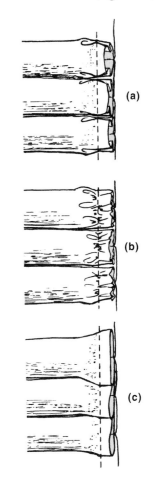

Fig. 11-41. Before basting across the empty ends of stuffed rolls, (a) pleat, (b) gather, or (c) flatten the casings.

NOTES & VARIATIONS

Actually, the circumference of a circle is 3.1416 times its diameter, but simplifying to three times the chosen diameter for the tubular casing of a roll stuffs out close enough to the estimate to justify the easier formula. However, if the fabric used for the casing is tightly woven and unyielding, allow a generous three times the diameter for casing measurement.

For rolls of unchanging diameter, the seamlines that construct the tubular casings are straight and equidistant from the fold. Seamline variations that deviate from the standard change the shape, the progress, and the size of the stuffed rolls: (1) Seamlines that are straight but slant toward the folds produce casings that stuff into rolls that taper (Fig. 11-42).

Fig. 11-42. Tapered rolls.

(2) Cross seams break the rolls into segments. For each break, flatten, center, and pleat the sides of the unstuffed casing to reduce its width to the diameter after stuffing. Topstitch straight across the pleated tube ((a) in Fig. 11-43). (3) Seamlines that split the entire casing, or separate portions of the casing, create two casings. Center the casing over its seam and topstitch down the center ((b) in Fig. 11-43).

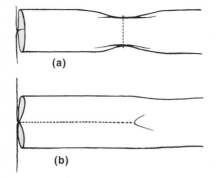

Fig. 11-43. Stuffed roll variations: (a) Topstitch across the pleated casing. (b) Topstitch down the center of the unstuffed casing.

One or both ends of a casing may be stitched closed before the roll is stuffed if access into the tube is available in seam openings. For rolls that encircle, sew the ends of the fabric together, matching the pre-marked seamlines. Stitch the seamlines together to construct the roll casings. Stuff through openings left in the seams.

Closing the ends of a stuffed roll by sewing the flattened casing to the background fabric encases the stuffing and also steadies the roll. If long, fat, horizontal rolls wobble on their seams, tack each stuffed-roll casing to the background fabric with hand stitching on each side of the construction seam.

Detached rolls are sewn and stuffed apart from the fabric to which they are applied. Cut a strip of fabric three times the roll diameter plus two seam allowances. Stitch the long edges together to form a tubular casing. Stuff the casing through the ends and/or through openings left in the seam.

For **a detached surface roll**, stitch the edges together with the right side of the fabric strip folded inside, and turn the tubular casing right side out before stuffing ((a) in Fig. 11-44). Surface rolls are hand stitched to a foundation with construction seams hidden underneath. If the casing strips are cut on the bias, the rolls can be applied to spacious curves.

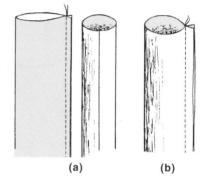

Fig. 11-44. Detached rolls: (a) Surface rolls stuffed after sewing. (b) In-seam rolls stuffed while sewing.

For **a detached in-seam roll**, stitch the edges of the fabric strip together with the right side on the outside. Pause while sewing to lift the presser foot and stuff softly ((b) in Fig. 11-44). To insert the roll into a seam joining two pieces of fabric, attach a zipper or cording foot to the machine. Matching edges, baste the roll to the right side of one fabric. Sew the second piece of fabric to the first with right sides together and the roll in between. Alternate construction: Sew the unstuffed casing into the seam joining two pieces of fabric, but leave stuffing openings in the seam. Stuff, and hand sew the openings closed.

XI-19 —Stuffed rolls that gradually increase in size.

XI-20—Construction that revolves around tapered rolls that hold the flimsy fabric upright, and detached in-seam rolls that stabilize the circular top and base.

XI-21—Cross-seams interrupting the rolls complicate the overall pattern.

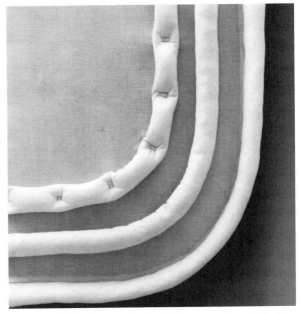

XI-22—Detached rolls with bias-cut casings applied in curves on the surface and in-seam at the edge.

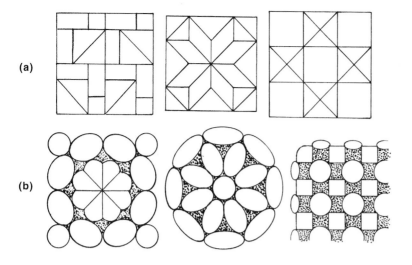

(a)

(b)

Fig. 11-45. Shapes with straight and curving sides arranged into designs for little pillows: (a) Joined into a solid unit. (b) Connected with open spaces as part of the design.

LITTLE PILLOWS

—plumped, geometric forms cut from doubled fabric, sewn around, turned, and stuffed. Fitted together into a planned arrangement, an assembly of little pillows is self-lined and reversible.

PROCEDURES

1. Compose a grid-based arrangement of adjoining geometric shapes, with or without see-through spaces between edges that touch (Fig. 11-45). Set the actual sizes of the components.

2. Draft patterns for the various shapes in the design:

   a. Draw an outline of each shape. Estimate a stuffed height/depth for each shape (Fig. 11-46). Enlarge each outline by one-fourth the height estimate. For example, if the estimated depth is ¼″ (6mm), draw another outline ¹⁄₁₆″ (1.5mm) outside the original; if the estimated depth is ½″ (1.3cm), extend the original outline by ⅛″

(3mm) all around.

Fig. 11-46. Little pillow profile. To estimate height, choose a realistic measurement for the imagined depth that stuffing will produce when inserted into the casing.

   b. For circles and ovals, the enlargement is the pattern (Fig. 11-47).

   c. For squares, rectangles, triangles, and other angled shapes, connect the enlarged outline to the corners of the original outline with curving lines (Fig. 11-48).

   d. Cut out the patterns. Indicate a small but reasonable opening for turning and stuffing. For little pillows, the pattern outline is the seamline. Seam allowances are added when cutting the fabric.

3. With a fabric-safe marking tool, trace pattern outlines onto the wrong side of the fabric, marking stuffing openings outside each outline. Allow enough space between adjacent outlines for seam allowances when cutting.

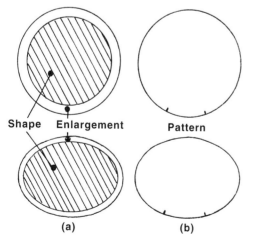

Shape   Enlargement   Pattern

(a)

(b)

Fig. 11-47. Round and oval patterns for little pillows: (a) Enlarge for estimated height. (b) Patterns without seam allowances, with stuffing openings marked.

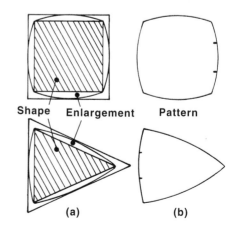

Shape   Enlargement   Pattern

(a)   **(b)**

Fig. 11-48. Square and triangular patterns for little pillows: (a) Shapes with enlargements tapered into the corners of the original outlines. (b) Patterns without seam allowances, with stuffing openings marked.

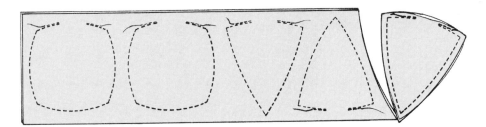

Fig. 11-49. Pillow outlines stitched, except for the openings, and cut out outside the seams.

4. With right sides together, pin the fabric with traced outlines over a second piece of fabric. Straight stitch by machine over each outline, starting and ending with backstitching on either side of the stuffing opening. Add a small but adequate seam allowance when cutting out the pillow casings (Fig. 11-49). Trim seam allowances diagonally across corners. Turn right side out.

5. Stuff each pillow until it is suitably plump, substantial, and stable (refer to "Stuffing" on page 229). Stuff pillows with straight sides until the edges straighten out. Stop stuffing round or oval pillows before the surrounding seam begins to buckle and pucker. Hand sew the openings closed with ladder stitching or tiny overhand stitching.

6. Arrange and join the pillows into the larger, pre-planned construction:
   - For a closed arrangement of pillows with straight sides: (1) To make sure that corners and edges abut precisely, especially on long seams, tack at intervals or baste with large ladder stitches before sewing together permanently. (2) Whip the edges together with tiny stitches invisible in front, or machine sew with zigzag, satin, or decorative stitching (Fig. 11-50).
   - For an open arrangement of round, oval, and straight-sided pillows: Hand sew the pillows together with tiny whipstitches at the points where they touch, or attach with ties. Connect straight-sided pillows with ties, faggotting, or tabs (Fig. 11-51).

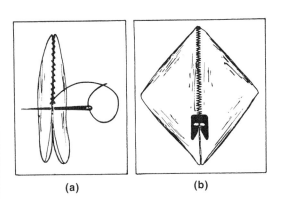

(a)   (b)

11-50. Sewing straight-sided little pillows together in closed arrangements (a) Catch fabric from the back seam of the pillows with tiny whip stitches. (b) Zigzag or satin stitch over the butted edges.

(a)   (b)   (c)   (d)   (e)

Tabbed Pillow Pattern

(f)

Fig. 11-51. Open attachments for little pillow arrangements (a & b) String ties. (c) Faggotting. (d) Ribbon ties. (e) Whipstitching at contact points. (f) Tabs that start with curved projections added to each side of the pillow pattern.

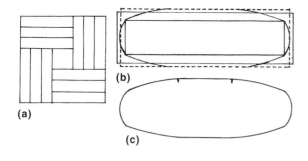

(a)

(b)

(c)

Fig. 11-52. (a) Little pillow design. (b) Enlarge for estimated height. Add to the long sides the amount deleted from the short sides (dashed line). Curve the corrected enlargement into the corners of the original outline. (c) Pattern with stuffing opening marked.

NOTES & VARIATIONS

When estimating depth for little-pillow patterns, vary the estimate with the overall size of the shape: Larger shapes are capable of more depth than smaller shapes. Designs that include shapes of various sizes will have different elevations when the stuffed pillows are assembled. After stuffing, pillows are usually a little plumper than the estimate. A construction that includes too many pillows wider than 4″ (10cm) square tends to become clumsy and cumbersome.

When devising patterns for shapes with sides that are dramatically different in size (elongated rectangles, triangles, and ovals), enlarge as usual, but reduce the enlargement of the short sides and add the amount eliminated from the short sides to the enlargement of the long sides (Fig. 11-52).

Two little pillow **variations**: (1) After turning the casing but before stuffing, outline a small shape in the center—a circle, a diamond, crossed rectangles, a clover-leaf—topstitching by hand or machine. (2) After stuffing, add a decorative tie or button in the center, attached by sewing down and back through the stuffing.

Peekholes are straight-sided pillows with see-through openings. Patterns are developed in the little pillow manner, but with seam allowances added around the outside and a "hole" outlined in the center. (1) Trace the outlines of the pattern on the lining, marking peekhole outlines. (2) For each peekhole, cut a front with the lining (3) Sew the front to the lining with right sides together, stitching over the peekhole outline. Cut out inside the seam, clip the seam allowance, and turn right side out. (4) Matching all edges, sew the two-layer peekholes together into the pre-planned arrangement. For accuracy, stitch over seamlines marked on the linings (Fig. 11-53). (5) Stuff each peekhole through one or two slits cut into the lining. (6) Unlike standard little pillows, an assembly of peekholes needs an outer lining to conceal and protect

the seam allowances and darned openings visible in the back. Tack the outer lining to the peekhole unit at intersections. From the front, the outer lining will be visible through and behind the peekholes. For variety, uncover a peekhole by cutting the outer lining away behind the opening, stitching the cut and turned edge to the inner lining around the peekhole.

Compared to the plump firmness of little pillows, **raised patchwork** seems deflated and soft. Raised patchwork is composed of straight-sided elements assembled with hand sewing or machine stitching into closed units—just like little pillows—except: (1) The patterns are *not* enlarged to compensate for height after stuffing, and (2) the amount of stuffing inserted inside the casing must be controlled to prevent the straight sides of the casing from curving inward—which would complicate closed assembly (Fig. 11-54). Because light stuffing distributed throughout the casing tends to shift inside large interiors, raised patchwork shapes have smaller dimensions. Casings may be prepared as described for little pillows; or they can be made by folding rectangles into squares and squares into triangles or rectangles, sewing together only the cut edges.

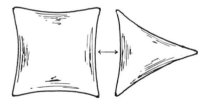

Fig. 11-54. Pillows with sides concaved by too much stuffed elevation in the center are difficult to sew into a closed construction.

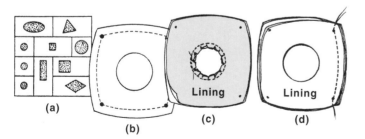

(a)

(b)

(c) Lining

(d) Lining

Fig. 11-53. (a) Design for little pillows with peekholes. (b) Pattern with seam allowance around the outside and peekhole in the center. (c) Peekhole prepared when the front and lining are stitched together. (d) Sewing the edges of two pillows-with-peekholes together.

XI-23—Closed arrangement of squares, triangles, and rectangles joined with hand stitching and satin stitching.

XI-24—Circles and ovals handstitched together into an openwork border.

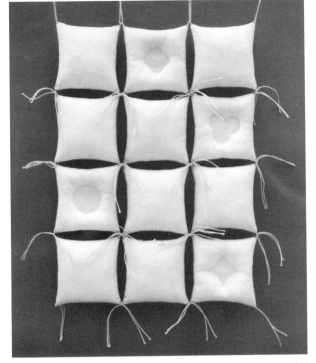

XI-25—Plump pillows with sides that curve inward because the pattern was not enlarged for estimated height. Designs topstitched in the center reduce the plumpness of four of the pillows.

XI-26—Sixteen squares: 3 unstuffed, 5 stuffed into pillows, and 8 with peekholes. Lining cut away behind the triangular peekhole opens it up to the space beyond.

BISCUITS

—cushiony mounds of fabric elevated from small, squared foundations that are sewn together. Pleats caught into the seams that edge each biscuit make room for the supportive stuffing.

PROCEDURES

1. Draw a square, adding seam allowances, for the base of the biscuit. Increasing the size of the base by the estimated height of the biscuit when stuffed, draw an enlarged square, including the seam allowances, for the biscuit pattern. For example: For a biscuit 1″ (2.5cm) high, enlarge a base 3″ (7.5cm) square to a 4″ (10cm) square. For a biscuit ½″ (1.3cm) high, enlarge a 3″ (7.5cm) base to 3½″ (9cm). Mark a center point on each side of the base and biscuit squares, and cut out the patterns (Fig. 11-55).

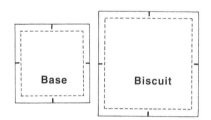

Fig. 11-55. Base and biscuit patterns with center points indicated.

2. From lining fabric, cut a base for each biscuit required for the planned construction. From the top fabric, cut a biscuit for each base. On the right side of each base and biscuit, mark the center points inside the seam allowances.

3. Matching corners and edges, sew each biscuit, right side up, to its base, stitching inside the seam allowance. Make a pleat in each side of the biscuit to reduce the biscuit to the size of the base:

   ♦ For a biscuit 1″ (2.5cm) larger than the base or less, make a single-fold pleat in each side (Fig. 11-56).

   ♦ For a biscuit 1″ (2.5cm) larger than the base or more, make an inverted pleat in each side (Fig. 11-57).

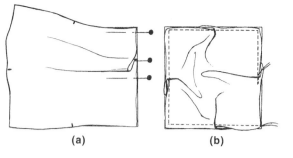

Fig. 11-56. To sew biscuits to bases with single-fold pleats (a) Pin as shown, making a pleat with its outside fold meeting the center mark. (b) Biscuit after stitching, with an opening for stuffing.

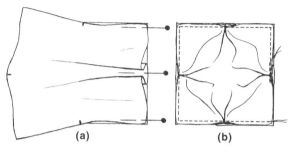

Fig. 11-57. To sew biscuits to bases with inverted pleats (a) Pin as shown, making an inverted pleat with both outside folds meeting in the center. (b) Biscuit after stitching, with an opening for stuffing.

♦ Sew each pleated side in turn. At the final side, stop sewing after felling the pleat to allow an opening for stuffing between the pleat and the corner.

4. Assemble the biscuits in rows. Stuff the biscuits to the softly rounded height allowed by the loose fabric released from the pleats (refer to "Stuffing" on page 229):

   ♦ With right sides facing, sew two rows of biscuits together with all openings located on the outside of each row. Stuff the biscuits. Topstitch the openings closed with a zipper foot. With right sides together, baste and sew an unstuffed row of biscuits to the stuffed row of biscuits, locating all openings on the side opposite the seam. Stuff, and continue adding rows with openings accessible on the outside (Fig. 11-58).

   ♦ Another method defers stuffing until all rows of biscuits have been stitched together. Eliminate the side openings when preparing the biscuits. Assemble and stuff the biscuits through slits cut into bases. After stuffing, hand sew the openings closed.

5. Line the biscuit construction to cover the exposed seam allowances in back. Tack the lining to the stuffed top at the cross seams.

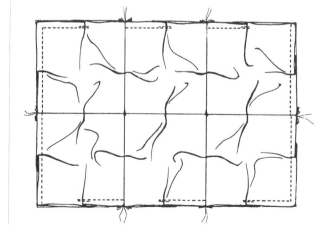

Fig. 11-58. Two rows of biscuits seamed together with cross seams matching and openings located on the outside edges. After stuffing, add more unstuffed rows to each side of the central unit.

NOTES & VARIATIONS

Biscuits are cushiony mounds, softly stuffed. To establish the roundness of a biscuit, never push stuffing into the corners of the squared base.

Sewing unstuffed rows to stuffed rows of biscuits becomes a clumsy task as the assembly increases in size. Section large constructions, leaving unstuffed rows where two sections will be joined, and stuff those rows through slits cut into the bases.

An alternate and speedier method of biscuit preparation starts with patterns for a block of biscuits: (1) Draw a grid of squares that combines the bases for four or more biscuits. Draw another grid of enlarged squares for the pleated top of the biscuits. Mark the pleat locations and add a seam allowance around both patterns. (2) With a fabric-safe marker, trace all grid lines (seamlines) and pleat markings onto the fabric cut for the base and the top. (3) Sew the top to the base. Pin match all parallel seamlines and pleat markings in one direction. Machine sew, forming pleats at every pleat location. Repeat in the cross direction (Fig. 11-59). (4) Assemble the entire biscuit construction. Stuff each biscuit through a slit cut into its base.

Although the traditional biscuit has a square foundation, a pleat on every side also enables biscuits to rise from non-square bases (Fig. 11-60). Enlarge the base pattern all around by an amount equal to one-half the desired elevation.

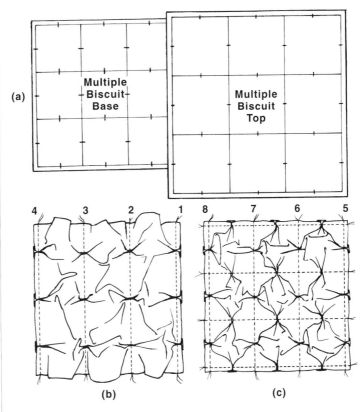

Fig. 11-59. To quick-sew a block of biscuits (a) Base and top patterns combining multiple biscuits, with pleat locations marked on seamlines. (b) Top and base stitched together in one direction with inverted pleats at marked locations; (c) stitched in the opposite direction. Seams are stitched as numbered.

Additional textures and levels may be introduced to a biscuit construction by including smooth, flat areas between the biscuits, leaving selected biscuits unstuffed and crumpled, and furrowing the billowing fabric in the center (refer to "Furrowing" on page 9).

Sausages are a biscuit variation. To justify the name, they are rectangular—long and slender but plump. They are constructed like biscuits in all respects but one:

Instead of a pleat on every side, only the two opposite sides have pleats, and those pleats are always centered in the smaller ends of the rectangles. For a sausage pattern, enlarge the base pattern in one direction, increasing the length of the short sides of the rectangle by the amount of the desired elevation.

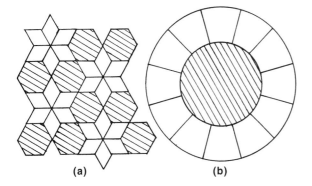

Fig. 11-60. Two unusual construction formats for biscuits: (a) Clusters of diamond-shaped biscuits separated by flat hexagons. (b) Circle surrounded by a ring of biscuits.

BISCUITS

XI-27—Traditional construction of biscuits that looks like its name.

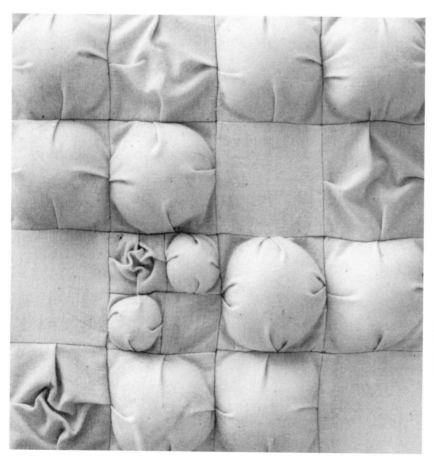

XI-28—Unstuffed and furrowed biscuits, and level squares of fabric, elaborate the pattern of reliefs in a biscuit construction.

XI-29—Triangular biscuits shaped with inverted pleats.

XI-30—Sausages varied with unpleated, softly stuffed rectangles centered inside five of the three-sausage squares.

PEAKS AND VALLEYS

—small, cone-shaped elevations of fabric, supported with stuffing, that rise from triangular or square foundations. Assembled into orderly arrangements, valleys caused by the construction seams separate the peaks.

PROCEDURES

1. Create a design of adjoining equilateral triangles with connecting squares (Fig. 11-61). Set the actual size of the components.

2. Draft a base pattern, without seam allowances, for each triangle and square in the design. Draft a peak pattern, without seam allowances, for each base pattern:

   ◆ For a triangular base pattern, the peak pattern is a square. Each side of the square equals the measurement of one side of the triangle (Fig. 11-62).

   ◆ For a square base pattern, the peak pattern is a pentagon. Each side of the pentagon equals the measurement of one side of the square (Fig. 11-63).

   ◆ Add seam allowances and sewing notations to each base and peak pattern. Cut out the patterns.

3. From lining fabric, cut a base for each peak in the design. From top fabric, cut a peak for each base. On the right side of each base and peak, lightly mark the points where the seams turn corners.

4. Sew each peak, right side up, to its base, stitching inside the seam allowance. Matching corner points and edges, sew from corner point to corner point around all sides of the base. At each corner, pivot with the needle down, adjust the next side of the peak to match the next side of the base, and sew to the next corner point. At the final corner, the extra side of the peak will form a loose fold (Fig. 11-64).

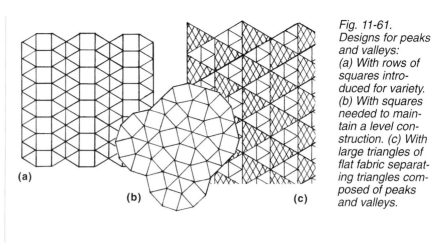

Fig. 11-61. Designs for peaks and valleys: (a) With rows of squares introduced for variety. (b) With squares needed to maintain a level construction. (c) With large triangles of flat fabric separating triangles composed of peaks and valleys.

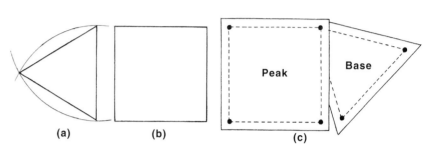

Fig. 11-62. (a) With a compass set to the measurement of one side of the peak's triangular base, draft a triangle with three equal sides. (b) Using the same measurement, draft a square for the peak. (c) Patterns with seam allowances, and circles (●) to mark the corners.

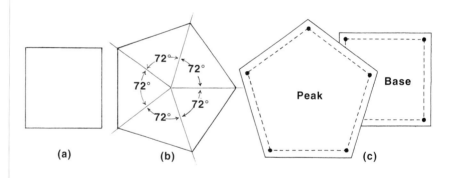

Fig. 11-63. (a) Draft a square base for a peak. (b) Using a protractor, draft a pentagon for the peak with sides that match the sides of the square. (c) Patterns with seam allowances, and circles (●) to mark the corners.

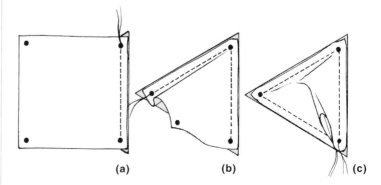

Fig. 11-64. (a) Sew one side of the peak to one side of the base. (b) Match and sew the next side, and (c) the next, leaving the extra side of the peak as an open fold at the corner.

5. Assemble the peaks as pre-planned, and stuff (refer to "Stuffing" on page 229):

• With right sides facing, sew the peaks together in rows with all loose folds located on the outside ((a) in Figs. 11-65 and 11-66).

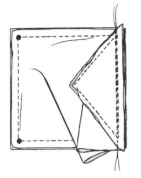

Fig. 11-65. Sew two peaks together with a seam just to the left of the first seam.

Push stuffing through the openings in the folds to stuff the peaks. After stuffing, pull down and match the edges of each fold to the outside edge of its peak and topstitch the folds down with a zipper foot ((b) in Fig. 11-66). With right sides together, baste and sew more unstuffed rows of peaks to the stuffed row of peaks, locating all loose folds on the outside. Stuff and continue adding rows.

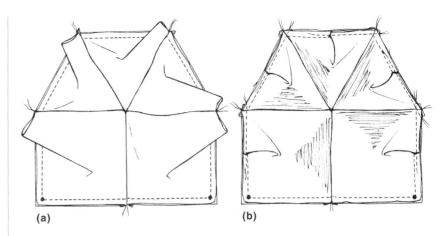

(a)   (b)

Fig. 11-66. (a) Peaks sewn together with open folds on the outside. (b) Folds topstitched to the sides of the peaks after stuffing.

• An alternate method schedules stuffing after all the peaks are assembled. When preparing the peaks, continue sewing to secure the fold of the peak to the base (Fig. 11-67). Sew the peaks together into the pre-planned arrangement. Stuff each peak through a slit cut into the base. After stuffing, hand sew the opening closed.

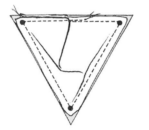

Fig. 11-67. Unstuffed peak with fold stitched down.

6. Line the assembly of peaks and valleys to cover the exposed seam allowances in back. Tack the lining to the stuffed top at the cross seams.

Notes & Variations

Sewing rows of unstuffed peaks to rows of stuffed peaks becomes cumbersome as the assembly increases in size. Divide large constructions into manageable sections, leaving unstuffed rows with folds stitched down where the sections will be joined. After sewing the sections together, stuff the peaks on either side of the seam through slits cut into bases.

Stuff the corners at the base of each peak as well as the tip of the pyramid. After stuffing, point each peak by moving adjacent stuffing up into the tip on the end of a sturdy needle inserted into the stuffing. A square peak will stuff higher at the tip than a triangular peak with the same side measurement. The larger the peak, the higher its elevation.

When assembling peaks and valleys, regulate the direction the folds face when stitched down. The folds are part of the overall design.

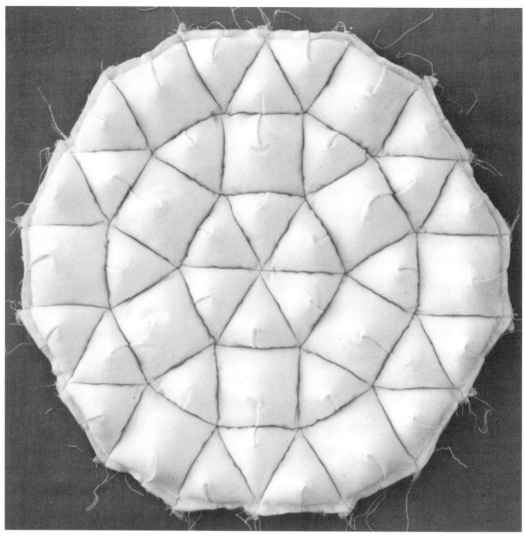

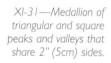

XI-31—Medallion of
triangular and square
peaks and valleys that
share 2" (5cm) sides.

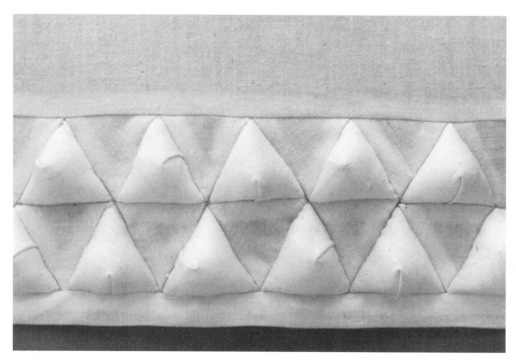

XI-32—Border
arrangement with the
valleys extended to
flat triangles between
the rising peaks.

Structured
Surfaces

*D*arts sculpt the fabric's surface into highs and lows. A shortened fold of fabric seamed to a point or between two points, a dart causes the level of the fabric to raise or drop in direct ratio to the amount of fabric it removes.

On the fabric's surface, darts appear as seams or as folds. Although the doubled layers of fabric that darts produce brace the structure they shape somewhat, darted forms are hollow, as if inflated, and collapsible—unless supported by other means.

DARTS

12 Using Darts

Note: This chapter begins with BASICS, indicated by a gray band located underneath the relevant columns.

DART BASICS

SECURING DART SEAMS

Because dart seams end and, with double-pointed darts, begin within the fabric, the cut thread where the seams stop must be secured or the stitching may unravel. Where it's appropriate:

1. **Tie the needle to the bobbin thread with a square knot:**

   - After stitching a dart on the *wrong* side of the fabric, tie the threads where the seam runs off the fabric.

   - After stitching a dart on the *right* side of the fabric, turn to the back. Snag both threads from the final stitch with a needle and pull them through to the back for tying.

   - After stitching a dart on the *right* side of the fabric, tie the threads together in front. Insert both threads into a needle, insert the needle into the final machine-needle hole, push it through to the back, and pop the knot through the fabric.

   Trim tied threads at least ½″ (1.3cm) from the knot.

2. **Reduce stitch length:**

   - When sewing a dart on the *wrong* side of the fabric, start reducing the stitch length before reaching the end of the seam, arriving at 0 as the seamline tapers out. Take three or four stitches at 0 before clipping the threads. To begin a double-pointed dart, reverse the procedure: Start at 0 and increase rapidly to regular stitch length.

   - When seaming *dart patterns on the wrong side* of the fabric, sew all dart seams with unusually small, tight stitches.

   - Clip the threads ½″ (1.3cm) from the stitching.

3. **Sew with a single thread when stitching a single-pointed dart.**
   (1) Tie the end of the bobbin thread to the end of the needle thread with a very tight, square knot. (2) Pulling on the needle thread, tug the knot through the needle. Rewind the needle thread onto the spool, moving the knot and the bobbin thread up through the threading guides and tension until the knot reaches the spool. (3) Begin stitching with the dart fold placed up against the needle, which should be down. At the first stitch, the thread will wrap around the fold, leaving no ends to tie or trim.

   To stitch dart patterns efficiently, fold and pin a row of darts and stitch without stopping to cut the threads between darts. After finishing one dart, pull out several inches of thread before starting the next dart. After seaming an entire row, cut the threads between the darts.

   For a dart pattern or dart improvisation seamed into the right side of the fabric, unclipped threads deliberately left to dangle or feather out from the ends of seams add their own kind of texture over the top of the dimensionalized structure.

SINGLE-POINTED DART

—a V-marked segment of fabric folded in half and stitched from the mouth of the V, which is always at the fabric's edge, to the vanishing point of the V, where the fabric elevates or dips.

PROCEDURES

1. Using a pattern of the flat shape to be dimensionalized, draft a pattern that will model the flat shape into a three-dimensional form with one or more single-pointed darts. The width at the mouth of the dart and the shaping of the dart seam—straight, curved inward, curved outward—affect the contour of the structured form (Fig. 12-1). Adapt one of the following methods:

Guess and trim:

For each dart, fold the pattern at the chosen dart position. Draw an arbitrary dart stitching line and cut on the line. Abut the sides of the cut and tape together. Trim the darted edge to conform to its pre-dart contour.

Note: *After the darted edge is trimmed, the outer measurements of the darted shape will no longer match the pre-dart measurements of the original pattern (Fig. 12-2).*

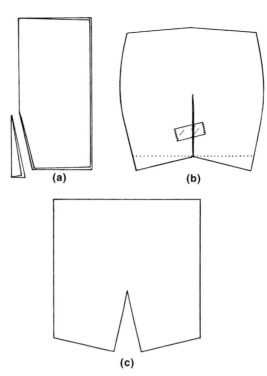

(a)   **(b)**

(c)

Fig. 12-2. Guess-and-trim dart pattern for a square: (a) Cutting the dart. (b) Dart sides taped together with the darted edge restored to straightness. (c) The pattern.

Slash and spread:

Estimate an elevation (or depth) for the darted pattern to achieve. For each dart, mark a point on the flat pattern where the elevation (or depth) will culminate at the end, or apex, of the dart. Connect the point to the edge of the pattern with a line that indicates the location and length of the dart.

a. **For a single dart:** (1) Extend the dart line drawn on the pattern straight across to the opposite edge. (2) Cut the pattern on the line,

stopping 1/16″ (1.5mm) short of the opposite edge. (3) Spread the cut until the opening at the edge equals *the estimated elevation/depth.* Stick a strip of paper behind the gap. (4) Using a compass, draft a dart as wide as the opening at the edge and as long as the original dart line (Fig. 12-3).

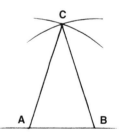

Fig. 12-3. To draft a balanced dart, set a compass to match the length of the dart. Place the point of the compass at A on one side of the mouth of the dart and draw an arc; repeat at point B. Connect C, where the two arcs intersect, to A and B with lines.

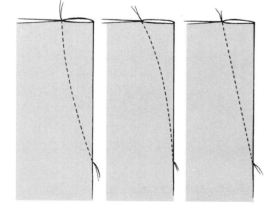

Fig. 12-1. Single-pointed darts.

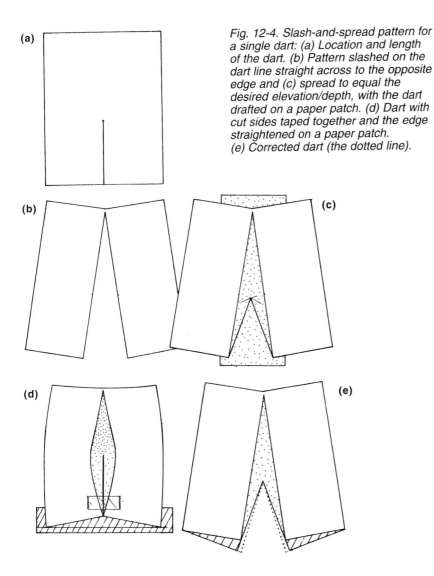

(a)

(b)

(c)

(d)

(e)

Fig. 12-4. Slash-and-spread pattern for a single dart: (a) Location and length of the dart. (b) Pattern slashed on the dart line straight across to the opposite edge and (c) spread to equal the desired elevation/depth, with the dart drafted on a paper patch. (d) Dart with cut sides taped together and the edge straightened on a paper patch. (e) Corrected dart (the dotted line).

(5) Cut the darts open. Restore the now slightly enlarged dart openings to correct width (Fig. 12-5). (6) To make darts on the other two sides, slash from one edge through the center extension to the opposite edge and repeat steps (1) through (5).

Note: *After the final corrections, the exterior measurements of the pattern will match the exterior measurements of the original, but interior measurement across the taped-together dart or darts will increase, and the darts will be longer than originally planned.*

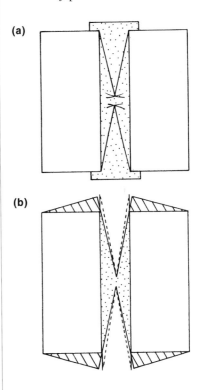

(a)

(b)

Fig. 12-5. Slash-and-spread pattern for two opposite darts: (a) Pattern cut apart and spread to equal one-half the desired elevation/depth, with the darts drafted on a paper patch. (b) Pattern with the contours of the darted edges and dart widths corrected.

Cut out the dart. (5) Abut the sides of the dart and tape together. Sticking a strip of paper beneath the darted edge, re-draw it from corner to corner to conform to the pre-dart contour. (6) Cut the dart open. Restore the extended and slightly enlarged dart opening to an opening equal to the estimated elevation/depth (Fig. 12-4).

b. For two opposite darts:
(1) Connecting the dart lines, cut the pattern apart from one edge to the opposite edge.
(2) Stick the pieces, separated by a distance equal to *one-half the amount of the desired elevation/depth*, to a strip of paper.
(3) Draft the darts with a compass, making each dart as wide at the base as the separation of the cut. Cut out the darts. (4) Abut the sides of the darts and tape together. Sticking a strip of paper behind each darted edge, restore the edges to their pre-dart contours.

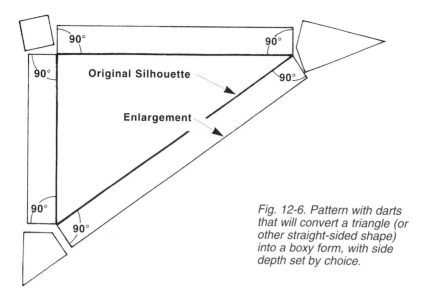

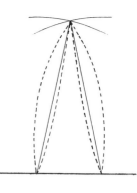

Fig. 12-6. Pattern with darts that will convert a triangle (or other straight-sided shape) into a boxy form, with side depth set by choice.

Fig. 12-7. Dart with seamlines drafted to curve inward or outward relative to straight guidelines (also refer to Fig. 12-3).

Enlarge and equalize:
Choose a desirable elevation/depth for the pattern to reach at the ends of the darts:

a. **To lift/lower a pattern with straight sides on darts at the corners:** (1) Trace the silhouette of the pattern on paper. (2) Enlarge the silhouette all around by *the amount of the desired elevation/depth.* (3) At each corner point, connect the pattern's silhouette to the enlargement with lines at 90-degree angles to both, thereby equalizing the lengths of the silhouette and enlargement between the corner lines. (4) Cut on the lines, which become the seamlines of the darts (Fig. 12-6). These corner darts change the original straight-sided pattern into a box-like form. If the corner darts proceed to a vanishing point inside the silhouette, the corners and sides will no longer be squared, but will slant inward.

b. **To develop a rounded form from a circular pattern using spaced darts:** (1) Trace the silhouette of the pattern on paper. On the traced silhouette, outline a central area where the three-dimensional form will reach maximum roundness. (2) Enlarge the silhouette all around by *one-half the amount of the desired elevation/depth* for the rounded form. (3) Divide the silhouette and enlargement into segments with straight lines that radiate out from a central point, noting that each segment will contain a dart. (4) Measure the length of the pattern's silhouette between two adjacent segment lines (use a measuring tape or strip of paper set on edge). (5) Compare the silhouette measurement with the enlargement measurement between the same two segment lines: The enlargement will be longer. The difference sets the width of the dart where it begins on the enlargement line. (6) For each segment, draft a dart with side seamlines that curve inward to a vanishing point at the previously outlined central area. Inward-curving darts produce outward-curving results that ease out at the vanishing points (Fig. 12-7).

Outward-curving darts produce inward-curving results that come to an abrupt stop at the vanishing points, and straight-sided darts, which also stop abruptly, make a form with straight sides. If each dart ended at the silhouette rather than inside the silhouette, and was drafted with straight sides, the result would be a round box rather than a curving dome or bowl (Fig. 12-8).

Note: *Patterns developed with the enlarge-and-equalize method will produce forms with exterior measurements that match the original shape, and interior measurements that match the original shape plus the amount added for elevation/depth.*

2. Trace the darted pattern, including the dart seamlines, onto the wrong side of the fabric. If the darts are to be visible on the outside of the form, trace the seamlines on the right side of the fabric with chalk, disappearing pen, or faint lines. Folding with seamlines matched, stitch each dart from the edge to the vanishing point (refer to "Securing Dart Seams" on page 267). For darts on the wrong side of the fabric, trim excessive fabric out of wide darts, and clip darts with seams that curve inward so that they turn right side out smoothly.

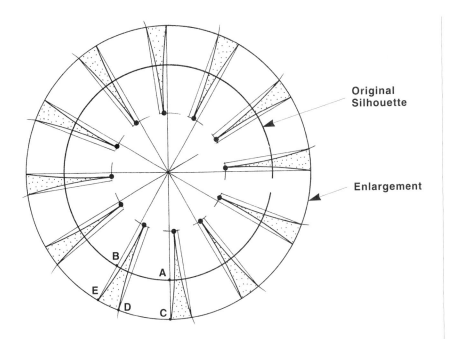

Original Silhouette

Enlargement

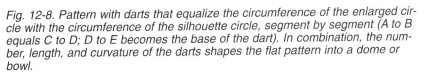

Fig. 12-8. Pattern with darts that equalize the circumference of the enlarged circle with the circumference of the silhouette circle, segment by segment (A to B equals C to D; D to E becomes the base of the dart). In combination, the number, length, and curvature of the darts shapes the flat pattern into a dome or bowl.

3. Press the darts, opening the seam allowances of trimmed darts. Heat press on a padded board; use a ham, a point presser, or any other pressing device that will aid the shaping of the fabric form. Finger press darts too small or abrupt for the iron.

4. To finish the edge of a darted form, bind or face the edge, line with a duplicate of the darted fabric, sew the edge to extensions, or hem before stitching the darts. To stabilize the outer shape of a darted form, sew the edges to a base cut from the original pattern.

NOTES & VARIATIONS

Use the guess-and-trim method for adventurous fun with darts. With one guiding principle in mind—elevation/depth increases with the amount removed by the darts—practice with paper and gummed tape. Try working spontaneously with the fabric to create experimental forms dimensionalized with straight and curving darts. Forego trimming and allow the edges to be unevenly contoured by the darts. Exploit the unpredictability of the method: explore "what would happen if."

When control is an issue, use the slash-and-spread or enlarge-and-equalize methods to develop patterns for three-dimensional forms.

For refined forms sculpted with multiple darts, enlarge and equalize produces the most precise and reliable results. Slash and spread lies somewhere in between the guess-and-trim and enlarge-and-equalize methods. It's neither as unpredictable as the former, nor as precise as the latter. It is the only method that adds around the darts as it reduces inside the darts, which causes an expansion in the middle of the darted form—an effect that can be advantageous when appropriately applied.

When drafting darts by slashing and spreading, the width of the desired elevation may be divided between two or more darts sharing the same edge. When planning the darts for a circular shape to be enlarged and equalized, more darts produce a more perfectly rounded form than less darts, and a silhouette with deep curves requires more darts to model into a smoothly rounded form than a slightly curving silhouette. For example, oval shapes require more darts at the steeply curving ends than at the shallow curves on the sides.

To understand the enlarge-and-equalize method better, visualize the original pattern shape as the silhouette or shadow of a three-dimensional form. Imagine the darts elevating or lowering the area of the pattern shape while keeping the outer size and shape, the silhouette/shadow, the same. For that result, a combination of three basic principles applies to dart formation: (1) Enlargement equals half the desired elevation/depth. (2) The amount of fabric removed by a dart at its widest point regulates the elevation/depth produced by the dart at its vanishing point. (3) After drafting the darts, the enlarged contour between any two points must match the size and reflect the shape of the original pattern between those same two points.

Neither the slash-and-spread nor enlarge-and-equalize methods guarantee that the elevation/depth specified before drafting the darts will stitch out exactly as anticipated. A single dart (slash and spread) and darts that stop at the silhouette (enlarge and equalize) are the most accurately predictable. Don't assume that a rounded form will be perfectly arched after the first pattern: Expect to test and readjust the curvature or length of the darts at least once. Little alterations make a crucial difference. After each test, record adjustments on the paper pattern. Seam allowances, ignored when drafting the darts, are added to final patterns or included when cutting the fabric.

If the vanishing points of two darts on opposite or adjacent edges are connected, the darts can be changed to a seam. For darts that require gradual, curved tapering, which becomes difficult to sustain when dart width tapers down to threads of the weave, *darts converted to seams* solves a stitching problem. Test and evaluate the seamlines crossing the structured surface for their decorative effect, and improve with slight alterations (Fig. 12-9).

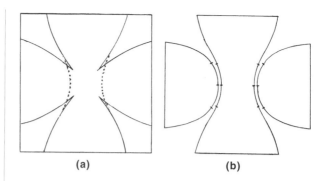

Fig. 12-9. (a) Pattern with corner darts connected with seamlines. (b) Three-piece pattern with contours adjusted to match when sewing. After testing, add seam allowances to the patterns.

Surface darts, which appear as tapered folds on the outside of the dimensionalized fabric, decorate as well as model the form. The darts may be turned to the side, or centered and flattened. At the base, side-felled darts slant upward, and, if wide, may continue beyond the seam allowance unless the seam allowance inside the dart is increased on the pattern, an adjustment recommended for inside as well as outside darts (Fig. 12-10).

Projecting darts, pressed or unpressed, are not stitched down at the base and extend out from the surface (clip and turn the seam allowance at the base to the inside of the dart). Unsuitable for surface darts: Curved-seam darts that require clipping to accommodate the roundness of the form.

The seams for *released darts* stop before reaching the apex of the darts, releasing folds that complicate the configuration of the fabric.

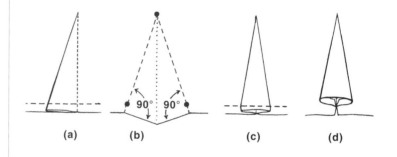

Fig. 12-10. Surface darts: (a) Felled to one side. (b) Adjusted on the pattern for matching edges at the base. (c) Centered over the dart seam. (d) Cone-shaped projecting dart hemmed at the base.

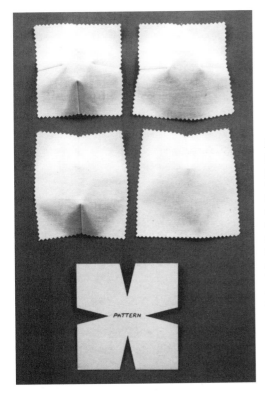

XII-1—Squares of stiffened muslin elevated by darts ³⁄₄" (2cm) wide at the edge. Four darts (upper left) elevate to 1¹⁄₂" (4cm); with three darts (upper right), and with two opposite darts (lower left), the center elevation reaches 1¹⁄₄" (3cm); one dart (lower right) elevates to ³⁄₄" (2cm) at the tip.

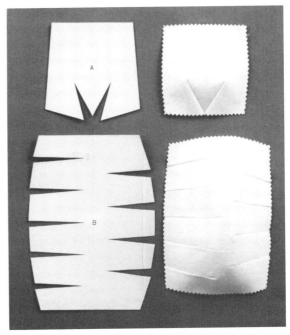

XII-3—Two patterns that divide the estimated elevation between two angled darts (pattern A), and five darts on one side and four darts on the opposite side (pattern B). The stiffened muslin forms elevate to ³⁄₄" (2cm) for pattern A and 2" (5cm) for pattern B.

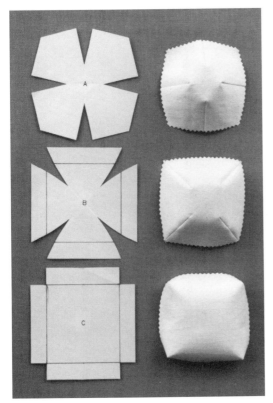

XII-2—Patterns drafted around silhouettes 3¹⁄₂" (9cm) square: Pattern A (slash and spread) with darts ³⁄₄" (2cm) wide creates a form 1¹⁄₂" (4cm) high. For patterns B and C, silhouettes enlarged ³⁄₄" (2cm) are equalized with corner darts that end inside the silhouette (B) and at the silhouette (C). Pattern B creates a slant-sided form that elevates to 1¹⁄₂" (4cm). Pattern C makes a straight-sided form raised to ³⁄₄" (2cm).

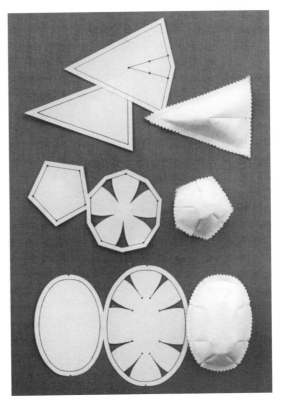

XII-4—Stiffened muslin forms seamed to foundations (the original pattern shapes) that control their contours at the edges.

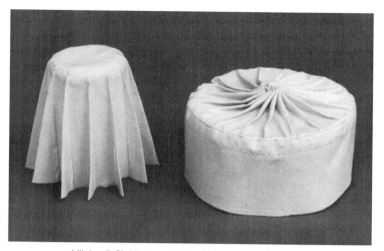

XII-5—Pieced construction of dart-structured muslin forms. For the large high-domed 4" (10cm) square, corner darts were converted to seams. Three smaller squares with released darts were stitched from unstiffened muslin.

XII-6—(left) Muslin cylinder with projecting darts, made from a pattern with a circular silhouette 3" (7.5cm) in diameter, enlarged by 4" (10cm), and equalized with 12 darts ending at the silhouette outline. (right) Long muslin strip modelled with adjoining darts along one edge into a round, boxy form.

SINGLE-POINTED DART

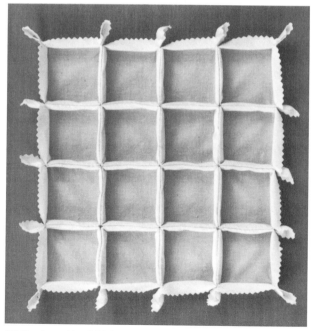

XII-7—Fragile muslin bowl 6" (15cm) in diameter, 4" (10cm) deep, with 16 inward-curving darts flattened by zigzag topstitching.

XII-8—Assembly of 16 boxy cells. Each cell is 2" (5cm) square surrounded by sides 3/4" (2cm) high. After sewing the corner darts, the edges of adjoining "boxes" were hand-stitched together, and each box was pushed down to create a cell. The tips of converging darts were tied together in back.

DOUBLE-POINTED DART

—a diamond-shaped segment of fabric folded in half lengthwise and sewn from tip to tip. Double-pointed darts structure internally, raising or lowering the fabric at both ends of the dart seam.

PROCEDURES

Review "Single-pointed Dart" on page 268, particularly the slash-and-spread procedures.

NOTES & VARIATIONS

The principle that relates the width of a dart at its widest cross-section to the amount of elevation or depth achieved at the end of the dart applies—in duplicate—to double-pointed darts (Fig. 12-11).

When the fold of a double-pointed dart remains underneath, the dart will pull the fabric down at each end unless the dart seam allowance is clipped, releasing the dart to open and move upward toward the tips. Because clipping to the stitching weakens the seam, reinforce the stitching to prevent breaks, particularly when usage involves strain. Double-pointed darts on the surface of a construction form a bridge between elevations at the ends.

Measuring from edge to edge across the seam, a double-pointed dart reduces fabric measurement beside its seam, and releases the full measurement of the fabric at each end of the dart and out to an edge that floats in waves. A row of double-pointed darts in soft fabric gradually releases fullness in a manner similar to gathering, but with reduction by folds. If the fabric is stiff, the waves at the edge will be sculptural—regular and as deep as the width of the darts. Double-pointed darts shape a cylinder of fabric like an hourglass. For the occasional application, where it's necessary to extend the sides to compensate for what the dart removes, add half the width of the dart to the edges that parallel the dart seam ((a) in Fig. 12-12).

For sculptural purposes, double-pointed darts shape the interior of the fabric, and single-pointed darts deal with the fullness of the fabric at the edge. Two single-pointed darts as wide as the double-pointed dart in the center reduce the measurements at opposite edges to the measurement across the center of the double-pointed dart. To gauge conformity easily, draft a double-pointed dart in the slashed spread between the vanishing points of single-pointed darts ((b) in Fig. 12-12).

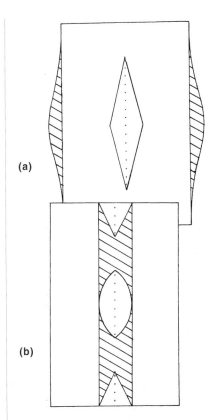

(a)

(b)

Fig. 12-12. (a) Double-pointed dart in a rectangle with sides enlarged to compensate for fabric removed by the dart. (b) Curving double-pointed dart drafted between two slashed-and-spread single-pointed darts.

Used together, single- and double-pointed darts create involved three-dimensional configurations. When the darts are varied with incurved and outcurved seams (Fig. 12-11), contouring possibilities increase. Adding to the structural possibilities, one double-pointed dart can be seamed across the center of another, shaping four peaks/dips around a low/high in the middle. Also, a double-pointed dart can cross the tip of another dart like a T, spreading out the flare at the end of the dart.

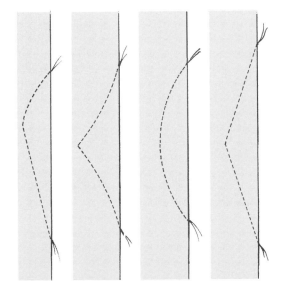

Fig. 12-11. Double-pointed darts with seams contoured to affect the modelling of the fabric form.

Dart patterns structure fabric into allover, three-dimensional designs. The wider the darts, the greater the dimensionality of the fabric construction. To create a dart pattern, use gridded paper to devise a repeating arrangement of small, double-pointed darts, combined with single-pointed darts at the fabric's edge. Cut out each dart on its seamline, converting the pattern into a stencil to use when tracing the design on the right or wrong side of the fabric (Fig. 12-13).

Because clipping the darts in a dart pattern weakens the strength of the darted framework, darts stitched on the wrong side of the fabric pull the fabric down at the ends. When stitched on the right side, the visible folds support height at each end. (Refer to "Securing Dart Seams" on page 267). To evaluate a dart pattern, it's essential to test with a square of fabric. Look at both sides of the stitched sample; they will be quite different. Measure the fabric before and after stitching the darts.

The before-dart measurement and the after-dart measurement yield a fraction to use when estimating the fabric required for dart patterning to a target measurement. After stitching a dart pattern, set with steam. Pin the low points of the relief to a padded surface and steam with an iron held just above the fabric. Allow to cool and dry before moving. To stabilize immovably, tack the low points of the relief to a stay.

Unusual formations result when slender darts are stitched into the fabric at random. *Dart improvisations* are spontaneously sculpted. The length, width, and direction of the darts, the separation between the darts, and alternating between right-side and wrong-side stitching, combine to control and diversify the relief that develops as the darts accumulate.

With dart patterns and improvisations, folds on the surface become figurative design elements more conspicuous, sometimes, than the sculpted fabric that underlies the folds. Thread ends left to dangle after knotting add a feathery flourish over the top.

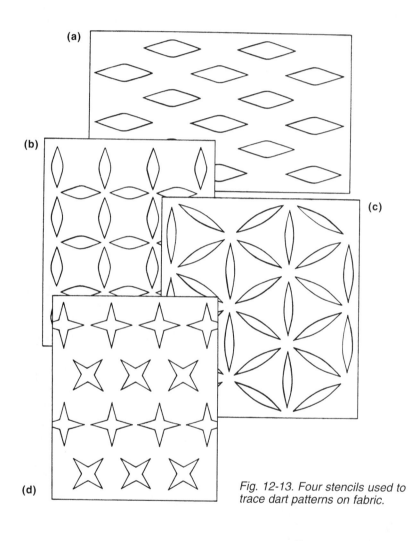

(a)
(b)
(c)
(d)

Fig. 12-13. Four stencils used to trace dart patterns on fabric.

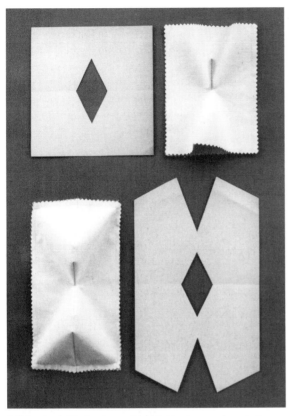

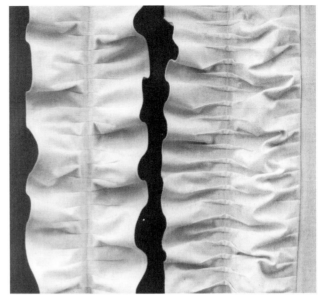

XII-10—(left) Muslin strip with a row of identical darts. As the clipped darts taper out, the ever-widening fabric falls into soft folds like a double-edged ruffle. (right) Double-pointed darts on the surface, felled by a centered seam, and single-pointed darts at the edge cause the fabric between the rows to puff and peak into swirling ridges.

XII-9—(top) Muslin elevated 1 ½" (4cm) at each end of a double-pointed dart ½" (1.3cm) wide in the center, with seam allowance clipped. (bottom) The same dart combined with single-pointed darts at the edges sculpts the muslin into a pair of pyramid-like shapes. Each stiffened muslin sample is stitched to a stay.

DOUBLE-POINTED DART

XII-11—Cylinders of muslin stiffened with iron-on interfacing, shaped with double-pointed darts internally, and single-pointed darts that reduce the diameters of the openings on two of the forms.

DOUBLE-POINTED DART

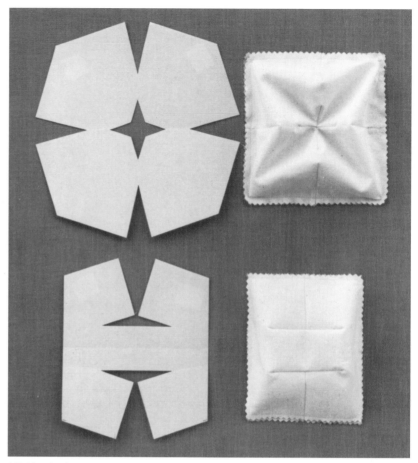

XII-12—(top) Darts that cross each other and (bottom) cross the tips of other darts change the configuration of forms grounded at the edges with single-pointed darts. Both examples are seamed to stays.

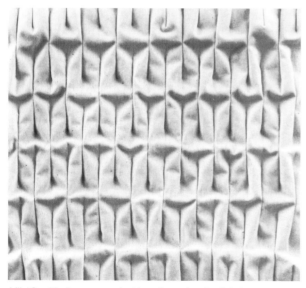

XII-13—Muslin patterned with a dimensionalized design (see (a) in Fig. 12-13 for the pattern).

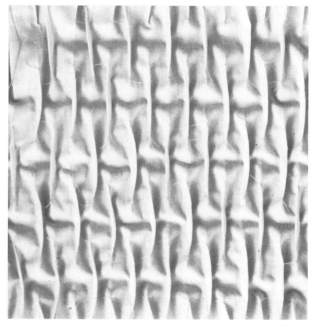

XII-14—Reverse side of photo XII-13.

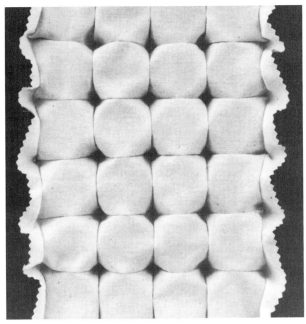

XII-15—Muslin structured to look like marshmallows in a box (see (b) in Fig. 12-13 for the pattern).

XII-16—Reverse side of photo XII-15 with peaks instead of hollows between the tips of the darts.

XII-17—Muslin configured with a hexagon arrangement of darts (see (c) in Fig. 12-13 for the pattern). The low points of the relief were tacked to a stiffened foundation.

DOUBLE-POINTED DART

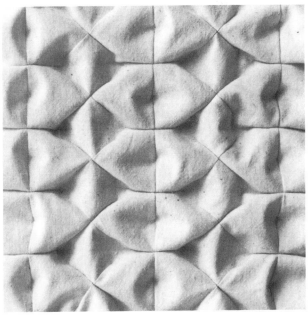

XII-18—Muslin stitched into a relief created with crossed double-pointed darts (see (d) in Fig. 12-13 for the pattern).

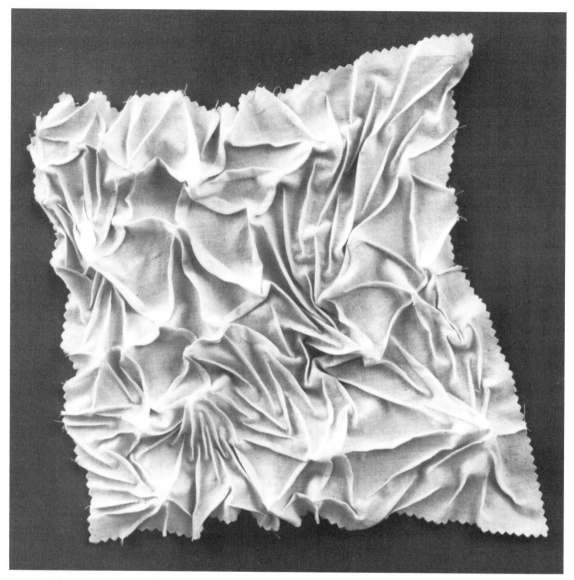

XII-19—Muslin reconstructed into a complex relief with an improvised composition of surface darts.

DOUBLE-POINTED DART

Mixed
Manipulations

PART SIX

*T*here are two kinds of *combinations*, combinations of techniques that synthesize into singular technique variations, and creative combinations that link two or more techniques into constructions that serve a functional, decorative, and artistic purpose. The first is a more limited group than the second, which is limited only by the desire to invent.

COMBINATIONS

13 Combinations

TECHNIQUE VARIATIONS

XIII-1 SMOCKED TUCKS—
Blind tucks smocked with
honeycomb stitching into
cellular formations over
broad, flat channels. The
sample is stable, almost rigid.

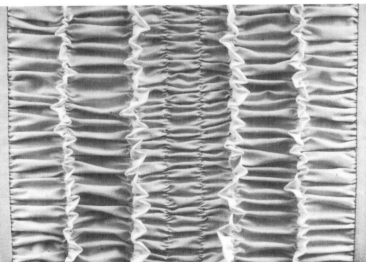

XIII-2 SHIRRED TUCKS—
Tucks with gathered
seams beside a centered
band of plain shirring.

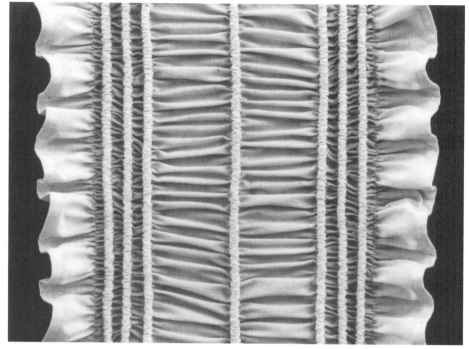

XIII-3 SHIRRED SURFACE CORDING (CORDED SHIRRED TUCKS)—Cords inserted and stitched in one operation, and bobbin-thread gathered as the casing fabric was gathered over the cord.

XIII-4 GATHERED CORDED TUBING—Tight- and loose-fitting casings gathered over cords while turning right side out. For contrast, a stuffed ball ends a length of smooth, corded tubing.

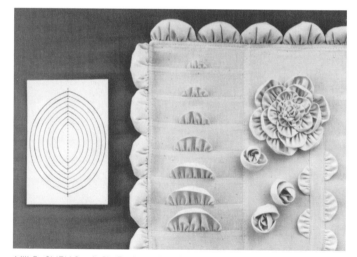

XIII-5 SHELLS—(left) Graduated oval patterns. (right) Folded in half and gathered until straight, graduated shells are inserted in seams, arranged into a large flower-like circle, and rolled into three bud-like shapes. Shells border an appliquéd band and stuffed shells border the sample.

XIII-6 DETACHED BALLS—(counterclockwise from upper right) Four balls (puffs with stuffing); three nested balls (ruffled puffs, stuffed, with edges gathered and tacked underneath); four ruffled balls (ruffled puffs, stuffed); four ruffled balls on bases (ruffled puffs, stuffed, on a base); and ball-centered, puffed circular shirring.

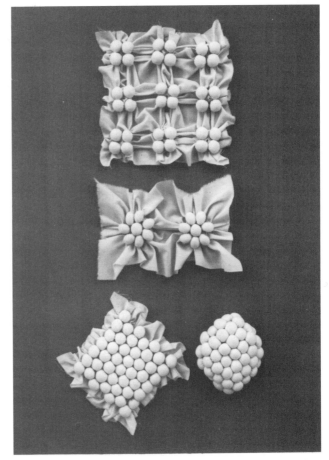

XIII-7 BALL GATHERING—(top) Two examples of spaced ball gathering (puff gathering, stuffed) include folds in the overall design. (bottom) Two examples of massed ball gathering with very closely spaced balls curving one of the samples.

XIII-8 BALL GATHERING—Heading of separated balls, hand appliquéd to a band, gathers a length of fabric.

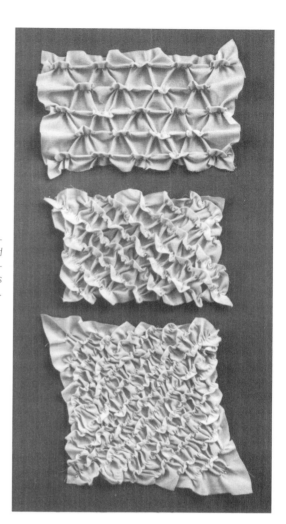

XIII-9 GATHERED DART PAT-
TERNS—Rows of double-pointed
darts, gathered on hand stitching, configure the fabric with irregular folds
between crescent-shaped projections.

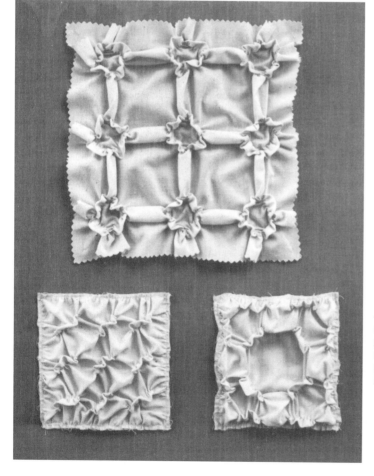

XIII-10 GATHERED DART PATTERNS—
(top) Separated clusters of four
gathered darts in a squared arrangement with pointed ends touching.
(bottom) Two samples stayed with
linings, ready for insertion.

XIII-11 DART GATHERING—Row of gathered double-pointed darts creates fullness in the released fabric and finishes the edge with scallops.

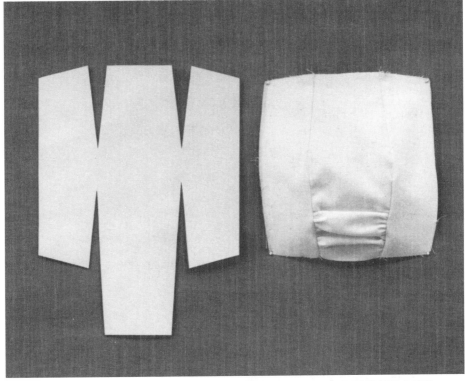

XIII-12 GATHERED SINGLE-POINTED DARTS— (left) The pattern. (right) Muslin test with one leg of two adjacent darts gathered before stitching the dart.

CREATIVE COMBINATIONS

XIII-13 Elevated form constructed from a circle of muslin over batting-padded lining, shaped with six single-pointed darts, surface textured with gathering and machine quilting, and finished with gathered piping and a ruffled ball.

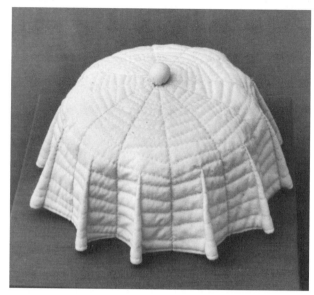

XIII-14 Elevated form created from a muslin circle machine-quilted to a batting-padded lining with nine, projecting, single-pointed darts; with an envelope-style edge finish and a ball on top.

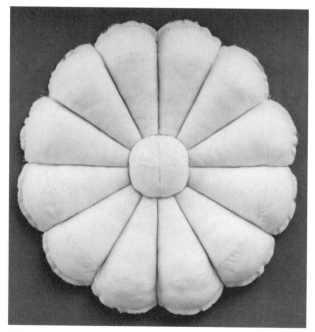

XIII-15 Thick, heavy, high-relief medallion with 12 stuffed segments (gusset-elevated forms) that start low on the inside and finish high at the edge, and a stuffed half-ball in the center (shaped with single-pointed darts converted into seams).

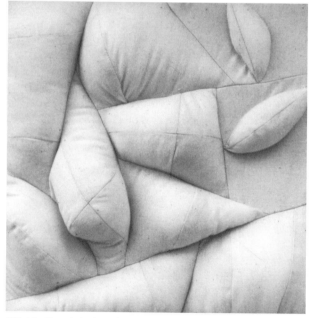

XIII-16 Organic-looking forms formed with single-pointed darts converted into seams, stuffed and pieced into a high-relief construction.

XIII-17—Broomstick pleating tacked to a stay over stuffed forms of gather-elevated appliqué.

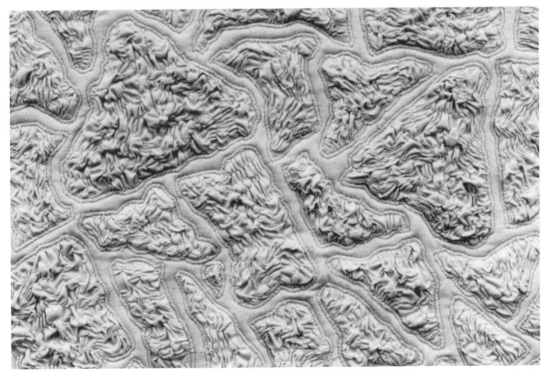

XIII-18—Fabric scraps meander-shirred with a gathering foot, appliquéd to a top/batting/lining foundation with satin stitching, which also quilts the layers.

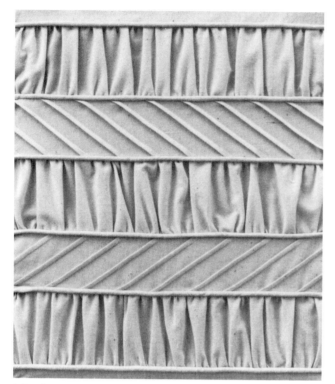

XIII-19 Bands of diagonal tucks alternating with bands of opposite-edge gathering, separated by rows of in-seam piping.

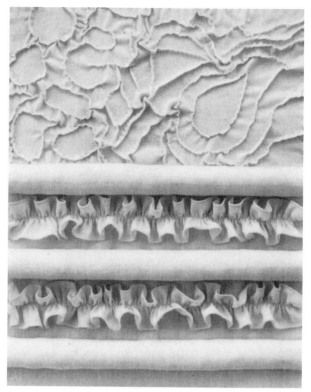

XIII-20 Three connected rolls with double-edged ruffles in between, topped with an overlay of improvised pattern tucking.

XIII-21 (from the top) Cabled tuck with balls tacked inside opened folds, snip-fringed ruffle, band of pleats formed on the Perfect Pleater, and a batting-padded machine-quilted cuff.

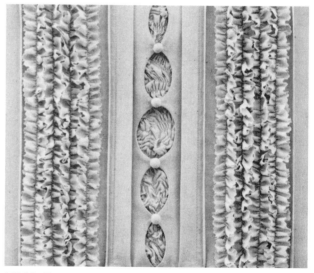

XIII-22 Keyhole tucks with balls at connecting points reveal an insert of meander shirring; at the sides, low massed ruffles between standing tucks.

XIII-23 Shirred border gathered on surface-corded seams; square of waffle shirring at the corner; with a firmly stuffed, detached roll finishing the edge.

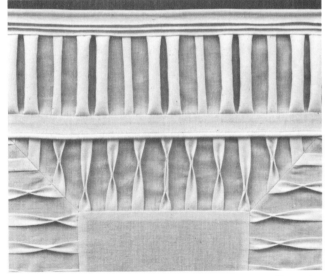

XIII-24 Borders dimensionalized with bow-tied tucks and stuffed and unstuffed centered tucks, outlined with piping and more tucks.

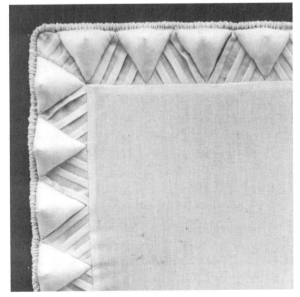

XIII-25 Border of peaks and valleys, with tucked separations, edged with gathered piping.

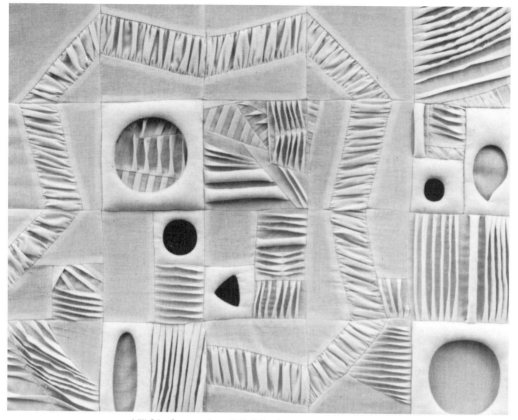

XIII-26 Construction of 4" (10cm) squares variously patterned with peekholes, stuffed and tucked manipulations, and a wandering path of opposite-edge gathering.

XIII-27 Yo-yos applied to a pleated foundation.

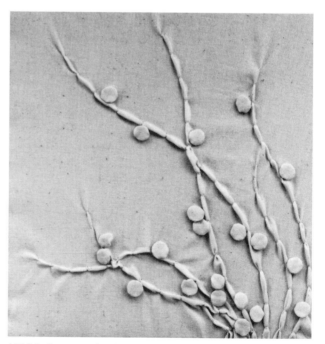

XIII-28 Reverse-tied tucks accented with puffs.

*XIII-29 Loose appliqué leaves,
appliquéd yo-yo flowers, one
flower with a ruffled edge
surrounding a furrowed
center, and a lightly
stuffed container
of undulating
tucks.*

*XIII-30 The
flowers: Seven
made from coiled
double-edged ruffles
with a ravelled-fringe
edge finish; two from
ball gathering surrounded
with furrowing; four from
gathered darts. Loose appliqué
leaves, tuck-patterned container.*

*XIII-31 Three-
dimensional floral
composition built with
a variety of manipulated
techniques: Double-edged
ruffles, single-edged ruffle, yo-
yos, ball gathering, furrowing, puffs,
balls, loose appliqué, and tucks.*

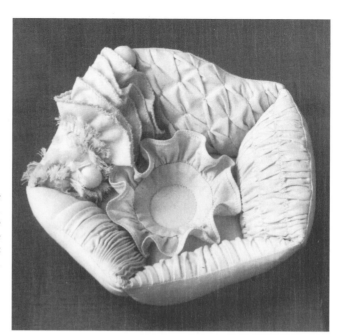

XIII-32 Five trapezoid-shaped little pillows with curving upper edges, attached to a pentagon-shaped little pillow with a circle topstitched in the center. Inside, various manipulations sewn to one side of all the pillows.

XIII-33 Manipulations integrated into abstract constructions of reliefs and tactile textures. Each surface was built over a top/batting/lining foundation, with the stitching that secures the manipulations incorporated into the quilting.

Appendix

HAND STITCHES

BACKSTITCH

—Strong, versatile hand stitch used where firm sewing is required for structural seams, for mending breaks in machine-stitched seams, and for hand quilting. Backstitches are also used to secure sewing thread at the beginning, replacing a knot in the end of the thread, and at the end of a row of stitching. Work backstitching from right to left (reverse all directions if left-handed). Bring a threaded needle up to the surface; insert the needle back into the fabric ⅛″ (3mm) to the right of the emerging thread. For an **even backstitch**, make a stitch ¼″ (6mm) long underneath and bring the needle out ⅛″ (3mm) in front of the emerging thread. For all succeeding stitches, insert the needle into the needle hole ending the previous stitch and bring it out ⅛″ (3mm) in front. Even backstitching looks like straight machine stitching ((a) in Fig. A-1). The **half backstitch** looks like running stitches. Making a stitch ½″ (1.3cm) long underneath, bring the needle out ¼″ (6mm) in front of the emerging thread. Insert the needle into the fabric ⅛″ (3mm) to the right of the emerging thread and bring it out ¼″ (6mm) in front ((b) in Fig. A-1). For **securing backstitches**, turn to the back behind the seam. Make two tiny backstitches, one over the other, looping the thread over the needle figure-eight style on the last stitch ((c) in Fig. A-1).

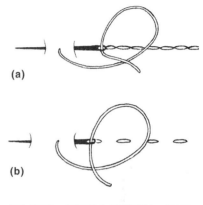

(a)

(b)

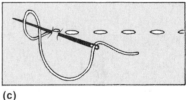

(c)

Fig. A-1. (a) Even backstitch. (b) Half backstitch. (c) Securing with backstitches.

BASTING

—Temporary hand stitching that holds fabric layers together in the desired alignment until permanent stitching is in place. Baste from right to left (reverse all directions if left-handed). For **even basting**, make long running stitches the same length in back as in front ((a) in Fig. A-2). For **uneven basting**, take small stitches with the needle separated by longer lengths of thread on the surface ((b) in Fig. A-2).

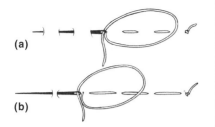

Fig. A-2. (a) Even basting.
(b) Uneven basting.

BLINDSTITCH

—Strong, inconspicuous hand stitch used to appliqué a folded edge to the right side of another piece of fabric. Blindstitching is worked from right to left (reverse all directions if left-handed). Bring the needle up underneath the folded edge of the appliqué, through two or three threads of the appliqué's fold, and pull out the thread. Insert the needle into the foundation fabric directly in front of the emerging thread at the edge of the fold; bring it out under the appliqué's fold ⅛″ (3mm) ahead, catching two or three threads of the fold in the stitch. After four or five stitches, pull the thread taut ((a) in Fig. 11-11 on page 237).

CATCHSTITCH

—Flexible hand stitch minimally visible in front, used to fasten pinked or taped single-fold hems, to secure the edges of facings, and to hold seam allowances flat against linings. Work from left to right (reverse all directions if left-handed) on the wrong side of the fabric. Bring the needle up through the fabric layer on the top, burying the knot between the layers. Moving forward at an angle, alternate between a backstitch in the fabric underneath and a backstitch in the edge of the fabric layer on top. Catch one or two threads of the fabric underlayer in each stitch; make

a larger backstitch in the fabric on top. Catchstitching looks like her-ringbone stitching (Fig. A-3).

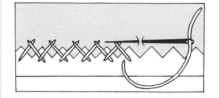

Fig. A-3. Catchstitch.

LADDER STITCH

—Concealed hand stitch used to close stuffing openings left in seams, and to attach the folded edges of appliqués to foundation fabric. Ladder stitching is worked from right to left (reverse all directions if left-handed). **To close openings in seams**, bring the thread out through the fold on one of the abutting edges. Crossing directly over to the opposite edge, take a stitch ⅛″ (3mm) long inside the fold. Moving straight across, take a stitch ⅛″ (3mm) long inside the opposite fold. After five or six stitches in opposite folds, pull the thread taut ((a) in Fig. A-4).

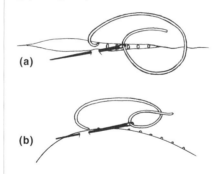

Fig. A-4. Ladder stitch: (a) Closing openings. (b) Appliqué.

To appliqué, bring the needle up through the foundation just under the folded edge of the appliqué. Take a stitch ⅛″ (3mm) long inside the appliqué's folded edge. Without moving forward, insert the needle into the foundation and bring it out ⅛″ (3mm) ahead, keeping the emerging thread just under the folded edge of the appliqué. After five or six stitches, pull the thread taut ((b) in Fig. A-4), and refer to ((b) in Fig. 11-11 on page 237).

OVERCAST STITCH

—Slanting hand stitch used to prevent cut edges from ravelling, to fell seam allowances, and to secure hems. When the stitches are pulled tight, overcast stitching gathers and rolls the edge to the back as the depth of the stitch collapses. Tiny overcast stitching is also used for pattern tucking. Work from right to left or left to right. **To prevent ravelling**, bring the needle out about ⅛″ (3mm) below the cut edge; move ahead ¼″ (6mm) for the next stitch, wrapping the edge with the thread (Fig. A-5).

Fig. A-5. Overcast stitch.

To fell seam allowances, catch the lining underneath before emerging ¼″ (6mm) ahead, and ⅛″ (3mm) to ¼″ (6mm) into the seam allowance. **To secure a single- or double-fold hem**, catch two or three threads of the fabric underneath before slipping the needle under the edge of the hem. **To gather**, start turning the edge to the back with a tiny, finger-creased fold before overcasting the edge with five or six stitches. Pause to gather and enclose the fold on tightly pulled thread before continuing.

OVERHAND STITCH

—Close, firm hand stitch used to join two folded or finished edges, or to appliqué a folded or finished edge to the fabric underneath. Overhand stitching can be worked from right to left or left to right. **To join two folded or finished edges**, align the edges with right sides facing. Tug the knot at the end of the thread inside a fold, or secure unknotted thread with two or three overlapping stitches. For each stitch, angle the needle forward ⅛″ (3mm) in the same direction, catching a tiny bit of each edge with the needle. When used **to appliqué** a folded or finished edge to the fabric underneath, overhand stitching is sturdy and visible (Fig. A-6).

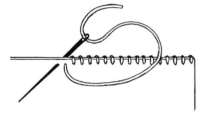

Fig. A-6. Overhand stitch.

RUNNING STITCH

—Basic hand-sewing stitch used for construction when seams will not be stressed, for gathering and shirring, and for quilting. It is also used to appliqué, topstitch, and hem with visible, decorative thread; and to sew tucks when softness is desirable. Working from right to left (reverse all directions if left-handed), load the needle with a series of forward moving, evenly spaced, in and out stitches, penetrating all fabric layers with each stitch. Pull the needle and thread out, and repeat. Unless the particular application dictates otherwise, stitch length and the space between stitches should be about ⅛″ (3mm) (Fig. A-7).

Fig. A-7. Running stitch.

SLIPSTITCH

—Hand stitch used to secure hems and facings in a manner that's barely visible inside and outside. Slipstitching is worked from right to left (reverse all directions if left-handed) on the wrong side of the fabric. Bring the needle out through and under the hem fold, or next to and under the edge of a single-fold hem or facing. Moving forward ¼″ (6mm), pick up one or two threads of the fabric immediately underneath and draw the needle out. Moving forward ¼″ (6mm), pick up two or three threads of the hem or facing and draw the needle out. After five or six stitches, pull the thread gently to secure the hem or facing (Fig. A-8).

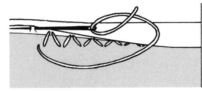

Fig. A-8. Slipstitch.

STABSTITCH

—Hand stitch accomplished with two actions: (1) Push the needle down and draw it all the way out of the fabric. (2) Push the needle back up to the surface and draw it all the way out of the fabric. Stabstitching is used when tacking and quilting.

TACKING

—Very closely spaced or overlapping hand stitches, often stabstitched, that join one element to another at contact points.

TAILOR TACKS

—Hand stitching used to transfer fold line, seamline, and other sewing notations from patterns to fabric with markers of thread, a method recommended for fabric that could be damaged by other marking substances. With small, sharp scissors, cut a hole in the pattern at every point to be marked on the fabric. Pin the pattern to the right side of the fabric. Working from right to left (reverse all directions if left-handed) with extra long doubled thread, unknotted, in the needle, make small stitches inside the holes cut into the pattern, leaving loose loops of thread between the stitches (Fig. A-9). Cut the loops in the center and gently remove the pattern. To mark two layers of fabric at once, leave very long loops between the stitches. Cut the loops and remove the pattern. Separate the fabric layers about ¾″ (2cm) and cut the threads between the layers.

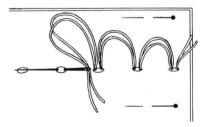

Fig. A-9. Tailor tacks.

WHIP STITCHING

—Hand sewing two folded or finished edges together with overhand stitching.

GLOSSARY

APPLIQUÉ
—(1) Smaller, shaped cutout of fabric applied to a larger expanse of fabric. (2) To attach a small cutout of fabric to foundation fabric with hand or machine stitching.

BIAS
—Direction that slants diagonally across woven fabric. The **true bias** moves at a 45-degree angle to the crossgrain and lengthgrain of the weave. The bias of woven fabric is stretchable.

BODKIN
—Slender, blunted tool with a large eye or a tweezer grip, designed to draw tape, ribbon, string, cord, or elastic through a casing.

CROSSGRAIN
—Direction of the **weft** yarns or threads that span woven fabrics from selvedge to selvedge. The crossgrain is more adaptable than the lengthgrain of the fabric.

EASE
—To match two unequal edges, one slightly longer than the other, and sew together smoothly by catching a tiny bit of fullness from the longer edge into each stitch.

EDGESTITCH
—To machine stitch through all layers 1/16" (1.5mm) from a folded edge or seamline with the fabric right side up.

FABRIC-SAFE MARKER
—Tool, device, or substance used to indicate seamlines, fold lines, match points, positions, and trace outlines, that does not deface the visible surface of the fabric in any permanent manner. *Always test the permanent removability of a substance on the intended fabric before using.* Markers include: (1) Pins and lightly pressed folds. (2) Scissor nips and notches in seam allowances. (3) Basting and tailor tacks. (4) Blackboard chalk, chalk pencils, chalk wheels, and chalk liners. (5) Air-erasable and water-erasable marking pens with fine-line, felt-tip points. (6) Colored pencils especially manufactured for use on fabric, or artist's pencils recommended as safe for fabric (e.g., pencils made by Berol), with a sharpener to maintain a point, and appropriate erasers. (7) Mechanical pencil with hard lead, or an artist's hard-lead drawing pencil sharpened to a pin point, with a white, fabric eraser or an art gum eraser. *Never use a soft lead pencil.* (8) Slivers of soap. (9) A track pressed into the top with a hera or the blunted point of a needle—which requires immediate stitching before it fades. (10) Lengths of narrow masking tape.

FACING
—Fabric seamed to a cut edge and turned to the back in order to finish the edge with a fold. Facings also function as stays. A **decorative facing** is turned to the front.

FINGER PRESS
—To flatten and open a short seam allowance during the construction process by pinching between the fingers or bearing down hard with a fingernail.

FLUTE
—To appliqué an edge hand-gathered on even running stitches in such a manner that the grooves between folds, each anchored with a stitch, are regular and distinct.

FOUNDATION
—Base fabric to which manipulated elements and appliqués are sewn. Foundation fabric is visible between and around the applied elements.

GRAIN
—The weave of woven fabric. Fabric is **on grain** when the crossgrain and lengthgrain yarns or threads interlace at a 90-degree angle. If the fabric is **off grain**, tug it across the bias to restore the crossgrain/lengthgrain to a 90-degree relationship. Iron with steam to set the corrected alignment.

HEM ALLOWANCE
—Fabric width to be turned under when finishing a floating edge.

IRON
—To use an iron with forward and backward, gliding movements, removing wrinkles and smoothing the surface of the fabric.

LENGTHGRAIN
—Direction of the **warp** yarns or threads that parallel the selvedges in woven fabrics. The lengthgrain is stronger and firmer than the crossgrain of the fabric.

LINING
—Fabric that underlies the surface fabric and matches it in size and shape. A lining conceals and protects construction details, functions as a stay, and, when sewn to the surface fabric with right sides together before turning to the back, finishes edges.

NEEDLE MODELLING
—Hand stitching using pulled thread to create dimpled or extended indentations in a stuffed surface. To make one stitch or a series, use the stabstitching technique to bring a long needle up from the back, through the stuffing, and out at the desired point on the surface. Taking a tiny stitch several threads-of-the-fabric wide, return the needle to the back. Pull on the thread to make an appropriate indentation in front, and secure the tension on the thread with several backstitches.

Nips

—Tiny cuts at fabric edges, inside the seam allowances, that mark points to match or fold positions.

Notches

—(▲) markings on the edges of patterns that indicate points to match, fold positions, etc. When transferred to fabric, notches are tiny V-shaped cuts inside seam allowances or projections outside seam allowances.

Pin Match

—To stab and pin two layers of fabric together at specific points; to synchronize and secure two seams or markings that must coincide exactly when stitched together.

Press

—To use an iron with pick-up and put-down movements, flattening and smoothing a limited area without disturbing previous manipulations or mussing seam allowances.

Quilt-As-You-Go

—Method of quilting that starts by subdividing large top/batting/lining projects into smaller segments which are quilted one at a time before assembly into the whole. Also called "lap quilting," "apartment quilting," and, in this book, "modular quilting."

Ruche, Ruching

—Closely gathered or finely pleated strip of fabric applied as trim. In contemporary fashion writing, often used as a synonym for any form of gathering or shirring.

Seam Allowance

—Space between the cut edge and the seamline. After sewing two edges together, seam allowances are pressed **open**—turned in opposite directions, or **closed**—turned in the same direction.

Selvedges

—Lengthgrain edges of woven fabric, loom-finished to prevent unravelling.

Stabilize

—(1) To secure gathered stitching or pleating by sewing to another piece of fabric; to prevent stretching or strain from disturbing a manipulation by attaching it to another piece of fabric; to stay. (2) To add firmness to fabric, preventing extensive stitching from pinching, drawing, and distorting the fabric.

Stabilizer

—Material, substance, or device used to add firmness to fabric. (1) **Permanent stabilizers** of woven or non-woven fabric, such as muslin, organdy, commercial interfacing, or batting-padded lining, are basted to the back of the fabric before stitching. Fusible interfacings are heat-bonded. Starch as a stabilizer is permanent until the fabric is washed. (2) **Temporary stabilizers** include typing-weight paper and specialized commercial products developed for that purpose, which are basted to the back of the foundation before stitching; and freezer paper which is heat-bonded to the back of the foundation with its shiny side down. After sewing, temporary stabilizers are carefully torn away from the stitches without distorting the even lay of the thread. Stretching the fabric taut in a hoop or frame also stabilizes temporarily.

Stay

—(1) To prevent a manipulation from coming undone, stretching out of shape, or moving out of place; to stabilize. (2) Stabilizing fabric invisibly stitched behind a manipulation. A **full stay** underlies the entire manipulation from edge to edge; a partial stay underlies the manipulated section of the fabric. A foundation, a facing, or a lining can also function as a stay. A **decorative stay** covers the source of a manipulation in front (e.g., a strip of fabric, tape, or ribbon seamed over rows of gathering or the head of a pleated arrangement).

Staystitching

—Straight stitching by machine through a single layer of fabric, beside the seamline within the seam allowance. Staystitching prevents the edge from stretching and, when the openings left in seams for turning right side out are staystitched, facilitates turning the seam allowances inside for hand-sewn closings.

Steam Block, Steam Press

—To use steam to re-shape, set, smooth, and refresh a foundation fabric with manipulated elevations, or a manipulated construction that would be flattened under the pressure of an iron. Stretching to the desired size and shape, pin the foundation or construction around its perimeter, and at critical interior points, to a padded surface. Arrange the folds of loose fabric, pinning to hold if needed. Steam with an iron moving slowly over and above the surface. Allow to cool and dry before unpinning. For hanging installations, adjust the folds and use a steamer.

Stitch-in-the-Ditch

—With the right side of the fabric up, to sew in the groove next to the ridge made by the fold of a closed seam allowance.

Straight-Grain

—Either the crossgrain or the lengthgrain of the fabric.

Straight of the Fabric

—Lengthgrain of woven fabric, which is indicated on patterns by a long, double-pointed arrow.

Suffolk Puffs

—English term for a form of patchwork composed of circles gathered into smaller circles. In America and in this book, Suffolk puffs are called yo-yos.

TEMPLATE

—Pattern or guide. Sturdy templates are cut from cardboard, plastic, or other substantial material resistant to the abrasion of repeated use.

TOPSTITCH

—To sew one or more rows parallel to an edge or seam on the right side of the fabric through all layers, using plain or decorative hand or machine stitching.

UNDERSTITCH

—To straight stitch by machine through a facing and all seam allowances, but not through the surface fabric, $\frac{1}{16}''$ (1.5mm) from the seam. Understitching prevents a facing from rolling to the front at the edge.

WADDING

—In Great Britain, a word meaning batting.

SELECTED BIBLIOGRAPY

BOOKS

While researching this book, I looked through any volume with a title that seemed appropriate to my subject and considered it worth the time if I found one little technique, idea, or even a hint that increased my manipulation data base. The list that follows doesn't include any of the numerous entries in my notes that consist of nothing more than a sketch or a definition—invaluable to me, but not enough to justify a reference for readers to consult. I do recommend the following:

Andrew, Anne. *Smocking*. London: Merehurst Press, 1989.

The Art of Sewing. The Editors of Time-Life Books. 16 vols. New York, NY: Time-Life Books, 1976.

Carr, Roberta. *Couture: The Art of Fine Sewing*. Portland, OR: Palmer/Pletsch Associates, 1993.

Carroll, Alice. *The Good Housekeeping Needlecraft Encyclopedia*. Sandusky, Oh: Stanford House, 1947.

Caulfeild, S. F. A., and Saward, Blanche C. *Encyclopedia of Victorian Needlework*. 2 vols. New York, NY: Dover Publications, Inc.; originally published by A. W. Cowan, London, 1882.

Cave, Œnone, and Hodges, Jean. *Smocking: Traditional & Modern Approaches*. London: B.T. Batsford Ltd, 1984.

Clabburn, Pamela. *The Needleworker's Dictionary*. New York, NY: William Morrow and Company, Inc., 1976.

Colby, Averil. *Quilting*. New York, NY: Charles Scribner's Sons, 1971.

Coleman, Elizabeth Ann. *The Opulent Era: Fashions of Worth, Doucet and Pingat*. Brooklyn, NY: The Brooklyn Museum in association with Thames and Hudson, 1989.

The Complete Guide to Needlework Techniques and Materials. Mary Gostelow, Consultant Editor. Secaucus, NY: Chartwell Books Inc. First published by Quill Publishing Limited, London, 1982.

Cunningham, Gladys. *Singer Sewing Book*. New York, NY: Golden Press, 1969.

Cunnington, C. Willett. *English Women's Clothing in the Nineteenth Century*. New York, NY: Dover Publications, Inc., 1990. Unabridged republication of work originally published by Faber and Faber, Ltd., London, 1937.

da Conceição, Maria. *Wearable Art*. New York, NY: The Viking Press (A Studio Book), 1979; Penguin Books, 1980.

Durand, Dianne. *Smocking: Technique, Projects and Designs*. New York, NY: Dover Publications, Inc., 1979.

Dyer, Ann. *Design Your Own Stuffed Toys*. U. S. Edition. Newton, MA: Charles T. Branford Company, 1970.

Ericson, Lois. *Texture...a closer look*. Self-published by the author, 1987.

Every Kind of Smocking. Kit Pyman, Editor. New York, NY: Henry Holt and Company, Inc., 1987.

Fanning, Robbie and Tony. *The Complete Book of Machine Quilting*. 2nd Edition. Radnor, PA: Chilton Book Company, 1994.

Fons, Marianne, and Porter, Liz. *Quilter's Complete Guide*. Birmingham, AL: Oxmoor House, Inc., 1993.

Gibbs-Smith, Charles H. *The Fashionable Lady in the 19th Century*. London: Her Majesty's Stationery Office for the Victoria and Albert Museum, 1960.

Gioello, Debbie Ann, and Berke, Beverly. *Fashion Production Terms*. New York, NY: Fairchild Publications, 1979.

Guild, Vera P. *Good Housekeeping New Complete Book of Needlecraft*. New York, NY: Good Housekeeping Books, 1971.

Haight, Ernest B. *Practical Machine-Quilting for the Homemaker*. David City, NE: self-published by author, 1974.

Hall, Carolyn Vosburgh. *Soft Sculpture*. Worcester, MA: Davis Publications, Inc., 1981.

_____. *The Sewing Machine Craft Book*. New York, NY: Van Nostrand Reinhold Company, 1980.

Hargrave, Harriet. *Heirloom Machine Quilting*. Lafayette, CA: C & T Publishing, 1995.

Hutton, Jessie, and Cunningham, Gladys. *Singer Sewing Book*. New York, NY: Golden Press, 1972. Earlier editions by Gladys Cunningham, 1969; and Mary Brooks Picken, 1953, 1949.

Ingham, Rosemary, and Covey, Liz. *The Costume Technician's Handbook*. Portsmouth, NH: Heinemann Educational Books, Inc., 1992.

Ireland, Patrick John. *Encyclopedia of Fashion Details*. London: B.T. Batsford Ltd, 1987.

Kimball, Jeana. *Loving Stitches: A Guide to Fine Hand Quilting*. Bothell, WA: That Patchwork Place, Inc., 1992.

Leman, Bonnie. *Quick and Easy Quilting*. Great Neck, NY: Hearthside Press, 1972.

Link, Nelle Weymouth. *Smocking and Gathering for Fabric Manipulation*. Berkeley, CA: Lacis, 1987. Originally published under the title *Stitching for Style: Fabric Manipulation for Self Trim*. New York, NY: Liveright Publishing Corporation, 1948.

Margolis, Adele P. *The Encyclopedia of Sewing*. Garden City, NY: Doubleday & Company, Inc., 1987.

Martin, Richard, and Koda, Harold. *Infra-Apparel*. New York, NY: The Metropolitan Museum of Art, 1993.

_____. *Haute Couture*. New York, NY: The Metropolitan Museum of Art, 1995.

McGehee, Linda F. *Texture with Textiles*. Shreveport, LA: self-published by the author, 1991.

Meilach, Dona Z. *Soft Sculpture and Other Soft Art Forms*. New York, NY: Crown Publishers, Inc., 1974.

Morgan, Mary, and Mosteller, Dee. *Trapunto and Other Forms of Raised Quilting*. New York, NY: Charles Scribner's Sons, 1977.

The New Butterick Dressmaker. New York, NY: The Butterick Publishing Co., 1927.

Penn, Irving. *Issey Miyake*. New York Graphic Society: Little, Brown and Company (Inc.), 1988.

Reader's Digest Complete Guide to Sewing. Pleasantville, NY: Reader's Digest Association, 1976, 1995.

Rodgers, Sue H. *The Handbook of Stuffed Quilting*. Wheat Ridge, CO: Leman Publications, Inc., 1990.

Scott, Toni. *The Complete Book of Stuffedwork*. Boston, MA: Houghton Mifflin Company, 1978.

Short, Eirian. *Introducing Quilting*. New York, NY: Charles Scribner's Sons, 1974.

Sienkiewicz, Elly. *Dimensional Appliqué: Baskets, Blooms & Baltimore Borders*. Lafayette, CA: C & T Publishing, 1993.

Simms, Ami. *How to Improve Your Quilting Stitch*. Flint, MI: Mallery Press, 1987.

The Singer Sewing Reference Library. The Editors of Cy DeCosse Incorporated in cooperation with the Singer Education Department. 31 vols. Minnetonka, MN: Cy DeCosse Incorporated, 1984.

Thom, Margaret. *Smocking in Embroidery*. New York, NY: Drake Publishers Inc., 1972.

Thompson, Sue. *Decorative Dressmaking*. Emmaus, PA: Rodale Press, 1985.

Victorian Fashions and Costumes from Harper's Bazaar 1867–1898. Stella Blum, Editor. New York, NY: Dover Publications, Inc., 1974.

The Vogue/Butterick Step-by-step Guide to Sewing Techniques. Editors of Vogue and Butterick patterns. New York, NY: Simon & Schuster, 1989.

The Vogue Sewing Book. Vogue Patterns. New York, NY: Butterick Publishing, 1975.

Waugh, Norah. *The Cut of Women's Clothes 1600-1930*. New York, NY: Theatre Arts Books, 1968.

Women's Institute of Domestic Arts & Sciences. *Decorative Stitches and Trimmings*. Scranton, PA: International Educational Publishing Company, 1929.

_____. *Designing and Decorating Clothes*. Scranton, PA: International Educational Publishing Company, 1929.

_____. *Dressmaking, Trimming, Finishing*. Scranton, PA: International Educational Publishing Company, 1936.

Yarwood, Doreen. *The Encyclopedia of World Costume*. New York, NY: Bonanza Books, 1986; originally published by Charles Scribner's Sons, 1978.

ARTICLES

I have a bulging file called "Clues" filled with tearsheets from magazines and newspapers—pictures of garments with intriguing details, textiles in home decorating situations, bits and pieces about process—and scribbled notes. Sources I didn't credit at the time provided information for this book. Material popped up where least expected, and where I expected to find it in the following periodicals:

Allen, Alice. "Improving the Bottom Line: How to choose hand- and machine-sewn hem finishes." *Threads*. Vol. #16 (April/May 1988): pp. 46-49.

Avery, Virginia. "Embellish with Scraps." *American Quilter*. Vol. II, #4 (Winter, 1986): pp. 21-24.

Breland, Nancy, and Weinrich, Judy. "It's a Frame Up! Taking the Drudgery out of Basting." *American Quilter*. Vol. XI, #1 (Spring 1995): p. 46.

Callaway, Grace. "Handsewing Stitches: Which to use when and how to sew them." *Threads*. Vol. #12 (Aug/Sept 1987): pp. 53-57.

Carr, Roberta. "Couture Quilting: Geoffrey Beene adds structure and decoration to both day and evening wear with channel stitching." *Threads*. Vol. #42 (Aug/Sept 1992): pp. 30-35.

_____. "Dior Roses: Add a touch of haute couture." *Threads*. Vol. #34 (Apr/May 1991): pp. 72-73.

Douglas, Sarah. "Smocking Meets the Flat Pattern: How to shape fabric into clothing with the pleater." *Threads*. Vol. #26 (Dec/Jan 1990): pp. 50-55.

_____. "What is This Thing Called Pleater? Creating texture with machine-made pleats." *Threads*. Vol. #21 (Feb/Mar 1989): pp. 54-57.

Duffey, Judith. "Quilt Meets Soft Toy: Padding and stitching add structure with less batting." *Threads*. Vol. #43 (Oct/Nov 1992): pp. 42-45.

Ericson, Lois. "A Surprising Turn of the Pleat: Simple techniques for jacket construction and fabric manipulation." *Threads*. Vol. #39 (Feb/March 1992): pp. 32-35.

_____. "Manipulating Fabric." *American Quilter*. Vol. V, #1 (Spring 1989): pp. 26-30.

Flynn, John. "Dots and Dashes: Quilting experiments in the art of stippling." *Threads*. Vol. #35 (June/July 1991): pp. 58-62.

Fons, Marianne. "Quilting Makes the Quilt: Design your own whole-cloth quilt." *Threads*. Vol. #33 (Feb/Mar 1991): pp. 50-53.

Gaugel, Barbara Conte. "My Small Obsession: A Touch of Tucking." *American Quilter*. Vol. IX, #4 (Winter 1993): pp. 18-19.

Goddu, Carol. "Relief Appliqué for Pictorial Quilts." *American Quilter*. Vol. VI, #1 (Spring 1990): pp. 48-50.

Hartman, Sember. "Sew Right! Mastering the Quilt Stitch." *American Quilter*. Vol. III, #1 (Spring 1987): pp. 44-45.

Jackson, Damaris. "Drawing a Line With a Sewing Machine: Free-motion embroidery for creative quilting." *Threads*. Vol. #20 (Dec/Jan 1989): pp. 30-33.

Kling, Candace. "Decorative Ribbon Work: Folding and stitching methods for turning fabric into flights of fancy." *Threads*. Vol. #12 (Aug/Sept 1987): pp. 58-61.

LaPierre, Jeanne E. "How to Stretch a Quilt." *American Quilter*. Vol. VIII, #4 (Winter 1992): pp. 64-65.

Loeb, Emiko Toda. "On the Reverse Side." *American Quilter*. Vol. IV, #4 (Winter 1988): pp. 33-35.

Lotta-Sellars, Jeanne. "Textured and Tailored: How to machine quilt garments without sacrificing shape." *Threads*. Vol. #55 (Oct/Nov 1994): pp. 37-41.

Mattfield, Elizabeth. "Practical Smocking: A fitting approach to fullness in garment design and embellishment." *Threads*. Vol. #19 (Oct/Nov 1988): pp. 36-38.

Morrison, Lois. "Layered Trapunto: A technique for raised quilting that you can stretch and frame or spread on the bed." *Threads*. Vol. #12 (Aug/Sept 1987): pp. 50-52.

Rathfon, Constance. "Quilt Batts—Which One's for You?" *Threads*. Vol. #58 (Aug/Sept 1995): pp. 65-67.

Saint-Pierre, Adrienne. "Embellishing with Fabric: Trims adapted from the nineteenth century decorate clothing in the twentieth." *Threads*. Vol. #50 (Dec/Jan 1994): pp. 66-69.

Schaeffer, Claire. "Clothing Connections: Variations on a seam." *Threads*. Vol. #22 (Apr/May 1989): pp. 24-29.

Shanks, Carol Lee. "Long Live Wrinkles! Add texture and shape to the simplest garments with just a twist." *Threads*. Vol. #58 (April/May 1995): pp. 58-61.

Shirer, Marie. "A Quilter's Picture Dictionary: Hand Quilting." *Quilter's Newsletter*. Vol. 227 (Nov 1990): pp. 58-59.

_____. "Basting the Quilt Layers with Running Stitches." *Quilter's Newsletter*. Vol. 268 (Dec 1994): pp. 32-33.

_____. "Basting the Quilt Layers with Pins or Tacks." *Quilter's Newsletter*. Vol. #269 (Jan/Feb 1995): p. 39.

Sienkiewicz, Elly. "Flowers from Baltimore Album Quilts: Tucks and gathers transform ribbon into lifelike blossoms." *Threads*. Vol. #44 (Dec/Jan 1993): pp. 40-43.

Simms, Ami. "Toward Smaller Quilting Stitches: Improve the variables of your environment; then learn to needle anew." *Threads*. Vol. #21 (Feb/Mar 1989): pp. 63-65.

Smith, Barbara. "Machine Quilting Tips: Using the Walking Foot." *Quilter's Newsletter*. Vol. #251 (April 1993): pp. 38-40.

_____. "Machine Quilting Tips: Using the Darning Foot." *Quilter's Newsletter*. Vol. #252 (May 1993): pp. 29-31.

Stewart, Helma S. "Floral Appliqué: Making a Three-dimensional Rose." *American Quilter*. Vol. VII, #1 (Spring 1991): pp. 18-22.

Tornquist-Smith, Lois. "Machine Gathering for Surface Texture." *Quilter's Newsletter*. Vol. #205 (Sept 1988): p. 51.

Townsend, Louise O. "Hand Quilting: What Does the Quilting Do?" *Quilter's Newsletter*. Vol. #229 (Jan/Feb 1991): p. 48.

_____. "Hand Quilting: Transferring the Design to the Quilt Top." *Quilter's Newsletter*. Vol. #230 (Mar 1991): p. 52.

_____. "Hand Quilting: Preparation for Quilting." *Quilter's Newsletter*. Vol. #231 (Apr 1991): p. 54.

_____. "Hand Quilting: Choosing a Frame, a Hoop, or One's Lap." *Quilter's Newsletter*. Vol. #232 (May 1991): p. 52-53.

_____. "Hand Quilting: About the Quilting Stitch." *Quilter's Newsletter*. Vol. #233 (June 1991): p. 41.

_____. "Hand Quilting: The Quilting Stitch from Start to Finish." *Quilter's Newsletter*. Vol. #234 (July/Aug 1991): pp. 44-45.

_____. "Hand Quilting: Tools for Designing and Drafting Quilting Patterns." *Quilter's Newsletter*. Vol. #235 (Sept 1991): p. 52.

_____. "Hand Quilting: Using Traditional and Printed Patterns." *Quilter's Newsletter*. Vol. #236 (Oct 1991): p. 60.

_____. "Hand Quilting: Designing Your Own Quilting Pattern." *Quilter's Newsletter*. Vol. #237 (Nov 1991): p. 52.

_____. "Hand Quilting: Designing Alternate Block and Border Quilting." *Quilter's Newsletter*. Vol. #238 (Dec 1991): pp. 50-51.

Wagner, Debra. "Debra Wagner Defines Machine Quilting." *American Quilter*. Vol. XI, #2 (Summer 1995): pp. 26-32.

Wakefield, Linda. "On Piping: The Basics and Beyond." *Threads*. Vol. #56 (Dec/Jan 1995): pp. 40-43.

COSTUME EXHIBITIONS

I'm indebted to the museums in my city that have textile and costume collections. I can't imagine having done this book without access to such primary source material. In particular, again and again, the striking exhibitions at these institutions gave me information, verification, and the inspiration to persevere:

The Galleries at the Fashion Institute of Technology, Shirley Goodman Resource Center, New York, NY.

The Metropolitan Museum of Art, The Costume Institute, New York, NY.

ENDNOTE

Each of the samples photographed for this book was "posed" for the camera. After pressing or steaming, samples were stretched and extensively pinned to a batting-padded board, or arranged and displayed against a neutral background. The purpose for all this preparation: To show each manipulated surface to best advantage for Mike Kagan to reveal with the light and shadow of black-and-white photography. The speckles apparent on the fabric are natural to unbleached muslin.

Work-in-progress on this reference came to a halt when I realized that if I continued on to the end of the outline I originally proposed, the size of the manuscript would seriously alarm my patient publisher. Robbie noticed that prairie points weren't included in the text. They were part of the chapters that would have followed if I hadn't decided to stop after covering the classic techniques, an appropriate and sufficient focus for one book. The rest could wait for another time.

Even so, letting go was difficult. There's always one more sample that could be made, not to mention that nagging question, "Have I overlooked something? Construction detail, variation, tip?" I tinkered through the final proofreading. But, eventually, the author has to say "enough" and give it over to the reader. Now it's your turn. I'd like to know what you discover, invent, and create. There's no such thing as the last word about manipulating fabric, only, that's it until....

Index

P lease see HAND STITCHES, pages 295–297, and GLOSSARY, pages 298–300, for explanations of additional terms not referenced in this Index.

All page numbers appearing in **bold** type refer to pages with photographs. The numbers in parentheses ( ) immediately following the **bold** page numbers indicate specific pictures on that page. Subheadings marked with an asterisk * appear elsewhere as main headings with supportive references.

A

---

page #—text & illustrations **page #(#,#)**—photographs (picture #s on that page) * *See also as a main heading*

single-edge gathering, 10–15
 contoured, 10–11, **14**(6)
 definition, 10
 draped, 10, **13**(5)
 fullness, 3, 10, **12**(1,2), **13**(3,4)
 stayed, 11, 12, **14**(7,8), **15**(10,11),
  19(16)
 tiered, 11, **15**(9)
 See also balls, gathering; gathered
  darts

single-pointed darts, 268–74
 converted to seams, 272, **274**(5),
  288(15,16)
 definition, 268
 drafting darts, 268, 270
 drafting enlarge-and-equalize
  patterns, 270–72, **273**(2,4),
  274(5,6,7,8), **288**(13,14)
 drafting guess-and-trim patterns, 268,
  271, **273**(1)
 drafting slash-and-spread patterns,
  268–69, 271, 272, **273**(2,3,4),
  274(5), **277**(9,10,11), **278**(12)
 released, 272, **274**(5)
 surface, 272, **274**(6), **288**(14)
 See also double-pointed darts;
  gathered darts

skewed applications, 16, **19**(16),
 20(20), 32, **37**(19)

slash-and-spread pattern drafting
 controlled flounce, 77–78
 darts, 268–69, 271, 272, 275
 elevated appliqué, 242–244
 gathering, 10–11, 12, 17

slashed tucks, 167–70
 definition, 167
 ravelled-fringe, 168, **170**(33)
 shark's teeth, 167–68, **169**(28,29,30)
 snip-fringed, 167, 168, **170**(31,32)

smocked tucks, **283**(1)

smocking, 124–47
 description, 124
 direct*, 138–40
 embroidery stitches*, 127–28
 English*, 129–37
 fabric required for, 125–26
 Italian*, 144–47
 managing the smocking-pleated edge,
  128–29
 North American*, 141–43
 using a smocking pleater, 126

smocking embroidery stitches, 127–28
 cable, 127, 131, 132, 138,
  140(12,13,14)
 cable, double, 127
 diamond, 127, 131, 132, 138
 feather, 128, 131, **136**(7)
 flowerettes, 128, 131
 honeycomb, 127, 132, 133, 138, 139,
  135(4,5), **136**(8), **137**(10),
  140(12,13,14), **283**(1)
 honeycomb, surface, 128, 131, 133,
  138, **140**(13,14)
 mock chain, 127, 131
 outline, 127, 132, 138, **136**(7),
  140(13,14)
 spool, 128, 131
 trellis, 127, 131, 138
 Vandyke, 128, 131, 132, 138,
  140(12,14)
 wave, 127, 131, 132, 138

smocking pleater
 Sally Stanley, **114**(28), **134**(2)
 using a, 126

spaced tucks. *See under* standard tucks

square knot, 179, 214

stabilizing gathered stitching, 6–9
 fluting appliquéd edges, 7–8, **19**(18),
  27(34), 298
 invisibly with facings, 8, 298
 invisibly with stays, 8, **13**(5), **14**(8),
  15(10), **18**(14,15), **19**(16,17,19),
  20(20,21), **24**(25), **25**(30), 299
 locating the stabilizing seam, 5
 visibly with bindings, 6–7, **15**(9),
  20(22), **24**(23)
 visibly with extensions, 7, 8, **15**(10),
  19(19), **20**(20,21), **24**(25), **25**(30)
 visibly with foundation stays, 7–8,
  14(6,7), **15**(11), **18**(15),
  19(17,18), **20**(21), **24**(24),
  27(34,35,36), 298
 visibly with ruffled edges, 8, **20**(21)
 visibly with stops, 9, **24**(23)
 See also circular flounce, stabilizing;
  glossary, stabilizer; shirring,
  stabilizing

standard tucks, 150–59
 blind, 150–51, **155**(3)
 centered, 150–51, 152, 153, **155**(5),
  291(24)
 cross, 154, **157**(10,11)
 definition, l50

designer, 154, **156**(9), **159**(17,18),
  292(26), **293**(30,31)
 doubled-and-centered tucks, l50–5l,
  152,153, **156**(6)
 graduated, 150–51, **155**(4)
 grainline deviations, 154, l59(16)
 mock pin, 154, **158**(14,15)
 pin, l50–5l, **155**(1), **158**(13)
 random,154, **157**(12)
 spaced, l50–5l, **155**(2), **290**(19),
  291(25)
 tapered, l50–5l, 152, 153–54,
  156(7,8), **159**(16)
 terminology, 151, 152
 See also connected rolls; shirred
  surface cording; shirred tucks;
  smocked tucks; surface cording

star gathering. *See* all-sides gathering

stays. *See under* stabilizing gathered
 stitching

stipple quilting. *See* hand quilting

stops, 9, **24**(23)

strips. *See* cutting fabric strips

stroking, 4, **19**(18)

stuffed appliqué, 236–41
 definition, 236
 eased, 238, **240**(8), 298
 frayed-edge, 238
 freezer-paper preparation, 238
 inserting stuffing, 237–38
 loose, 239, **241**(11), **293**(29,30,31)
 sewing by hand, 236, 237,
  240(7,8,9), **246**(12)
 sewing by machine, 236–37,
  240(7,8), **241**(10,11)
 stacked, 238–39, **240**(9), **241**(10)

stuffed quilting, 230–35
 definition, 230
 inserting stuffing, 231, 232
 layered, 233, **235**(5,6)
 reversed, 233, **235**(4)
 sewing by hand, 230–31, **234**(1,3),
  235(4,5,6)
 sewing by machine, 230, 231,
  234(2,3)
 trapunto, 191, 232, **234**(1)
 See also hand quilting; hand-sewn
  corded quilting; machine quilting;
  machine-sewn corded quilting

page #—text & illustrations   **page #(#,#)**—photographs (picture #s on that page)   * See also as a main heading

About the Author

Colette Wolff says that she could write an autobiography around the garments, needlework, quilts, stuffed toys, and textile art associated with memorable events in her past. "My grandmother introduced me to embroidery at a very early age. Before I was 10, my mother taught me how to sew on my grandmother's treadle sewing machine," she remembers. "Since then, fabric, needle and thread, and the sewing machine have been constants in my life."

Although she hasn't written that autobiography, Colette Woof has been writing about cloth-related subjects for more than 25 years, contributing articles and designs to most of the major craft, sewing, and textile publications, and teaching and lecturing as well. In 1969, she began designing cloth dolls and animals and publishing patterns for **Platypus**, a mail-order business she still owns and operates. During the last ten years, her interests have converged around exploring the techniques for creating low- and high-relief sculpted cloth with a

series of dimensionalized "quilted tapestries." *The Art of Manipulating Fabric* is the printed result of those continuing studies.

Colette Wolff lives and works in Manhattan, New York City.